# CONSENTING CHILDREN

Since 1905, the *Proceedings of the British Academy* series has provided a unique record of British scholarship in the humanities and social sciences. Each themed volume drives scholarship forward and is a landmark in its field. For more information about the series, please visit www.thebritishacademy.ac.uk/proceedings

PROCEEDINGS OF THE BRITISH ACADEMY • 279

# CONSENTING CHILDREN

## AUTONOMY, RESPONSIBILITY, WELL-BEING

Edited by
LISA FORSBERG, ISRA BLACK,
AND ANTHONY SKELTON

*Published by* THE BRITISH ACADEMY
*Marketed and distributed by Liverpool University Press*

*Published by The British Academy*
*10–11 Carlton House Terrace, London SW1Y 5AH*

*Marketed and distributed by Liverpool University Press*
*4 Cambridge Street, Liverpool L69 7ZU*


*First edition published in 2025*


*British Library Cataloguing in Publication Data*
*Data available*

*Library of Congress Cataloguing in Publication Data*
*Data available*

*Typeset by Newgen Publishing UK*

*ISBN 978-1-83-624567-4 (print)*
*ISBN 978-1-83-624950-4 (pdf)*
*ISBN 978-1-83-624957-3 (epub)*
*ISSN 0068-1202*

*The manufacturer's authorised representative in the EU for product safety is:*
*Easy Access System Europe, Mustamäe tee 50, 10621 Tallinn, Estonia*
*https://easproject.com (gpsr.requests@easproject.com)*

# Contents

# Table of Cases

## Australia

## Canada



## England and Wales

## France



## Ireland



## United States



## European Court of Human Rights

# Table of Legislation

## Australia



## Canada



## England and Wales

## France



## Scotland



## United States



## International Treaties and Conventions

# Notes on Contributors

**David Archard** is Emeritus Professor of Philosophy, Queen's University Belfast, having previously taught at the Universities of Ulster, St Andrews, and Lancaster. He has published extensively in the areas of applied ethics, political philosophy, and philosophy of law, especially on the topics of children, the family, sexual consent, and the public role of philosophy. He is the author of *Children: Rights and Childhood*, third edition (Routledge, 2014) and the co-editor (with Colin Macleod) of *The Moral and Political Status of Children* (OUP, 2002).

**Isra Black** is Associate Professor in Law, University College London, having previously taught at the University of York. His expertise lies at the intersection of health law and philosophy. He has published on the law of medical treatment (particularly as it concerns adolescents), mental capacity law, end of life decision-making (e.g. refusals of treatment and assisted death), health and human rights law, as well as the theorisation of health law as an area of legal practice and scholarly enquiry, among others. He is the author of articles appearing in *Journal of Ethics and Social Philosophy*, *Law Quarterly Review*, and *Oxford Journal of Leal Studies*.

**Jo Bridgeman** is Professor of Healthcare Law and Feminist Ethics, University of Sussex. Her research adopts a critical feminist perspective informed by and developing the feminist ethics of care in consideration of parental, professional and state responsibilities to children. She has published widely on the medical treatment of children, including the care of children with complex needs, parental responsibility for children undergoing treatment for cancer, and withholding/withdrawal of life-sustaining treatment from a child. Her most recent book is *Medical Treatment of Children and the Law: Beyond Parental Responsibilities* (Routledge, 2020).

**David O. Brink** is Distinguished Professor of Philosophy, University of California, San Diego. He has published extensively in the areas of ethical theory, the history of ethics, moral psychology, political philosophy, and jurisprudence, including on juvenile justice and criminal responsibility. He is the author of a large number of important and influential articles which have appeared in, among other journals, *Ethics*, *Criminal Law and Philosophy*, and *Texas Law Review*. He is the author of four books, the most recent of which is *Fair Opportunity and Responsibility* (OUP, 2021).

**Emma Cave** is Professor of Healthcare Law, Durham University. She publishes widely in the field of health law, which she teaches at undergraduate and postgraduate levels. Her research focuses on understanding and shaping the ambits of patient choice and emerging biotechnologies. The seventh edition of her co-authored book (with

Margaret Brazier and Rob Heywood) *Medicine, Patients and the Law* (Manchester University Press) was published in 2023 and her 2004 monograph *The Mother of All Crimes* (Routledge) on criminalisation of the child born alive was reissued in 2018.

**Mary Donnelly** is Professor of Law, University College Cork. Her primary research interests lie in medical/capacity law and consumer protection. Her work in medical/capacity law relates primarily to the interplay between individual autonomy and state intervention/protection. She has published extensively on capacity and consent, as well as death on neurological criteria. She is the author of *Healthcare Decision-Making and the Law: Autonomy, Capacity and the Limits of Liberalism* (CUP, 2010) and of *Consent: Bridging the Gap Between Doctor and Patient* (Cork University Press, 2002), as well as numerous important journal articles on a wide range of topics.

**Jennifer Epp** is Assistant Professor of Philosophy, Huron University College. She works primarily in the areas of ethics, feminism, and epistemology. She has published on children's rights and sexual agency, among other topics. She teaches courses on embodiment, gender and sexuality, normative ethics, the history of political philosophy, reconciliation, and the philosophy of sex, love, and friendship.

**Lisa Forsberg** is Senior Research Fellow, Uehiro Oxford Institute, and Research Fellow in Philosophy, Somerville College, University of Oxford. Her main research interests lie in normative and practical ethics, and in the philosophy of medical and criminal law. Her publications have appeared in *Modern Law Review*, *Law Quarterly Review*, *Journal of Ethics and Social Philosophy*, and *Philosophical Quarterly*, among other journals.

**Andrew Franklin-Hall** is Associate Professor of Philosophy, University of Toronto. His research areas include ethics, philosophy of the emotions, social and political philosophy, bioethics, and philosophy of education. He has published articles on these topics in, among other journals, *Ethics*, *Journal of Applied Philosophy*, *Philosophical Quarterly*, and *Social Theory and Practice.*

**Steph Jowett** is Lecturer in Health Law, Queensland University of Technology. Her research focuses on a range of socio-legal issues, especially on the intersection of children's health and law. She has published on consent for medical treatment of young people, access to healthcare for trans youth, adolescent decision-making capacity and the law, consent for involvement of children in health research, among other topics. Her publications appear in leading Australian and international peer-reviewed journals. She is the author of *Consent for Medical Treatment of Trans Youth* (CUP, 2022).

**Maximilian Kiener** is Junior-Professor of Philosophy and Ethics in Technology, Hamburg University of Technology, where he leads the Institute for Ethics in Technology, and a Research Associate of the Uehiro Oxford Institute at the

University of Oxford. He researches in the areas of moral and legal philosophy, with a particular focus on consent, responsibility, and artificial intelligence. He is the author of *Voluntary Consent: Theory and Practice* (Routledge, 2023) and of articles in *Journal of Moral Philosophy* and *Philosophical Studies*.

**Barry Lyons** is Associate Professor in Medical Ethics and Law, Trinity College Dublin. His research interests relate to the interface between law and medicine, especially concerning children and the definition of death, as well as to the role of negative emotions in medicine, where he has investigated the role of shame in clinical practice, patient experience, and medical student education. He has published articles in *Bioethics*, *Clinical Ethics*, *Legal Studies*, and *Medical Law International*, among many others.

**Sir Jonathan Montgomery** is Professor of Healthcare Law, University College London. His primary area of research is healthcare law, an area of research that he played an instrumental role in defining. He has made important theoretical contributions to this and other areas. He has published numerous influential articles and book chapters. He is the author of *Health Care Law* (OUP, 2002) and (with Priscilla Alderson) *Health Care Choices: Making Choices with Children* (Institute for Public Policy Research, 1996). In 2019, he was awarded a knighthood for services to Bioethics and Healthcare Law.

**Peter Schaber** is Emeritus Professor of Applied Ethics, University of Zurich. He researches in the areas of ethics and practical ethics, especially on the ethics of consent and related issues. He has published widely on these topics. His work has appeared in the journals *Ethical Theory and Moral Practice*, *Journal of Ethics*, *Journal of Applied Philosophy*, *Journal of Moral Philosophy*, among many others. He is the editor (with Andreas Müller) of *The Routledge Handbook of the Ethics of Consent* (Routledge, 2018).

**Anthony Skelton** is Professor of Philosophy, University of Western Ontario. He has published in the areas of applied ethics, the history of ethics, legal philosophy, and normative ethics, especially on the nature of children's well-being. His publications have appeared in *Journal of Ethics and Social Philosophy* and *Law Quarterly Review* and in volumes published by Cambridge University Press and Routledge Press. He is the co-editor of *Bioethics in Canada*, 2nd edn (OUP, 2019).

**Meghan Winsby** is a doctoral candidate in philosophy, University of Western Ontario. She researches primarily in the areas of applied ethics and normative ethics with a special emphasis on the treatment of children. She is currently working on her dissertation entitled *The Prospective Stance: Developing Moral Agency and Agents*.

# Acknowledgements

The editors owe a debt of gratitude to a great many people for their support in bringing this volume to fruition. We wish to thank John Coggon for his feedback on the book proposal submitted to the British Academy, the authors of the volume's chapters for their contributions and their patience, the many colleagues who generously agreed to provide expert peer review of the chapters, an anonymous reader for their helpful suggestions on the manuscript, and the British Academy, especially Portia Taylor, Yas Afshar, Lizzie Evans, and Ting Baker. We acknowledge each other's equal contribution to editing of this volume.

Lisa Forsberg offers thanks to the British Academy Postdoctoral Fellowship scheme (award pf170028), the European Research Council (grant number 819757), and the Uehiro Foundation for Ethics and Education.

Anthony Skelton wishes to acknowledge the support of the Graham and Gail Wright Distinguished Scholar Award programme, the Rotman Institute of Philosophy, and the Faculty Scholar programme at the University of Western Ontario. In addition, Anthony wishes to thank Douglas Jasey for editorial assistance.

We began our work on law and philosophy as they relate to adolescents during a residency at the Fondation Brocher in 2015. We gratefully acknowledge its enduring contribution.

# Consenting Children: Introduction

LISA FORSBERG, ISRA BLACK, AND ANTHONY SKELTON

CHILDREN—INDIVIDUALS BELOW THE legal age of majority—are treated differently compared to adults in many domains, including in healthcare, education, employment, and criminal justice. It is a settled fact that this differential treatment is sometimes appropriate. It seems permissible to prevent younger children from forgoing routine medical treatment and to spare children of all ages from the harshest criminal punishments, including for serious crimes. In other cases, the permissibility of differential treatment is far less clear. It is not obvious that we may impose life-prolonging medical treatment on an adolescent whose decision-making capacity matches that of a competent adult whose refusal would be respected.

That children are treated differently to adults in a range of contexts—and indeed that children are treated differently to one another—is not without controversy. This makes it both practically and theoretically important to clarify and engage with the justification of when and why it is permissible to do so. Because the justifications of children's differential (and, often, paternalistic) treatment typically appeal to foundational normative considerations, they provoke considerable controversy and disagreement in law and in philosophy—as the chapters in *Consenting Children* reveal. This calls out for sustained investigation of the kind on display in this volume.

The purpose of this introduction is to acquaint readers with the themes explored in *Consenting Children*, to provide readers with a summary of the chapters to follow, and to situate the volume's contributions. Our ambition is for the volume's contributions to lay the groundwork for future engagement in the legal and philosophical literature with the controversies raised by arguments about children's autonomy, responsibility, and well-being, and the myriad interactions between them. We anticipate that the chapters in this volume will serve as an indispensable critical reference for scholars working in the broad range of disciplines dealing with the treatment of children. We hope, further, that the volume demonstrates the potential of the study of children to generate insights into thinking about consent, autonomy, responsibility, and well-being more broadly.

*Proceedings of the British Academy*, **279**, 1–12, © Authors 2025.

## Themes

*Consenting Children* grapples with the differential treatment of children in a variety of contexts. The study of these is revealing of cross-cutting themes—autonomy, responsibility, and well-being—that invite reflection on our treatment of children—compared to adults and compared to each other.

Consider first the domain of healthcare. Younger children do not, typically, have the decision-making capacity to give or to refuse medical or healthcare consent. In the typical case, decisions about healthcare interventions fall to those having decision-making authority over the child in question, such as a parent. The exercise of such authority is guided and constrained by concern for the best interests of the child. However, it is not always clear exactly what treating a child in accordance with their best interests involves. There is uncertainty in particular around the relative ethical significance of the interests of parents, of the interests of the adult the child in question will one day become, and of the present interests of the child themselves. Regarding the last, it is settled that a child's preferences for or against treatment are given some consideration, while typically assigned lower weight according to age. But this approach leaves unresolved the precise normative status of younger children's views and their relationship to the child's well-being at a time and across time.

As children age, the complexity intensifies. While older children's well-being is a central focus in healthcare, it is not the only factor that seems worthy of moral consideration. One notable feature of older children—particularly adolescents—is that they often have or are developing their own inventory of values and seem capable of making autonomous decisions about their lives in a variety of domains (including healthcare). This does not mean, however, that such children are treated as if they are adults or that their autonomous choices always trump their putative best interests. On the contrary, it is common with respect to at least some healthcare decisions that the scope of adolescents' autonomous choice is limited. For example, regarding life-prolonging medical interventions, an adolescent may give a valid consent and thereby authorise treatment, while their valid refusal will lack the power to block treatment determinatively. When and why adolescents are treated differentially is hard to determine. Evaluating and attempting to justify our practices involves considering the nature of adolescent autonomy, consent (refusal), legal and decision-making capacity (or competence), as well as well-being (ill-being), in new and novel ways. It is of utmost importance to consider how these consequential factors interact with each other in legal and ethical thinking (and practice).

Healthcare is not the only domain in which the question of when it is permissible to grant the consent of adolescents the same power as it has in the case of typical adult agents (and why) is controversial. In the domain of sex and sexual activity, when two people (each) above the age of majority validly consent to sexual activity, then that activity is—other things equal—permissible. Yet what makes for permissible sex in cases where the participants are adolescents raises several difficult issues.

First, there is presence and determination of an age of consent. In most jurisdictions, there exists an age of consent to sexual activity that is lower than the age of majority, for example, 14, 15, or 16 and 18 years of age, respectively. Opting for a status-based approach—that is, fixed according to age—*as well as* a functional approach—fixed according to decision-making capacity—for consent to sexual activity seems appropriate. (Whereby a child's functional capacity to engage in sexual relations is relevant only on passing the age of consent.) Yet, it is also puzzling. It is far from clear what makes for the validity of consent to sexual activity at a defined age and accounts for its normative power to permit sexual activity with another. Why, for example, should consent given by a 16-year-old legally permit sexual intercourse but consent by a 15-year-old should not? We require an answer to this question in cases where both parties possess the relevant functional decision-making capacity and satisfy all other conditions of valid consent. Second, law or prosecutorial policy might permit a younger adolescent—for example, a 12- or 13-year-old—to consent to sex but only with other adolescents of a defined range—for example, up to two years older. How might a 12-year-old's valid consent to sexual activity permit sex with a 14-year-old but not with a 16-year-old? A plausible line of enquiry here might be to consider what consent in minors protects and whether that is the same as in the case of adults. Third—and related to the first two issues—there seem to be problems specific to children's consent to sex concerning the latter's scope and value, as well as how best to provide the resources to facilitate and to protect both refusal of and consent to sex. These issues and questions represent instances of a more general puzzle this volume addresses: how to explain the demarcation of children's consent from adult consent, and the consent of some children from that of others.

Moving to our practices of praising and blaming, rewarding and punishing—what we might call the domain of responsibility—an enduring difficulty is how to stand in relation to children in these regards, as well as how to explain and justify our stances. Our responsibility practices vis-à-vis children are adultlike—for we deploy familiar responsibility concepts in familiar ways—and yet we do not treat children as adults in this domain, in virtue of children's immaturity and stage of development.

In 'Freedom and Resentment', P. F. Strawson's groundbreaking discussion of reactive attitudes, he expresses genuine puzzlement as to the appropriate treatment of children in the context of parenting.[1] Strawson notes that we can neither regard children as we do adults—as the full participants in interpersonal relationships who are thus fitting objects of reactive attitudes—nor can we regard them purely from what he calls the objective stance, the stance from which children would

[1] P. F. Strawson, 'Freedom and Resentment', *Proceedings of the British Academy*, 48 (1962), 187–211.

be regarded merely as something to manage or train like a pet potbelly pig. As Strawson put it:

> [Parents] are dealing with creatures who are potentially and increasingly capable of holding, and being objects of, the full range of human and moral attitudes, but are not yet truly capable of either. The treatment of such creatures must therefore represent a kind of compromise, constantly shifting in one direction, between objectivity of attitude and developed human attitudes. Rehearsals insensibly modulate towards true performances. The punishment of a child is both like and unlike the punishment of an adult.[2]

Holding children responsible for their actions or thinking of them as fitting targets of certain reactive attitudes—for example, blame, praise, and resentment—is at once an appropriate and a difficult enterprise. Reactive attitudes target the will of individuals subject to them. We might blame children and resent them for bad conduct because it results from a bad will (the will to harm). We also praise children for various good deeds or for their achievements. These practices come naturally. And, yet, they are perplexing. It is a near truism that while younger children have some degree of autonomy, they lack a fully (or even significantly) developed will and so cannot be entirely fitting targets of reactive attitudes. An explanation is needed for our invocation of reactive attitudes in children's regard.

Strawson did not elaborate on the ways in which the punishment of a child is and is not like the punishment of an adult. Figuring out exactly where the differences lie and their implications for punishing children is of great significance to the well-being and life prospects of children—not least in the context of criminal justice. When an individual under the age of 18 commits a criminal offence, her crime is typically dealt with under a youth justice system that is distinct from the adult justice system. Although this makes sense from the point of view of reducing recidivism, of enhancing the prospects of rehabilitation, and of meeting the unique needs of young offenders, it may seem hard to justify treating youths who wilfully commit very serious offences like murder and rape under this system. It will be especially hard in cases where the child who commits the crime meets the threshold of criminal responsibility for adults. A justification is needed, then, for treating youth criminals differentially from adults who commit similar serious crimes. A further puzzle arises when we consider the fact that children in some jurisdictions may be held criminally responsible at a much earlier age than they are able to give legally determinative consent to medical treatment or to sex. Why should the age of legal culpability be younger in general than the age of legally determinative consent?

Underlying the foregoing discussion is the observation that although differences in capacities may go some way towards explaining the differential treatment of children compared to adults, as well as some children compared to others, capacities cannot alone do all the work in all the cases. An appeal will need to be made

[2] Strawson, 'Freedom and Resentment', 204–5.

to other (normative) factors to clarify (and justify) differential treatment but what those are is an open and disputed question. Hence, this volume.

## Chapter summaries

This volume comprises 15 chapters and is divided into three separate sections. The chapters engage with a range of topics related to the differential treatment of children (including their consent) from the perspectives of both law and philosophy.

Part I of *Consenting Children* is entitled 'Children's Consent and Capacity'. It comprises four chapters. In 'Setting the Standard(s) for Capacity: Are Children Different?', Mary Donnelly and Barry Lyons argue that the capacity tests in the law of England and Wales for children under the age of 16 and for adults, respectively, have distinct origins. The former test is governed by the notion of *Gillick* competence, while the latter is governed by the provisions in the Mental Capacity Act 2005. Each standard for capacity has been designed to serve a different purpose and has solicited different judicial reactions. The standards have therefore evolved and function in different ways. As a result, Donnelly and Lyons argue, there is no possibility of the standards converging. In medical decision-making involving children under the age of 16, Donnelly and Lyons suggest, much less emphasis is placed on competence than in the case of adults. Children deemed to be autonomous or competent do not always thereby have the authority to make their own medical decisions. In the case of adults, however, there is no difference between being autonomous and having authority to makes one's own medical decisions, and so if an adult is deemed competent and autonomous they have the authority to decide their own medical treatment.

In 'Competence for Minors in Medical Decision-Making: A Life-Stage Approach', Andrew Franklin-Hall attempts to provide a rationale for the differential treatment of the medical decisions of adults and minors with decision-making capacity, respectively. Typically, adults in possession of decision-making capacity have the authority to determine their own medical treatment. This is generally not true for adolescents. Franklin-Hall draws a distinction between two accounts of competence, decision-based competence and abilities-based competence. On the first account, a patient is competent when they make no significant mistakes in reasoning and their decision is roughly in line with their values; on the second account, competence is a matter (merely) of possessing certain abilities at the time one makes a decision, including the capacity to appreciate and understand the information one is given and to weigh the costs and benefits of one's treatment options, and so on. We treat adolescent and adult medical decision-making differently because, Franklin-Hall argues, we apply the former account of competence to adolescents but the latter to adults. The reason we apply the decision-based account of competence to adolescents has to do with their stage of life. Adolescence is a probationary period in which adolescents are being prepared for assuming full responsibility for their lives.

In ‘Asymmetry of Adolescent Decision-Making Capacity and Rational Choice’, Isra Black examines the existence of, and normative support for, one specification of what he terms the ‘asymmetry of capacity thesis’ in English law, namely, a legal doctrine that holds that an individual may possess the capacity to consent to a medical intervention and yet lack the capacity to refuse the same. Black advances two main arguments. First, he argues that doctrinally or institutionally, the asymmetry of capacity thesis is not a feature of the English adolescent medical treatment case law. Second, and normatively, Black argues that neither of two prominent ways of explaining and justifying the asymmetry of capacity thesis—the *risk-relative* account of capacity, and Stephen Gilmore and Jonathan Herring’s distinction between *refusal of consent* and *refusal of treatment*—succeed. Black concludes that if the asymmetry of capacity thesis is part of English law, it should not be; if it is not part of English law, we should not embrace it within this legal order. At least, not in virtue of either of these views.

In ‘Minors and Sexual Consent’, Jennifer Epp broadens the discussion of children’s consent to sex beyond the age at which children gain the capacity and have the authority to consent to (especially) sexual intercourse. Epp examines not only the conditions under which children may validly consent to a range of sexual activities (including but not limited to sexual intercourse) but also the relationship between consent to sexual activity and the value of sex for children with capacity, as well as the impact that oppression and oppressive social conditions have on children’s ability to validly consent to sexual activity and to express sexual agency. Insight into these issues, Epp contends, is important to making sense of the duties we owe to children in respect of their sexual autonomy.

Part II of *Consenting Children* is entitled ‘Children’s Consent and Other Parties’. It comprises eight chapters. In ‘Children and Consent: Best Interests, Parents, and a Child’s Views’, David Archard explores two questions related to medical decision-making involving children who lack capacity. What does giving parents or caregivers the power to decide on children’s medical treatment comprise, and what role (if any) should children’s own views have in decision-making about their own healthcare? What having the power to choose for children in a medical setting involves, Archard contends, is having the *tendency* to choose what is in the best interests of children. In the absence of this tendency, parents have no such power to choose. Children’s attitudes about their own medical treatment warrant consideration because they have the capacity to express preferences, and because treatment happens *to* them, and so they will live with the effects (positive and negative) of it. This reveals, according to Archard, that we have two obligations to children: to promote their best interests and to listen to their voices.

In ‘The Interaction of Children’s Capacity Regimes and Parental and Judicial Powers: A “Strictly” Legal View’, Sir Jonathan Montgomery reviews the legal structure in England for the governance of healthcare decisions to explain why children’s capacity regimes are of limited significance in the protection of young people’s rights, including the right to exercise autonomy. Children’s consent rights are, he argues, fragile—as evidenced by the application of the capacity test, of limited value in the context of extensive professional discretion over treatment selection, and weak since they may be overridden by others (both parents and judges). The legal structure of patient autonomy can be considered as analogous to that of ownership, which is understood as constituted by a bundle of rights and powers. Measures aimed at enhancing children's say in their lives should, Montgomery argues, concentrate less on capacity questions and more on how best to define the obligations of others. It is the latter's power that most constrains the young person's ability to determine what treatment they are given; Montgomery concludes that their modulation will be most likely to enhance children's autonomy.

In 'A Future-Orientated View of Autonomy', Emma Cave addresses the issue of how to reconcile the commitment to respecting a child's competent choices with the requirement to do what is in their best interests (however conceived). Cave's focus is on the medical decisions of children below the age of 16. She argues that there are a variety of ways under the law of England and Wales in which the medical decisions of children found to be competent are restricted or limited and held not to be determinative. Cave describes and clarifies four ways in which children's competent decisions are limited. These include using the judicial power to override children's choices; requiring the valid consent of both a child and their parents (or guardians) to medical treatment; using age-centred controls expressed in legislation; and capitalising on the adaptability of criteria for competence. Cave sees the merits and clarity of respecting as determinative a competent child's medical decision (as is the case with adults), come what may. But she also recognises that by permitting limitations to the medical decisions of competent children, 'policy makers are given greater scope to move from denial of treatment or a requirement that all cases come before the court to determine best interests, to one that accommodates the views of potential individual child recipients and potentially allows more timely access to treatment'.

In 'Medical Treatment Refusals by Teenagers and the Law: Justice That Is More Caring?', Jo Bridgeman argues that in legal cases involving teenagers refusing consent to medical treatment, courts should appeal to both considerations of justice and care in deciding what to do. According to Bridgeman, in the legal cases she considers, courts employ hierarchical reasoning in their decision-making, giving priority to avoiding serious harm over other considerations, including the relationships the teenagers value and the responsibilities to others that they take most seriously. If there is conflict between what may save a teenager's life or prevent them from experiencing serious harm and the responsibilities that teenagers feel to their family or to their religious convictions, the former wins out on the court's reasoning. The difficulty with this approach is that it neglects to engage the reasoning of the teenagers which explicitly appeals to relationships and responsibilities. The remedy for this, Bridgeman suggests, is for courts to decide these cases by reference to value hierarchies and rights as well as relationships and responsibilities, in so doing integrating what Carol Gilligan calls the ethics of justice and the ethics of care. This will, Bridgeman says, issue in a more caring form of justice.

In 'Consent to Medical Treatment for Trans Youth in Australia', Steph Jowett critically engages with the Australian legal framework governing consent to medical treatment for trans youth, where gender-affirming care for minors has received significantly more judicial attention—over an extended period—than in England and Wales. Jowett argues that the law is afflicted with endemic cisgenderism; it places conditions on trans youth obtaining (gender-affirming) medical treatment that are not applied to cis youth in any other medical treatment context. These more burdensome conditions result in significant harms. Jowett maintains that to remove the discrimination associated with the differential treatment of trans youth, Australian law needs to be reformed to include, among other provisions, a statutory presumption of capacity treating the decisions of those aged 16 years and over the same as those of adults and statutory clarity on the role of parental consent in cases where a youth is declared competent to make their own treatment decisions. These reforms will, Jowett suggests, go some way toward facilitating proper access to healthcare resources for trans youth.

In 'On Sharing the Normative Power of Consent', Peter Schaber brings the concept of shared normative powers to bear on the 'concurrent consents doctrine', that is, the rule according to which the valid consent of an adolescent to medical treatment is determinative of its legal permissibility, whereas an adolescent's valid refusal of the same is not—parents or a court retain the power to consent concurrently with the adolescent, overriding the refusal if the power is exercised. After explaining the concept of normative powers, Schaber elucidates what it means to share a normative power with others. He then considers whether the concurrent consents doctrine involves the sharing of normative powers and whether the rule is morally defensible. Schaber concludes that the limitation of adolescents' normative power of consent is justified in cases where the interest in having normative control served by the full power of consent is outweighed by the interest in being protected from being severely harmed.

In 'Treating Adolescents Differently', Anthony Skelton, Isra Black, and Lisa Forsberg—this volume's editors—develop a well-being-based justification of the asymmetrical treatment of adolescent consent and refusal in the context of healthcare to justify the differential and paternalistic treatment of adolescents more generally. The core of Skelton, Black, and Forsberg's view is a variabilist theory of what is fundamentally and non-instrumentally prudentially good for adolescents, which includes the prudential value of what they call shielding—or the value of being insulated from full responsibility for their choices. This theory of well-being, they argue, explains why adolescents may be treated differentially and paternalistically in numerous domains. It is good for them to be shielded because it allows for a variety of freedom from making certain kinds of decisions in the absence of a safety net provided by others in supportive and caring relationships. Skelton, Black, and Forsberg argue that their account of the justification of differential and paternalistic treatment of adolescents has attractive implications for a range of cases and holds up well in the face of philosophical criticism.

In 'Children and Ineffective Consent', Lisa Forsberg considers different ways in which consent can in some sense be ineffective in terms of guiding consent-receivers' behaviour and their relevance in the context of the 'concurrent consents doctrine', which allows for children's consent to be supplanted with a consent by parents and courts in some cases. Forsberg argues that the way in which children's consent is sometimes ineffective in changing our duties is better explained by views that focus on our duties to children and, in particular, how concern for their well-being structures our duties, such that they are less consent-sensitive, than it is by views that hold children's consent to be invalid due to deficiencies in the consent given or in the consent-giver.

Part III of *Consenting Children* is entitled 'Children's Responsibility'. It comprises three chapters. In 'The Prospective Stance: Children and Responsibility', Meghan Winsby examines our practice of praising and blaming young children. She argues that existing views addressing children's responsibility fail to capture the full extent of what is involved in such practices. She advocates for a normative competence view which holds that young children may be fully responsible for their behaviour in some cases but not in others. Whether they are depends on the developmental status of their normative competence which, she argues, is substantial in more cases than traditional views allow. Winsby goes on to argue that the best way through which to clarify our practice of holding children responsible, of praising and blaming them, is to adopt a prospective—forward looking—stance toward children. From this stance, we stand prepared to hold children responsible, paying close attention to their developing moral competencies for opportunities to attribute full-blown praise and blame to them.

In 'Consent and Responsibility: How (Not) to Justify Diverging Thresholds for Minors', Maximilian Kiener assesses the moral justification of diverging age thresholds for criminal responsibility and for consent to medical treatment. Kiener argues that although the conditions for valid consent and moral responsibility include competence, information, and voluntariness, the conditions operate differently in the two cases. For example, while drunkenness may render one's consent to sexual intercourse invalid because of its effect on competence, it does not mitigate one's responsibility for driving under the influence, even if in both cases one behaved in ways that one knew would render one incompetent to consent or act responsibly. The differences rest on facts about what we owe to each other. We owe it to others not to exploit their drunkenness to obtain sex and not to enhance the extent to which we wrong them or expose them to harm. Turning back to the diverging age thresholds, Kiener argues that even though the conditions of responsibility and valid consent behave differently in different contexts, understanding such differences still reveals that at least some existing diverging age thresholds lack moral justification. Whether a child's consent is valid, or a child is criminally responsible, will be issue- and context-specific and dependent on what we owe to children.

In 'What's Special About Juvenile Justice', David O. Brink discusses the trend in the USA of transferring juvenile criminal offenders to adult courts where they are subject to lengthier and significantly more punitive sanctions. Brink argues for what he calls the asymmetry thesis: other things equal, juvenile crimes ought to be punished less severely than adult crimes. After considering and rejecting a political rationale for the asymmetry involving appeal to the fact that juveniles are denied the vote, Brink presents a case in favour of a developmental rationale. On this view, the asymmetry is justified on grounds that juveniles are less mature than adults: they are in general less normatively competent and have diminished control over their volitions and understanding of normative reasons and their gravity. This makes them, in general, less culpable than and therefore less deserving of punishment than adult offenders. Together with various pragmatic considerations, Brink argues that the immaturity of juveniles justifies a rejection of the current practice in the USA respecting the transfer of juvenile offenders to adult court for sentencing and punishment.

## Consenting children: origins, focus and future

*Consenting Children* brings together many papers that were presented at the 'Children's Consent: Philosophy and Law in Conversation' workshop held at Exeter College, Oxford, in March 2019. The workshop was co-organised by the volume's editors, together with Jonathan Herring. It was designed to bring together academics working in philosophy and law to explore children's consent to medical treatment, in addition to a range of closely related issues, including children's values, well-being, responsibility, and decision-making capacity. The event sought to facilitate a broader, interdisciplinary understanding of these matters, as well as of the nature of childhood and of consent and responsibility more broadly.

We are pleased to have been able to attract additional scholars at a range of career stages and holding a diversity of perspectives to contribute to this volume and so to expand its remit. We hope that this volume contributes to the ongoing and perennially important issue of the proper treatment of children—and their consent, autonomy, responsibility, and well-being.

*Consenting Children*'s chapters focus on children's consent and other notions in a healthcare context, while also including important contributions to discussions of children's responsibility for criminal and other kinds of behaviour and consent to sex. The emphasis on healthcare reflects the fact that medical decision-making is the domain where discussions of children's consent, and differential treatment of children more broadly, have achieved perhaps the highest degree of theoretical and practical sophistication—especially in law but also in philosophy. As a result, healthcare provides a rich setting for deeper engagement with the legal and philosophical issues related to children's consent.

Moreover, the healthcare context provides a valuable basis for thinking about consent, autonomy, responsibility, and well-being across a variety of social domains.

Importantly, the insights these chapters offer are not limited to the medical domain. The views developed in the chapters on medical decision-making may be generalised and applied to other contexts. Chapters by Skelton, Black, and Forsberg, as well as by Kiener and Montgomery, for example, defend views applicable to the domains of education and employment and to discussions of the limits of parental authority and of protecting the vulnerable. There is much here that might facilitate conversations about a broad range of children's rights and responsibilities, as well as the interests of other parties.

Many of the chapters on medical decision-making focus, to some extent, on the approach to children's consent taken in the law in England and Wales. The principal reason for the attention to English law is that the English *Gillick* case lays the foundation for much common law legal doctrine on minor capacity and agency (including in Australia and Canada),[3] but also because the subsequent English legal authorities (especially *Re R* and *Re W*) appear to challenge (or 'retreat' from) *Gillick*,[4] yielding fertile conditions for academic debate. The English law focus is relevant to other common law jurisdictions where the contours of the jurisprudence on children's consent remains unclear (perhaps especially Ireland and New Zealand) and potentially susceptible to development in a similar direction to England and Wales.

Discussion of the *Gillick* doctrine is also relevant to non-common law or hybrid jurisdictions, to the extent that legal rules may recognise minors' autonomy (to some degree), for example, 'mature minor' doctrines in US jurisdictions, and laws governing '*la capacité de discernement*' and equivalent concepts in civilian jurisdictions.

*Consenting Children* also includes chapters that present academically fruitful perspectives on legal practices in other jurisdictions. Jowett's chapter on children's consent to gender-affirming medical interventions takes place against the backdrop of the more advanced state of development of Australian case law compared to that of England and Wales, and Brink's chapter on juvenile justice philosophically engages with youth criminal justice in the USA, and in particular the controversial practice of transferring youth offenders to the adult criminal justice system.

English law—especially the legal and academic contestation of *Gillick*, as well as its interaction with *Re R*, *Re W*—is also a useful tool for eliciting and elucidating the normative issues relevant to children's consent. Indeed, many of the chapters whose focus is English law explore issues of normative significance relevant to any community in which conflicts between children, parents, professionals, and state institutions may arise in a variety of contexts. For example, Schaber's philosophical analysis of the more abstract notion of normative powers uses the English

[3] *Gillick v West Norfolk and Wisbech AHA* [1986] AC 112.

[4] *Re R (A Minor) (Wardship: Consent to Treatment)* [1992] Fam 11 (CA); *Re W (A Minor) (Medical Treatment: Court's Jurisdiction)* [1993] Fam 64 (CA).

'concurrent consents' doctrine as a focal point for his discussion, Bridgeman's analysis of English minor medical treatment cases offers an inspiring vision for how feminist and care ethics might enhance the 'ethics of justice' operative in our treatment of children, and Cave's examination of the restrictions on the medical choices of children in England and Wales reflects on the normative implications of balancing children's competent views and their best interests.

Readers less familiar with English law, and with existing legal scholarship on children's consent, will find helpful orientation on the rules governing the legal validity and legal effectiveness of children's consent—and how this regime contrasts with that applicable to adults—in chapters by Black and by Donnelly and Lyons. All chapters, whether more legal or philosophical, contain a primer on the key doctrinal or normative concerns to facilitate accessibility of the subject matter for a wide variety of readers.

*Consenting Children* offers a set of perspectives on the differential treatment of children, especially related to children's consent and capacity, decision-making powers, responsibility, autonomy, and well-being, among other topics. It aims to deepen our understanding of these topics within specific domains. However, as we have endeavoured to show in this brief introduction, and as our contributors show, many of the arguments and insights presented here have broader relevance and can be applied to many contexts. The chapters in this volume contribute to an ongoing dialogue—one we hope will continue to grow to include a wider range of voices and jurisdictions, each bringing out new challenges and new insights.

# Part I

# Children's Consent and Capacity

1

# Setting the Standard(s) for Capacity: Are Children Different?

MARY DONNELLY AND BARRY LYONS

THE FOUNDATIONAL ACADEMIC narrative in respect of the decision of the House of Lords in *Gillick v West Norfolk and Wisbech AHA*[1] is that it was a victory for children's rights, protecting children's autonomy and privacy from parental intrusion and control.[2] The legal tool to deliver this protection was the individualised evaluation of each child's decision-making ability, subsequently known as *Gillick* competence. Yet, the standard for *Gillick* competence has always been problematic, not least because of the evident difference between *Gillick* competence and other capacity standards.[3] This difference became especially apparent following the introduction of the Mental Capacity Act 2005 (MCA). For the most part, the MCA applies to young people over the age of 16 years.[4] This means that different standards are applied in respect of the same task to children under the age of 16 years and to young people aged 16 and 17 years.[5]

These inconsistencies have led a number of commentators to advocate change. For some, including the current president of the Family Division writing extra-judicially, the solution lies in incorporating elements of the MCA standard into the standard for

[1] *Gillick v West Norfolk and Wisbech AHA* [1986] AC 112.

[2] See, for example, J. Eekelaar, 'The Emergence of Children's Rights', *Oxford Journal of Legal Studies*, 6 (1986), 161–86; J. Fortin, 'The *Gillick* Decision: Not Just a High-Water Mark', in S. Gilmore, J. Herring and R. Probert (eds), *Landmark Cases in Family Law* (Oxford, Hart Publishing, 2011), pp. 199–224.

[3] See B. Lyons, 'Dying to be Responsible: Adolescence, Autonomy and Responsibility', *Legal Studies*, 30 (2014), 257–78; E. Cave, 'Goodbye *Gillick*? Identifying and Resolving Problems with the Concept of Child Competence', *Legal Studies*, 34 (2014), 103–22.

[4] See Code of Practice to the Mental Capacity Act 2005 (London, Department of Constitutional Affairs, 2007) paras 12.6–12.25.

[5] Note that, for clarity, this chapter uses 'children' to refer to those under the age of 16 years and young people for those aged 16 and 17 years.

*Proceedings of the British Academy*, **279**, 15–30, © Authors 2025.

*Gillick* competence.[6] For others, a more radical solution is needed. Thus, Emma Cave advocates the application of the MCA standard alongside another test 'which is specifically designed to encapsulate those factors that render some young people functionally incapacitated'.[7] The question of standards has been before the courts and received conflicting responses. In *Re S (Child as Parent: Adoption: Consent)*, Cobb J chose to 'read across to, and borrow from, the relevant concepts and language' of the MCA in applying the standard for *Gillick* competence.[8] In contrast, in *NHS Trust v X (In the Matter of X (A Child) (No. 2))*[9] Sir James Munby delivered a strong (albeit *obiter*) endorsement of the distinction. He considered that *Gillick* competence and decision-making capacity as understood at common law and under the MCA were 'both historically and conceptually quite distinct';[10] the former was a matter for 'child and adolescent psychology'; the latter was in the 'realm of psychiatry'.[11]

This chapter explores the distinction between the standards for MCA capacity and *Gillick* competence in respect of healthcare decision-making. With this in mind, we start by looking back, identifying the different roles played by *Gillick* competence and by MCA capacity in establishing the boundaries of law in the changing medico-legal landscape of the 1980s and early 1990s. Because of these different roles, the two standards developed in distinct ways and have come to reflect different understandings of autonomy. Capacity serves as a gatekeeper for decision-making authority (referred to here as the autonomy/authority vision), while *Gillick* competence has come to play a distinctly less authoritative role. For this reason, we argue that, while there is some scope for the incorporation of elements of the MCA standard into the standard for *Gillick* competence, as the role of *Gillick* competence has evolved and reduced, this is likely to be of limited practical relevance.

## Drawing the boundaries of law

The latter part of the 20th century saw profound changes in the ways in which law and medicine interacted.[12] In respect of both children/young people and adults with impaired capacity, this period saw courts having to engage in the task of boundary

[6] A. McFarlane, 'Mental Capacity: One Standard for All Ages', *Family Law*, 41 (2011), 479–85; see also V. Chico and L. Hagger, 'The Mental Capacity Act 2005 and Mature Minors: A Missed Opportunity?', *Journal of Social Welfare and Family*, 33 (2011), 157–68.

[7] Cave, 'Goodbye *Gillick*', 119.

[8] [2017] EWHC 2729 (Fam), [15]. This approach was approved and applied in *Bell v Tavistock and Portman NHS Foundation Trust* [2020] EWHC 3274 (Admin), [116]–[118]. This aspect of the judgment was not addressed in *Bell v Tavistock and Portman NHS Foundation Trust and Ors* [2021] EWCA Civ 1363, with the Court of Appeal finding at [83] that a comparison between *Gillick* competence and MCA capacity did not assist in the case in question.

[9] [2021] EWHC 65 (Fam). Hereafter referred to as *Re X*.

[10] [2021] EWHC 65 (Fam), [73].

[11] [2021] EWHC 65 (Fam), [73].

[12] From the rich body of literature on the dynamics of these changes see D. Rothman, *Strangers at the Bedside: A History of How Law and Bioethics Transformed Medical Decision-Making* (New York, Basic

drawing, identifying when and how the law should intervene in decisions which had hitherto been left to the discretion of parents and the medical profession.

**Locating oversight of adolescent decision-making**

As is well known, the decision in *Gillick* concerned an application by Mrs Gillick for a declaration that guidance on family planning services issued to area health authorities was unlawful. This guidance had been developed by the Department of Health and Social Security in response to policy concerns regarding the levels of teenage pregnancies. It stated that, in exceptional cases, a doctor exercising his or her clinical judgement could decide whether to prescribe contraception to a girl under the age of 16 years. It also expressed the hope that attempts would always be made to persuade children who attended clinics to involve their parent or guardian at the earliest stage of consultation, and that it would be most unusual to provide contraceptive advice to such children without parental consent.

The ambition of Mrs Gillick's request can sometimes be missed. Doing what she had asked would have involved expanding the legal role to encompass the monitoring of public policy evaluations. It is unsurprising that the House of Lords was unenthusiastic about taking on this role. As described by Lord Bridge, '[i]n cases where any proposition of law implicit in a departmental advisory document is interwoven with questions of social and ethical controversy, the court should, in my opinion, exercise its jurisdiction with the utmost restraint'.[13] Faced with the request, the House of Lords sought to draw the boundaries of law's involvement. While recognising that the law had a role in adolescent decision-making and that this was not a matter to be resolved solely in the private realm of the family, the House of Lords located the day-to-day operation of law's role outside the legal sphere. Lord Scarman explained why the medical profession was a better locus for decisions in this regard:

> The truth may well be that the rights of parents and children in this sensitive area are better protected by the professional standards of the medical profession than by 'a priori' legal lines of division between capacity and lack of capacity to consent since any such general dividing line is sure to produce in some cases injustice, hardship, and injury to health.[14]

Thus, the necessary nuance to deal with the inherent challenges was better found somewhere other than the courts.[15] The consequent uncertainty was the price to be paid in order to 'keep the law in line with social experience'.[16]

---

Books, 1991); J. Miola, *Medical Law and Medical Ethics: A Symbiotic Relationship* (Oxford, Hart, 2007); K. Veatch, *The Jurisdiction of Medical Law* (Abingdon, Routledge, 2007).

[13] [1986] AC 112, 194.

[14] [1986] AC 112, 191.

[15] See J. Harrington, 'Privileging the Medical Norm: Liberalism, Self-determination and the Refusal of Treatment', *Legal Studies*, 16 (1996), 348–67.

[16] [1986] AC 112, 119.

The key speeches in *Gillick* diverge on the impact of a finding that a child meets the standard for competence. Lord Scarman viewed competence as the gatekeeper for the transfer of decision-making authority from parent to child,[17] while Lord Fraser's guidelines incorporated a best interests evaluation as part of the process.[18] Viewed through this lens, we can see the subsequent Court of Appeal decisions in *Re R (A Minor) (Wardship: Consent to Treatment)*[19] and *Re W (A Minor) (Medical Treatment: Court's Jurisdiction)*[20] less as the frequently cited 'retreat from *Gillick*'[21] and more as an inevitable unfolding of the role of law in adolescent decision-making. This unfolding will be returned to below, but first we turn to the different role played by capacity in establishing the boundaries of the law in respect of adults.

## Establishing the boundaries of capacity law

For decisions involving adults with impaired capacity, the negotiation of law's boundaries emerged in *Re F (Mental Patient: Sterilisation)*.[22] Here, the House of Lords recognised the court's inherent (declaratory) jurisdiction to authorise a medical intervention (in this case, non-consensual sterilisation) where a person lacked decision-making capacity. In so doing, the House of Lords filled a gap which had been left by the abolition of the *parens patriae* jurisdiction. This jurisdiction had been abolished by the Mental Health Act 1959 based on the policy view at that time that medical and personal matters were not an appropriate subject for law and that decisions where an adult lacked decision-making capacity should be left to medical discretion.[23] While affirming the applicability of the inherent jurisdiction, the House of Lords was also clear in its reinforcement of medical discretion. The Court found that it was not necessary for medical professionals to obtain a judicial declaration prior to making an intervention (although it did describe an application to court in a case such as *Re F* as 'highly desirable').[24] In spite of the Court's reassurance, *Re F* was followed by a steady stream of court applications relating to a range of different issues. Arising from these decisions and subsequent court directions, by degrees the situations in which court involvement was required became established.

While *Re F* concerned the allocation of decision-making authority where a person lacks capacity, the decision did not address what capacity involves. By the time this question came to be considered by the courts in *Re C (Adult: Refusal*

[17] [1986] AC 112, 188–9.

[18] [1986] AC 112, 174.

[19] [1992] Fam 11. Hereafter referred to as *Re R*.

[20] [1993] 3 WLR 758; [1993] Fam 64. Hereafter referred to as *Re W*.

[21] As described in G. Douglas, 'The Retreat from *Gillick*', *Modern Law Review*, 55 (1992), 569–76.

[22] [1990] 2 AC 1.

[23] See K. Jones. *A History of Mental Health Services* (London, Keegan and Paul, 1972) on the pendulum-like movements between legalism and medicalism in mental health law.

[24] [1990] 2 AC 1, 57 *per* Lord Brandon.

*of Medical Treatment)*,[25] the role of law in this sphere had already become well established and the declaratory jurisdiction was routinely being used. This meant that Thorpe J's three-part test for capacity fitted into quite a different legal setting to the novel landscape being carved out in *Gillick*. The standard for capacity was derived from the evidence provided by one of the medical experts, a psychiatrist, Dr Eastman. However, Dr Eastman's evidence was not a result of a psychiatric analysis but was, in fact, based on the position which had been adopted by the Law Commission in its Consultation Paper No. 129.[26]

When the MCA came into force in 2007, decisions involving adults lacking capacity had already been thoroughly incorporated into the legal system. The MCA affords a statutory defence for persons who do an act in connection with the care or treatment of P provided the person reasonably believes that P lacks capacity and that the act is in P's best interests.[27] This was intended to obviate the need for recourse to court in most instances. However, the Code of Practice to the MCA outlines a relatively long list of circumstances in which an application to court should still be made.[28] Accordingly, while the vast majority of day-to-day decisions under the MCA are made informally, formalised assessments of capacity and referrals to the Court of Protection are an integral part of the legal environment in respect of adult capacity. As will be seen below, the role of *Gillick* competence has evolved in an entirely different way.

## Standards in operation: convergence and divergence

The MCA gave a statutory basis to the common law standard for capacity, which had been established in respect of healthcare in *Re C (Adult: Refusal of Medical Treatment)*[29] and refined in *Re MB (An Adult: Medical Treatment)*.[30] The statutory formulation is that a person lacks capacity where s/he is unable to make a decision for him/her self because s/he cannot understand relevant information; retain the information; use or weigh the information as part of the decision-making process; or communicate the decision.[31] The MCA also provides extensive scaffolding for the operation of the standard. This responds to the unavoidable uncertainties in determining whether or not a person has the required abilities by protecting individuals from being inappropriately found to lack capacity. Among the measures included are the (controversial) diagnostic threshold, which requires that the person's

[25] [1994] 1 WLR 290.
[26] *Ibid.*, 295.
[27] MCA s 5.
[28] Code of Practice to the Mental Capacity Act (London, Department of Constitutional Affairs, 2007) para 8.18–8.24.
[29] [1994] 1 WLR 290.
[30] [1997] 2 FCR 541.
[31] MCA s 3(1).

inability to make a decision must arise from 'an impairment of, or disturbance in the functioning of, the mind or brain'[32] and a statutory presumption of capacity.[33] Other scaffolding of the MCA standard includes a requirement that all practicable steps to help the person whose capacity is in question to make the decision should be taken before the person is found unable to make a decision;[34] a requirement that a person should not be treated as unable to make a decision merely because s/he makes an unwise decision;[35] and a requirement that a lack of capacity may not be established merely by reference to a person's age or appearance or to a condition or aspect of behaviour which might lead others to make unjustified assumptions about the person's capacity.[36] The operation of the MCA standard is by no means problem free.[37] Commentators point to assessor subjectivity;[38] excessive judicial deference to medical opinions in preference to other forms of knowledge;[39] a lack of forensic testing of medical evidence;[40] and limited systemic or structured engagement with the MCA abilities.[41] While there is undoubtedly room for improvement,[42] it is still fair to say that, at this point, the MCA standard is well established, solidly grounded in jurisprudence, and generally workable.[43]

The standard for *Gillick* competence pre-dated the common law test for capacity in respect of adults by almost a decade and the MCA standard by almost two. Moreover, as described above, the House of Lords in *Gillick* was more concerned to allocate the task of assessment to medical professionals rather than with setting out clear guidance for the operation of the standard. The House of Lords expressed its confidence that the medical profession would refine and develop the standard. However, this did not happen and instead, as José Miola has shown, guidance provided by the medical profession simply restated the legal position without further elaboration.[44]

32 MCA s 2(1).

33 MCA s 1(2).

34 MCA s 1(3).

35 MCA s 1(4).

36 MCA s 2(3).

37 See House of Lords Select Committee on the Mental Capacity Act 2005, *Mental Capacity Act 2005: Post Legislative Scrutiny* HL Paper 139 (London, Stationary Office, 2014), pp. 33–40.

38 See M. Donnelly, *Healthcare Decision-Making and the Law: Autonomy, Capacity and the Limits of Liberalism* (Cambridge, Cambridge University Press, 2010), pp. 160–9.

39 J. Lindsey, 'Competing Professional Knowledge Claims About Mental Capacity in the Court of Protection', *Medical Law Review*, 28 (2020), 1–29.

40 P. Case, 'Negotiating the Domain of Mental Capacity: Clinical Judgement or Judicial Diagnosis', *Medical Law International*, 16 (2016), 174–205.

41 N. Kane, A. Ruck Keene, G. Owen, and S. Kim, 'Applying Decision-Making Capacity Criteria in Practice: A Content Analysis of Court Judgments', *PLoS ONE*, 16 (2021), 1–16.

42 See suggestions in S. Kim, N. Kane, A. Ruck Keene, and G. Owen, 'Broad Concepts and Messy Realities: Optimising the Application of Mental Capacity Criteria', *Journal of Medical Ethics*, 48 (2022), 838–44.

43 A. Ruck-Keene, N. Kane, S. Kim, and G. Owen, 'Mental Capacity: Why Look for a Paradigm Shift?', *Medical Law Review*, 31 (2023), 340–57.

44 See Miola, *Medical Ethics*, p. 185; see also J. Harrington, 'Of Paradox and Plausibility: The Dynamic of Change in Medical Law', *Medical Law Review*, 22 (2014), 305–25 at 308.

### *Gillick* competence in the courts

Given its unstable foundations, it is no surprise that the test for *Gillick* competence has turned out to be imprecise and highly malleable. As discussed below, very little is known about how medical professionals assess *Gillick* competence. However, from the relatively small number of cases before the courts, we can see overt manipulation of the standard so as to incorporate broader outcome-based considerations. This has included the elevation of the standard to essentially unattainable levels in some treatment refusal cases,[45] on the stated basis that the court 'should be very slow to allow an infant to martyr himself'.[46] A similar elevation of the standard may be seen in the (now deprecated) decision of the Divisional High Court in *Bell v Tavistock and Portman NHS Foundation Trust* in respect of consent to puberty blockers.[47] Although recognising that 'in achieving *Gillick* competence it is important not to set the bar too high',[48] the Court went on to outline a detailed set of information which needed to be understood, including 'an understanding of the immediate and long-term consequences of the treatment, the limited evidence available as to its efficacy or purpose, the fact that the vast majority of patients proceed to the use of cross-sex hormones, and its potential life-changing consequences for a child'.[49] Given the scope of what was required, it is unsurprising that the Divisional Court identified 'enormous difficulties' for a child under the age of 16 in reaching this standard.[50]

We can also see the standard being reduced so as to ensure a suitable outcome. In *An NHS Trust v A, B, C and A Local Authority*, Mostyn J found that A, who had just passed her 13th birthday, was competent to consent to the termination of her pregnancy in spite of the fact that doubts had been raised from earlier meetings because A was uncommunicative[51] and the medical evidence indicated that it was difficult to say whether she understood every nuance of the conversation. The standard applied was described as 'sufficient understanding and intelligence'[52] and the court was clear that, once this was reached, the matter of best interests was not relevant.[53] In the emergency context in which this case was heard,[54] there is no doubting the convenience of the finding of competence, given that the medical expert (whose evidence was quoted in full by the court) found it difficult to assess

[45] *Re E (A Minor) (Medical Treatment)* [1993] 1 FLR 386; *Re L (Medical Treatment) (Gillick Competency)* [1998] 2 FLR 810.
[46] *Re E* [1993] 1 FLR 386, 394.
[47] [2020] EWHC 3274 (Admin); *Bell v Tavistock and Portman NHS Foundation Trust and Ors* [2021] EWCA Civ 1363.
[48] [2020] EWHC 3274 (Admin), [130].
[49] [2020] EWHC 3274 (Admin), [151].
[50] [2020] EWHC 3274 (Admin), [151].
[51] [2014] EWHC 1445 (Fam), [8].
[52] [2014] EWHC 1445 (Fam), [10].
[53] [2014] EWHC 1445 (Fam), [10].
[54] A and her family had not become aware of the pregnancy until four days prior to the hearing at which point she was over 21 weeks pregnant and very close to the statutory cut-off of 24 weeks.

whether termination of the pregnancy would be in A's best interests. Ultimately, neither the court nor the expert seemed comfortable taking responsibility to make a judgement regarding the termination. The effect of this 'reinstatement' of *Gillick* competence[55] was to leave the ultimate responsibility for a profoundly difficult choice with an evidently vulnerable 13-year-old.[56]

## Moves toward convergence

The strongest authority for convergence in standards is found in *Re S (Child as Parent: Adoption: Consent)*, where Cobb J found that the question of whether a child had 'sufficient understanding and intelligence to enable him or her to understand fully what is proposed'[57] (in this case consent to adoption) should be assessed on the basis of the abilities outlined in the MCA.[58] Cobb J also affirmed the applicability of a functional approach, describing assessment of *Gillick* competence as decision-specific and child-specific, and noted that lack of competence in another sphere does not mean a lack of competence in respect of the decision at issue.[59] Cobb J justified the integration of the MCA abilities into the standard for *Gillick* competence on the basis that this provided consistency in approach in respect of consent to adoption regardless of whether the parent was aged over 16 years. It would be, he said, 'illogical if the court applied a materially different test of capacity/competence depending on which side of their 16th birthday the parent fell'.[60] As shown below, incorporating the MCA abilities into the standard for *Gillick* competence may reduce inconsistency, but it does not remove it. A more persuasive case for incorporation is that the MCA abilities provide necessary structures in assessing *Gillick* competence. Abstract terms from *Gillick* such as maturity or intelligence are of little instructional value and inevitably lead to the kind of malleability identified above. While the MCA standard is not free from difficulties, its task-specific and ability-focussed approach does at least provide a workable basis for engagement with the task of assessment. The assessor has something to measure and a standard to measure it with.

Some aspects of the MCA scaffolding can also be applied to *Gillick* competence. In *Re S (Child as Parent: Adoption: Consent)*, Cobb J supported the

[55] K. Moreton, '*Gillick* Reinstated: Judging Mid-Childhood Competence in Healthcare Law: *An NHS Trust v ABC & A Local Authority* [2014] EWHC 1445 (Fam)', *Medical Law Review*, 23 (2015), 303–14 at 308.

[56] Contrast the decision in *Re X (A Child) (Capacity to Consent to Termination)* [2014] EWHC 1871 (Fam) where Munby J found it to be in the best interests of a girl (aged 13 years and 9 months) with significant difficulties to have a termination of her pregnancy (this finding according with the views of the girl).

[57] *Gillick v West Norfolk and Wisbech AHA* [1986] AC 112, 188–9 *per* Lord Scarman.

[58] [2017] EWHC 2729 (Fam), [18]. The birth mother was aged under 16 years and had intellectual disabilities; she wished to consent to the adoption but questions arose regarding her competence in this regard.

[59] [2017] EWHC 2729 (Fam), [17].

[60] [2017] EWHC 2729 (Fam), [19].

incorporation of the MCA requirement that all practicable steps should be taken to support the child to make the decision about adoption,[61] including the provision of age-appropriate information.[62] This approach is in line with contemporary children's rights-based approaches to decision-making, discussed further below. However, the core elements of the MCA scaffolding—the presumption of capacity, the protection of unwise decisions, and the diagnostic threshold—do not apply to children. For children, therefore, the standard for *Gillick* competence has to do all of the normative work on its own. This means that assessments cannot but be infused by judicial values as well as by the emotional backdrop against which the decisions are made (a theme to which we return below).

## *Gillick* competence: a peripheral role in contemporary context

Within the traditional liberal formulation of autonomy, capacity is centrally important because it serves as the gatekeeper for decision-making authority (referred to below as *the autonomy/authority vision*).[63] The person with capacity can make decisions for themselves while decisions are made for the person found to lack capacity on the basis of an evaluation of their best interests. The autonomy/authority vision represents the approach in respect of adults under the MCA,[64] although the increased importance of the wishes and feelings/beliefs and values of a person lacking capacity has resulted in a more subjective, person-centred assessment of best interests.[65] In contrast, *Gillick* competence plays a much more peripheral role, both in law and in clinical practice.

### De-linking *Gillick* competence and autonomy/authority

As described above, the decision in *Re R* presaged the de-linking of *Gillick* competence from legal authority, with Lord Donaldson finding that the parental right to consent survived even if the child were found to be *Gillick* competent.[66] This was

[61] [2017] EWHC 2729 (Fam), [41].
[62] [2017] EWHC 2729 (Fam), [42].
[63] See Donnelly, *Healthcare Decision-Making and the Law*, pp. 90–1.
[64] Note however, the growth in the usage of the inherent jurisdiction in respect of vulnerable adults who fall outside of the MCA: see *Re SA (Vulnerable Adult with Capacity: Marriage)* [2005] EWHC 2942 (Fam); see generally, M. Dunn *et al.*, 'To Empower or to Protect? Constructing the "Vulnerable Adult" in English Law and Public Policy', *Legal Studies*, 28 (2008), 234–53; J. Herring and J. Wall, 'Autonomy, Capacity and Vulnerable Adults: Filling the Gaps in the Mental Capacity Act', *Legal Studies*, 35 (2015), 698–719.
[65] See e.g. *Aintree University Hospitals NHS Foundation Trust v James* [2013] UKSC 67; *Wye Valley NHS Trust v B* [2015] EW/COP 60.
[66] [1992] Fam 11.

followed by *Re W* where judicial authority to override a minor's decision was found to subsist until the minor achieved the age of majority. In both cases, the Court of Appeal identified difficulties with the way in which *Gillick* competence had been assessed by the relevant medical professionals/court of first instance.[67] However, the Court chose not to revisit or refine the standard or indeed to utilise the provisions of the Mental Health Act 1983,[68] preferring a more extensive re-alignment of decision-making authority not just for children but also for young people up to the age of 18 years.[69] Moreover, the Court did not restrict the de-linking to refusal of life-sustaining treatment but was clear that this applied in principle to all treatment refusals, including for example, a child or young person's refusal of abortion (although Lord Donaldson was confident that the operation of 'medical ethics' would prevent the 'hair-raising' possibility of an abortion being carried out against the wishes of the child/young person).[70]

The de-linking of competence/capacity from decision-making authority evoked a good degree of academic criticism,[71] although the position has also had its academic defenders.[72] The ongoing applicability of the Court of Appeal's position was affirmed

[67] In *Re R* [1992] 1 Fam 11 the medical expert had given evidence that the young woman, aged 15 years, had sufficient maturity and understanding to make the decision (to refuse anti-psychotic medication) and that she was rational at the time. This led Lord Donaldson to note (at 25) that it was clear that the test for *Gillick* competence was capable of being misunderstood. In *Re W* [1992] 3 WLR 758, 769, Lord Donaldson indicated that Thorpe J had erred at first instance in finding the young woman to have capacity because he had not taken 'sufficiently into account (perhaps because the point did not emerge as clearly before him as it did before us), … that it is a feature of anorexia nervosa that it is capable of destroying the ability to make an informed choice'.

[68] See M. Brazier and C. Bridge, 'Coercion or Caring: Analysing Adolescent Autonomy', *Legal Studies*, 16 (1996), 84–109.

[69] *Re W* [1992] 3 WLR 758.

[70] *Re W* [1992] 3 WLR 758, 767. The reference to 'medical ethics' as used here is best understood as referring to the professional ethical standards of the medical profession rather than to individual moral choices by medical professionals: on this distinction, see C. Foster and J. Miola, 'Who's in Charge? The Relationship Between Medical Law, Medical Ethics and Medical Morality', *Medical Law Review*, 23 (2015), 505–30.

[71] From the substantial body of literature, see e.g. G. Douglas, 'The Retreat from *Gillick*'; J. Murphy, 'W(h)ither Adolescent Autonomy?', *Journal Social Welfare and Family Law*, 14 (1992), 529–44; M. Freeman, 'Rethinking *Gillick*', in M. Freeman (ed.), *Children's Health and Children's Rights* (Leiden/Boston, MA, Martinus Nijhoff, 2006), pp. 201–17; J. Coggon, 'Varied and Principled Understandings of Autonomy', *Health Care Analysis*, 15 (2007), 235–55; E. Cave and J. Wallbank 'Minors' Capacity to Refuse Treatment: A Reply to Gilmore and Herring', *Medical Law Review*, 20 (2012), 423–49.

[72] See e.g. N. Lowe and S. Juss, 'Medical Treatment – Pragmatism and the Search for Principle', *Modern Law Review*, 56 (1993), 865–72 and S. Gilmore and J. Herring, '"No" Is the Hardest Word: Consent and Children's Autonomy', *Child and Family Law Quarterly*, 23 (2011), 3–25. See also the philosophical justification of the 'concurrent consents doctrine' (whereby consent may be given by the child/adolescent or by the person with parental responsibility or by the court) in A. Skelton, L. Forsberg and I. Black, 'Overriding Adolescent Refusals of Treatment', *Journal of Ethics and Social Philosophy*, 20 (2021), 221–47. Note also the endorsement of the Court of Appeal's position by the Irish High Court in *HSE v JM and Anor* [2013] IEHC 13 and *XY a minor suing by her guardian ad litem Raymond McEvoy v HSE* [2013] IEHC 490.

by Sir James Munby in *Re X*.[73] The case concerned a 15-year-old girl with severe sickle cell disease requiring ongoing blood transfusions, which she refused. Following a detailed and wide-ranging analysis,[74] which encompassed the implications of the Human Rights Act 1998, the MCA, the decision of the Supreme Court of Canada in *AC and Others v Manitoba (Director of Child and Family Services)*,[75] as well as changes in societal norms, Sir James concluded that 'the learning' in *Re R* and *Re W* emerged unscathed.[76] Any change was a matter for Parliament and not for the courts.[77]

Significantly, Sir James Munby also described it as 'conventional wisdom' that the judicial right of veto was not restricted to treatment refusals but also extended to 'vetoing some procedure to which the child has consented' in circumstances where 'the consequences of the child's decision is likely to be serious risk to life or death'.[78] It is not clear what exactly Sir James had in mind here. One possibility is organ donation, which, in *Re W*, Lord Donaldson had identified as a situation in which doctors could not rely on the consent of a minor without also having parental consent.[79] As Lord Donaldson had noted, organ donation falls outside of s 8 of the Family Law Reform Act 1969, which refers to consent to 'surgical, medical and dental treatment' (including diagnostic and ancillary procedures) and which would not encompass surgery for the purposes of organ donation.[80] It is difficult to see many circumstances beyond organ donation in which s 8 would not apply (i.e. where the intervention does not constitute 'treatment') and in which there is also a serious risk to life or death. Nonetheless, this further reinforces the different level of decision-making authority associated with *Gillick* competence (and, indeed, MCA capacity in young people).

The courts' de-linking of *Gillick* competence and decision-making authority reflects a similar stance to that in evidence in the manipulation of the standard for *Gillick* competence discussed earlier. This reflects a range of extra-legal considerations. One is the impact of emotion on judicial decision-making in this sphere.[81] This is perhaps best summarised by Sir Mark Hedley who writes (extra-judicially) about why he defends 'the basic right of society to protect those under 18 from the consequences of refusing treatment'[82] as follows: 'The death of a child resulting

[73] [2021] EWHC 65 (Fam). For commentary, see E. Cave, 'Confirmation of the High Court's Power to Override a Child's Treatment Decision: *A NHS Trust v X (In the Matter of X (A Child) (No. 2)) (Re X)* [2021] EWHC 65 (Fam)', *Medical Law Review*, 29 (2021), 537–46.

[74] In addition to the parties, the High Court invited submissions from the Children and Family Court Advisory Support Service (Cafcass).

[75] [2009] SCC 30.

[76] [2021] EWHC 65 (Fam), [162].

[77] [2021] EWHC 65 (Fam), [162].

[78] [2021] EWHC 65 (Fam), [2].

[79] [1992] 3 WLR 758, 767.

[80] [1992] 3 WLR 758, 767.

[81] On the role of emotion in the task of judging, see S. Roach Anleu and K. Mack, *Judging and Emotion: A Socio-Legal Analysis* (Abingdon, Routledge, 2021).

[82] M. Hedley, *The Modern Judge: Power, Responsibility and Society's Expectations* (Bristol, Lexus Nexus, 2016), p. 45.

from a refusal of treatment should be a decision for which some adult bears responsibility. One also has to recognise that judges need to sleep that night too, and that is not perhaps always irrelevant to a decision to overrule a refusal.'[83]

This approach also reflects a different conception of temporality at work in decisions involving children, which is not just concerned with the present—the time at which the decision is to be made. Instead, it involves a consideration of a life-yet-to-be-lived. The future-facing vision is perhaps most effectively summarised by Sir James Munby P's description of the judicial role in *Re X*:

> [O]ur objective must be to bring the child to adulthood in such a way that the child is best equipped both to decide what kind of life they want to lead—what kind of person they want to be—and to give effect so far as practicable to their aspirations. Put shortly, our objective must be to maximise the child's opportunities in every sphere of life as they enter adulthood.[84]

For Sir James, this judicial objective explains why the court could exercise its discretion 'to require a teenager to submit against their wishes to lifesaving medical treatment'.[85] As he paraphrased Nolan LJ in *Re W*, 'the duty of the court is to ensure so far as it can that children attain the age of 18 at which an individual is free to do with his life what he wishes'.[86] This future-facing vision also explains the spectre of regret which haunted the Divisional High Court in *Bell v Tavistock and Portman NHS Foundation Trust*.[87] Recounting her regret at the decision to begin a female to male medical transition at the age of 16 with the prescription of puberty blockers by Gender Identity Development Service (GIDS), Quincy Bell described how she 'started to realise that the vision I had as a teenager of becoming male was strictly a fantasy and that it was not possible', leaving her feeling 'more lost, isolated and confused than I did when I was pre-transition'.[88] This led the Divisional Court to conclude that 'adolescents find it difficult to contemplate or comprehend what their life will be like as adults and that they do not always consider the longer-term consequences of their actions is perhaps a statement of the obvious'.[89]

These judicial approaches to temporality reflect elements of Joel Feinberg's influential conception of the child's 'right to an open future'.[90] This 'right' is premised on

[83] Hedley, *The Modern Judge*, p. 46.

[84] [2021] EWHC 65 (Fam), [21]. In this, Sir James Munby was quoting from his own judgment in *Re G (Education: Religious Upbringing)* [2012] EWCA Civ 1233, [80].

[85] *Re G (Education: Religious Upbringing)* [2012] EWCA Civ 1233, [81].

[86] *Re G (Education: Religious Upbringing)* [2012] EWCA Civ 1233, [81] from [1993] Fam 64, 94.

[87] [2020] EWHC 3274 (Admin).

[88] [2020] EWHC 3274 (Admin), [81].

[89] [2020] EWHC 3274 (Admin), [141].

[90] J. Feinberg, 'The Child's Right to an Open Future', in W. Aiken and H. LaFollette (eds), *Whose Child?: Children's Rights, Parental Authority and State Power* (Totowa, NJ, Rowman & Littlefield, 1980), pp. 124–53; *The Moral Limits of the Criminal Law: Harm to Self* (New York, Oxford University Press, 1986), pp. 325–6. An alternative philosophical justification is the concept of 'shielding' (the 'idea that it is prudentially good for an adolescent to be free from making consequential decisions without a safety net' identified by Skelton *et al.* 'Overriding Adolescent Refusals', 240.

the view that certain children's rights are distinct to those of adults and should be understood as 'rights-in-trust' or 'anticipatory autonomy rights'. These rights 'look like adult autonomy rights … that are to be saved for the child until he is an adult but which can be violated "in advance", so to speak, before the child is even in a position to exercise them'.[91] Feinberg is concerned with the child who 'cannot very well exercise his free choice until later when he is more fully formed and capable'.[92] Nonetheless, this future-facing conception of autonomy can be contrasted with the largely synchronous view of autonomy which is adopted in respect of adults.[93] For the purposes of the discussion here, the significant point to be noted is that given that decisions about *Gillick* competence involve a balance of autonomy and protection, the conceptualisation of autonomy as something that happens in the future reduces the significance of autonomy in the present. Moreover (although this argument has not been tested in the courts), if an open future is conceptualised as something to which a child has a right, judicial protection of anticipatory autonomy could be regarded as a matter of duty, creating a presumption against a finding of *Gillick* competence where the stakes are high.

### *Gillick* competence in clinical practice

There is remarkably little data about how (and indeed whether) *Gillick* competence operates in clinical practice. Such data as there is indicates that interpretations of the applicable standard are variable and confused,[94] and that external factors (such as the child's appearance and age and the assessor's philosophical perspectives and idiosyncratic heuristics)[95] impact on decisions about *Gillick* competence. There is also evidence of professional discomfort in proceeding on the basis of *Gillick* competence alone without the consent of parents.[96]

Most of the time, it would seem that lack of parental consent is not a problem in clinical practice. Regarding Mrs Gillick's concerns about contraception and

[91] Feinberg, 'The Child's Right',125–6.

[92] Feinberg, 'The Child's Right', 125.

[93] See e.g. *Ms B v An NHS Trust* [2002] EWHC 429 (Fam) where Butler-Sloss P rejected the argument that Ms B should wait until she had experienced the one-way weaning programme (from life-sustaining ventilation) before making the decision to have ventilation withdrawn.

[94] See e.g. R. Stretch *et al.*, 'A Qualitative Study to Assess School Nurses' Views on Vaccinating 12–13 year old School Girls Against Human Papillomavirus Without Parental Consent', *BMC Public Health*, 9 (2009), 254; F. Woods *et al.*, 'What Constitutes Consent When Parents and Daughters Have Different Views About Having the HPV Vaccine: Qualitative Interviews with Stakeholders', *Journal of Medical Ethics*, 37 (2011), 466–71; T. Bartholomew and T. Carvalho, 'Medical Practitioners' Competence and Confidentiality Decisions with a Minor: An Anorexia Nervosa Case Study', *Psychology, Health and Medicine*, 12 (2007), 495–508.

[95] A. Teoludska and T. Bartholomew, 'Queensland General Practitioners Applications of the "Mature Minor" Principle: The Role of Patient Age and Gender', *Journal of Law and Medicine*, 18 (2010), 390–401.

[96] See Stretch *et al.*, 'A Qualitative Study'.

abortion, there is no evidence that prescription of contraception to under 16s has been a source of concern or complaint.[97] Ellie Lee's study of abortion found that all but three of the 51 children interviewed who had terminated their pregnancies had informed their parents before the referral for abortion.[98]

Outside of the abortion/contraception context, it would seem that most of the time, children, parents, and clinicians make decisions and work out solutions to disputes which may involve varying degrees of negotiation, compromise and support but which have little to do with whether or not the child is *Gillick* competent.[99] Child involvement and respect for the views of children (irrespective of *Gillick* competence) is a fundamental ethical premise in paediatric care. Thus, the GMC 0–18 Guidance[100] emphasises the importance of involving children and young people in decisions about their healthcare.[101] Medical professionals must take children and young people's views seriously;[102] provide information to children and young people which is easy to understand and appropriate to their age and maturity;[103] and talk directly, and listen, to children and young people who are able to take part in discussions about their care.[104] This approach also coheres with the obligations which arise under article 12 of the United Nations Convention on the Rights of the Child,[105] which requires that the child who is capable of forming their own views has the right to express these views and that these views must be given 'due weight in accordance with the age and maturity of the child'. Studies suggest that this approach is also in line with children's preferences.[106]

This process is very different to the autonomy/authority approach which underpins the MCA. The dissonance is usefully displayed in the Divisional High Court

[97] This assertion is based on analysis of the GMC Annual Reports on *The State of Medical Education and Practice in the UK* available at www.gmc-uk.org/about/what-we-do-and-why/data-and-research/the-state-of-medical-education-and-practice-in-the-uk (accessed 13 October 2021) and NHS complaints data available at https://digital.nhs.uk/data-and-information/publications/statistical/data-on-written-complaints-in-the-nhs (accessed 13 October 2021) (although neither is sufficiently disaggregated to allow for a definitive conclusion).

[98] E. Lee, 'Young Women, Pregnancy and Abortion in Britain: A Discussion of "Law in Practice"', *International Journal of Law, Policy and the Family*, 18 (2004), 283–304 at 290–1. Two of the three were from 'particularly disrupted and unstable backgrounds and were out of touch with their birth parents'.

[99] See e.g. the resolution of several cases involving a child's refusal of an organ transplant: see L. Hagger, *The Child as Vulnerable Patient: Protection and Empowerment* (Farnham, Ashgate, 2009), p. 14; E. Cave 'Adolescent Consent and Confidentiality in the UK', *European Journal of Healthcare Law*, 16 (2009), 309–31.

[100] *0–18 Years: Guidance for all Doctors* (London, GMC, 2007).

[101] GMC Guidance para 14.

[102] GMC Guidance para 16.

[103] GMC Guidance para 17.

[104] GMC Guidance para 19.

[105] General Assembly Resolution 44/25, 20 November 1989.

[106] See e.g. P. Alderson, *Children's Consent to Surgery* (Buckingham, Open University Press, 1993), pp. 154–63; M. Donnelly and U. Kilkelly, 'Child-Friendly Healthcare: Delivering on the Right to be Heard', *Medical Law Review*, 19 (2011), 27–54 at 37.

in *Bell v Tavistock and Portman NHS Foundation Trust*.[107] Here, the Court recounts its request for statistical material on how often the GIDS had not prescribed puberty blockers to someone because they were found not to be *Gillick* competent and were informed that this information could not be provided.[108] Evidencing a degree of scepticism, the Court notes its 'strong impression' that it was 'extremely unusual' to refuse puberty blockers on the grounds of lack of *Gillick* competence and that instead the approach was 'to continue giving the child more information and to have more discussions until s/he is considered *Gillick* competent or is discharged'.[109] This, of course, makes a great deal of sense within a framework based on negotiation, compromise and support and very little in one based on formal assessment of *Gillick* competence.

The negotiation/support approach does not always lead to happy outcomes and sometimes it may be impossible to reach a solution without recourse to the courts. As recognised by Hayden J in *An NHS Foundation Trust v A, M, and P*, the balance to be struck between negotiation and referral to court is a difficult one.[110] In this case, by the time the application for the insertion of a nasojejunal (feeding) tube for a severely malnourished 15-year-old girl came to court,[111] the girl's condition had deteriorated substantially and her life was at risk.[112] While accepting that 'time and care should always be spent exploring the possibilities of an agreed way forward in a patient's best interest',[113] Hayden J noted 'crucial time can sometimes be lost trying to secure acquiescence',[114] and that '[t]here are occasions where it is simply the right course to go to court directly'.[115]

While recourse to the courts clearly remains a necessary element of decision-making for children, this is not to be regarded as the norm. There is clear legal authority for this position from the Court of Appeal in *Bell v Tavistock and Portman NHS Foundation Trust*.[116] In overturning the Divisional High Court's guidance that court intervention was appropriate for the prescription of puberty blockers to children under 16, the Court of Appeal affirmed that it was 'for clinicians to exercise their judgement knowing how important it is the consent is properly obtained, according to the particular individual circumstances, as envisaged by *Gillick* itself, and by referencing to developing understanding in this difficult and controversial area'.[117]

[107] [2020] EWHC 3274 (Admin).
[108] [2020] EWHC 3274 (Admin), [44].
[109] [2020] EWHC 3274 (Admin), [44].
[110] [2014] EWHC 920 (Fam), [18].
[111] The girl suffered from persistent vomiting which clinicians found did not appear to have a physical cause, a conclusion which both the girl and her mother rejected: [2014] EWHC 920 (Fam), [4].
[112] [2014] EWHC 920 (Fam), [17].
[113] [2014] EWHC 920 (Fam), [18].
[114] [2014] EWHC 920 (Fam), [18].
[115] [2014] EWHC 920 (Fam), [18].
[116] [2021] EWCA Civ 1363, [89].
[117] [2021] EWCA Civ 1363, [93].

## Conclusion

This chapter has approached the question of whether children are different when it comes to the standard for capacity in law as a question of 'social fact'.[118] We have argued that, from the outset, *Gillick* competence has played an entirely different role in law to that of capacity in respect of adults now statutorily codified in the MCA. From these different origins, the two standards have evolved in distinct ways. As a result, they now reflect different underpinnings and evoke different judicial responses. This means that while a reasonable case may be made for the incorporation of elements of the MCA standard into the standard for *Gillick* competence, there is no possibility of the two standards converging. This is not to deny that the divergence in approach can lead to arbitrary conclusions. Neither a sixteenth, nor indeed an eighteenth birthday, represents a step change in decision-making ability. The ongoing legitimacy of competence/capacity based distinctions is not because they accurately divide children, young people, and adults but rather, and only insofar as, because they represent the most effective way to structure the balancing of autonomy and protection in the relevant categories.

We have also argued here that as the law has evolved, *Gillick* competence has become largely peripheral to contemporary healthcare decision-making involving children. The courts have long rejected the autonomy/authority model in respect of *Gillick* competence in the more difficult cases, including treatment refusal and organ donation and in the wake of Sir James Munby's endorsement in *Re X*,[119] this does not look set to change. In clinical practice, a different framework applies, grounded in negotiation, compromise, and support, a position which is also underpinned by the Convention on the Rights of the Child. There is, of course, ample scope for critical engagement with the question of how (and whether) this framework is actually delivered upon in clinical practice. We suggest that for the future, it is here, rather than in the operation of *Gillick* competence that the more interesting questions will lie.

[118] As described in E. Durkheim, *The Rules of Sociological Method* (1895), p. 142, social facts are 'manners of acting, thinking and feeling external to the individual, which are invested with a coercive power by virtue of which they exercise control over him'.

[119] [2021] EWHC 65 (Fam). For commentary, see Cave, 'Confirmation of the High Court's Power'.

# 2

# Competence for Minors in Medical Decision-Making: A Life-Stage Approach

ANDREW FRANKLIN-HALL

THE CENTRAL FUNCTION of patient competence (or capacity) determinations is to settle whose medical decisions have final authority. On the standard view, we may paternalistically override a patient's decision only when he is incompetent to make his own choice.[1] Historically, adults have been presumed competent unless shown otherwise, whereas those under the age of medical consent were deemed incompetent as a matter of status. However, many jurisdictions now hold that some minors are mature enough to count as competent to make their own decisions.[2] This is often referred to as the 'mature minor doctrine'. But this raises an important question. Should the standard for competence be the same when applied to adults and minors?

The usual assumption is that there is, indeed, a single standard for judging competence, whatever the subject's age. I will make the contrary case, that adults and minors should be held to different standards. Part of the difficulty, here, is that we are not always clear on the nature of adult competence either. I believe adults are entitled to a *robust* right to autonomy. As long as they have the ability to make a reasonable decision with access to all the available information, adults have the right to make their own choice, even if the decision they ultimately reach is unreasonable, as judged by their own values and convictions. By contrast, I think we should defer to a questionable or risky decision of an adolescent only if it is sensible in light of what is important to her, in spite of the fact that she has the abilities an adult would need to lay claim to the more robust right of autonomy. Taking this more protective stance toward the young is justified, I think, because we can fairly conceive of adolescence as a time-limited probationary stage of life during which we are

[1] Allen E. Buchanan and Dan W. Brock, *Deciding for Others: The Ethics of Surrogate Decision-Making* (Cambridge, Cambridge University Press, 1989), p. 27.

[2] Seminal 'mature-minor doctrine' cases in English, American, and Canadian law include: *Gillick v West Norfolk and Wisbech Area Health Authority* [1985] 3 WLR 830 (HL); *In re EG* 549 NE 2d 322 (Ill 1989); *A v Manitoba* [2009] 2 SRC 181.

*Proceedings of the British Academy*, **279**, 31–47, © Authors 2025.

protecting young people from serious mistakes, while at the same time recognising that, if an important decision cannot be postponed, then it ought to be made in light of what she—not what someone else—cares about. Although this view is not commonly articulated, I think it actually accounts for some strands of our practice better than the more familiar alternatives.

I will proceed as follows. After sorting out some different senses of the word 'competence', I distinguish two broad conceptions: one that appeals to the subjective reasonableness of the decision, the other that appeals to the possession of abilities requisite for making a subjectively reasonable decision. When it comes to adults, I argue that the abilities-based view is superior but that most of us are more protective of adolescents. I then explain why it is justifiable to employ the more restrictive reasonable-decision-based standard when we are dealing with minors.

## Meanings of competence

According to conventional wisdom, it is important to respect the patient's decision about her own medical care but not when the patient is—to put it vaguely—acting seriously irrationally or in significant ignorance. For example, a patient suffering from intensive care unit (ICU) delirium might insist he needs to go to the office or an Alzheimer's patient might refuse medication which he doesn't remember needing. We don't think we should defer to such 'choices'. But in what sense must a decision be irrational to justify overriding it? What if a patient refuses a needed injection simply out of an aversion to needles? In outline, there is broad agreement on the relevant principle: *a decision about a proposed treatment is authoritative when it is voluntary, adequately informed, and made by a competent patient.* Things get controversial, however, once we try to fill this principle out in detail. Here our focus will just be on one part of that principle: the nature of competence.

Before considering different accounts, we should sort out some of the different meanings of the word. In general, 'competence' refers to an ability to do something.[3] Often, in law and ethics, we are concerned with a person's epistemic or deliberative abilities. If Brown is competent to testify as an expert on structure fires, then he has the relevant knowledge to offer an informed opinion on such matters. But 'competence' can also refer to the subject's *authority* to exercise a legal or normative power. If I insist that Green's court was not competent to hear my case, I am saying that the court lacks jurisdiction, not casting aspersions on the personal abilities of the judge. This second sense can refer to the authority of individuals as well—e.g. 'It was within his competence to say that he would not appoint a new trustee.'[4] In some countries, the law prefers the word 'capacity' to 'competence',

[3] 'Competence' in *Black's Law Dictionary* (St Paul, MN, Thomson Reuters, 2014).

[4] 'Competence' in *The Oxford English Dictionary Online*, March 2025. https://www.oed.com/dictionary/competence_n (accessed 25 July 2025).

and the same ambiguity is even *more* prominent here. A 'capacity' can quite naturally refer to a person's natural ability to do something (e.g. 'he has little capacity for thinking through problems of any complexity') or to an individual's authority to exercise certain legal powers (e.g. 'I was acting in my capacity as executor of my father's will').[5]

Let's call the first of these meanings the *natural-abilities sense* (or competence$_A$) and the second the *legal-power sense* (or competence$_P$).[6] The kind of competence$_P$ relevant to our subject is patient 'decisional authority': roughly, the formal power to give, withhold, and/or rescind consent to medical treatment.[7] As Dan Brock and Allen Buchanan put it, when a patient has decision-making authority, his decisions 'must be respected by others and accepted as binding', whereas the decisions of patients without this authority may be set aside, and the final decision made for them by a surrogate on the basis of the patient's best interests.[8]

Regrettably, it is common for usage to slide between competence$_A$ and competence$_P$, but I think the distinction is generally familiar. There is, however, a third meaning of the word that is not well understood, even though it is key to the philosophical debate. To bring this third meaning into resolution, let us ask what connection there might be between competence$_A$ and competence$_P$. A common thought is that competence$_A$ *grounds* competence$_P$. That is, it is in virtue of having the relevant natural psychological abilities to a sufficient degree that one properly has the legal power to make one's own medical decision. This is a plausible view but not an analytic truth. Something other than the possession of certain natural abilities might ground decisional authority. For example, in an influential early essay, Loren Roth, Alan Meisel and Charles Lidz canvas five possible standards of competence: (a) making a choice, (b) making an objectively 'reasonable' choice, (c) making a choice based on 'rational' reasons, (d) the ability to understand the relevant factors relating to making a choice, and (e) actual understanding of those factors.[9] Of these, only (d) represents a genuine ability. The others involve actual performance of the decision-making task in a particular way (or the performance of some preliminary to that task). They are not formal conceptions of authority or competence$_P$ either. What, then, are they conceptions of? Like (d), they identify facts about the decision-maker or his decision that purport to *ground* decision-making authority (competence$_P$). When philosophers offer accounts of competence, this is generally what they are talking about. So, let us call this 'competence in the power-grounding sense' (or competence$_G$).

[5] See the entries on 'capacity' in the *OED* and *Black's Law Dictionary.*

[6] I shall focus on legal powers, but we could also consider non-legal, normative powers more generally.

[7] Dan W. Brock, 'Decisionmaking Competence and Risk', *Bioethics*, 5 (1992), 105–12 at 105.

[8] Buchanan and Brock, *Deciding for Others*, p. 27.

[9] Loren H. Roth, Alan Meisel, and Charles W. Lidz, 'Tests of Competency to Treatment', *American Journal of Psychiatry*, 134 (1977), 279–84.

## Two conceptions of competence

Our quarry is an account of the facts that ground decision-making authority (competence$_G$). Before we consider the *ability* to make a decision, however, let's consider, first, the paradigm case of patient decision-making, which goes something like this: the doctor explains to the patient the diagnosis, the symptoms he can expect, the prognosis without treatment, and the possible interventions along with their benefits, chances of success, and possible complications or side effects. The patient then takes that information and decides, often in dialogue with his medical team and loved ones, which option is best for him given his values and plans. If the patient is initially unsure what is important to him in this situation, his deliberation may need to involve deeper reflection on the nature of his values, which may also involve conversation with others. When the patient reaches a decision made in light of the relevant available information, and that follows reasonably well from his values, then we may say that he has made an *autonomous decision.*

This ideal of the autonomous decision is often presented as the ultimate aim of the shared decision-making process between doctor and patient.[10] Now, competence determinations also seem to have something to do with respecting or promoting the patient's autonomy. But what exactly is the connection? Let's focus on just two possible views.

One says that a patient is competent$_G$ so long as his choice is reasonably autonomous in the above sense. On this *decision-based* conception, competence is undermined when something goes seriously wrong with the patient's actual decision-making process: the patient makes a significant mistake in reasoning, refuses to accept the plain facts, is swayed by some errant passion, or otherwise comes to a conclusion that is deeply at odds with his own values. Competence, therefore, is tied to subjective rationality. Though competence$_A$ is a precondition for competence$_G$, the latter does not consist in the former.

An alternative position is that the patient is competent$_G$ so long as he is *capable* of making an autonomous decision in the above sense, even if his ultimate decision is not at all consistent with what is important to him. What matters, therefore, is not the character of the actual decision but certain properties of the decision-maker at the time of the decision, namely, that one possesses, to a sufficient degree, the epistemic and deliberative abilities for understanding and appreciating the information relevant to the decision,[11] for effectively comparing the pros and cons of different courses of action, for evaluating those options in the light of one's enduring values, for resisting contrary inclinations, and so on. One needs to possess these abilities,

[10] See, for example, Terrence F. Ackerman, 'Why Doctors Should Intervene', *The Hastings Center Report*, 12 (1981), 14–17; Ruth R. Faden and Tom L. Beauchamp, *A History and Theory of Informed Consent* (New York, Oxford University Press, 1986), esp. ch. 7; Dan W. Brock, 'The Ideal of Shared Decision-Making', in his *Life and Death: Philosophical Essays in Biomedical Ethics* (Cambridge, Cambridge University Press, 1993), pp. 55–79.

[11] Thus, the abilities-based model, while not decision *based*, remains decision *relative*.

furthermore, *at the time of the decision*; it is not enough to possess them most of the time.[12] On this *abilities-based* approach, then, competence$_G$ *does* consist in competence$_A$.

You might suppose that the ordinary, common-sense understanding of what grounds decision-making authority is, as the second view says, the possession of certain natural abilities.[13] But when we turn to what is easily the most thorough and influential account of patient competence in the philosophical literature—that found in Buchanan and Brock's *Deciding for Others*—we get a different picture. Buchanan and Brock do, indeed, gloss competence as 'decision-making capacity', and they outline certain 'capacities needed for competence', which include the kinds of abilities for understanding, deliberation, and decision that I mentioned above.[14] But these capacities, they observe, are possessed and exercised by degrees, and when they finally come to articulating the criterion for assessing competence, they say that what matters is the quality of the 'decision-making process' itself:

> The evaluation of the patient's decision making will seek to assess how well the patient has understood the nature of the proposed treatment and any significant alternatives, the expected benefits and risks and the likelihood of each, the reason for the recommendation, and then whether the patient *has made a choice that reasonably conforms to his or her underlying aims and values*.[15]

In fact, at least when the choice seems questionable from a medical point of view, Buchanan and Brock hold that, for a patient to make a competent decision, there should be 'no significant mistakes in the patient's reasoning and decision making' and that the decision should be 'reasonably related to the patient's interests' as defined by his own values.[16] This, then, is a decision-based, not an abilities-based, account of the facts that ground decision-making authority.[17]

These two conceptions of competence seem rooted in concern for two different values—both of which often travel under the name of 'autonomy'. Daniel Brudney and John Lantos distinguish these, dubbing them 'authenticity' and 'agency'.[18] Whereas *authenticity* is the value of choosing in a way that expresses or conforms to

[12] I assume we can make sense of the idea that people sometimes fail to make reasonable decisions they were capable of making. If, as sceptics allege, no satisfactory analysis is available of this ability to do otherwise, then that is an objection to this model.

[13] Eric Vogelstein says this is the orthodox view (which he rejects). I think most writers *say* that competence is about possessing abilities, but if you look closely, their accounts are not always truly abilities based. See Vogelstein, 'Competence and Ability', *Bioethics*, 28 (2014), 235–44.

[14] Buchanan and Brock, *Deciding for Others*, pp. 18, 23–5.

[15] Buchanan and Brock, *Deciding for Others*, p. 56. Emphasis added.

[16] Buchanan and Brock, *Deciding for Others*, p. 54.

[17] In other writing, Brock does seem to assume an abilities-based model. See Brock and Steven A. Wartman, 'When Competent Patients Make Irrational Decisions', in Brock (ed.), *Life and Death* (Cambridge, Cambridge University Press, 1993), pp. 80–92.

[18] Daniel Brudney and John Lantos, 'Agency and Authenticity: Which Value Grounds Patient Choice?', *Theoretical Medicine and Bioethics*, 32 (2011), 217–27. See also David Enoch, 'Hypothetical Consent and the Value(s) of Autonomy', *Ethics*, 128 (2017), 6–36.

one's enduring values, *agency* is the value of being able to make one's own choice, to exercise one's will, especially over one's own life and affairs. The decision-based conception appears closely related to the value of authenticity. As Buchanan and Brock put it, 'The interest in self-determination ... is people's interest in making important decisions about their lives for themselves according to their own values and aims'.[19] Thus, we deem a person incompetent when his choice is seriously disconnected from those attitudes that ought to govern his behaviour. The connection between authenticity and the abilities-based model is looser. People with the requisite abilities do ordinarily make important decisions in line with their values. But, as the phenomena of weakness of will and recklessness indicate, it is possible to err. It is, therefore, the exercise of agency that seems more directly protected by the abilities-based view. The point of competence determinations, so understood, is to ensure that a person's choice is appropriately connected to her agency, that it is genuinely her decision, that she bears direct responsibility for it, even if it runs contrary to her values.[20] A person's decision is her own, in this sense, only if making a subjectively reasonable decision was realistically within her power. Such a person, we may say, has the necessary abilities for accountable agency in this context. By contrast, if we say that a person was incompetent, we mean the choice was determined by internal factors that either prevented the agent from enjoying a real opportunity to be guided by his standing values *or* that prevented him from applying his values in light of the available relevant information.[21] In such cases, the agent does not seem directly responsible or accountable for his choice;[22] thus, it would be a mistake for anyone to fault him for making a *bad* decision, since it wasn't really his decision at all.

Appreciating the connection between competence and concepts like control and accountability permits us to be more precise about when a patient can be said to lack the ability to make his own decision. What matters is not whether there were factors that influenced the person to decide in an irrational way (there always are) but whether those factors were significant enough to deprive the person of a fair or reasonable opportunity to make an autonomous decision. If a person is procrastinating a needed operation out of an ordinary aversion to surgery, we probably

[19] Buchanan and Brock, *Deciding for Others*, p. 229. Isra Black has pointed out to me that, while the decision-based approach in Buchanan and Brock may appeal to the notion of authenticity, one might defend a decision-based view without appealing to the subject's deep values. Perhaps one could say that a decision counts as competently made as long as it is free of material errors of fact and free of significant mistakes in reasoning. But if the underlying value is not authenticity, then what is it? Is this a different way of thinking about respect for agency? This is an interesting possibility, but I will have to leave further exploration of it to another day.

[20] Carl Elliott, 'Competence as Accountability', *Journal of Clinical Ethics*, 2 (1991), 167–77.

[21] A person might be prevented from exercising accountable agency by certain external factors as well—like coercion or lack of access to information. The abilities constituting competence only comprise the internal conditions necessary for exercising accountable agency.

[22] If I get so inebriated that I cannot think clearly, then I am still *indirectly* responsible for whatever decision I make, even if I couldn't have decided reasonably at the time. I cannot explore the matter here, but competence seems related to our direct, not our indirect, responsibility for a decision.

wouldn't regard that as a responsibility-excusing incapacity. But if the aversion was powerful enough, perhaps rooted in past trauma, then we might. Likewise, it is not just any refusal to accept the facts that vitiates competence. There may be cases of pathological denial where we think the patient cannot be held responsible for ignoring the truth. But often people just refuse to accept what they are told on good authority and instead believe what they wish were true. Typically, we do not consider that a symptom of an incapacity but as the manifestation of an epistemic vice for which they bear responsibility.[23]

## Adult competence: the case for the abilities-based view

Which account of competence$_G$ should we prefer? Consider, first, just the case of adults. It seems that, to decide this, we need to reflect on how much we care about authenticity and agency.

Little need be said to motivate the importance of authenticity. Most of us do think there's something good about a person's life bearing the imprint of his projects and concerns. Indeed, when we mourn someone's passing, we often find it consoling to reflect on the ways that his life was successfully shaped by his passions and convictions, even when they are rather different from our own.

But the value of agency might seem more puzzling. What is so good about the bare fact of choosing?[24] After all, if I make a bad decision, it seems all the worse to regard it as an 'unforced error'. I would suggest that the chief importance of agency lies, not in its teleological 'goodness', but in its deontological significance. That is, it is plausible to think that a part of respecting others as moral equals consists in recognising each person's final authority over his own life, at least insofar as the interests of others are not immediately concerned. The moral importance of respecting this authority might be understood in different ways, but I think of it as bound up with the broadly Kantian notion that we should interact with others as reasoning agents in a relation of basic practical equality.[25] On this view, we do not have licence to interfere with another person's choices simply because we might make better choices, even as judged by her own standards. Rather, we can interfere only when we cannot sufficiently attribute the choice to the person's agency—it was not really *her choice* at all.[26]

23 On epistemic vices and our responsibility for them, see Quassim Cassam, *Vices of the Mind: From the Intellectual to the Political* (Oxford, Oxford University Press, 2019).

24 Brudney and Lantos, for example, don't think agency is so valuable.

25 Garrett Cullity, *Concern, Respect, and Cooperation* (Oxford, Oxford University Press, 2018), ch. 2. See also Stephen Darwall, *The Second-Person Stance* (Cambridge, MA, Harvard University Press, 2006) and Arthur Ripstein, *Freedom and Force: Kant's Legal and Political Philosophy* (Cambridge, MA, Harvard University Press, 2009).

26 This resembles Joel Feinberg's 'soft paternalism', though I place more importance on the individual's possession of the requisite abilities rather than on the voluntariness of the choice. See Feinberg, *Harm to Self* (New York, Oxford University Press, 1986), p. 12.

I think both values are important. But I submit that the best way of doing justice to each in the medical context is to adopt the abilities-based conception of competence. Here is why. To respect a person's agency is to recognise her as having content-independent authority over a decision.[27] As long as the choice has the right formal character – namely, that it was made by a person with the present ability to make an informed choice in line with his values – then we ought to defer to the choice regardless of whether it seems like a sensible decision.[28] Let's call this 'robust authority', in that it doesn't depend on the content of the decision.[29] The decision-based model, however, does employ a content-based test in asking whether the patient's choice is reasonably consistent with her own values.[30] Therefore, if we follow this approach, there's no room to protect agency.

Agency *is* protected, of course, if we adopt the abilities-based view. But this doesn't mean we have to neglect the value of authenticity; there are other ways of recognising it. As I've indicated, an essential aim of the doctor–patient-shared-decision-making process is that of helping the patient make a decision that is right for him, given what he deems most important. Suppose that a patient is inclined to make a choice that will frustrate his most deeply held plans, perhaps because he is swayed by wishful thinking. Just because the patient is competent on the abilities-based view doesn't mean that the doctor ought to immediately abandon the patient to his irrationality and wash her hands of the matter. On the contrary, this would be a suitable occasion for the doctor to try to find a way of reaching the patient and encouraging him to reconsider her decision. For example, it might help if a trusted family member were brought into the conversation. The doctor *should* 'intervene' in such a case; it is just that she should not override his final decision. In this way, we can give each value its due.

An example that, I think, supports the intuitions behind the abilities-based conception is the tragic case of Apple founder and former CEO Steve Jobs. In 2003, Jobs was diagnosed with a rare but often curable form of pancreatic cancer. Doctors recommended immediate surgery, but Jobs refused, disliking the idea of his body being 'opened'. According to his biographer, Walter Isaacson, Jobs instead chose

[27] On authority and content-independent reasons, see Joseph Raz, *The Morality of Freedom* (Oxford, Oxford University Press, 1986), ch. 2.

[28] Though doctors should not perform medically inappropriate treatments just because patients want them.

[29] This resembles 'treating someone's will as decisive' in Daniel Groll, 'Paternalism, Respect, and the Will', *Ethics*, 122 (2011), 692–720.

[30] An anonymous reviewer has pointed out to me that a decision-based model could still recognise the patient's content-independent authority, as long as it only required that the decision was the outcome of the proper process and did not require (pace Buchanan and Brock) that the decision be in line with the patient's values. For instance, it might require that the patient actually understand his options and have given them consideration in consultation with the doctor. Although I am inclined to reject this view as well, what is most important to me is the distinction between views that require the decisions be authentic versus those that require (perhaps along with other process requirements) only the capacity for making an authentic decision.

to self-treat the cancer with 'a strict vegan diet, ... acupuncture, a variety of herbal remedies, and occasionally a few other treatments he found on the Internet'.[31] Friends and family deplored how unreasonable Jobs' initial response to his diagnosis was. Some attributed it to his inclination 'to ignore stuff he doesn't want to confront' and engage in 'magical thinking', as though 'he could will things to be as he wanted'.[32] Nine months later, as his condition worsened, he reversed course and opted for the surgery after all. But it was, apparently, too late. The cancer had spread, and after a long illness, he finally died from resulting complications in 2011 at the age of 56. Although it is impossible to be sure that an earlier surgery would have saved him, Barrie R. Cassileth, the chief of integrative medicine at the Memorial Sloan Kettering Cancer Center, opined that the delay 'likely cost him his life'.[33] And, according to Isaacson, Jobs himself later regretted not going ahead with the operation sooner.[34] But though his initial refusal to undergo surgery seems irrational given his goals in life, no one seems to have seriously regarded him as incapable of making a reasonable decision. After all, that's why his friends and family were so angry with him. They certainly did not think his refusal was sensible given his values, and some earnestly tried to get him to change his mind. They were surely right to do so. But I think most of us would agree that it would have been wrong to go further and override his decision to refuse treatment, just because (in the words of Buchanan and Brock) it did not *reasonably conform to his underlying aims and values*.[35] He had a right to use his own faculties to make up his own mind about what was best for him. As it happens, he made a mistake. But the possibility of mistakes comes with having the authority to make your own decisions. If that's our verdict, then, at least when we are dealing with adults, we seem to be appealing to an abilities-based criterion of competence, not a decision-based one.

## Competence for minors: the single-standard model

How, then, should we think about competence as it relates to minors? As a preliminary, let me say a word about who counts as a 'minor'. Just about everywhere, there is a fixed age—often 18—at which a person is recognised as legally independent of his parents and as an adult for most purposes. Generally, then, our topic is persons younger than about 18. But things are a little more complicated than that. In a few

[31] Walter Isaacson, *Steve Jobs* (New York, Simon & Schuster, 2011), p. 454.

[32] Isaacson, *Steve Jobs*, pp. 454–5.

[33] Liz Szabo, 'Book Raises Alarms About Alternative Medicine', *USA Today*, 18 June 2013. https://www.usatoday.com/story/news/nation/2013/06/18/book-raises-alarms-about-alternative-medicine/2429385/ (accessed 25 July 2025).

[34] See Isaacson's interview on *60 Minutes* (21 October 2011).

[35] Buchanan and Brock, *Deciding for Others*, p. 56. Someone might say that Jobs' reckless refusal *was* authentic since it was consistent with his reckless character. But I doubt this is the relevant sense of authenticity.

jurisdictions, the age of medical consent is lower than the standard age of majority. And, in many places, minors can consent without parental notification to some forms of treatment (like treatment of sexually transmitted disease). Moreover, you might think that, although some people should be treated as minors, the law has drawn the line at the wrong place. All this is just to say that the extension of the word 'minor' is not simple. Different views will take different positions, not only on the nature of minority competence but also on who counts as a minor.

Now, if we adopt the abilities-based conception of adult competence, then the simplest position is to apply the same standard to the young. This could be done in a few different ways. We could use our abilities-based standard to make categorical generalisations on either side of a designated age. For example, we might maintain that, since those younger than (say) 18 usually fail to meet the standard, while those older than 18 tend to satisfy it, we will pick 18 as the standard age of consent. While such rough generalisations may be satisfactory in some domains, they increasingly appear problematic in medicine, since the decisions that need to be made are so consequential for the life of the patient, and since it is actually feasible in the medical context to make individual assessments (unlike, say, prior determination of capacity to give sexual consent). So, let's assume that we are applying the standard of competence in a more case-by-case manner. There are basically two ways of doing this. We might say that, just as the presumption of adult competence is rebuttable by sufficient evidence, the same ought to be true of the presumption of incompetence of minors. The other approach is to say that everyone is presumed competent until shown otherwise.[36] Occasionally, it will be necessary to distinguish these two versions of the view, but much of what I have to say applies to each of them.

The Single-Standard Model is attractive in its theoretical simplicity, and it provides a sensible explanation as to why we don't usually recognise young children as having the authority to make their own decisions. A five-year-old child, for example, will probably lack the ability to appreciate the gravity of certain outcomes or deliberate rationally about probabilities. Furthermore, we may worry whether it really makes sense to treat the avowed beliefs and values of younger children as genuinely their own, as opposed to those of (say) their parents. For this reason, a young person may be incapable of bringing her values to bear on a decision, given that she doesn't really have values of her own in the first place. How to decide whether a person's values are authentically hers is, of course, a difficult question in its own right. Presumably, we will look to such things as whether the values seem to be deeply internalised, whether the youth can articulate their importance in her own words, whether she has been exposed to other perspectives and has had much opportunity to critically reflect on her values, and so on. In any case, the bottom line here is that there are abundant reasons to think that young children will lack various abilities necessary for competence.

[36] See, for example, Ontario's *Health Care Consent Act*, 1996, S.O. 1996, c. 2, Sched. A, §4.

The harder question is whether the Single-Standard Model handles adolescents, who are so much more like adults, in a plausible way. My suspicion is that, if we fairly apply the same competence-standard to adults and adolescents, then we are going to get results that will be hard to accept. On the abilities-based approach, recall, there will be cases in which a competent individual makes decisions that are quite unreasonable, even as judged by her own values and plans. I think that we are going to be reluctant, however, to let an adolescent, who apparently has all the abilities that an adult would need to count as competent, make a choice that is extremely harmful (from a medical point of view) and subjectively unreasonable.

Consider the following case:

> CASSIE: Cassie is a 16-year-old just diagnosed with leukaemia. The doctors are optimistic about her prospects if she receives prompt and aggressive treatment. In fact, they think the probability of a full recovery in that case is about 85 per cent. On the other hand, if the cancer is left untreated, her prognosis is grim; she will probably be dead inside of two years. Although Cassie understands what her doctors tell her, she is from the start unsettled by the prospect of chemotherapy. This aversion only grows once she starts following a holistic medicine group on social media, and she is soon persuaded that, whatever her doctors may say, her condition can be more effectively treated with natural remedies than with the 'poison' the doctors are prescribing. Moreover, she resents that her doctors have not presented this alternative treatment as an option, and she is coming to believe that doctors only prescribe chemotherapy drugs because they are bribed by the pharmaceutical companies. Since she has not yet reached the age of medical consent in her jurisdiction, she asks to be recognized as a mature minor who can make her own decision.[37]

Of course, in a briefly sketched hypothetical case like this, there is no way of determining whether the patient has the requisite abilities or not. My point is only that she might well possess them. After all, the case bears a striking resemblance to the Steve Jobs example. As I have been emphasising, the mere fact that someone makes a subjectively unreasonable decision does not show that the person lacks the abilities for accountable agency. And yet, even if we were convinced that Cassie had the abilities an adult would need to count as competent, I still think we would be loath to let a 16-year-old make such a disastrous choice. On the other hand, there have been influential court cases in which minors have been allowed to refuse medical treatment on religious grounds.[38] What this suggests is that many of us are inclined to let adolescents with adult-like capacities make their own decisions but only if the content of those decisions seems reasonable in light of the young person's own values and convictions. In other words, we *are* applying a different standard to adolescents—namely, a decision-based or authenticity standard. That may look dubious, but I will argue in the next section that it can be justified.

[37] Compare the Connecticut case of *In re Cassandra C* 112 A 3d 158 (Conn 2015). For background, see https://sciencebasedmedicine.org/the-sad-but-unexpectedly-hopeful-cancer-saga-of-cassandra-callender/ (accessed 25 July 2025).

[38] The key mature-minor cases in American and Canadian law (*In re EG* and *AC v Manitoba*) both involve Jehovah's Witnesses refusing blood transfusions.

Before I do so, however, let me anticipate one response. Someone might agree that we shouldn't let Cassie refuse treatment but insist that this is because her unreasonable refusal is all the evidence we need to reach the conclusion that she probably lacks the requisite abilities. This argument will be on the firmest ground if we are working within a framework in which the young person is presumed incompetent and a strong case needs to be established to rebut the presumption. By contrast, when dealing with a normal adult, the same evidence, by itself, is usually not enough for a determination of incompetence, and this is because, here, the burden of proof faces the other way. That's an important argument, and maybe that's the whole explanation. No doubt this whole issue deserves fuller consideration than I can give it here. Presently, I will only observe that, if it turns out that we are, as a rule, ready to defer to the unreasonable decisions of apparently competent adults, whereas we almost never defer to the unreasonable decisions of adolescents, and if we cannot point to any difference in the abilities of the adult and the minor, then that suggests to me that we are not just relying on different presumptions. Whether we are forthright about it or not, we seem to be actually applying different standards to the two sorts of cases.

## Competence for minors: the life-stage model

Could it be appropriate to apply a different competence standard to adults and to minors? I have said that respecting a person's agency over her own affairs is one part of recognising her as a moral equal: that we each possess authority over our own lives. The view we have just been considering assumes that a person must immediately acquire full decision-making authority just when she adequately develops the capacity for making accountable decisions about her life.[39] But I want to suggest a different way of thinking about this.

As I see it, what is fundamental to respecting another as a moral equal (in this connection) is recognising that she has a life of her own to lead—she has a right to 'life-authorship', if you will. But the property of being the author of one's own life is a global one, referring to the character of a life as a whole. As a consequence, just when the young person is first handed over the reins to his life is not particularly important as far as the duty of respect is concerned, so long as this transfer of authority does eventually happen, it is not delayed too long, and everyone is treated in the same way. After all, we do not usually think that the limited freedom of childhood, though necessary, diminishes our ability to make our lives our own. Neither, I contend, does a tutelage that extends beyond childhood proper and through adolescence. This merely prolongs this preparatory stage before the projects that define adult life have been begun in earnest.

To draw that intuition out into the open, suppose that, in the country of Florin, people are recognised as adults at the age of 17, while in Guilder, the age of

[39] Allowing, of course, that the boundaries for adequate possession of these abilities are vague.

majority is 19. Now, just for the purposes of this example, let's assume that everyone acquires the capacity for accountable agency on their seventeenth birthday. Does it follow that, from the whole-life perspective, the people of Florin have more of an opportunity to lead their own lives than the people of Guilder? Does the society of Guilder fail to respect the moral equality of 17- and 18-year-olds? No, the ideal of leading one's own life is just not that sensitive to the timing of when we become full adults. In both countries, individuals will have plenty of time to assume full authority over their lives and make the sorts of decisions about career, place of residence, and family that shape people's lives. Therefore, both societies adequately recognise the moral equality of all. Of course, if the people of Guilder did not count as adults until the age of 50, and the average lifespan were what it is now, then that would be another matter. That *would* presumably be too late for the beginning of independence. But I assume that there is a range of ages which we might reasonably pick as the conventional beginning of adulthood.

If the line between childhood and adulthood is not marked by the acquisition of the abilities that underlie accountable agency, then how do we draw it? Basically, by considering the consequences. If young people generally benefit from having a longer preparation for adulthood, then we may, consistent with the duty to respect the equal right to life-authorship, legitimately delay adolescents' ability to enter into certain adult paths. Instead, we may keep them integrated in the formative institutions of the family and the school. During this imposed moratorium on adult pursuits, we aim at fostering more than the minimal abilities necessary for accountable agency. After all, that would be a pretty modest aim of education—to raise children just so they don't need wards as adults. Before letting the young leave the nest, we want to give them the time to develop really good judgement and to gain as much insight as they can into what is really worthwhile in life. But when a young person does reach the socially recognised age of adulthood, she becomes her own master, as long as she has at least reached the threshold for accountable agency. In this way, we can do justice to our more perfectionist intuitions about raising children as well as our anti-perfectionist intuitions about respecting people's authority over their own lives.[40]

What age would be suitable for the onset of adulthood? I claim no special insight into this. Much will depend on local economic and cultural facts, including existing rites of passage. Perhaps the age of 18 is appropriate for many modern societies today. Of course, if you are convinced that a period of limited freedom in later adolescence is *not* generally beneficial, that it does not foster healthy maturation, then even if it were consistent with the duty of respect, it would lack justification.[41] I simply assume, here, the conventional view that it is beneficial.

[40] Andrew Franklin-Hall, 'On Becoming an Adult: Autonomy and the Moral Relevance of Life's Stages', *The Philosophical Quarterly*, 63 (2013), 223–47. See also the similar view defended in Joel Anderson and Rutger Claassen, 'Sailing Alone: Teenage Autonomy and Regimes of Childhood', *Law and Philosophy*, 31 (2012), 495–622.

[41] See Monika Betzler, 'The Moral Significance of Adolescence', *Journal of Applied Philosophy*, 39 (2022), 447–61.

But suppose you accept all that. This does not seem very helpful for thinking about important decisions that arise in the life of the adolescent that cannot be postponed without effectively deciding the matter one way or another. And, of course, medical decisions often have this character of *forced, momentous choices*. How, then, should we deal with these?

Keep in mind that we are assuming that the adolescent in question is someone who already has the requisite minimal abilities for accountable agency, including a set of values that can sensibly be said to really be her own. In that case, I think that out of a concern for the value of authenticity we ought to let the young person make a decision that is expressive of her own priorities, even if the choice is controversial or seems inadvisable from a strictly medical point of view. Further, if the young person does not yet know what is important to her, or how those values bear on the decision, then she has a right to figure these things out and decide accordingly. After all, if a decision has to be made that will have such important consequences on the youth's life, what other person's values have a stronger claim to guide us? It is only by recognising the adolescent's right to make a decision based on her own values that we can really honour the fact that the young person's life is ultimately her own.

But this is still a *limited* form of autonomy, for I am also suggesting that we should not defer to an adolescent's decision that is harmful (from a medical point of view) and subjectively unreasonable.[42] That kind of robust authority should, of course, be extended to adults as a part of recognising their moral equality. But, as I have just been saying, we can recognise others as equals, and thus as having the right to inherit this authority of life-authorship upon reaching the conventional start of adulthood, without thinking that this full authority must kick in as soon as a person is capable of accountable agency. In this way, we are letting the young person put her values into practice when faced with a forced momentous decision, but we are not entirely taking off the guardrails. Rather, we continue to shield the person from the worst effects of grave mistakes.[43]

But what if the adolescent's choice, though inconsistent with his values, is actually the medically advisable option? Perhaps out of fear, the youth chooses the option most likely to save his life rather than the one most in line with his religious convictions (which he typically regards as paramount).[44] Since the medically advisable choice has a lot to say for it, it will be hard in practice to distinguish these cases from those in which the young person is changing his mind about his priorities. But suppose we stipulate the facts are as described. This is a challenging case, but I

[42] As James Anderson has pointed out to me, this is not so unlike the standard we apply to substitute decision-makers for adult patients, since proxies are not entitled to make reckless or negligent decisions but must decide in line with the wishes or values of the patient.

[43] On the value of 'shielding', see Anthony Skelton, Lisa Forsberg, and Isra Black, 'Overriding Adolescent Refusals of Treatment', *Journal of Ethics and Social Philosophy*, 20 (2021), 221–47.

[44] My thanks to an anonymous reviewer for encouraging me to address this question.

think we should treat the decision as valid.[45] The adolescent lacks robust autonomy because he does not have the authority to make a decision that is subjectively unreasonable *and* harmful from a common-sense and medical point of view. If the young person can take responsibility for his choices, there is no reason why he shouldn't be allowed to make decisions that don't do him any harm.[46] Someone might object that the decision *is* harmful from his own evaluative perspective. Perhaps so, but while medical professionals have a responsibility to *defer* to decisions based on values that run counter to medical values, they don't have the responsibility—perhaps not even the authority—to ensure that patients avoid the temptation of goods like life and health while remaining true to particular religious or ethical doctrines.[47]

I think that this life-stage approach accounts for some of the ways that the mature minor doctrine is actually applied. Whatever they *say* they are doing, courts are not typically just looking to see whether the young person has the abilities an adult would need to count as competent. Few courts would recognise an adolescent as 'mature' if he were acting as Steve Jobs did. The only people likely to be deemed mature minors by the courts are those who are making sensible choices that are in line with values and convictions that the young person has thought seriously about.[48] That is a higher standard of competence than we require of adults. This difference cannot be explained because the stakes are allegedly higher when we are dealing with an adolescent. The stakes are essentially the same when we are dealing with a 25-year-old patient.

Moreover, I submit that the life-stage account is more compelling than the alternatives. For instance, someone might say that, during the probationary stage of adolescence, we need not even defer to a young person's subjectively reasonable decision

[45] Alternatively, we could hold that the adolescent is incompetent to make this decision. In that case, a substitute decision-maker will have to be involved. And we might claim (consistent with current practice) that substitute decision-makers cannot refuse medically essential treatment for minors on religious or other controversial grounds. This, then, would bring us back to the medically advisable option which the adolescent originally chose.

[46] One might compare Buchanan and Brock's view that the threshold for competence requires subjective reasonableness only when the choice in question is potentially harmful and not obviously the best option from a medical point of view. Where there are few risks or the choice is quite reasonable from a medical perspective, the decision is held to a lower standard, requiring only a basic understanding of the choice made (*Deciding for Others*, pp. 51–7).

[47] This may seem to be in tension with my claim, above, that doctors ought to help the patient make a decision that is right for her, given what she deems most important. But my idea is that there is a difference between cases in which the best option, even from a medical point of view, depends on the patient's aims and values (e.g. what is more important: controlling anxiety or maintaining a normal libido?) and those in which the patient's religious or ethical convictions call, in some contexts, for choosing against the kinds of goods that medicine promotes (life, health, etc.). If a patient chooses health-related goods over her religious convictions, we should not expect the doctors to push back, even if the decision is not subjectively reasonable.

[48] Court decisions are frequently ambiguous between claiming that the adolescent patient must have the capacity to make a mature decision and that her decision must itself exhibit maturity. However, as James Anderson reminds me, in the real world, authorities also sometimes deem adolescents mature only if their decisions are 'objectively reasonable' in the sense of being medically advisable.

about some forced, momentous question—for that, too, is a perquisite of adulthood. But, as I have said, it is hard to see why, if a decision has to be made, someone else's values should take precedence over the person whose life it is (assuming, again, that the young person is capable of exercising accountable agency).

To run to the other extreme, one might say that we should treat adolescents who are capable of accountable agency just like adults in these circumstances: let them make their own decisions and bear whatever consequences may come. That is a coherent position; I just think that the life-stage model offers a better balance between the young person's interest in autonomy and our protective responsibilities toward those in the transitional stage between childhood and adulthood.

Some say that, when choices need to be made about an adolescent's care, the decision-making process should, so far as possible, be a shared one between the adolescent, her guardians, and her medical team. This is quite plausible as a moral ideal. But I am asking where final authority lies when we can't reach consensus. The shared decision-making model doesn't provide us with that.

A final position, which has received considerable attention recently, is to say that young people should be able to consent to treatment proposed by their doctors, but should not be able to refuse life-saving treatment.[49] As I see it, though, this approach draws the line at the wrong place. Consider:

> DANA: Like Cassie, Dana is a 16-year-old leukaemia patient. However, Dana has already been through two rounds of chemotherapy and each time the cancer has returned. The doctors are eager to try one more round of treatment, although they admit that the odds of driving the cancer into long-term remission are only about 15 per cent. Her parents are even more adamant that the treatment is worth one more try. But Dana disagrees. She believes that, since the odds are that she is at the end of her life no matter what she does, she would rather ensure that her final months be as comfortable as they can be so that she can make something of the time she has left.

I think we ought to respect Dana's decision, notwithstanding the fact that she is refusing life-saving treatment. She is, to be sure, making a controversial decision, but it remains a reasonable one in that it is consistent with all available information and is in line with what is most important to her. I think that the reason why the idea of an asymmetry between consent and refusal looks plausible in the first place is that we are thinking about examples more like Cassie's, where the refusal has little to be said for it. But Dana's story shows that this is just one sort of case. Whether a treatment has a chance of saving the patient's life is not the critical issue.

To my mind, then, our life-stage model looks the most reasonable. This means an abilities-based standard for adults and a decision-based standard for minors. But is the decision-based standard really a standard of *competence* at all? Or would it

[49] Neil C. Manson, 'Transitional Paternalism: How Shared Normative Powers Can Give Rise to the Asymmetry of Adolescent Consent and Refusal', *Bioethics*, 29 (2015), 66–73; Faye Tucker, 'Developing Autonomy and Transitional Paternalism', *Bioethics*, 30 (2016), 759–66; Skelton, Forsberg, and Black, 'Overriding Adolescent Refusals of Treatment'.

be more accurate to say that, even if an adolescent is competent, we should defer to his decision only if it is subjectively reasonable? Because of the aforementioned ambiguities of the word 'competence', which I have discussed above, we could put it either way. I have presented an account of the facts that should ground the legal power of giving and withholding medical consent for adolescents. Therefore, in my terminology, this is a theory of competence$_G$. However, the theory says that, in determining whether to defer to an adolescent's decision, the sufficient possession of the abilities that underlie accountable agency are not decisive. Thus, this is not an account of competence$_A$.

## Conclusion

To say an adult has the mind of a child is to suggest that he lacks the capacity to care for himself. But to allege that he is acting like a teenager is usually only to impute vices like recklessness or short-sightedness, not incapacity. This suggests that older adolescents are often thought to sufficiently possess the abilities an adult would need to count as competent. As I have said, you might conclude that we should, therefore, treat adolescents like adults in medical decision-making. I disagree. When confronted with an important medical decision that cannot be postponed, an adolescent who would qualify as competent if she were an adult should be allowed to make a decision that is in line with her own values. But it remains justifiable to protect adolescents from foolhardy decisions, since we can fairly treat adolescence as a probationary stage, during which certain protections remain in place, but which is nonetheless on life's path to the more robust freedom we accord to adults. Although that robust autonomy is owed to people as moral equals, it is not necessarily owed to them at every stage of life. What is essential is that it is known that such independence will be assumed as a matter of course by everyone capable of exercising it at the conventional start of adulthood. We should, therefore, think of 'mature minors', whose decisions are owed deference, not as adolescents who merely possess the minimal capacities adults would need to decide for themselves but as young people whose decisions, though perhaps controversial in content, nonetheless actually approach the ideal of subjective reasonableness and thoughtfulness.

# 3

# Asymmetry of Adolescent Decision-Making Capacity and Rational Choice

ISRA BLACK

CONSIDER THE FOLLOWING proposition. Call it the *asymmetry of capacity thesis*.[1]

> For a set of options, the functional decision-making capacity required to choose any one option may differ to the functional decision-making capacity required to choose any other option.

In this contribution, I consider the existence of, and normative support for, the asymmetry of capacity thesis in English law. In particular, I take an interest in one specification of the proposition: a legal doctrine holding that an individual may have the capacity to consent to a medical intervention and yet lack the capacity to refuse the same.[2]

I advance two main arguments. First, I develop scepticism as to whether legal authority exists for the asymmetry of capacity thesis in the adolescent medical treatment case law (where it is thought to have emerged). Second, I argue that neither of two prominent ways of explaining and justifying the asymmetry of capacity thesis—the *risk-relative* account of capacity,[3] and Stephen Gilmore and Jonathan Herring's distinction between *refusal of consent* and *refusal of treatment*[4]—succeed.

[1] I shall often use 'capacity' as shorthand for 'functional decision-making capacity'.

[2] I am open to the asymmetry of capacity thesis manifesting in other ways—for example, as a capacity to refuse, but not to consent asymmetry: see e.g. *Bell v Tavistock and Portman NHS Foundation Trust* [2020] EWHC 3274 (Admin). But it is not necessary to consider more than one specification in what follows.

[3] See e.g. A. E. Buchanan and D. W. Brock, *Deciding for Others: The Ethics of Surrogate Decision Making* (Cambridge, Cambridge University Press, 1989); A. Buchanan and D. W. Brock, 'Deciding for Others', *The Milbank Quarterly*, 64 (1986) 17–94; I. Wilks, 'The Debate Over Risk-Related Standards of Competence', *Bioethics*, 11 (1997) 413–26; R. Lawlor, 'Cake or Death? Ending Confusions About Asymmetries Between Consent and Refusal', *Journal of Medical Ethics*, 42 (2016) 748–54.

[4] S. Gilmore and J. Herring, '"No" is the Hardest Word: Consent and Children's Autonomy', *Child and Family Law Quarterly*, 23 (2011), 3–25.

*Proceedings of the British Academy*, **279**, 48–77, © Authors 2025.

If the asymmetry of capacity thesis is part of English law, it should not be; if it is not part of English law, we should not embrace it within this legal order. At least, not in virtue of either of these views.

My discussion proceeds as follows. First, since this is a law *and* philosophy endeavour, I explain my methodology. Second, I outline the English legal regime(s) for adolescent medical treatment. Third, I investigate whether the case law admits of the asymmetry of capacity thesis. (I suggest that it does not.) Fourth, I explore whether the asymmetry of capacity thesis survives rational reconstruction. Working from the distinction between a decision's legal *validity* and its legal *effectiveness* identifiable in the law of medical treatment, I establish that the norms that govern decision-making capacity are not substantive in the sense that they require agents choose reasonable or best outcomes—as determined by third parties in a relation of authority or responsibility vis-à-vis the agent—in order to make legally valid decisions. I then argue that a subjective standard of instrumental rationality best explains the legal tests for functional capacity posited in the Mental Capacity Act 2005 (MCA 2005) and set out by the House of Lords in *Gillick v West Norfolk and Wisbech AHA*.[5] Armed with these two arguments, I show why risk-relative and refusal of consent/refusal of treatment defences of asymmetry of capacity fail to provide normative support for the thesis' incorporation into English law.

## Methodology

As telegraphed above, rational reconstruction is the mode of analysis I shall employ. I should set out what this involves in general, as well as the potentially specific way in which I understand the exercise. In terms of generalities, Neil MacCormick writes:

> In legal scholarship—in legal dogmatics, that is to say—rational reconstruction means the production of clear and systematic statements of legal doctrine, accounting for statute law and case law in terms of organizing principles, relating actual or hypothetical decisions both to their factual bases and to governing norms elaborated out of the authoritative materials.[6]

This statement invites two related observations/clarifications. First, the raw materials—statute, case law, etc.—matter. As Neil MacCormick observes: 'Even anomalous cases or statutes are real decisions and real laws ["institutional facts"], whose effects must be taken into account at the same time as they may be put to one side ...'[7]

Second, the ontological status of legal material requires that we read the complex of legal sources relevant to a domain—such as healthcare decision-making—charitably, so that we might fairly claim a *grounding* relation between the outcomes

[5] *Gillick v West Norfolk and Wisbech AHA* [1986] AC 112.

[6] N. MacCormick, 'Reconstruction After Deconstruction: A Response to CLS', *Oxford Journal of Legal Studies*, 10 (1990), 539–58 at 556.

[7] MacCormick, 'Reconstruction', 557.

of rational reconstruction and legal materials. My gloss on MacCormick is that for an analysis to count as rational reconstruction, one must show a sufficient degree of *fidelity* to the sources.

The general statement of method above has implications for the kind of work I seek to do in this chapter, integrating legal and philosophical content and methods. One is that the requirement of fidelity constrains legal and philosophical ordering of relevant material: our theorising should not stray from a charitable interpretation of the sources if it is to qualify as rational reconstruction. Hence MacCormick's injunction that principles used to systematise legal doctrine relate to the relevant facts, as well as governing norms, and the latter are themselves elaborated out of a selection of authoritative materials. We should be mindful not to read *too much* into the sources. Another is that we should not read *too little* into legal materials either. I take from the preceding discussion that a central element of rational reconstruction in law is its *internal perspective*. As Jan M. Smits observes, '[t]he legal system is not only the subject of the inquiry, it also provides the normative framework for analysis ... the doctrinal approach the law is intelligible in its own terms'.[8] Put another way, law itself sets the standards that comprise law. I take the internal perspective seriously. But I suggest that we ought not to understand it in a limiting way: one that would exclude the insights other disciplines offer—philosophy in my case—just when legal actors (wittingly or unwittingly) invoke or evoke phenomena that exist both as part of the law and outside law.[9]

The methodological claim that underpins this chapter is that where law and other bodies of knowledge share or have similar concepts/conceptions, principles, norms, etc., we may look to non-legal knowledge to help us elucidate law (and vice versa). It is appropriate and helpful to attempt to integrate law and philosophy when discussing the law of medical treatment, since the law engages philosophical discourse in this domain.

## A précis of English law on adolescent medical treatment

English law gives no general licence to health professionals to interfere physically with the bodies of patients, including minors: '[a]ny invasion of the body of one person by another is potentially both a crime and a tort'.[10] Thus, in the usual run of things,[11] professionals—like other members of the public—require consent if

[8] J. M. Smits, 'What Is Legal Doctrine? On the Aims and Methods of Legal-Dogmatic Research', in E. L. Rubin, H. W. Micklitz, and R. van Gestel (eds), *Rethinking Legal Scholarship: A Transatlantic Dialogue* (Cambridge, Cambridge University Press, 2017), pp. 207–18.

[9] See e.g. I. Black, L. Forsberg, and A. Skelton, 'Transformative Choice and Decision-Making Capacity', *Law Quarterly Review*, 139 (2023), 654–80.

[10] *Airedale NHS Trust v Bland* [1993] 1 AC 789 (HL) 891 (Lord Mustill).

[11] For example, outside situations of emergency or abandonment for minors aged 15 years or younger: *Gillick* 181–2, 188 (Lord Scarman), 194 (Lord Bridge), 204–5 (Lord Templeman); or incapacity for individuals aged 16 years or older: MCA 2005, ss 5, 4.

the touching of another is to be lawful.[12] The merits of the intended treatment are irrelevant in the absence of consent.[13]

For the purpose of explaining the law and the analysis that follows, it is helpful to distinguish between rules that govern the legal *validity* and the legal *effectiveness* of consent to—or refusal of—medical treatment, respectively.[14]

## Validity rules

The validity of consent to or refusal of medical treatment is determined by three individually necessary and jointly sufficient conditions. First, the individual's decision must cover (or correspond to) the intervention proposed. This condition is typically met by adducing evidence that the individual has been adequately informed, that is, 'informed in broad terms of the nature of the procedure which is intended'.[15] Second, the individual must have decision-making capacity. Third, the choice must be voluntary, that is, the individual's will must not have been overborne by third-party influence.[16] Since my focus is on asymmetry of capacity, I stipulate that the cover and voluntariness conditions are fulfilled.

The legal regimes for capacity differ for minors aged 15 years or younger and those aged 16 or 17 years. Minors aged 15 years or younger are rebuttably presumed to lack capacity—by default, they are unable to take legally valid medical decisions.[17] A minor in this age category may rebut the presumption of incapacity by satisfying the conditions of the *Gillick* test. In outline, a minor has capacity when they '[achieve] a sufficient understanding and intelligence to enable him or her to understand fully what is proposed'.[18]

The MCA 2005 governs the capacity of individuals aged 16 years and older.[19] Thus, minors aged 16 and 17 years are rebuttably presumed to have capacity in

[12] *Bland* 891 (Lord Mustill). Health interventions do not fall within the category of 'physical contact which is generally acceptable in the ordinary conduct of daily life' for which no consent is required: *Collins v Wilcock* [1984] 1 WLR 1172 (DC) 1177 (Robert Goff LJ). Were that the case, the issue of whether consent offers a legal defence would not arise. Where health professionals differ to the general public is that they may with consent—or consent by operation of law, or some other legal justification (see e.g. references at n 11)—cause bodily injury above some 'critical level' in the course of treatment 'performed in accordance with good medical practice': *Brown (Anthony Joseph)* [1994] 1 AC 212 (HL) 258–59 (Lord Mustill). This is the 'medical exception'; see P. Lewis, 'The Medical Exception', *Current Legal Problems*, 65 (2012), 355–76; L. Forsberg, 'The Scope of the Medical Exception in Criminal Law', *Modern Law Review*, 88 (2025), 237–66.

[13] *Bland* 864 (Lord Goff).

[14] So far as treatment involves physical interference with the patient's body. Let us leave aside the difficult issue of which rules are applicable to interventions that do not involve touching.

[15] *Chatterton v Gerson* [1981] QB 432, 443 (Bristow J).

[16] *Re T (Adult: Refusal of Treatment)* [1993] Fam 95 (CA Civ) 117 (Butler-Sloss LJ).

[17] *Gillick.* Usually, decisions concerning a minor's healthcare are taken by persons exercising parental responsibility in the former's regard: Children Act 1989, s 3(1). However, the courts may override parental decisions in the event that the latter conflict with a minor's best interests: see e.g. *An NHS Trust v SR* [2012] EWHC 3842 (Fam).

[18] *Gillick* 188–9 (Lord Scarman).

[19] MCA 2005, s 2(5).

virtue of section 1(2) of the Act. MCA 2005, section 2(1) sets out the conditions for rebutting the presumption of capacity in individual cases: 'a person lacks capacity in relation to a matter if at the material time he is unable to make a decision for himself in relation to the matter because of an impairment of, or a disturbance in the functioning of, the mind or brain'.

Section 3(1) of the Act explains that being unable to do any of the following makes for inability to take a decision: '(a) to understand the information relevant to the decision, (b) to retain that information, (c) to use or weigh that information as part of the process of making the decision, or (d) to communicate his decision …'

If a minor in the relevant age category rebuts the presumption of incapacity by meeting the *Gillick* standard, or has capacity under the MCA 2005 regime, their medical decision—whether consent or refusal—is legally *valid*.

## Effectiveness rules

In contrast to the general position for adults,[20] adolescents may often see their legally valid healthcare decisions deprived of legal *effect*. Under the 'concurrent consents' doctrine developed in the post-*Gillick* Court of Appeal cases of *Re R* and *Re W*, parents or the court retain the power to consent to treatment in a minor's regard—and thereby make its provision lawful—notwithstanding that the latter has validly refused the intervention.[21] This is especially the case when an adolescent refusal of treatment, if respected, risks serious harm or death.[22] As it plays out in English legal doctrine, therefore, the concurrent consents doctrine involves an asymmetry 'in the normative power of consent to and refusal of medical treatment'.[23] This asymmetry of legal effectiveness is distinct from asymmetry of capacity; the latter goes to legal validity. In due course, the concurrent consents doctrine will assist with our rational reconstruction of the asymmetry of capacity thesis. But first we need to establish whether the asymmetry of capacity thesis obtains in English law.

[20] For adults, the legal effectiveness of consent or refusal of treatment usually tracks the validity of an individual's decision: *Bland* 864 (Lord Goff). One example of when it does not is when the intervention offered, e.g. assisted death, lies outside the medical exception: *Bland* 865 (Lord Goff).

[21] *Re R (A Minor) (Wardship: Consent to Treatment)* [1992] Fam 11 (CA) 23–4 (Lord Donaldson MR); *Re W (A Minor) (Medical Treatment: Court's Jurisdiction)* [1993] Fam 64 (CA) 84 (Lord Donaldson MR). See A. Skelton, L. Forsberg, and I. Black, 'Overriding Adolescent Refusals of Treatment', *Journal of Ethics and Social Philosophy*, 20 (2021), 221–47 at 222–4 for doctrinal exposition of the concurrent consents doctrine, which differs across minors aged 15 years and younger and minors 16 or 17 years of age, respectively.

[22] *Re W* 81–2 (Lord Donaldson MR), 88 (Balcombe J), 94 (Nolan LJ). For a recent application of this approach, see *Re E (Children: Blood Transfusion)* [2021] EWCA Civ 1888.

[23] Skelton, Forsberg, and Black, 'Overriding', 221.

## Is there authority for the *asymmetry of capacity thesis* in English legal doctrine?

Recall that on the asymmetry of capacity thesis:

> For a set of options, the decision-making capacity required to choose any one option may differ to the decision-making capacity required to choose any other option.

As I note in the introduction, two accounts of the asymmetry of capacity thesis feature in the academic literature. The first is the *risk-relative* conception of capacity; the second is Gilmore and Herring's distinction between refusal of consent and refusal of treatment. It is helpful to introduce these theories and consider their doctrinal support.

So there is no suspense, I contend that we should be sceptical of any claim that either account forms part of English law. The *risk-relative* account has received sustained attention in the bioethics literature.[24] Yet, its doctrinal grounding is at best equivocal. Gilmore and Herring develop their account of refusal of consent/refusal of treatment distinction out of *Gillick*, *Re R*, and *Re W*. As such, their version of the asymmetry of capacity thesis will enjoy doctrinal support if their reading of the case law is persuasive; I argue that it is not.

### The risk-relative account of capacity

Allen Buchanan and Dan Brock argue for a risk-relative account of capacity, according to which: 'the standard of competence ought to vary with the expected harms or benefits to the patient of acting in accordance with a choice … just because a patient is competent to consent to a treatment, it does not follow that the patient is competent to refuse it, and vice versa'.[25]

On this view, the principle of *risk* plays a role in setting the standard of capacity.[26] When different risk-benefit ratios exist for the options available to the agent, this is commensurate with differing standards of competence across the options.[27] For example, Buchanan and Brock argue that: 'consent to a low-risk life-saving procedure by an otherwise healthy individual should require a *minimal* level

[24] See references at n 3 and e.g. M. R. Wicclair, 'Patient Decision-Making Capacity and Risk', *Bioethics*, 5 (1991), 91–104; G. S. Cale, 'Continuing the Debate over Risk-Related Standards of Competence', *Bioethics*, 13 (1999), 131–48; E. Vogelstein, 'Competence and Ability', *Bioethics*, 28 (2014), 235–44; N. J. Pickering, G. Newton-Howes, and S. Walker, 'Risk-Related Standards of Competence Are a Nonsense', *Journal of Medical Ethics*, 48 (2022), 893–8; T. Douglas, 'Pragmatic Argument for an Acceptance-Refusal Asymmetry in Competence Requirements', *Journal of Medical Ethics*, 48 (2022), 799–800.

[25] Buchanan and Brock, *Deciding for Others*, p. 34.

[26] See Cale, 'Risk-Related Competence', 139–40; Wilks, 'Risk-Related Competence', 424–5.

[27] Wilks, 'Risk-Related Competence', 419.

of competence, but refusal of that same procedure by such an individual should require the *highest* level of competence'.[28]

Understood in this way, as Rob Lawlor observes, the risk-relative account allows for: 'asymmetry of standards of competence, between consent and refusal ... someone could be competent *enough* to consent to treatment, but not competent enough to refuse treatment'.[29]

What legal authority exists for the risk-relative account? Buchanan and Brock argue that 'the decision-relative concept of competence [which they argue to be risk-relative] better coheres with our basic legal framework'.[30] However, they offer no primary analysis of legal materials, and the secondary analyses cited provide no authority for the risk-relative account.[31] In any event, neither Buchanan and Brock nor their sources analyse English law.

John Harris proclaims that in the English case of *Re W*—concerning an adolescent with anorexia nervosa—the Court of Appeal decided 'that a child might be competent to consent to treatment but not to refuse it'.[32] If true, this would indicate that risk-relative capacity has some foothold in English health law. As it happens, the Court held nothing of the sort. In *Re W*, the trial judge finds W to have decision-making capacity.[33] The Court of Appeal proceeds on this basis, since the issue on appeal is the existence and scope of the concurrent consents doctrine.[34] As noted above, the latter doctrine—which involves an asymmetry of legal effectiveness—comes into play when an individual has made a legally valid decision according, *inter alia*, to the relevant standard for capacity. That the concurrent consents doctrine exists cannot tell us whether the standard for capacity is risk-relative. Moreover, such *obiter* that exist on the standard for capacity in *Re W* are inconclusive. Balcombe LJ remarks that, 'In logic there can be no difference between an ability to consent to treatment and an ability to refuse treatment'.[35] This statement aligns with the position that Harris imagines the Court to reject, namely:

> you need to understand the nature of the course of action to which you are consenting, which, in medical contexts, will include its probable and possible consequences and side effects and the nature of any alternative measures which might be taken and

[28] Buchanan and Brock, *Deciding for Others*, p. 34 (emphasis added).

[29] Lawlor, 'Cake or Death?', 749.

[30] Buchanan and Brock, *Deciding for Others*, pp. 61–2.

[31] See Buchanan and Brock, *Deciding for Others*, ch. 5. Gaylin's defence of risk-relativity is normative, rather than doctrinal: 'Competence: No Longer All or None', in W. Gaylin and R. Macklin (eds), *Who Speaks For the Child: The Problems of Proxy Consent* (New York, Plenum Press, 1982), pp. 27–54. Whereas Capron's discussion of the 'mature minor doctrine' provides no indication that the asymmetry of capacity thesis obtains in the cases cited: 'The Competence of Children as Self-Deciders in Biomedical Interventions', in W. Gaylin and R. Macklin (eds), *Who Speaks for the Child: The Problems of Proxy Consent* (New York, Plenum Press, 1982), pp. 57–114.

[32] J. Harris, 'Consent and End of Life Decisions', *Journal of Medical Ethics*, 29 (2003), 10–15 at 12.

[33] *Re W* 80, 84.

[34] *Re W* 76. W's capacity is doubted by Lord Donaldson MR in virtue of her diagnosis of anorexia nervosa, but Thorpe J's first instance finding is not disturbed: *Re W* 80–1.

[35] *Re W* 88.

> the consequences of doing nothing … So, to understand a proposed treatment well enough to consent to it is to understand the consequences of a refusal. And if the consequences of a refusal are understood well enough to consent to the alternative then the refusal must also be competent.[36]

However, Balcombe LJ's dictum is not enough to dispose of the risk-relative account. If we take the latter as its proponents wish it understood, the symmetricity of *ability* to understand and appreciate across the available options is not determinative of whether capacity is risk-relative, since the relevant asymmetry lies instead in risk being the standard that sets the *sufficiency* of an agent's reasoning.[37] I return to the tenability of this view later. Here, it suffices to say that this conception of the risk-relative account finds no doctrinal support in *Re W* either; one must look elsewhere.

In *Re R*, we find statements that support a relationship between capacity and the gravity or seriousness of medical treatment. For Farquharson LJ, '[p]lainly the capacity to consent will vary with the gravity of the treatment proposed'.[38] And Lord Donaldson MR, in comments about the 'developmental' nature of *Gillick* capacity, observes that: 'at one age [a child] will be quite incapable of deciding whether or not to consent to a dental examination, let alone treatment. At a later stage it will be quite capable of both, but incapable of deciding whether to consent to more serious treatment.'[39]

Farquharson LJ does not elaborate further. Lord Donaldson MR does; and in the *dicta* that follow it is far from clear that his Lordship holds the view that capacity is risk-relative across the options available to the agent: 'what is involved is not merely an ability to understand the nature of the proposed treatment … but a full understanding and appreciation of the consequences both of the treatment in terms of intended and possible side effects and, equally important, the anticipated consequences of a failure to treat'.[40]

A plausible construction of Lord Donaldson MR's view is that his Lordship considers the capacity required to take treatment *decisions* to increase, according to respective stakes. The stakes set the standard of capacity for a decision, but the standard of capacity does not vary between whichever option—consent or refusal—is thought (if at all) to make the decision of greater or lesser consequence. On this account, capacity is risk-relative, though not in the same way argued by risk-relativists in the literature. Crucially, the 'stakes-relative' conception of capacity we find in *Re R* is incompatible with the asymmetry of capacity thesis.

There is very limited evidence elsewhere in the English doctrine for the proposition that the risk-relative account is part of positive law. Perhaps the

36 Harris, 'Consent', 12.
37 Lawlor, 'Cake or Death?', 749.
38 *Re R* 31.
39 *Re R* 25.
40 *Re R* 26.

strongest—albeit equivocal—support is found in first instance decisions that set a high bar of capacity to refuse treatment. For example, in *Re S*, Johnson J— addressing S's refusal of a life-prolonging blood transfusion—held:

> It does not seem to me that her capacity is commensurate with the gravity of the decision which she has made. It seems to me that an understanding that she will die is not enough. For her decision to carry weight she should have a greater understanding of the manner of the death and pain and the distress.[41]

We might read Johnson J compatibly with the interpretation of Lord Donaldson MR's *dicta* above—since the decision is high stakes, a high standard of capacity is required no matter which option is chosen. But one might conjecture that 'the decision' refers only to the *option* that S chose, namely refusal. This would allow for—but not ensure—risk-relativity between the options of consent and refusal: the standard of capacity for refusal was high for S because of the life-ending consequences of refusal; whereas the comparative risks for consent were lower and with it the standard of capacity. I say that risk-relativity may not be ensured, since it is questionable whether the cost-benefit analysis turns out this way when, for example, the minor in question—like S—belongs to a religious minority for whom negative consequences may attach to treatment acceptance or imposition.

To conclude on the risk-relative account of capacity, its doctrinal grounding is, at best, equivocal. We might doubt whether the law has embraced this asymmetry of capacity.

## The refusal of consent/refusal of treatment distinction

Gilmore and Herring identify the following distinction in the English adolescent medical treatment case law:

> 1 A 'rejection of proposed treatment' [their shorthand: 'refusal of consent']. Here the child is offered the option of consenting to a particular treatment. The child considers the proposed treatment and indicates that he or she does not consent to it; or, in other words, declines to provide consent to that particular treatment.
> 2 A 'refusal of treatment'. Here the child has decided not to have any treatment whatsoever. It is not merely the patient's wish to decline particular treatment, but a decision to refuse all treatment, a conscious decision to incur the consequences of a total failure to treat.[42]

[41] *Re S (A Minor) (Consent to Medical Treatment)* [1994] 2 FLR 1065 (Fam) 1076; See also *Re E (A Minor) (Wardship: Medical Treatment)* [1993] 1 FLR 386 (Fam) 391 (Ward J).

[42] Gilmore and Herring, 'No', 7. For critical discussion, see E. Cave and J. Wallbank, 'Minors' Capacity to Refuse Treatment: A Reply to Gilmore and Herring', *Medical Law Review*, 20 (2012), 423–49.

Out of this distinction of refusal of consent and refusal of treatment,[43] Gilmore and Herring build their version of the asymmetry of capacity thesis. On their view, the capacity required to refuse consent differs from the capacity required to refuse treatment, save when the respective choices relate to the same informational 'content', namely 'where there is only one treatment *available*':[44]

> It does not necessarily follow from the fact that a child has capacity to consent (and corresponding capacity to decline consent) to certain specific treatment that he or she will have capacity to refuse all treatment … the child who is simply considering whether or not to accept a particular proposal, will not necessarily have addressed all matters pertaining to the refusal of all treatment (not least because he or she may only have been told by the doctor about the proposed treatment).[45]

How sound is Gilmore and Herring's reading of the doctrine? Let us start with their analysis of the House of Lords decision in *Gillick*. There are difficulties here, both in respect of the finer points made, and in respect of how these individual points feed into the refusal of consent/refusal of treatment distinction.

The ratio in *Gillick*, as stated by Lord Fraser, is that:

> Provided the [minor] … is capable of understanding what is proposed, and of expressing his or her own wishes, I see no good reason for holding that he or she lacks the capacity to express them validly and effectively and to authorise the medical man to make the examination or give the treatment which he advises.[46]

Lord Scarman agrees with Lord Fraser,[47] though his Lordship formulates the *Gillick* capacity test in different language:

> as a matter of law the parental right to determine whether or not their minor child below the age of 16 will have medical treatment terminates if and when the child achieves a sufficient understanding and intelligence to enable him or her to understand fully what is proposed.[48]

Specifying the *Gillick* test to the context of contraceptive advice and treatment, Lord Scarman holds that:

> there is much that has to be understood by a girl under the age of 16 if she is to have legal capacity to consent to such treatment. It is not enough that she should understand the nature of the advice which is being given: she must also have a sufficient maturity to understand *what is involved*. There are moral and family questions, especially her relationship with her parents; long-term problems associated with the emotional

[43] Cave and Wallbank helpfully put the distinction as between 'refusal of a *particular* treatment' and 'refusal of *all* treatment': 'Minors' Capacity', 425. Nothing hangs on the terminology and I shall articulate the distinction more formally later.

[44] Gilmore and Herring, 'No', 7 (emphasis added).

[45] Gilmore and Herring, 'No', 8.

[46] *Gillick* 169.

[47] *Gillick* 176.

[48] *Gillick* 188–9.

> impact of pregnancy and its termination; and there are the risks to health of sexual intercourse at her age, risks which contraception may diminish but cannot eliminate.[49]

Gilmore and Herring argue that 'the most straightforward way to read what Lord Fraser says' is that 'in relation to consenting to treatment, the understanding required is merely an understanding of that which is proposed by way of treatment'. Further, they argue that on Lord Scarman's specification, the capacity to consent to treatment does not require understanding of 'the consequences of a failure to treat':[50]

> His test is directed to an understanding of the contraceptive treatment proposed and its wider implications … If his Lordship were intending to state that the girl had also to understand what would happen if there was no treatment (no contraception) then he might have been expected to emphasise not just pregnancy and its termination, but a number of other factors including the nature and pain of birth, the burdens of caring for a baby and so forth.[51]

Gilmore and Herring then buttress the above with a pragmatic argument: were capacity to consent to treatment evaluated in part on the basis of a minor's grasp of what refusal entails, few would have the capacity to consent—whether to contraception or to other interventions.[52]

What should we make of these arguments? Let us take them in turn, then globally. Gilmore and Herring's first claim is that 'what is proposed' should be understood restrictively as the treatment *offered* and its implications,[53] rather than (as 'in some quarters') as 'what is involved': what is proposed plus understanding 'the consequences of not having treatment'.[54] As an initial response, it is *prima facie* implausible to hold that decisions in respect of 'what is proposed' do not encompass comparative judgements between alternative states of affairs. Understanding and appreciation of what is proposed might just require a grasp of what is involved.[55] I articulate this point later. Even in the context of the *dicta* in *Gillick*, Gilmore and Herring's restrictive reading of 'what is proposed' is far from straightforward. This is because the Law Lords appear to treat the terms 'propose' and 'involve' as synonymous. Lord Scarman uses 'what is proposed' when stating the test of *Gillick* capacity and 'what is involved' when specifying to the context of contraceptive advice and treatment. Lord Fraser also uses 'propose' and 'involve' interchangeably.[56] This would not be a problem for Gilmore and Herring, except they have made something of the difference and will later rely on it in their exegesis of *Re R* and *Re W*.[57]

49 *Gillick* 189 (emphasis added).
50 Gilmore and Herring, 'No', 11.
51 Gilmore and Herring, 'No', 10–11.
52 Gilmore and Herring, 'No', 11.
53 For example, that contraception is not 100 per cent protective against pregnancy.
54 Gilmore and Herring, 'No', 10.
55 In this respect, I agree with Cave and Wallbank, 'Minors' Capacity', 429, 433, and with Harris, 'Consent', 12 (text quoted at n 36).
56 *Gillick* 169–70.
57 Gilmore and Herring, 'No', 13–15.

Gilmore and Herring's second claim attempts to address the synonymity issue: so far as Lord Scarman's speech goes, 'what is involved' should not be read to include an understanding of the consequences of refusal; rather, it means 'what is proposed', namely what is offered. This is a rather strained reading. And an argumentative strategy freighted with risk. For one, Gilmore and Herring seem committed to the view that Lord Scarman meant *exhaustively* to specify the information relevant to capacity for the purposes of contraceptive advice and treatment. For another, later *Gillick* capacity cases show that a grasp of what non-treatment entails is required. In *Re X (A Child) (Capacity to Consent to Termination)*, Munby J accepts the following expert evidence for incapacity:

> although X would understand termination and its effect—the death of her baby—she did not have a full understanding of what the pregnancy would involve—the later stages and the birth—and only a very limited understanding of what having a child means, the responsibilities it entails and the impositions it would place upon her.[58]

Here, what makes for X's incapacity is a lack of understanding and appreciation of exactly the kind of information Gilmore and Herring allege Lord Scarman deliberately omitted from the information relevant to *Gillick* capacity. Of course, Gilmore and Herring's article predates *Re X*. The point is that their reading of *Gillick* has left them hostages to fortune.

Gilmore and Herring's third claim is that, practically, the bar of capacity to consent would be set too high if minors were required to understand and appreciate what refusal entails. Again, I will expand on my doubts whether it is conceptually possible or normatively desirable to prize apart grasp of consent and refusal aside later. As a doctrinal matter, it is not evident from the speeches in *Gillick* that their Lordships were looking to make it easy for minors to have capacity to consent to (as opposed to refuse) medical treatment.[59]

There is a more global issue with Gilmore and Herring's treatment of *Gillick*: its support for the refusal of consent/refusal of treatment distinction is not obvious. Cave and Wallbank note 'some ambiguity as to whether Gilmore and Herring are drawing a distinction between consenting and refusing, as well as between consenting/refusing particular treatment and refusing all treatment'.[60] I agree. Gilmore and Herring's discussion on *Gillick* is devoted to arguing for a distinction between the respective capacities required *to consent* to and *to refuse* treatment, given variance in the capacity-relevant information. In order for *Gillick* to ground the refusal of consent/refusal of treatment distinction doctrinally, Gilmore and Herring would

[58] *Re X (A Child) (Capacity to Consent to Termination)* [2014] EWHC 1871 (Fam) [13]. There is no suggestion in *X* of variance of the information relevant to capacity according to the option favoured by X—keeping the baby—at the time of the capacity test.

[59] *Gillick* 189 (Lord Scarman) (text quoted at n 49). If one worries about the demandingness of the capacity test, one might narrow the scope of the information relevant to the *decision*, as opposed to the information relevant to the *options*. For discussion, see Black, Forsberg, and Skelton, 'Transformative Choice'.

[60] Cave and Wallbank, 'Minors' Capacity', 428.

have to show the House of Lords to engage with their conceptions of 'no consent' and 'no treatment' and to show how the capacity to refuse consent is equivalent to grasping what is *offered*, while the capacity to refuse treatment is equivalent to grasping what is *involved*. Of course, Gilmore and Herring do not do this because it is impossible. Rather, they use the analysis of *Gillick* to build a conception of the asymmetry of capacity thesis, according to which the information relevant to capacity (and therefore capacity itself) *is option-sensitive*. If one consents, the informational basis against which capacity is assessed is thinner; if one refuses, the informational basis against which capacity is assessed is thicker. But the fact that *Gillick* in and of itself does not support the refusal of consent/refusal of treatment distinction leaves much work outstanding. Gilmore and Herring still need doctrinal support for their option-sensitive, variable information account of the asymmetry of capacity. Enter the cases of *Re R* and *Re W*.

With regard to *Re R*, Gilmore and Herring argue that Lord Donaldson MR takes cognisance of the distinction between 'what is proposed' and 'what is involved' as they interpret it, and 'indeed between a refusal of consent to specific treatment and a refusal of all treatment'.[61] Gilmore and Herring appeal to the fact that R was proposing to refuse all treatment, and Lord Donaldson MR's evaluation of the expert evidence on capacity.[62] Let us take the former for granted, although the position is potentially more complex.[63] On the latter, the expert witness in question—Dr R—stated in his written evidence that '[R] is of sufficient maturity and understanding to comprehend the treatment being recommended and is currently rational'.[64] Under oral examination, the relevant part of the exchange with regard to capacity is as follows:

> Q. … having regard to her development and maturity, [does] she [understand] the nature of the implications of the treatment proposed … ? A. Yes, I felt that she is mature enough to understand the nature of the proposal. When I saw her on [4 July] she was rational and, I thought, of sufficient understanding to be able to make a decision in her own right.[65]

Consideration of the evidence and Lord Donaldson MR's engagement with it invites several observations. First, it is unclear whether the expert witness found R to have capacity at the relevant time merely on the basis of understanding of 'what is proposed' as understood by Gilmore and Herring. The terms 'treatment

61 Gilmore and Herring, 'No', 13.

62 Gilmore and Herring, 'No', 13.

63 R was refusing sedative and anti-psychotic medication. The success of this refusal would have led to her discharge from the adolescent psychiatric unit where she was receiving a course of treatment for which medication was sometimes necessary: *Re R* 20. Whether an individual refuses treatment depends rather on how narrowly or widely the notion is drawn. See (in a different context) J. Coggon, 'Alcohol Dependence and Anorexia Nervosa: Individual Autonomy and the Jurisdiction of the Court of Protection; *An NHS Foundation Trust v Ms X* [2014] EWCOP 35; (2014) 140 BMLR 41', *Medical Law Review*, 23 (2015), 659–67.

64 *Re R* 19–20.

65 *Re R* 20.

being recommended' and 'sufficient understanding to be able to make a decision' are ambiguous. Moreover, 'the nature of the proposal' should be understood in the context of the question put by counsel. Second, regardless of how we interpret it, the expert witness found R to have capacity to refuse on the basis of understanding 'what is proposed'. This approach to capacity seems option-insensitive—the information relevant to capacity is invariable across the options of consent and refusal. Third, Lord Donaldson MR clearly rejects the expert witness' approach to capacity.

> it is far from certain that Dr. R. was saying that R. understood the implications of treatment being withheld, as distinct from understanding what was proposed to be done by way of treatment—'the nature of the proposal' which I take to have been intended as a paraphrase of Lord Scarman's 'to understand fully what is proposed'.[66]

Importantly, however, it is not clear that Lord Donaldson MR rejects an option-insensitive approach to the capacity-relevant information in favour of an option-sensitive distinction between capacity to consent—evaluated against 'what is proposed'—and capacity to refuse—evaluated against 'what is involved'. It is open to us to conclude, *pace* Gilmore and Herring, that his Lordship views an understanding of the 'implications of treatment being withheld' as necessary for capacity across the options. Indeed, this option-insensitive conception of *Gillick* seems a better fit with what Lord Donaldson MR says on the developmental nature of *Gillick* capacity in *Re R*, insofar as his Lordship appears to speak of a *single* capacity test.[67] Finally, it is hard to see how *Re R* provides authority for Gilmore and Herring's refusal of consent/refusal of treatment distinction. Again, the most we can say is that to the extent that *Re R* is authority for the proposition that the information relevant to capacity is option-sensitive, it does so only for the respective capacities to consent and to refuse treatment. Refusal of consent is not in the doctrinal picture.

In respect of *Re W*, Gilmore and Herring merely argue that '[i]t is evident from Balcombe LJ's judgment that the court at first instance received evidence only on W's ability to understand the treatment which was proposed'.[68] Again, this view turns on the ambiguous meaning of the expert witness' utterance 'understands what is proposed as treatment'.[69] Moreover, the limited *obiter* that *might* acknowledge the refusal of consent/refusal of treatment distinction seem hostile to it. As Cave and Wallbank observe, Lord Donaldson MR mentions that W was 'not in fact refusing all treatment',[70] and thus ought to have been competent to refuse consent, insofar as she understood the treatment proposal (on Gilmore and Herring's meaning); yet his Lordship speaks of 'W being unable to refuse *any* treatment (including specific treatment) for her anorexia nervosa'.[71]

66 *Re R* 20.
67 See text at nn 39 and 40.
68 Gilmore and Herring, 'No', 14.
69 *Re W* 84.
70 *Re W* 79.
71 Cave and Wallbank, 'Minors' Capacity', 431 (original emphasis).

To summarise on the refusal of consent/refusal of treatment distinction, I am not convinced that Gilmore and Herring's reading of *Gillick*, *Re R*, and *Re W* supports the asymmetry of capacity thesis, that is, provides authority for varying the information relevant to capacity according to the option chosen by the agent. Even if the doctrine reflects the asymmetry of capacity thesis, it merely leads to a doctrinal distinction between the capacity to consent and to refuse treatment, rather than the refusing consent/refusing treatment distinction for which Gilmore and Herring argue.

Before we move on, we should note, with Gilmore and Herring,[72] that for adolescents subject to the MCA 2005, the information against which we evaluate capacity is invariant across the options available to the agent. Capacity is assessed relative to a *decision*,[73] and the MCA 2005, section 3(1) functional test employs a notion of capacity-relevant information that 'includes information about the reasonably foreseeable consequences of—(a) deciding one way or another, or (b) failing to make the decision'.[74] Therefore, if the capacity-relevant information (and therefore capacity itself) is option-sensitive for minors 15 years of age or younger, the same is not true of minors aged 16 or 17 years.

Of course, my argument in respect of the refusal of consent/refusal of treatment distinction, as well as the risk-relative conception of capacity above, is simply that these conceptions of the asymmetry of capacity thesis are not *currently* features of English legal doctrine. I do not claim that they could not be. As such, it is important to proceed to the next stage of my analysis: whether, given the underlying commitments of English capacity law, we ought to accept some version of the asymmetry of capacity thesis.

## Should English law embrace the asymmetry of capacity thesis?

In this section, I consider the asymmetry of capacity thesis against what I establish to be norms governing the functional element of English capacity law. My analysis has three stages. First, I employ the concepts of legal validity rules and legal effectiveness rules to demonstrate that whether an individual has functional capacity does not turn on the substantive rationality of their decision. Second, I aim to show that the evaluative norms that best explain the nature and operation of the functional test of capacity are those of instrumental (or procedural) rationality. Third, I consider the tenability of the asymmetry of capacity thesis in light of these conclusions.

72 Gilmore and Herring, 'No', 12–13.

73 MCA 2005, ss 1–3.

74 MCA 2005, s 3(4).

## Legal validity rules, legal effectiveness rules, and substantive rationality

I shall employ the distinction between legal validity rules and legal effectiveness rules to demonstrate that the norms governing the capacity element of legal validity are not those of substantive rationality.[75] That is, I show that possessing functional capacity does not require an agent to assign (dis)value to some option independent of their own conative state,[76] for example, by aligning their decision with what third parties such as a doctor or a court regard as the reasonable or 'best interests' choice. This is the case for both adults and adolescents. For clarity of argument, I shall consider the former, simpler case ahead of the latter.

English health law applicable to adults recognises the 'principle of self-determination', according to which:

> respect must be given to the wishes of the patient, so that if an adult patient of sound mind refuses, however unreasonably, to consent to treatment or care by which his life would or might be prolonged, the doctors responsible for his care must give effect to his wishes, even though they do not consider it to be in his best interests to do so ...[77]

> If the patient is capable of making a decision on whether to permit treatment and decides not to permit it his choice must be obeyed, even if on any objective view it is contrary to his best interests. A doctor has no right to proceed in the face of objection, even if it is plain to all, including the patient, that adverse consequences and even death will or may ensue.[78]

The principle of self-determination is best understood as an effectiveness rule. In the above-cited passages from *Bland*, Lord Goff and Lord Mustill, respectively, note that the wishes of the patient prevail, but only if the patient is of 'sound mind' or 'capable of making a decision', that is, only if they have capacity; the principle kicks in, if you will, once the issue of the validity of an individual's decision has been settled. Further, the principle of self-determination is a very *extensive* effectiveness rule: considerations of reasonableness or 'best interests' from the physician's (or court's) point of view do not, *inter alia*, licence overriding of a patient's valid refusal, namely, imposing treatment.[79] This has significance for our investigation

[75] Substantivism about rationality is the view according to which: '[a]n agent can have a reason to have a desire whether or not the agent can rationally reach this desire from the beliefs and desires that he or she has'. See B. Hooker and B. Streumer, 'Procedural and Substantive Practical Rationality', in A. R. Mele and P. Rawling (eds), *The Oxford Handbook of Rationality* (New York, Oxford University Press, 2004), pp. 57–74.

[76] By conative state, I mean an individual's '... desires, her values, what she wants, her likes and dislikes, attitudes that record how she would like the world to be': R. Pettigrew, *Choosing for Changing Selves* (Oxford, Oxford University Press, 2020), p. 12.

[77] *Bland* 864 (Lord Goff).

[78] *Bland* 891 (Lord Mustill). See also e.g. *Re MB (An Adult: Medical Treatment)* [1997] 2 FCR 541 (CA) 553 (Butler Sloss LJ).

[79] See I. Black, 'Refusing Life-Prolonging Medical Treatment and the ECHR', *Oxford Journal of Legal Studies*, 38 (2018), 299–327.

of the governing norms of capacity law. For if the substantive rationality of a patient's decision cannot settle whether a decision is effective, substantive considerations ought not to determine whether that decision is valid either. The reason being that were the legal validity of healthcare decisions a matter of reasonableness, best interests, or the like, it would be incoherent to hold such concerns irrelevant to legal effectiveness, since by necessity all valid decisions would possess the excluded quality. We can conclude, therefore, that substantive rationality is irrelevant to adult capacity.

For adolescents, the relevant effectiveness rule is the concurrent consents doctrine, according to which a minor's legally valid refusal of treatment may be overridden by parents or the court on best interests grounds.[80] Minors, therefore, are in a different position to adults: substantive considerations clearly bear on whether their healthcare wishes prevail. As Lord Donaldson puts it in *Re W*, a 'paramount' concern for minors' best interests:

> involves giving them the maximum degree of decision-making which is prudent. Prudence does not involve avoiding all risk, but it does involve avoiding taking risks which, if they eventuate, may have irreparable consequences or which are disproportionate to the benefits which could accrue from taking them.[81]

Minors' valid refusals of treatment, then, are merely *pro tanto* legally effective.[82] The fact that substantive rationality *is* relevant to the legal effectiveness of minors' healthcare decisions does not, however, mean that substantive concerns dictate the legal validity of such decisions. For were it the case that minor capacity turns on whether an individual chooses the option that aligns with what a health professional or a court considers to be in their best interests, it would not have been necessary for Lord Donaldson to fashion the concurrent consents doctrine out of *Gillick* in *Re R* and *Re W*—capacity law would do the necessary work. Thus, for minors, as for adults, the capacity element of legal validity is not a matter of substantive rationality. In the next section, I argue that we should understand functional capacity as a matter of instrumental (or procedural) rationality.

## Functional capacity as instrumental rationality

Elsewhere, Lisa Forsberg, Anthony Skelton, and I argue that the *operative standard* of functional capacity in English law—for adults and adolescents—is that of instrumental rationality (or 'rational choice').[83] That is, an individual's functional decision-making ability is 'evaluated by reference to … whether an individual behaves in accordance with what they value most, in light of what they believe'.[84]

[80] See *Effectiveness rules* above.

[81] *Re W* 82.

[82] Of course, if no override is forthcoming, health professionals have no permission to treat.

[83] Black, Forsberg, and Skelton, 'Transformative Choice', 670–2.

[84] Black, Forsberg, and Skelton, 'Transformative Choice', 671.

More precisely, one's decision is instrumentally rational if, facing a *choice*, one selects the *option* that is the better *means* to the *outcome* (or *end*) *most valued*, as determined by one's *subjective valuations* of the possible outcomes weighted for one's *credences* (degrees of belief) in those outcomes obtaining.[85]

Instrumental rationality provides the best explanation for the legal tests of functional capacity stated by legal actors—in statute (the MCA 2005) and in case law (*Gillick*)—and applied by the same in case law. In respect of the MCA 2005, respect for a plurality of values is a principle of the legal regime: 'A person is not to be treated as unable to make a decision merely because he makes an unwise decision.'[86] Moreover, Forsberg, Skelton, and I note the tight fit between an instrumental standard of rationality and the section 3(1) functional test:

> The *understanding* criterion in s.3(1)(a) of the Act corresponds to grasping descriptively what the set of options entail. The *using* or *weighing* criterion in s.3(1)(c) of the Act requires an individual to appreciate the outcomes given what they currently most value, to assign probabilities, and to select the best option. The MCA 2005 s.3(1)(b) *retaining* criterion is essential to understanding, using or weighing.[87]

Further, we highlight the wealth of—pre- and post-MCA 2005—adult capacity case law that 'exemplifies a judicial commitment in principle to … evaluation of capacity on the basis of an individual's own values, as opposed to what is [substantively] rational'.[88] To cite but one instance here, in *King's College NHS Foundation Trust v C*, MacDonald J held that:

> [An individual] is entitled to make her own decision [whether to accept treatment] based on the things that are important to her, in keeping with her own personality and system of values and without conforming to society's expectation of what constitutes the "normal" decision in this situation (if such a thing exists) …[89]

In respect of *Gillick* capacity, one should not be misled into thinking that '[being] capable of understanding what is proposed' or '[achievement of] sufficient understanding and intelligence to enable him or her to understand fully what is proposed' discloses a conception of capacity that assesses bare understanding of

[85] As the discussion progresses, it may on occasion be helpful to employ a simple formal schema, according to which: C is (or is identical to, the same as, =) a choice. *S* = a situation (or manner, or state of affairs). The set of options available in *S* from which C is made is (*x*, *y* …). (*x*, *y* …) belong to (or are elements of, Î) *S*. Thus the choice of *x* from the set of options (x, y) in some situation = C(*x*|*S*). The binary relations consistent with the instrumental rationality of C(*x*|*S*) include weak preference (*x* is at least as good as *y*, or x *R y*), strict preference (*x P y*, equivalent to («) [*x R y* & ~(*y R x*)]), and indifference (*x I y* « [*x R y* & y *R x*]). See A. Sen, *Collective Choice and Social Welfare*, expanded edn (Cambridge, MA, Harvard University Press, 2017), ch. 1.

[86] MCA 2005, s 1(4).

[87] Black, Forsberg, and Skelton, 'Transformative Choice', 671.

[88] Black, Forsberg, and Skelton, 'Transformative Choice', 671.

[89] *King's College Hospital NHS Foundation Trust v C* [2015] EWCOP 80 [97]. See also *Heart of England NHS Foundation Trust v JB* [2014] EWHC 342 (COP) [1], [7] (Peter Jackson J); *Ms B v An NHS Hospital Trust* [2002] EWHC 429 (Fam) [14–27] (Butler-Sloss LJ); *Bland* 864 (Lord Goff).

information (or mere assimilation of relevant knowledge).[90] As Forsberg, Skelton, and I observe,[91] Lord Scarman speaks of both the minor's ability to 'appraise' the information relevant to the decision[92] and her faculty of 'appreciation'.[93] Both of these capacities go beyond mere understanding and add substance to Lord Scarman's references to the minor's 'intelligence' and 'maturity' in the statement and specification of the *Gillick* test.[94] Appraisal 'involves the exercise of judgement',[95] whereas appreciation entails 'the ability to apply information, including consequences of the decision, to oneself'.[96] Moreover, evaluation of a minor's appreciation and exercise of judgement takes place against the canvas of their own subjective values. We note that: 'It is implicit in *Gillick* itself that a minor with capacity may consent to contraceptive treatment, but they are not *required* so to do: they will not lack capacity merely because they consent to or refuse treatment.'[97]

In combination, these factors lend support to the argument that *Gillick* capacity is underpinned by the norms of instrumental rationality.

I would add one further point to what we argue elsewhere: were *Gillick* capacity truly an understanding-only conception of capacity, this would make the functional test that applies to adolescents less demanding than that applicable to adults (and now minors aged 16 and 17 since the MCA 2005). As Benjamin Freedman observes, 'tests that focus upon understanding eliminate the notion of competence in favor of the notion of information'.[98] Of course, one must be wary of anachronism. A functional test for adult capacity was not specified in English law until *Re C* in 1993,[99] and it is not until the Law Commission's report on *Mental Incapacity* in 1995 that we find explicit official mention of the now familiar criteria of understanding, using, and weighing of relevant information.[100] Yet, I would suggest that in invoking notions synonymous with the use or weighing of relevant information, Lord Scarman had something more demanding in mind for *Gillick* capacity than mere understanding, which is readily explainable in terms of instrumental rationality.

90 *Gillick* 169 (Lord Fraser), 188–9 (Lord Scarman), respectively.

91 Black, Forsberg, and Skelton, 'Transformative Choice', 672.

92 *Gillick* 189.

93 *Gillick* 189–90, citing *Johnston v Wellesley Hospital* (1970) 17 DLR (3d) 139 (ON SC) 143 (Addy J).

94 *Gillick* 188–9.

95 Black, Forsberg, and Skelton, 'Transformative Choice', 672.

96 N. B. Kane, A. R. Keene, G. S. Owen, and S. Y. H. Kim, 'Applying Decision-Making Capacity Criteria in Practice: A Content Analysis of Court Judgments', *PLoS ONE*, 16 (2021), e0246521 at 10.

97 Black, Forsberg, and Skelton, 'Transformative Choice', 672 (original emphasis).

98 B. Freedman, 'Competence, Marginal and Otherwise: Concepts and Ethics', *International Journal of Law and Psychiatry*, 4 (1981), 53–72 at 63.

99 *Re C (Adult: Refusal of Treatment)* [1994] 1 WLR 290 (Fam).

100 Law Commission, *Mental Incapacity* (Law Com No. 231, 1995) paras 3.15–3.17. The notion of appreciation receives mention in one of the consultation papers: Law Commission, *Mentally Incapacitated Adults and Decision-Making: A New Jurisdiction* (Consultation Paper No. 128, 1992) para 3.21.

## Is the asymmetry of capacity thesis tenable?

If the norms that govern functional capacity in English law are indeed those of instrumental rationality, we have a basis on which to assess the tenability of acceptance of the asymmetry of capacity thesis in this jurisdiction. I shall thus work through the risk-relative account of capacity and the refusal of consent/refusal of treatment distinction, including various matters I have identified and parked in the course of the preceding discussion, using instrumental rationality as the evaluative frame.

### *Against risk-relativity*

Harris' complaint about the risk-relative account of capacity seems to go to the salience of preference relations to rational choice.[101] On a binary choice, for example, an agent's credence-weighted subjective valuation of an option, $x$, requires comparison to the credence-weighted subjective valuation of the other option, $y$ (equivalent to not $x$). The choice of $x$ or $y$ will be instrumentally rational only if certain preference relations—weak preference, strict preference, indifference—obtain between $x$ and $y$. Thus, for a medical treatment decision for which there is one available treatment, we evaluate an agent's capacity on the basis of their choice set against the relative credence-weighted subjective values for consent and refusal. Say that an agent strictly prefers consent to refusal but opts for refusal. On a capacity qua instrumental rationality view, the agent fails to choose the option that is the better means to their most valued outcome and thus lacks capacity.

Were proponents of the risk-relative account of capacity committed to the position that an agent can have capacity to consent to treatment without having formed a comparative judgement (of the right kind) about consent *and* refusal, the theory would be *very* implausible. Such position is tantamount, as Lawlor writes, to the claim that one 'could be competent *to a certain degree* to consent to treatment, but then be less competent to refuse that same treatment'.[102] Harris dismisses such a view as 'palpable nonsense'.[103] However, risk-relativists need not downplay, ignore, or reject the salience of preference relations to capacity. Harris' argument attacks a straw man. Indeed, Lawlor goes as far as saying, 'I do not know of anyone who does defend this asymmetry'.[104]

That Harris' argument fails is not a sufficient reason to embrace the asymmetry of capacity thesis on the basis of risk-relativity, however. Recall that at the heart of the risk-relative account lies the claim that an asymmetry of the capacity required to choose $x$ rather than $y$ (or vice versa) may arise because the *standard* that sets the

[101] Harris, 'Consent', 12 (text quoted at n 36).
[102] Lawlor, 'Cake or Death?', 749 (original emphasis).
[103] Harris, 'Consent', 12.
[104] Lawlor, 'Cake or Death?', 749.

*sufficiency* of an agent's reasoning is determined by the notion of risk.[105] The challenge for risk-relativists is to relate risk to capacity in a way that supports asymmetry of capacity.

Neil Pickering, Giles Newton-Howes, and Simon Walker observe that in Lawlor's and Ian Wilks' defences of the risk-relative account,[106] the property of difficulty makes for a *conceptual* connection between risk and capacity.

> The risk-relative approach tells us that we should set [the] required level of competence in relation to the risk of choices and that the more risky a choice, the more demands we should place on the person's capacities to adjudge the person competent. To make a more risky choice, a person must be able to perform a more difficult one.[107]

Against this view, Pickering *et al.* argue that: 'there is no reason at all to think that there is any systematic relationship between decisions which are difficult and decisions which are risky. Difficult decisions are not necessarily risky ones, and risky decisions are not necessarily difficult ones.'[108]

I agree. At best, some difficult decisions are risky decisions.[109] I may struggle to choose between tomato- or oil-based pasta sauce tonight, but no particular risk inheres in the choice of either. (Suppose that both are apt to please me to some sufficient degree; the difficulty arises because both options are, on balance, good, but this is also what de-risks the choice.) And the choice to run some obvious risk—refusal of a blood transfusion, perhaps—may not be difficult at all, given an agent's character, values, and reasons. Accordingly, an account that relies on difficulty as the feature of decisions that makes the capacity to choose *x* over *y* vary according to risk is not plausible.[110]

Interestingly, Pickering *et al.* suggest that our judgements about whether an individual has capacity to choose a *prima facie* risky option may rely not on difficulty but, rather, *inter alia*, 'some good reason ... [that] show[s] the values and beliefs that lead to their decision'.[111] One might see potential here to develop an alternative footing for the risk-relative account that exploits a connection between *riskiness* and *reasons*. Accordingly, we might explain risk-relativity in terms of differential demands on the *cogency* of the reasons that underpin an agent's drawing of preference-relations.

Suppose—as is most often the case in the adolescent medical treatment case law—that refusal is perceived by health professionals to be the riskier option relative to consent. On a riskiness and reasons account, as the risk of refusal increases

105 Lawlor, 'Cake or Death?', 749.

106 Lawlor, 'Cake or Death?'; Wilks, 'Risk-Related Competence'.

107 Pickering, Newton-Howes, and Walker, 'Risk-Related Competence', 897.

108 Pickering, Newton-Howes, and Walker, 'Risk-Related Competence', 897.

109 To this extent, I would not even make the concession that '[i]t seems intuitive that it is harder to make a more difficult decision': Pickering, Newton-Howes, and Walker, 'Risk-Related Competence', 897.

110 A symmetrical 'stakes-relative' conception of capacity that relied on difficulty would fail for the same reasons.

111 Pickering, Newton-Howes, and Walker, 'Risk-Related Competence', 897.

relative to consent, so the strength of reasoning (in terms of its cogency) required for capacity to refuse increases, too. *Mutatis mutandis*, the strength of reasoning required for capacity to consent decreases—though perhaps not below some de minimis threshold. Thus, an individual may need to offer strong reasons for preferring refusal over consent in order to have capacity but might give quite weak reasons when the chosen option is consent.[112]

The connection between riskiness and reasons just set out is normative.[113] This might seem promising insofar as connecting riskiness and reasons through an account of why an agent *ought* to give better reasons for the choice of *y* rather than *x* avoids the conceptual shoehorning that undermines the risk and difficulty account. However, risk-relativists must now supply normative support for the determination whether an option available to an agent is risky. I argue that such support is either unavailable or of little practical significance when the norms governing functional capacity are those of *instrumental* rationality.

The worry that pervades the critical literature on the risk-relative account is that judgements of riskiness seem either to *impose* the value of risk aversion on the agent or (supposing that the value of risk aversion is held) to impose a certain *distribution* or *specification* of that value to the options of consent to and refusal of medical treatment. For example, Gita Cale argues that: 'substantiating the notion of asymmetrical competence seems [*inter alia*] ... to require the unjustified condition that risks and outcomes be evaluated in terms of and in accordance with normative values that originate outside of the individual being assessed.'[114]

The complaint can be expressed in terms of substantive and subjective value. The risk-relativist might be thought to set the risks attendant on an option substantively—riskiness is a function of reasons independent of an individual's conative state. The critic might reply that how risky an option is for an agent depends on the subjective valuation of the outcomes that may obtain as a result of their choice.

It is perhaps helpful to distinguish between the concept of risk as probability that some outcome obtains in virtue of an agent's choice and that of risk (or riskiness) as a normative (often negative) evaluation of some option. It is not implausible that the notion of risk as probability is substantive. I need not take a general position on whether it is tenable to hold that, as a normative matter, there exist substantively—as opposed to subjectively—risky options. Rather, I argue that—in the institutional context of English capacity law—it is problematic to use substantive values to determine the riskiness of options and, consequently, the cogency of reasons that an agent must give in order to have capacity. This is because making a substantive connection between risk and reasons sits in tension with instrumental rationality as the normative basis for the test of functional capacity.

My misgivings go to the burdens and potential costs for individuals who hold idiosyncratic or unconventional values of setting the cogency of reasons required

112 See Freedman, 'Competence', 64–6.

113 See Cale, 'Risk-Related Competence', 139–40.

114 Cale, 'Risk-Related Competence', 148.

for capacity according to a substantive evaluation of riskiness across the available options. If the risks, substantively evaluated, do not break evenly across the options, an individual with idiosyncratic or unconventional values will face greater demands going against the grain than an individual whose subjective values align with the substantive values used to set the risk-relative standard. On a risk-relative standard, minorities, eccentrics, and the marginalised—among others—may all need to do more to evince that their decisions are instrumentally rational. An individual who, for example, refuses treatment against medical advice would be subject to a more rigorous capacity assessment process *and* asked to give stronger reasons for their choice. Yet why should they? Adding a substantive gloss to a test of instrumental rationality strikes me as illiberal and inegalitarian. Illiberal in that it establishes a modal—what most people would choose—or socially privileged—what would align with professional advice—evaluation of the relevant states of affairs, which operates as a procedural and substantive obstacle to individuals acting on their own conceptions of the good. Inegalitarian to the extent that it treats people differently in ways inconsistent with formal (or procedural) justice—since the degree of rationality required for a valid medical decision is inconstant across individuals—as well as on grounds potentially attributable to moral luck.[115] For these reasons, we should reject a risk-relative account of capacity that determines the riskiness of options by appeal to substantive values.[116]

The risk-relativist might object, however, that (normative) risk for the purposes of the risk-relative account is indeed subjective. As Mark Wicclair observes,[117] between the article and book versions of *Deciding for Others*, Buchanan and Brock appear to retreat from the view that professional norms and values determine the expected harms and benefits consequent on consent or refusal of treatment, respectively,[118] to that according to which:

> [t]he net balance of expected benefits and risks of the patient's choice in comparison with other alternatives will usually be determined by the physician … focus[ing] on the expected effects of a particular treatment option in forwarding the patient's underlying and enduring aims and values, to the extent that these are known. When the patient's aims and values are not known, the risk/benefit assessment will balance the expected effects of a particular treatment option in achieving the general goals of health care …[119]

Buchanan and Brock do not abide by this prescription in what follows. They speak of rebuttable presumptions that certain choices are risky.[120] And their illustration of

[115] There is, of course, more to say about how substantive accounts risk-relativity are inegalitarian.

[116] I suggest that 'procedural' accounts of risk-relativity such as that recently defended by Douglas, 'Acceptance-Refusal Asymmetry' ought also to be rejected, since it is doubtful whether they are merely procedural in character. It is difficult to see how testing the selection of an option more rigorously than another is not raising the bar substantively for the former choice.

[117] Wicclair, 'Capacity and Risk', 93–4.

[118] Buchanan and Brock, *Deciding for Others*, p. 34.

[119] Buchanan and Brock, *Deciding for Others*, p. 52.

[120] Buchanan and Brock, *Deciding for Others*, p. 53.

when more or less demanding standards of capacity apply seems entirely to track 'the goals of health care'.[121] To the extent that a best interpretation of their position is available, it may be that, as Wicclair writes: 'although the general goals of health care should be the basis for deciding whether patients' decisions are "high risk" and trigger a strong standard of decision-making capacity, patients' underlying and enduring aims and values should guide risk/benefit assessments if patients satisfy the criteria associated with the strong standard'.[122]

Yet if this is Buchanan and Brock's view, substantive values are indeed active in determining whether an option is more risky and thus whether more cogent reasons will be needed to justify its choice over other(s). If the individual supplies reasons meeting the required standard (and thereby has capacity), only then will their subjective evaluation of the risks prevail. The concession seems trivial, tantamount to, 'if you have capacity, we shall then treat you as though you have capacity'.

Quite apart from what Buchanan and Brock actually believe, if we take seriously the idea that subjective values determine risk, the risk-relative account appears to become redundant. Consider the example of a haemophiliac Jehovah's Witness offered a life-saving blood transfusion. On a subjective approach to risk, as Pickering *et al.* observe, 'receiving a blood transfusion sacrifices an eternity of bliss for a few uncertain years of human life'.[123] The 'risky' option is consent and the 'safe' option is refusal. But this distribution of risk raises the question of what work to identify individuals who lack capacity the risk-relative account does that a risk-neutral approach does not? On the latter, an individual's capacity is a function of whether their chosen option tracks what they have most reason to value (weighted for their credences); this approach achieves plausible outcomes without intensifying or relaxing the reason-giving requirements across the options.[124]

I would argue that risk-relativists face a dilemma.[125] On the first horn, 'going substantive' about risk makes for a higher standard of capacity—a requirement of cogent reason-giving—when individuals choose contrary to professional norms

[121] Buchanan and Brock, *Deciding for Others*, p. 52, Table 1.1.

[122] Wicclair, 'Capacity and Risk', p. 94.

[123] Pickering, Newton-Howes, and Walker, 'Risk-Related Competence', 897.

[124] As such, one might also doubt the utility of procedural accounts of risk-relativity based on subjective risk, such as Douglas' in 'Acceptance-Refusal Asymmetry'.

[125] In 'Competence and Ability', Vogelstein defends a rationality-based account of capacity, according to which an agent has capacity if and only if: (a) they hold rational beliefs about what treatment option is best (epistemic rationality); and (b) they choose either (i) in line with those rational beliefs (practical rationality); or (ii) not significantly out of line with those rational beliefs (mild, not wild practical irrationality). Vogelstein suggests that his account is 'neutral' vis-à-vis risk-relativity. That is, tolerance of mild irrationality might fluctuate according to the relative riskiness of the options: 'one might advocate a risk-relative or sliding-scale view according to which the level of irrationality that would make someone incompetent depends on the risk-profile of the relevant decision … someone's decision is not *wildly* irrational, yet is still irrational enough to make that person incompetent given the riskiness of the relevant decision'. It is not obvious that sometimes, individuals who make irrational decisions have capacity and Vogelstein merely provides intuitive support by way of an example. Even if Vogelstein has an argument for his position, he, nevertheless, faces my dilemma about the nature of risk.

and values. The putative appeal of this view is that it makes it harder to have the capacity not to follow medical advice. However, this offends against the view that capacity is a matter of instrumental rationality. On the second horn, 'going subjective' about risk loses the risk-relative account its utility and intuitive appeal. Either way, we should not accept a risk-relative conception of the asymmetry of capacity thesis in English Law.

### *Rejecting the refusal of consent/refusal of treatment*

Above, I argued that Gilmore and Herring's reading of the adolescent medical treatment case law yields a conception of the asymmetry of capacity thesis according to which:

> the information relevant to capacity (and therefore capacity itself) *is option-sensitive*. If one consents, the informational basis against which capacity is assessed is thinner; if one refuses, the informational basis against which capacity is assessed is thicker.

Prior to discussing whether we should accept this view, I should clarify how, if the capacity-relevant information varies across the options available to an agent, the capacity required to choose any one option changes. I submit that we should understand this in terms of difference of *nature*, rather than *difficulty*.

Consider an example involving different decisions. Say that on two separate visits to the gelateria my choices are (pistachio, nocciola) and (pistachio, nocciola, stracciatella), respectively. These are different decisions in substance, since in the latter case the gelatiere has added stracciatella to the menu. Relatedly, the enquiry as to whether I choose my gelato well (or rationally) is different in *nature* in the two-gelato choice compared to the three-gelato choice. To wit, the capacity required in the two- and three-gelato choices is different in *nature*. Note, however, that the three-gelato choice is not necessarily more *difficult*; whether it is depends on further facts about the situation and my values—imagine I dislike chocolate.

Consider now the asymmetries identified in our analysis of Gilmore and Herring above. For a consent/refusal asymmetry, we might represent this as the claim that if an agent consents to a specific treatment option ($x$), their capacity is evaluated against the set of information (treatment) $\leftrightarrow$ ($x$), whereas if an agent refuses ($y$), their capacity is evaluated against (treatment, ~treatment) $\leftrightarrow$ ($x$, y). And for a refusal of consent/refusal of treatment asymmetry, if an agent consents or refuses consent, their capacity is evaluated against the set of information (treatment, ~treatment) for *a specific* treatment option—($x_1$, ~$x_1$)—whereas if an agent refuses treatment, their capacity is evaluated against (treatment, ~treatment) for *every available* treatment option—($x_1$, ~$x_1$… $x_n$, ~$x_n$) $\leftrightarrow$ ($x$, $y$). If the capacity-relevant information is option-sensitive in this way, we evaluate capacity *as if* the agent takes *different* decisions. Yet, the asymmetry of capacity in play is only contingently one of *difficulty* (or greater or lesser capacity).

Let us turn to the evaluation of these asymmetries, guided by my account of functional capacity as instrumental rationality. Gilmore and Herring's analysis of *Gillick* seems to support a consent/refusal asymmetry according to which the capacity to take a decision requires a grasp of mere understanding of the treatment offered rather than a grasp of both what treatment and non-treatment entail.[126] However, this asymmetry is incoherent as an asymmetry of capacity. If the capacity to consent to a treatment option is evaluated against the set of information (treatment) rather than (treatment, ~treatment), there is no decision—no choice between alternative states of affairs—whose rationality is assessable for the purposes of capacity. No such worry arises in respect of the refusal of consent/refusal of treatment asymmetry; we would assess capacity against at least a pair of options, whether the option exercised is consent, refusal of consent, or refusal of treatment.

Certainly, Gilmore and Herring are alive to the fact that the assessment of capacity must bite on a *decision*, for they acknowledge that when only one treatment is *available*, the capacity to refuse consent is equivalent to the capacity to refuse treatment.[127] We might consider, therefore, Gilmore and Herring's refusal of consent/refusal of treatment distinction to be an attempt to rescue *some* asymmetry in the capacity required to consent or to refuse, respectively. Is it worth saving?

Gilmore and Herring need to provide a rationale for the option-sensitivity of the information relevant to capacity. That the refusal of consent/refusal of treatment distinction is analytically tenable is not sufficient to justify its application.

Gilmore and Herring initially suggest that the risk-relative account of capacity might justify the refusal of consent/refusal of treatment distinction.[128] However, the risk-relative account offers no 'off the shelf' justification to the refusal of consent/refusal of treatment distinction, since it is a theory of the asymmetry of *sufficiency* of an agent's reasoning, rather than asymmetry of *capacity-relevant information.* Gilmore and Herring would need an argument for how risk connects to option-sensitivity of the information relevant to capacity. Moreover, any new specification of the risk-relative account in support of the refusal of consent/refusal of treatment distinction must address the concern, *inter alia*, above about the imposition of the value of risk aversion (or a distribution of this value) on an agent against background norms of instrumental rationality.

Gilmore and Herring's principal argument is that individuals' medical decisions merit differential respect according to whether the choice is 'weakly' or 'richly' autonomous.[129] A weakly autonomous decision 'represent[s] no more than a whim or casual preference and may not involve a careful consideration of the

[126] Gilmore and Herring, 'No', 10–11.

[127] Gilmore and Herring, 'No', 7.

[128] Gilmore and Herring, 'No', 20.

[129] Gilmore and Herring, 'No', 21–2. This distinction utilises the conceptions of autonomy developed in J. Coggon, 'Varied and Principled Understandings of Autonomy in English Law: Justifiable Inconsistency or Blinkered Moralism?', *Health Care Analysis*, 15 (2007), 235–55.

consequences'.[130] A richly autonomous decision 'reflect[s] a genuine part of the person's life vision, made with a full understanding of the consequences'.[131] On Gilmore and Herring's view, we might *respect* weakly autonomous consents (or even refusals when the stakes are low), yet require refusals to be richly autonomous when the stakes are such that an individual risks death or serious harm as a result of their preferred choice.[132]

This argument creates a justificatory puzzle. It is not clear how these claims about the *quality* of autonomy and its relation to norms governing the legal *effectiveness* of individuals' decisions underpin the refusal of consent/refusal of treatment distinction, the latter being a matter of legal *validity*. In the spirit of charity, let us see if a connection can be made.

First, if we think of capacity assessment as a matter of process, as well as substance, it may be important to orient the process such that it helps us determine whether an individual's legally *valid* decision should be legally *effective*, where—as in the case of adolescents' medical decisions—the latter is not entailed by the former. Perhaps Gilmore and Herring's thinking is that the capacity to consent—evaluated against the set of options ($x_1$, $\sim x_1$)—will at least evidence weak autonomy, whereas the capacity to refuse all treatment—evaluated against the set of options ($x$, $y$)—will robustly evidence rich autonomy?

Even were we to accept the general claim about the instrumental value of capacity assessment processes, I am not sure that it works to justify the refusal of consent/refusal of treatment distinction. For one, it is not clear whether an asymmetry of the capacity relevant information across consent and refusal enlightens us as to the rationality—and thus respect-worthiness—of an individual's decision. Recall that on Gilmore and Herring's view, the assessment of capacity to consent and to refuse treatment, respectively, are discrete exercises. Unless the choice is binary—($x_1$, $\sim x_1$) $\leftrightarrow$ ($x$, $y$)—the information relevant to the decision changes according to option chosen. In the case of three or more options, if an individual consents, no issue of their capacity to refuse anything other than the option to which they are consenting arises; if an individual refuses, their capacity to consent to or to refuse every available treatment option is assessed.[133] Thus Gilmore and Herring's proposal does not involve assessing capacity comparatively according to whether the agent chooses the same option in the consent and refusal of treatment situations, respectively. While expansion or contraction of the set of options available to an agent facing a choice *may* provide insight into whether an individual's decision is instrumentally rational,[134] this is not what is going on in the refusal of consent/refusal of treatment scenario.

130 Gilmore and Herring, 'No', 21.

131 Gilmore and Herring, 'No', 21.

132 Gilmore and Herring, 'No', 22.

133 Presumably, if an individual refuses consent, this triggers further enquiry as to their capacity to consent to *another* treatment.

134 This issues of contraction and expansion consistency are difficult and that there is insufficient space to explore them here: see A. Sen, 'Internal Consistency of Choice', *Econometrica*, 61 (1993), 495–521; Sen, *Collective Choice*, ch. 2.

For another, as noted above, the refusal of consent/refusal of treatment distinction is only of relevance when an individual faces a trinary choice or more. This raises the question of how much procedural assistance the refusal of consent/refusal of treatment distinction would provide in elucidating the depth of individual's reasons for refusal. Of course, this is an empirical matter, but since binary choices are frequent in healthcare, this limits the scope of application of Gilmore and Herring's distinction.[135]

Second, even if asking an individual to reason through more content gives us better access to the instrumental rationality of their choice, it does not follow that we will receive deep justification of the kind Gilmore and Herring ascribe to 'rich' autonomy. A normative framework of instrumental rationality assesses whether an individual's choice accords with what they have most reason to value, in light of what they believe; it does not dictate the content of their values or the attributability of values to a life plan.

Third, it is questionable whether, by restricting the capacity-relevant information in the case of consent or refusal of consent to ($x$, $\sim x$) for the relevant option when others are on the table, we will get a decision that meets the standard of an autonomous decision—contextually or all things considered. In respect of the former, an individual's decision may be instrumentally rational in respect of the binary choice of ($x$, $\sim x$); the issue is that they face a choice situation that is trinary or more. In respect of the latter, Gilmore and Herring's notion of 'weak' autonomy is question-begging. It seems entirely arguable whether decisions reflecting 'no more than a whim or casual preference' or involving inadequate deliberation exemplify (even weakly) autonomous choice.

In respect of the second and third points above, then, I doubt whether the refusal of consent/refusal of treatment distinction tracks the autonomy goods that purport to justify it, either in terms of 'rich' or 'weak' autonomy.

Finally, I worry about Gilmore and Herring's appeal to the 'need to balance autonomy interests against other values, including the well-being of the patient' to animate the refusal of consent/refusal of treatment distinction.[136] In their view, autonomy comes in degrees and exercises of autonomy that fail to exemplify deep convictions should not trump other important values.[137] To the extent that Gilmore and Herring are making an argument in respect of legal validity rules, they seem to espouse a substantive approach to the assessment of capacity to refuse

[135] There is some indication that Gilmore and Herring subscribe to the view that capacity to refuse should be evaluated against *notionally available* treatment options, rather than those *offered*, since they say 'the child who is simply considering whether or not to accept a particular proposal, will not necessarily have addressed all matters pertaining to the refusal of all treatment (not least because he or she may only have been told by the doctor about the proposed treatment)': 'No', 8. Yet, it seems highly problematic to evaluate an individual's capacity against treatment options they lack fair/equal opportunity to consider.

[136] Gilmore and Herring, 'No', 21–2.

[137] Gilmore and Herring, 'No', 21–2.

treatment—one requiring that the individual invoke 'thick' values in their reasoning. This substantive approach appears to sit poorly with the more formal approach to autonomy that is operative in the legal doctrine—functional capacity as instrumental rationality. Gilmore and Herring ask of the agent who refuses treatment not only that they draw appropriate connections between their values and beliefs, but also that such values are 'life vision' in nature. I have two concerns: why set the bar for capacity in this way? and why set the bar's height asymmetrically?

Regarding the first concern, an objection to my argument is that, charitably, Gilmore and Herring might merely be thought to demand a high degree of critical reflection of the agent, *within* a framework of instrumental rationality. What is required is greater coherence or systematisation of values, rather than values of a certain content. And we might reasonably disagree about the degree of critical reflection required for capacity. For the sake of argument, I shall concede this point, though it raises a further worry: why set the bar for critical reflection so high? Here, analysis of my second concern is revealing. Differentially mandating the demonstration of 'weak' and 'rich' autonomy across the options of consent/refusal of consent and refusal of treatment, respectively, relies on the medical assessment of how the adolescent's best interests (including their well-being) are distributed across the options. Thus we encounter anew the issues of liberty and equality raised in discussion of the risk-relative account. Gilmore and Herring's distinction operates such that individuals with unconventional values are held to a higher standard of capacity than individuals whose values align with medical norms. The refusal of consent/refusal of treatment distinction is only facially respectful of capacity as instrumental rationality; it allows substantive values to creep into the standard of rationality that an individual must demonstrate in order to have capacity.

## Conclusion

I have argued that, doctrinally or institutionally, the asymmetry of capacity thesis—either in the form of the risk-relative account or Gilmore and Herrings refusal of consent/refusal of treatment distinction—is not a feature of English adolescent medical treatment law. I have also argued that, normatively, we ought not to accept either conception of the asymmetry capacity thesis as part of the law. At least so long as the norms that underpin the legal regime for decision-making capacity remain those of instrumental rationality. The justification for the asymmetry of capacity thesis cannot be that the degree of capacity (other things equal, autonomy) required for legal validity ought to track the degree of instantiation of some other value (risk aversion, well-being, etc.) quite apart from whether it is subjectively held or subjectively held to the same degree by the agent.

To close, I should clarify that nothing I have argued necessarily militates against the laudable aim of protecting adolescents from instrumentally rational but substantively 'bad' decisions through judicious use of the concurrent consents doctrine.[138] I object to substantive values determining (asymmetrically) the legal standard of decision-making capacity—a validity rule—given the latter's normative underpinnings. It is an open question whether the liberty and equality critiques I have developed also bite on the effectiveness rule that allows parents or the court to override adolescents' medical decisions.

[138] Skelton, Forsberg, and Black, 'Overriding'.

# 4

# Minors and Sexual Consent

JENNIFER EPP*

WHEN PEOPLE THINK about children and sexual consent, they usually focus on a single question: at what age is consent to sexual intercourse legally determinative? The question about the legal age of consent to sexual intercourse is important. However, focusing solely on this question obscures three other important ones about consent in childhood.

First, and perhaps most obviously, sexuality encompasses a much wider range of activity than intercourse. Given this, what sorts of childhood activities count as sexual and how should consent be involved? Second, focusing on *when* children may consent to sexual activity might lead one to neglect questions about *how* children gain that capacity. What conditions enable or undermine a child's ability to give valid sexual consent? Third, while there are probably good reasons to designate a specific age of valid consent in law, a focus on legal consent leaves out a considerable number of important ethical questions about consent. For example, is there something particularly valuable about sexuality in childhood? What does the developmental process of gaining the capacity to consent imply about adult obligations to support children and adolescents as they acquire the skills and information necessary to do so? How should adults respond to children's sexual choices while the latter are developing the capacities necessary to consent or once they are able to consent? If children can be subject to oppression, how might that affect their ability to consent and how should adults respond? These questions cannot be answered adequately solely in legal terms, especially if good consent laws are to track moral considerations.

With these sorts of questions in mind, in this chapter I attend to some of the conditions required for minors to consent to sexual activity. I use the term 'sexual activity' broadly to include, without being limited to: flirting, holding hands with a crush, kissing, cuddling, masturbation, sexting, sending nude pictures, sensual

* I wish to thank Samantha Brennan for discussion and to Jacob Fehr for research assistance.

non-genital contact, intercourse, oral–genital and anal–genital contact, and many other activities that arouse, express, and/or satisfy physical attraction or desire. The desire for romance and emotional connection are often but not always involved.

I have already referred to children as a group. However, within the category 'child' (here covering the period between infancy and late adolescence) there are different developmental stages, often though not always correlated with age, that affect a child's ability to validly consent to sexual activity. As the chapter proceeds, I will discuss the ways in which developmental differences warrant different understandings of, and limits on, what to count as sexual activity and consent. I am writing from within a Canadian context, which informs the examples I have chosen. Finally, I wish to emphasise that nothing written here should be used to support child abuse or paedophilia in any way.

The chapter proceeds as follows. The first section describes consent in general and sexual consent in particular. The second section focuses on what it would mean for children to be sufficiently informed to give sexual consent, while the third section asks whether sexual consent is different from non-sexual consent in childhood by asking about the value of sexuality for children. The fourth section details the potential effects of oppression on consent, touching on disability, race, and gender. Finally, in the fifth section, I discuss the implications of treating consent as relational as well as some of the limitations of thinking about childhood sexuality through the lens of consent.

## Consent and sexual consent

Throughout the chapter, I will refer both to 'consent' and 'valid' or 'invalid' consent. The term 'invalid consent' here indicates either that consent was not successfully given or that any consent that was successfully given was not of the right sort to bind or release people from a moral and/or legal duty or waive the consenter's claim rights. By contrast, I take valid consent to be, almost always, morally transformative.[1] Typically, transformation occurs because consent removes features of an act or activity that would otherwise make it impermissible. For example, what would otherwise be sexual assault is instead consensual sexual activity if all parties validly consent. Other things being equal, consent transforms the moral and legal landscape.

Consent is considered valid only when certain conditions obtain. In particular, consent qualifies as valid only if one is competent, informed, and voluntary. Consent is invalid if one or more of these conditions are not met. An uninformed, incompetent, or unduly influenced individual (e.g. a coerced, manipulated, or deceived

[1] By contrast, see Franklin G. Miller and Alan Wertheimer, 'Preface to a Theory of Consent Transactions: Beyond Valid Consent', in Franklin G. Miller and Alan Wertheimer (eds), *The Ethics of Consent: Theory and Practice* (Oxford, Oxford University Press, 2010), pp. ix–xv.

individual) may consent. However, under such conditions: (1) consenters do not waive their claim rights or incur obligations via consent; (2) recipients (or consent-receivers) are not released from a moral or legal duty to act or not to act in the ways consented to toward the consenter, and (3) consent-receivers ought not act on a consenter's offer of consent. Whether or not it would be wise or good rather than simply permissible for a recipient to act on another person's valid consent is a separate question.

Must any further conditions be met to enable valid *sexual* consent? In addition to the conditions above, sexual consent may need to be expressly granted, specific, and revocable in order to be valid. First, if sexual consent must be expressly granted, then in order for person B to permissibly act on person A's sexual consent, person A must actively communicate their agreement to a particular action or activity, whether verbally or non-verbally. Unless explicitly negotiated otherwise, simply allowing something to happen without saying no does not count as the right sort of consent when dealing with sexual activity, if it counts as consent at all.[2] I discuss this condition in more detail below.

Second, if sexual consent must be specific, then one does not consent to 'have sex' (here used as a catch-all phrase). Instead, one consents (or not) to particular sexual activities while engaging sexually with others. Consent to one type of sexual activity does not provide blanket consent to everything else. This accords with the common-sense belief that, for instance, consent to kissing does not entail consent to genital touching. The reverse is also true; consent to a 'more serious' sexual activity does not entail consent to 'less serious' activities. The specificity requirement suggests that in order to enable consensual sexual activity, people must discover, articulate, and respect various boundaries, their own and their partner's.

Third, sexual consent is revocable, both before and during sexual activity. Consent to begin is not consent to continue. If so, then when someone agrees beforehand to do something sexual, they are neither bound later on to do it, nor must they continue against their will. Revoking consent reinstates a partner's duties to stop/avoid the previously consented to action or activity. Revoking sexual consent may disappoint or anger someone and that person *may* have had a right to expect you to do what you consented to do, but revoking sexual consent is not morally forbidden.[3] The implication is that sexual consent is on-going so that all parties have a responsibility to stay aware of whether or not their partners are still consenting.

Referring to 'consenters' and 'recipients' may make it seem that passive consenters are having something done to them by active consent-receivers. However, willingly receiving another person's sexual attention is an action and most sex involves people doing things to and with each other. I suggest that attention to

[2] See James Rocha 'Aggressive Hook Ups: Modelling Aggressive Casual Sex on BDSM for Moral Permissibility', *Res Publica*, 22 (2016), 173–92 at 173.

[3] See Hallie Liberto, 'The Problem with Sexual Promises', *Ethics*, 127 (2017), 383–414. Liberto argues in addition that promisees may not accept sexual promises and that promisors cannot be compelled to uphold such promises.

mutuality reveals that *all* parties involved in consensual activity must consent. Recipients are under no obligation to undertake an activity simply because a consenter consents to it. Recipients must also consent to participate. This means that everyone involved in consensual sexual activity is both a consenter and recipient. Consent should be mutual for an activity to proceed and anyone involved may withdraw consent.

Finally, for the purposes of this chapter, I will stipulate that valid consent requires communication,[4] and that consent is well understood as a form of agreement.[5] For the remainder of the chapter, sexual consent will be considered valid, and hence morally transformative, when the consenter voluntarily and expressly agrees to a specific activity or set of activities as a sufficiently informed and competent agent who can revoke their consent before or during the agreed upon activity. The consenter might also need to agree to the right sort of activity in order to give valid consent.

## Sufficiently informed consent in childhood

Everything I have said so far refers to consent and sexual consent in general. Does anything change when children or adolescents are the consenting parties? One of many significant differences between adults and children of any age is simply the amount of life experience that members of each group are likely to have. Life experience is an important source of information. As a result, children are likely in general to be less informed than adults about quite a few things, sex included. With that in mind, the focus in this section is on what it might mean for children to be sufficiently informed to consent to sexual activity. A child's degree of competence and voluntariness also affect their ability to give sufficiently informed consent, and I touch on these themes as well.

There are at least two ways in which one might fail to be informed. One might not *have* information and one might not *understand* the information one does have. Adolescents and even younger children know and understand quite a lot of things. However, they also lack and are sometimes unable to understand information, in particular about sexuality, for a number of reasons. These reasons include sexual inexperience, nascent cognitive, epistemic, and relational competencies, and information policing and constructed ignorance by adults. I suggest that lack of information can but does not necessarily prevent valid consent, while an inability to understand is a

[4] In defence of this claim, see Tom Dougherty, *The Scope of Consent* (Oxford, Oxford University Press, 2021). See also Monica R Cowart, 'Understanding Acts of Consent: Using Speech Act Theory to Help Resolve Moral Dilemmas and Legal Disputes', *Law and Philosophy*, 23 (2004), 495–525, and Renee Jorgensen Bolinger, 'Moral Risk and Communicating Consent', *Philosophy and Public Affairs*, 47 (2019), 179–207.

[5] For an overview of some alternate accounts of consent see K Chadha, 'Sexual Consent and Having Sex Together', *Oxford Journal of Legal Studies*, 40 (2020), 619–44.

more serious barrier. Someone who lacks information may be unable to consent if that lack means that she does not understand the choice she is being asked to make.[6] An inability to understand crucial information, however, may indicate an incompetence which would invalidate consent even for people who are sufficiently informed.

## Constructed deficits in information about sexuality

Consider, first, artificial deficits in information as impediments to consent. Nancy Tuana argues that 'ignorance should not be theorized as a simple omission or gap', instead it is 'in many cases, an active production'.[7] In other words, ignorance can be purposefully constructed, 'actively preserved … sustained, cultivated',[8] even intentionally 'disseminated'.[9]

We see this in the case of children who are regularly taught euphemistic and inaccurate names for their body parts or processes. In my family, menstrual products were called 'stuff' and one's vulva was called an 'in between'. Adults in other families name vulvas 'foo foo' or a 'front bum' while calling one's penis a 'willy'.[10] Similarly, people often say that pregnancy happens in a woman's 'tummy'. This despite evidence that knowledge of correct names for sexed body parts is both protective against sexual abuse and autonomy-enhancing.[11] People also sometimes disseminate inaccurate information about the possibilities for becoming pregnant or catching a sexually transmitted infection or they refuse to talk about sexuality with children at all.

Obfuscated and inaccurate information about sexuality does not come only from parents. As Tuana suggests, lack of knowledge can be institutionalised in politicised practices. Abstinence-only sex education programs are prime examples. These programmes purposefully avoid teaching children about contraception and non-abstinent ways to prevent sexually transmitted infections. Moreover, they and many non-abstinence-based curricula refuse to address sexual orientation, gender identity, sex outside of marriage, affirmative consent, pleasure, and more.[12] Such

[6] Joseph Millum and Danielle Bromwich, 'Informed Consent: What Must Be Disclosed and What Must Be Understood?', *American Journal of Bioethics*, 21 (2021), 46–58 at 53n5.

[7] Nancy Tuana, 'Coming to Understand: Orgasm and the Epistemology of Ignorance', *Hypatia*, 19 (2004), 194–232 at 195.

[8] Tuana, 'Coming to Understand', 194.

[9] Tuana, 'Coming to Understand', 196.

[10] Anonymous, 'Child Friendly Words for Vagina', *Netmums*, 7 September 2013. https://www.netmums.com/coffeehouse/being-mum-794/parenting-advice-192/985598-child-friendly-words-vagina.html (accessed 15 July 2025).

[11] Maureen C Kelly and Sandy K Wurtele, 'Toward Prevention of Childhood Sexual Abuse: Preschoolers' Knowledge of Genital Body Parts', in Maria S. Plakhotnik and Sarah M. Nielsen (eds), *Proceedings of the Seventh Annual College of Education Research Conference: Urban and International Education Section* (Miami, FL, Florida International University, 2008), pp. 74–9.

[12] John Santelli, Mary Ott, Maureen Lyon, Jennifer Rogers, Daniel Summers, and Rebecca Schleifer, 'Abstinence-Only Education Policies and Programs: A Position Paper of the Society for Adolescent Medicine', *Journal of Adolescent Health*, 38 (2006), 72–81.

information may be omitted in response to political pressure or conservative or religious values for fear of corrupting children or causing them to experiment with sexual behaviour too early, despite the fact that comprehensive sex education is associated with minor *delays* in initiating intercourse.[13] Where such beliefs operate, childhood sexual ignorance may be jealously guarded in ways that can harm children.[14]

Sex education ought to both accurately inform children and help them understand that information in age-appropriate ways. Programmes that misinform or withhold the sort of information described above aim to limit childhood agency in relation to sexuality. They aim to control children's choices by ensuring abstinence until marriage, heterosexuality, binary gender identification, traditional family structures, and so on. To the extent that such programmes prevent children from being informed enough to consent to sexual activity, they succeed—they prevent children from making informed, consensual decisions about deeply personal and meaningful aspects of their lives. Yet, as research on abstinence-only sex education has shown, children will still engage in sexual activity. Surely it would be better to support rather than undermine their ability to give or refuse sufficiently informed consent. That means neither that children should make decisions without guidance (see section 'What's so special about sexuality in childhood?'), nor that children must be informed about everything related to sexuality in order to consent to sexual activity.

Practice in informed decision-making is necessary for becoming autonomous, and it is also a necessary part of learning to make decisions that are prudent. To decide well, children must learn many things, including: to seek out and apply credible information, to consider the consequences of ignoring that information, to understand that others interpret information differently, and to consider and arrive at their own interpretations based on their own needs, goals, and values. This sort of learning takes practice. It also takes information, even controversial information, with which to practise. Adults in care-giving roles have a responsibility to provide good information to children while teaching them how to understand and evaluate that information because of their responsibilities to both ensure children's well-being and support their development of autonomy.[15]

[13] Pamela K. Kohler, Lisa E. Manhart, and William E. Lafferty, 'Abstinence-Only and Comprehensive Sex Education and the Initiation of Sexual Activity and Teen Pregnancy', *Journal of Adolescent Health*, 42 (2008), 344–51.

[14] They may be shamed or lack language with which to communicate about their bodily well-being, or they may be subject to unnecessary medical treatment. See, for example, Lauren Bialystok, 'The Politics Behind Ontario's Sex- Ed Curriculum', Macleans, 29 August 2019. https://www.macleans.ca/opinion/the-politics-behind-ontarios-sex-ed-curriculum/ (accessed 15 July 2025); Heitham Ajlouni, Azhar Daoud, Saleh Ajlouni, and Kamel Ajlouni, 'Infantile and Early Childhood Masturbation: Sex Hormones and Clinical Profile', *Annals of Saudi Medicine*, 30 (2010), 471–4 at 472.

[15] These are not conflicting goals. See Jennifer Epp and Samantha Brennan, 'Childhood and Sexuality', in Anca Gheaus, Gideon Calder, and Jurgen De Wispelaere (eds), *The Routledge Handbook of the Philosophy of Childhood and Children* (New York, Routledge, 2019), pp. 271–81.

There are two other reasons to be suspicious of adult-constructed child ignorance. First, children, and especially older children, may already have autonomy rights that can be violated. Second, some forms of information withholding are bad for children, regardless of their degree of autonomy. For example, 2SLGBTQIA+ children or children from queer families can feel isolated, depressed, and confused not because of their identities but because they are erased from public representations of family, love, and full humanity. This is a harm that is perpetuated via constructed ignorance. This suggests that caregivers, educators, and public officials must think carefully about the relation between information, autonomy, and well-being for many reasons, not least of which is that constructed ignorance can illegitimately interfere with a child's ability to give valid consent.

So much for artificial informational constraints on childhood sexual consent. What of deficits in information and understanding that are not purposefully imposed?

## Developmental deficits in information and understanding

When very young children are flourishing, they enjoy their bodies and enjoy physical connection with trusted people. They are sensual, exploring sensations, their bodies, and the world. They know many things, both physical and relational, that they like and do not like, and they have the ability to request and refuse physical contact. It is developmentally typical for young children to touch their genitals whether out of curiosity, for pleasure, or to alleviate boredom and distress.[16] Young children may also engage with other young children in play that involves genital touching. This is typical, harmless, and even beneficial behaviour and young children likely give their own meanings to and have their own understandings of their sexual activity. Those understandings, in part, make an activity the kind of activity it is ('playing doctor' rather than adult roleplay, for example). Consent to a shared activity between children of the same developmental stage does not, therefore, require children to have an *adult* understanding of that activity, unless a more mature understanding is required to understand and evaluate risk.

Young children do not typically engage in adult-like sexual activity, which if present may indicate abuse.[17] They have not begun puberty, they do not have the biological or conceptual resources to experience or understand sexuality in adult or adolescent ways, and they may still be developing a theory of mind with which to understand others. In other words, young children are not typically asexual, but they have significantly limited (or no) sexual experience, understanding, and capacity. This degree of limitation prevents children from knowing what they

[16] Ajlouni *et al.*, 'Infantile and Early Childhood Masturbation', 471.

[17] Kevin Borg, Christina Snowdon, and Deborah Hodes, 'Child Sexual Abuse: Recognition and Response When There Is a Suspicion or Allegation', *Paediatrics and Health*, 24 (2014), 536–43.

are being asked to agree to when they are faced with sexual requests or invitations from people who are more mature. A person cannot consent to something at all, let alone validly, when they do not understand what they are being asked to do. Therefore, young children cannot validly consent to and should never be involved in interpersonal sexual activity with anyone who is not at the same developmental stage mentally or physically.

Children who have begun the process of puberty during middle childhood are likely to have more information through experience than their younger counterparts, as are teenagers. Their growing experience may come from an increased interest in sexuality as their bodies change, sex education in schools that becomes more detailed for older children, as well as from greater exposure to media and internet sources, discussions with friends or parents, and from their own explorations whether alone or with other children. Given the social, physical, emotional, and cognitive changes that progress during puberty, they are also likely better able to understand that information. As both experience and understanding increase, older children and teens therefore become better positioned to consent to a broader range of sexual activity with appropriate partners.[18]

That is not to say, however, that older children or even teenagers are very experienced. Children in middle childhood still typically lack adult or teen levels of desire and experience, and they may find more mature expressions of sexuality off-putting. Teen sexual activity increases with age for a variety of behaviours; however, quite often even older teens lack sexual experience in some significant way; for instance, many have not engaged in intercourse or oral–genital sex.[19] This means they lack knowledge about, for example, what particular sexual experiences are like, which (if any) sexual activities they will enjoy, how relationships between sexual partners can operate, and some of the *lived* rather than theoretical potential consequences of sexual behaviour, such as pregnancy, social status changes in one's peer group, emotional connections, positive and/or negative effects on self-esteem, and pleasure, sexual transmitted infections, and so on. This is a deficit that cannot be remedied by anyone, young person or not, without lived experience. If so, and if consent to new experiences is to be possible, then this sort of information

[18] Millum and Bromwich suggest that in order to give valid consent, a person only needs to understand that she is being asked for consent and what she is being asked to allow others to do: 'Informed Consent', 53n5. If so, then children's lesser understanding of sexuality does not prevent consent. However, both information (including about risks and benefits) and some degree of understanding are required if one is to know what one is being asked to do or allow.

[19] Joyce C. Abma and Gladys M. Martinez, 'Sexual Activity and Contraceptive Use Among Teenagers in the United States, 2011–2015', *National Health Statistics Reports*, 104 (Hyattsville, National Center for Health Statistics, 2017), 1–23; Trisha Tulloch and Miriam Kaufman, 'Adolescent Sexuality', *Pediatrics in Review*, 34 (2013), 29–37; World Health Organization, 'Contraception Within the Context of Adolescents' Sexual and Reproductive Lives: Country Profile: Cambodia', *World Health Organization*, 2020. https://apps.who.int/iris/handle/10665/339327 (accessed 15 July 2025); Jokin de Irala, Alfonso Osorio, Silvia Carlos, Miguel Ruiz-Canela, and Cristina Lopez-del Burgo, 'Mean Age of First Sex: Do They Know What We Mean?', *Archives of Sexual Behaviour*, 40 (2011), 853–5.

deficit should not be thought, on its own, to invalidate consent. Young people may, however, need to know that they lack information about the topics above in order to understand the choices before them, a prerequisite for valid consent. They may also need at least some knowledge of the most likely risks and benefits of an activity in order to know what the activity itself is or entails.

## What's so special about sexuality in childhood?

Children in middle childhood and adolescence voluntarily choose to engage in potentially transformative and risky activities by, for instance, participating in potentially injurious or body-changing sports, performing on social media, and learning to drive. In Canada, children in Ontario who are older than seven must consent in order for adoption to proceed, while in other Canadian jurisdictions consent is required at 12 years or older.[20] If children are able to validly consent to these activities, does it follow that they have the capacity to consent to sexual activities? Is expressing sexuality somehow different from other potentially risky and transformative activities in ways that vitiate consent? To begin to answer these questions, I will consider some of the benefits and risks for children that accompany sexual activity.

Sexuality is not just a good for adults. Much philosophical work on childhood evaluates it and the way we treat children on the basis of the adult person the child will become, reflecting a general bias towards childhood as a time of preparation in which one acquires the knowledge, skills, and maturity to lead a successful adult life. This is especially true in relation to sexuality. While development into adulthood is morally significant, Samantha Brennan and I have argued that sexual health and happiness are also present goods of childhood, especially in later adolescence. We have also argued that children's knowledge of their own bodies and pleasures is an important aspect of their ability to give consent.[21]

But why is sexual activity important and how is it good for children? Sexuality is a site of deep relationship with oneself and potentially with others. Sexual expression is intimately embodied, sensed and felt directly, viscerally experienced. Even flirtation can cause an internal thrill. Sexual activity may also involve connections with others, physically, socially, and emotionally. By exploring sexual activity, children not only experience themselves directly, they learn about, develop, and express, many deeply important aspects of their personal identities. Sexual orientation is one such aspect, whether in relation to hetero, bi, or homosexuality, but also allo or asexuality, romance and monogamy or non-monogamy.[22] By exploring sexuality, children learn about and define their values and beliefs about sex and

[20] Nicholas Bala and Claire Houston, *Article 12 of the Convention on the Rights of the Child and Children's Participatory Rights in Canada* (Department of Justice Canada, 2015), Section III D.

[21] Epp and Brennan, 'Childhood and Sexuality', 271n40.

[22] 'Allosexuals' experience sexual attraction towards others and are not asexual.

relationships. They learn about their bodies, pleasures, desires, limits, needs, and boundaries. Where consent is supported, they also learn that they belong to themselves. Positive, agentic sexual experience can help one's body to feel like home.

Further, sexual expression, in sex-positive contexts that support consent, provides children with opportunities to develop positive self-regarding attitudes. These include self-trust, worth, respect, confidence, positive body and self-image, and freedom from shame about their physicality. In expressing sexuality with others, children may come to feel desirable, connected, valued, competent, self-directing, safe, and deserving of pleasure and respect. A sense of freedom and connection, pleasure, beauty, and agency is possible for children who are allowed to explore their sexuality safely and under their own direction. More importantly, sexual expression is part not only of learning or becoming but of *being* oneself. We are ourselves partly by expressing our sexuality and through it we may come to inhabit our bodies as our own.

I do not want to idealise sexuality. Sexual activity can also do the opposite to the above. People can feel rejected, shamed, undesirable, distrustful of themselves as they choose to do things they do not want, they may feel alienated from their bodies, violated, or any number of deeply painful things that undermine well-being. Eli Clare argues, further, that sexual abuse is a tool to position children in hierarchies of dominance and subordination.[23] I will take up this potential harm and its relation to consent in 'Oppression and consent' below by discussing oppression. The answer to these challenges, however, cannot be to avoid sexuality altogether or to attempt to protect children by denying their ability to consent when it exists. Even so, it is important to take into account some of the unique risks associated with sexuality.

First, some kinds of sexual activity carry the possibility of pregnancy and of bringing another person into existence. Carrying a pregnancy to term is life changing for more than one life, and it creates the radical vulnerability of infancy. If birth parents do not choose adoption for their children, their roles, responsibilities, and life possibilities change markedly. In addition, parents and sometimes extended families may be legally and relationally linked for a very long time. Adoption, too, changes lives, with potential emotional and psychological costs and benefits for multiple people. Few other activities have such significant outcomes. This ought to be taken seriously when thinking about whether an adolescent has enough understanding and competence to consent to intercourse.

However, risk of unwanted pregnancy is greatly diminished through access to comprehensive sex education, healthcare, and contraceptives. Consider the case of the Netherlands where 23 per cent of boys and 21 per cent of girls report having sex by the age of 15, but the country has one of the lowest teen pregnancy rates in the world.[24] Formal and informal social support systems can also reduce

[23] Eli Clare, *Exile and Pride* (Durham, Duke University Press, 2015).

[24] K Paige Harden, 'A Sex-Positive Framework for Research on Adolescent Sexuality', *Perspectives on Psychological Science*, 9 (2014), 455–69 at 456.

the risk of harm to children, whether as potential child-parents or as infants. If so, then discounting adolescent sexual consent is not automatically a justified response to the risk of unwanted pregnancy. Moreover, the kind of sex that can result in pregnancy is only one of many possible sexual activities, making the possibility moot in relation to considering childhood sexual consent in toto.

A second feature of sexual activity that makes it risky is the moral landscape within which it occurs. The morality of various kinds of sexual activity is contested and fraught in ways that driving, adoption, and sports are not. Children in conservative contexts who fail to act according to sexual norms that represent many forms of sexuality as deviant, whether justified or not, may be ostracised, bullied, disowned, denied opportunities, and they may face discrimination, violence, and oppression. In such a landscape, in order to consent to more complex forms of sexual expression children may need to be aware of these social risks and prepared to appreciate and evaluate them in order to understand the choices they are making. To do so, they will need some degree of moral agency. This is appropriate since it is possible to harm others or to treat them unethically through sexual activity, even if sexuality is not inherently bad or wrong.

Third, sexuality is risky because it carries the potential for children to be exploited. This is true in other areas of life as well (especially with respect to child labour), but the connection to well-being, agency, and visceral, bodily selfhood is deep here. Therefore, the risk is grave. This risk, far from supporting the claim that children cannot consent to sexual activity, supports helping children to develop the ability to consent and refuse, recognising children's expressions of consent and refusal, and helping their expressions to be effective and respected. This would involve a huge amount of social change since it would mean dismantling systems of oppression that create vulnerability and facilitate exploitation and abuse. Making that change will, in part, consist in practical, domain specific, on-the-ground efforts to protect children's agency. This is not to deny that adults may sometimes need to override childhood agreement and perhaps consent in order to ensure well-being. Protecting against childhood sexual exploitation and abuse requires multiple different kinds of intervention,[25] and where children have been groomed or otherwise taught to acquiesce, their agreement does not count as valid consent since it is not uncoerced and voluntarily given. However, children's agency and protection are not always or necessarily in conflict. Children with the capacity to consent and refuse can be involved in, though not responsible for, their own protection.[26]

Consent is central to one's sense of self, to self-understanding, moral agency, self-ownership, and autonomy. It is also central to one's current and future

[25] Stephen Smallbone, William L. Marshall, and Richard Wortley, *Preventing Child Sexual Abuse* (London, Willan, 2008).

[26] Samantha Brennan and Jennifer Epp, 'Children's Rights, Well-Being, and Sexual Agency', in Alexander Bagattini and Colin Macleod (eds), *The Nature of Children's Well-Being: Theory and Practice* (New York, Springer 2015), pp. 227–46.

well-being and development. Voluntary sexual activity requires a sense of bodily security and control. If all this is so, it is risky and potentially harmful to deny that children can give valid consent to sexual activity when they reach a certain degree of understanding and competence and when they make uncoerced decisions. Further, paying attention to sexuality as a good of childhood, as described in the beginning of this section, reveals the moral significance of sexism, homophobia, transphobia, racism, ableism, and other forms of oppression in undermining children's sense of self and agency. Therefore, I move on to consider some of the effects of oppression on a child's ability to consent.

## Oppression and consent

Children are not immune to oppression, including in relation to sexuality. Given that they are developing both their sense of self and agency, they may even be especially vulnerable to it. With this claim, I move from thinking about the personal risks and harms of sexual exploitation and abuse, including in relation to consent, toward a discussion of political risks and harms. Clare provides motivation for this shift:

> sexual and physical violence against children isn't only … power run amok, but also a form of social control. … [through which] adults teach children bodily lessons about power and hierarchy, about being boys, being girls, being children, being black, being working-class, being disabled. What better way to maintain a power structure – white supremacy, male supremacy, capitalism, a binary and rigid gender system – than to drill the lessons of who is dominant and who is subordinate into the bodies of children.[27]

In this section, then, I ask about the effects of oppression on children's sexual consent.[28] I will begin by arguing that oppression can make it harder for children to develop the capacity to consent. Next, I will demonstrate that oppression can make it difficult for children to use the capacities that they have developed either by making their consent invalid or by making their valid consent less effective or ineffective. The discussion is a beginning and much more remains to be said.

[27] Clare, *Exile and Pride*, pp. 149–50.

[28] How to conceptualise oppression is disputed. See Amy Allen, 'Feminist Perspectives on Power', *The Stanford Encyclopedia of Philosophy*, 28 October 2021. https://plato.stanford.edu/entries/feminist-power/ (accessed 15 July 2025). See also Marilyn Frye, 'Oppression', in Marilyn Frye (ed.), *The Politics of Reality* (Trumansburg, NY, Crossing Press, 1983), pp. 1–16; Combahee River Collective, 'A Black Feminist Statement (1977)', in Cherrie Moraga and Glora Anzaldua (eds), *This Bridge Called My Back: Writings by Radical Women of Color* (New York, Kitchen Table/Women of Color Press, 1981), pp. 234–44; and Patricia Hill Collins, 'Symposium on West and Fenstermaker's "Doing Difference"', *Gender and Society*, 9 (1995), 491–513.

## Oppression inhibits development of the capacity to consent

Iris Young argues that oppression exists when, as members of a particular social group, people are unjustly deprived of the institutional conditions needed to fully develop their capacities.[29] For the purpose of discussion, I will understand 'capacity' as a skill or ability. One has that skill or ability when they are sufficiently good at using it to regularly accomplish a corresponding task. Oppressive contexts may make it difficult for children to both develop and use the capacity to give and refuse valid consent in three ways. First, oppression can erode the relational or informational supports that children need to give valid consent. Second, children who are oppressed may have limited opportunities to practise consent and refusal where practice is part of the developmental process of becoming able to give consent. Third, children who are oppressed may find it difficult to develop positive, self-regarding attitudes supporting consent, including self-trust, self-esteem, and self-respect.

All three challenges arise in the following example, which discusses children's developing capacity to consent in the context of disability. Consider eroded informational supports first. Children with disabilities receive sex education at much lower rates than their abled counterparts.[30] This may be due in part to stereotypes that portray people with disabilities as asexual and undesirable, or that interpret disabled sexuality as pathological and threatening to the health of the body politic.[31] Such stereotypes survive in part as a result of cultural imperialism,[32] wherein abled people produce cultural representations of disabled people who, for their part, are afforded little opportunity to represent their own sexuality.[33] When children who are disabled do receive formal sex education, it regularly lacks information specific to disabled sexuality: how to have sex in a wheelchair; that non-genital orgasm is possible; appropriate relational boundaries with personal support workers, how to manage support worker involvement in facilitating sexual encounters, etc. In addition, adults and caregivers may demonstrate heightened discomfort in talking about sex with teens with disabilities[34] while sending 'negative messages … about

[29] Iris Marion Young, 'Five Faces of Oppression', in *Justice and the Politics of Difference* (Princeton, NJ, Princeton University Press, 1990), pp. 39–65.

[30] Lauri J. East and Treena R. Orchard, 'Somebody Else's Job: Experiences of Sex Education Among Health Professionals, Parents and Adolescents with Physical Disabilities in Southwestern Ontario', *Sexuality and Disability*, 32 (2013), 335–50.

[31] Melinda Hall, *The Bioethics of Enhancement: Transhumanism, Disability, and Biopolitics* (Lanham, MD, Lexington Books, 2016).

[32] Cultural imperialism is one Young's five faces of oppression. See Young, *Justice and the Politics of Difference*, pp. 53–55.

[33] Loree Erickson, 'Out of Line: The Sexy Femmegimp Politics of Flaunting It!', in Tristan Taormino *et al.* (eds), *The Feminist Porn Book* (New York, The Feminist Press, 2013), pp. 355–64.

[34] East and Orchard, 'Somebody Else's Job', 336n82; Sonali Shah, '"Disabled People Are Sexual Citizens Too": Supporting Sexual Identity, Well-Being, and Safety for Disabled Young People', *Frontiers in Education*, 21 (2017), 1–5.

their possibility of a sexual life and marriage as adults'.[35] This means that disabled children are less likely than abled children to have informal access to information about their own sexual possibilities.

As a result of oppression-related constructed ignorance, children with disabilities may be made less able to consent to sexual activity than their peers. As Lauri East and Treena Orchard put it:

> adolescents with physical disabilities do not always receive the necessary combination of comprehensive sex education within school environments, specialized information from health professionals, and informal sex education from family and peers that they require in order to gain the knowledge and skills needed to understand their own sexual capabilities and make informed decisions about their sexual health and intimate relationships.[36]

The same is true for children with intellectual or developmental disabilities, some of whom can become capable of giving valid consent.

Some information deficits mean that children who *do* have the capacity to consent will not be able to do so validly. They may be able to give consent but not *informed* consent, making their consent invalid. Other information deficits interfere with *developing* the capacity to consent. In order to be capable of consenting, people need to be able to make decisions, not necessarily good decisions but ones based on an adequate understanding of themselves, their circumstances, others, and their options. If children are not informed enough to understand their own capabilities, rights, and recourses, or to understand the sorts of sexual possibilities that exist, along with some of the risks, benefits, and social meanings of those possibilities, then they do not yet have an understanding of what they are being asked to do or allow. If so, they are not yet capable of validly consenting. The children described above are at risk of being in just this sort of situation; as a result of oppression, they are denied information that they need to become competent sexual decision-makers.

Developing a skill or ability takes practice. Constructed ignorance prevents practice in informed decision-making. However, information access is not the only thing preventing practice. Parents and caregivers of disabled children sometimes have more control for a longer period of time over their children's social activities than do parents of abled children. This is the case when a society's social institutions in combination with the manifestation of a child's disability make her more than usually dependent on, as well as socially and/or legally subject to, her carers. Disabled children are also heavily monitored by medical professionals, while their social behaviour may be measured and pathologised. Parents and caregivers of disabled children may therefore have an unusual degree of influence over their

[35] Diana J. H. G. Wiegerink, Marij Roebroeck, Mireille Donkervoort, and Henk Stam, 'Social and Sexual Relationships of Adolescents and Young Adults with Cerebral Palsy: A Review', *Clinical Rehabilitation*, 20 (2006), 1023–31 at 1028.

[36] East and Orchard, 'Somebody Else's Job', 335n82.

children's opportunities to explore sexuality, particularly with others. In practice, parents may both enable and prevent sexual and romantic connections.[37] However, where stereotypes, stigma, and discrimination operate, and where carers are able to override their children's sexual and relationship decisions in part for those reasons, children with disabilities will have fewer opportunities for practising consent.[38] By limiting practice opportunities, oppression can therefore once again impede development of the capacity to consent.

Finally, oppression can interfere with developing the sorts of self-understandings and self-regarding attitudes involved in seeing oneself as a sexual being with the potential and right to give and refuse sexual consent. In the above example, disabled children are discounted as sexual beings and, like the 2SLGBTQIA+ children described earlier, they are erased from public representations of healthy sexuality, love, and full humanity.[39] Their desires are monitored, pathologised, and made ineffective. This is marginalisation, a form of oppression according to Young. Such erasure harms children:[40]

> [t]he stigma, limited communication, and inadequate resources in relation to sexuality and disability can have detrimental effects on the physical and psychological health and well-being of disabled young people. It can lead to confusion about their sexual identity, reduced self-esteem, and self-doubt about their status as a sexual being.[41]

Children in this situation may feel ashamed of their sexual desire, and they may doubt their standing to give and refuse sexual consent. They may also be less able to decide how to act, while at the same time being more vulnerable than usual to manipulation and coercion. If, as Trudy Govier argues, the procedural autonomy necessary for consent 'is possible only if one has, and can maintain against criticism, a sense of one's own basic competence and worth',[42] then this form of oppression interferes with developing the capacity to consent.

## Oppression undercuts the effectiveness of valid consent

So far, I have demonstrated that oppression can unjustly limit a child's ability to develop the capacities needed to consent. In addition, when children who are subject to oppression do develop the capacity to give valid consent, oppression can

[37] Michel Desjardins, 'The Sexualized Body of the Child: Parents and the Politics of "Voluntary" Sterilization of Children with Intellectual Disabilities', in Robert McRuer and Anna Mollow (eds), *Sex and Disability* (Durham, Duke University Press, 2012), pp. 69–85.

[38] Wiegerink *et al.*, 'Social and Sexual Relationships', 1030.

[39] Erickson, 'Out of Line'; Esther Ignagni, Ann Fudge Schormans, Kristy Liddiard, and Katherine Runswick-Cole, '"Some People Are Not Allowed to Love": Intimate Citizenship in the Lives of People Labelled with Intellectual Disabilities', *Disability & Society*, 31 (2015), 131–5.

[40] For discussion of harms of being desexualised, see Clare, *Exile and Pride*, pp. 119–41.

[41] Shah, '"Disabled People Are Sexual Citizens Too"', 2.

[42] Trudy Govier, 'Self-Trust, Autonomy, and Self-Esteem', *Hypatia*, 8 (1993), 99–120 at 103–4. See also Robin Dillon, 'Self-Respect: Moral, Emotional, Political', *Ethics*, 107 (1997), 226–43.

create conditions that make that consent ineffective. This occurs when members of dominant groups are given licence to deny, ignore, or override their consent or refusal. It also occurs when oppression creates conditions within which well-meaning others are less able to recognise consent from children who are members of oppressed groups.

Consider disability once again, this time in relation to a double bind.[43] On the one hand, children who are disabled are at a much greater risk of sexual abuse during which their non-consent is ignored or denied. This is the case for many reasons, most of which are not a direct result of impairment and which include, for example: substandard sex education; ableist beliefs that disabled children are not harmed as much by sexual violence and abuse as their abled counterparts; and institutional settings that exacerbate isolation and vulnerability in some cases by making disclosure of violence possible only via perpetrators.[44]

On the other hand, because they are stereotypically interpreted as asexual, when children who are disabled do consent to sexual activity that activity may be interpreted as abuse. Thus, their consent may go unrecognised. Further, in direct opposition with stereotypes of asexuality, people who are disabled have been figured as sexually dangerous—whether because their sexual activity would pollute the health of the body politic[45] or because they are represented as hypersexual and depraved, unconstrained by morality or reason.[46] These discourses have been used to justify strict controls on disabled people's sexual agency, especially once they reach puberty, making their sexual consent legally and/or practically ineffective when it is overridden.[47]

## Does the argument generalise?

I have addressed ableism as an exemplar of oppression. However, other forms of oppression operate in similar ways both to inhibit the development of children's capacities to consent and to undermine those capacities where they do exist. One more set of examples should suffice to make this claim plausible. The examples arise from within interlocking systems of oppression that operate together and support each other. Analysis of these interconnections is beyond the scope of this chapter. Therefore, the examples address three aspects in turn: gendered racism, patriarchy, and homophobic masculinity, all within a colonial framework. After giving these examples, I will explain how they interfere with both developing and effectively using the capacity to consent.

Consider gendered racism first. As a group, Black men and women have been hypersexualised and treated as property, while Blackness is defined as by nature

[43] Frye, *The Politics of Reality*, p. 3.
[44] Shah, '"Disabled People Are Sexual Citizens Too"', 3.
[45] Hall, *The Bioethics of Enhancement*.
[46] Desjardins, 'The Sexualized Body of the Child', 69–70.
[47] Erickson, 'Out of Line'.

dangerous.[48] To maintain propertied White male political and economic control, Black men continue to be represented as sexually dangerous and animalistic. Black women are then figured as promiscuous, sexually aggressive, and strong. Both sets of stereotypes have been used to justify horrific acts of political violence, including lynching, rape, and forced reproduction to produce children born into slavery. In this system, White men are positioned as guardians of an endangered and fragile White female sexuality against the threat of Black male sexuality and Black female promiscuity.[49]

What can happen to childhood sexual consent in these circumstances? First, Black boys and girls are endangered and simultaneously depicted as undeserving of protection. Nelson Zounlomè and others, for example, demonstrate that 'stereotypes regarding Black women's hypersexuality can predispose men to believe (or claim to believe) that Black women are more interested in sexual activity than they are, exacerbating their likelihood of experiencing sexual violence'.[50] This applies also to girls. Further, if Blackness means uncontrolled lust, promiscuity, and sexual availability, then Black female non-consent is defined out of existence, ostensibly justifying rape. If it does appear, because of stereotypes about 'strong Black women', sexual violation can be taken as less harmful for Black girls than for White girls.[51] In addition, stereotypes that represent Black women and girls as single mothers who 'burden the system' may lead to efforts to prevent Black girls from choosing (that is, consenting) to be sexually active and bear children.[52]

Black boys, for their part, must worry about potentially deadly violence if they consent to engage sexually with White girls. White girls' consent to sexual activity with Black boys can then be treated as irrelevant 'for their own protection' when Black male sexuality is, by definition, represented as dangerous. In this context, Black boys' respect for consent from their partners gets denied—dissolved into what Angela Davis names 'the myth of the black rapist'.[53] These stereotypes also deny Black boys representations of romantic, non-animalistic sexual beauty and desire that could inform their understanding of their own sexual possibilities.[54]

[48] George Yancy, *Black Bodies, White Gazes: The Continuing Significance of Race*, second edition (Lanham, MD, Rowman and Littlefield Publishers, 2008), p. xxxiv.

[49] Angela Davis, 'Rape, Racism and the Myth of the Black Rapist', in *Women, Race, and Class* (New York, Vintage Books, 1983); Ayumu Kaneko, 'The Politics of the Black Rapist Myth', *Gender History*, 3 (2007) 5–18.

[50] Nelson O. O. Zounlomè Y. Wong, Elyssa Klann, Jessica David, and Nat Stephens, '"No One … Saves Black Girls": Black University Women's Understanding of Sexual Violence', *The Counselling Psychologist*, 47 (2019), 873–908 at 885.

[51] Zounlomè *et al.*, '"No One … Saves Black Girls"', 891–2.

[52] Hill Collins, 'Mammies, Matriarchs, and Other Controlling Images', in *Black Feminist Thought* (Boston, MA, Unwin Hyman, 1990), pp. 69–92.

[53] Davis, *Women, Race, and Class.*

[54] Wesley Morris, 'Last Taboo: Why Pop Culture Just Can't Deal with Black Male Sexuality', *New York Times*, 27 October 2016. https://www.nytimes.com/interactive/2016/10/30/magazine/black-male-sexuality-last-taboo.html (accessed 15 July 2025).

Next, consider capitalistic patriarchy wherein women and girls have been treated as the property or perpetual wards of fathers and husbands who 'protect' them. In this context, other men may treat women's consent or lack thereof as irrelevant. For example, girls often learn to say 'I have a boyfriend' instead of 'I'm not interested' to get men to leave them alone.[55] Or they signal to men that they are already 'taken' to avoid harassment. Their lack of consent, and even their sexual orientation if they are lesbians,[56] is not seen as enough to justify rejection; being claimed by another man is required. Similarly, men may ask a girl's father or boyfriend for permission to engage with her sexually without asking her what she thinks about this possibility. Doing so bypasses her consent or lack thereof entirely, treating it as irrelevant.[57] This happened to me when I was 14 and a 21-year-old male 'suitor' asked a man in my family for permission to become sexual with me. He did so in front of but without addressing me on the topic at all. No one responded as if anything was amiss other than me. I later learned that another male relative threatened the would-be-suitor with violence if he proceeded, again without consulting me. My opinion, let alone my consent, was bypassed and treated as irrelevant. I doubt that I am alone.[58]

The situation, however, is more serious than described so far. Consider, again, contexts where women and girls have been treated as the property or perpetual wards of men for the purposes of maintaining class status, racial purity, and economic dominance. In those contexts, female sexuality and fertility is tightly controlled, whether by laws that permit heritable chattel slavery or by those that sanction child removal and female confinement, often with the involvement of religious institutions. In these situations, a girl's consent to participate in sexual activity, or to bear or not to bear children, can be discounted as morally and politically irrelevant and women's, girl's, and infant's lives are endangered. Think here, for example, of Ireland's mother and baby homes where unwed young mothers were sent after being ostracised from their communities between 1922 and 1998. Children were separated from their mothers, and almost 9000 infants and children died and were buried in unmarked mass graves.[59]

[55] Sophie Gallagher, 'Is "I Have a Boyfriend" Really the Only Chat-Up Rejection that Works?', *Huffington Post*, 7 August 2019. https://www.huffingtonpost.co.uk/entry/i-have-a-boyfriend-is-this-the-only-rejection-that-really-works_uk_5c99fd3ce4b07435554a2dab (accessed 15 July 2025).

[56] TIMTAM, 'Dude Followed Me to My Car and Blocked Me in with His Work Van so He Could Hit on Me. Do These People Genuinely not Realize This Is Unacceptable Behavior?', *Reddit*, 12 November 2021. https://www.reddit.com/r/Feminism/comments/qsic3h/dude_followed_me_to_my_car_and_blocked_me_in_with/ (accessed 15 July 2025).

[57] Requests to fathers for sexual access to daughters cannot be excused as parental prerogative in sexist contexts given that mothers are not accorded the same prerogative. For an argument that parental consent should not be required alongside a competent child's consent to sexual activity, see Quill Kukla, 'Taking Children's Autonomy Seriously as a Parent', *APA Newsletter on Feminism and Philosophy*, 19 (2020), 14–17.

[58] Throwawayaway56789, 'Thoughts on Someone Asking for Your Partner's Permission First?', *Reddit*, 23 October 2021. https://www.reddit.com/r/polyamory/comments/qe5tz9/thoughts_on_someone_asking_for_your_partners/ (accessed 15 July 2025).

[59] BBC, 'Irish Mother and Baby Homes: Timeline of Controversy', *BBC*, 13 January 2021. https://www.bbc.com/news/world-europe-54693159 (accessed 15 July 2025).

Think also of colonial attempts to control Indigenous sexuality and family structures for the purposes of land dispossession and the destruction of Indigenous governance systems based on kinship.[60] During this process, Indigenous children were also removed from their families and communities, suffering abuse and often dying in residential schools, being removed and adopted into White families during the Sixties Scoop, or even now being removed into care in part because of discrimination in the funding of social services for Indigenous communities.[61] In addition, Leanne Betasamosake Simpson provides a detailed account of the ways in which colonial and settler society targets Indigenous women and Two-Spirit or Indigiqueer people's sexual expression and body sovereignty in order to destroy Indigenous nationhood.[62] In this case, bypassing, undermining, and attacking consent is a tool of genocide.

Finally, consider homophobic constructions of masculinity. The systems of oppression described above define normative masculinity not only as abled and White but as demanding dominance and heterosexual sexual appetite and prowess.[63] While this definition privileges many heterosexual men as agents, giving them licence to access women sexually and social status when they live up to this image, it is also harmful to them. Boys who are subject to this definition of masculinity may fail to learn that they can choose not to have sex or heterosexual sex. This lack of understanding interferes with their capacity to give valid consent because in order to meaningfully agree to something one must also be able to refuse it. Spencer, a person commenting on a blog post about 'how not to rape', describes this experience:

> I was never really brought up to understand that I could or should say no myself … I was taught under the presumption that I should want to go as far as she'll let me, which … isn't necessarily true. I thought setting boundaries was her job and respecting them was my job, and that mentality unfortunately led to a lot of regrets … it is vital to not only challenge the false presumption that silence is consent, but also to challenge the presumption that just because she says you can, means you should.[64]

Defining masculinity as necessarily sexual also makes boys' actual sexual consent irrelevant since it is presumed always to exist. Sexual abuse by women directed at

[60] Erin Hanson, 'Marginalization of Aboriginal Women', *University of British Columbia*. https://indigenousfoundations.arts.ubc.ca/marginalization_of_aboriginal_women/ (accessed 15 July 2025).

[61] *Indigenous Foundations*, 'Sixties Scoop' (University of British Columbia). https://indigenousfoundations.web.arts.ubc.ca/sixties_scoop/ (accessed 15 July 2025); and E. Hanson, D. Gamez, and A. Manuel (*Indigenous Foundations*, University of British Columbia, September 2020). 'The Residential School System'. https://indigenousfoundations.arts.ubc.ca/the_residential_school_system/ (accessed 15 July 2025). And *First Nations Child and Family Caring Society of Canada et al v Attorney General of Canada* 2016 CHRT 2.

[62] Leanne Betasamosake Simpson, 'The Sovereignty of Indigenous People's Bodies', in Leanne Betasamosake Simpson (ed.), *As We Have Always Done* (Minneapolis, MN, University of Minnesota Press, 2017), pp. 95–118.

[63] See Tom Shakespeare, 'The Sexual Politics of Disabled Masculinity', *Sexuality and Disability*, 17 (1999), 53–64.

[64] Spencer, 21 March 2013 (4:22 p.m.) comment on Abby Norman, 'The Day I Taught How Not To Rape', *Accidental Devotional*, 19 March 2013. https://web.archive.org/web/20201127090056/https://abbynorman.net/2013/03/19/the-day-i-taught-how-not-to-rape/ (accessed 15 July 2025).

boys may then go unrecognised when it is interpreted as consensual and 'lucky' since boys are thought automatically to want sex with women. In that situation, a boy's non-consent is violated. Boys who are asexual, gay, or bisexual are also harmed by these definitions when they are discounted as men and pressured to seek out and/or consent to unwanted heterosexual sex.

The representations of male and female sexual roles that Spencer identifies are also dangerous to women and girls who are charged with the responsibility of creating limits for male sexual desire. That positioning is used to silence female victims of abuse and sexual assault when abusers and bystanders blame them for failing to fulfil their proper role as gatekeepers.[65] This perspective, alongside the presumption of men's control and ownership of sexual access to women described above, conceptually erases the possibility that women and girls might choose to prioritise and explore their own pleasure and desire, making it less safe for them to do so.

In many of the examples given above, children's consent is presumed to be either always present or irrelevant.[66] If and when children in such situations are capable of consenting, their consent or refusal can be easily overridden, often violently. These are not individual incidents of violation. Instead, they are patterns of behaviour supported by legal and social institutions that distribute opportunities to control and access other people's bodies based on social group membership. Hypersexualising Black children and presuming male ownership of female sexuality enables consent violation and sexual violence. Legally permitting confinement in places of abuse and death either to punish, regulate, or eradicate Indigenous, queer, and female sexual agency reveals the violability of consent, sexual or not, as foundational to colonial and heteropatriarchal social control.[67] These forms of oppression unquestionably interfere with targeted children's effective use of their consent capacities.

Do these forms of oppression limit children's access to institutional conditions needed to develop the capacity to consent? Yes, in many ways. First, being subject to consent violations, including sexual violence, can inhibit one's ability to consent. As a defence mechanism, some children will choose to do things they would not otherwise do as a form of self-protection; if you would do it to yourself first, no one else can harm you by making you do it. Decisions for that reason are fear based and should not qualify as consensual. Consent violations also communicate, viscerally, that targeted children are not entitled to direct what happens to their bodies. As a result, they may become afraid, ashamed, or unworthy to practise giving, refusing, and receiving consent.

[65] Milena Popova, *Sexual Consent* (Cambridge, MA, MIT Press, 2019), p. 74.

[66] Disabled children's consent, by contrast, may be presumed never to be present. Violence, one of Young's five faces of oppression, occurs here, too, as presumed incompetence is used to justify institutionalisation and involuntary sterilisation. This eugenic practice also targets people by race and class. See Hall, *The Bioethics of Enhancement*, and Desjardins, 'The Sexualized Body of the Child'.

[67] This statement could just as easily be made about white supremacy, expressed in Black and Indigenous confinement in carceral systems. Disturbingly, sexual violence is dismissed as a humorous feature of these systems.

Next, as with ableism earlier, gendered racism, patriarchy, and homophobic masculinity construct ignorance. They each promote stereotypes resulting in widespread mistaken beliefs. Children from targeted groups may internalise stereotypes in ways that inhibit their consent capacity. Boys who believe they must always want and choose sex, girls who believe they are never entitled to do so, and racialised children who are not shown representations of their gentleness and romantic capacity may find it harder to understand themselves or to realise that they can say yes, no, or seek out different ways to express themselves sexually. They may lack self-knowledge, self-trust, and self-respect. All of these abilities are needed, in some measure, in order to be capable of consenting validly. Finally, the examples given above discourage children from developing consent skills through practice—practice in saying yes and no, in proposing alternatives, expressing needs and desires, seeking adult protection and support as well as better information, exploring non-oppressive sexual possibilities, and more.

I have now made the case that oppression can limit children's access to institutional conditions needed to fully develop their capacity to consent. I have also argued that oppression can create conditions that make children's consent ineffective where it does exist. I do not wish to deny, however, that agency–including children's agency–exists under oppression.[68] Oppression is not inescapable, nor is it totalising. Harmful, unjustly limiting, destructive yes, but people resist and give meaning to their lives outside of oppressive discourse and practices. They form communities, alliances, and seek joy and even sexual pleasure as modes of resistance essential to survival.[69] In order to help children live well, and to do justice to them, adults cannot stop at identifying danger and damage. We must be alert to and supportive of children's sexual agency—developing or extant. Speaking at the Barnard Conference on Sexuality, a major salvo in the feminist sex wars, Amber Hollibaugh puts it this way:

> I want to be unafraid to be the erotic person I created in my own fantasies as a 12-year old girl … We must demand that our pleasure and need for sexual exploration not be pitted against our need for safety. Feminism is a liberation movement; it needs to fight with that recognition at its center.[70]

[68] Quill Kukla, 'A Nonideal Theory of Sexual Consent', *Ethics*, 131 (2021), 270–92; Maria C. Lugones, 'Structure/Antistructure and Agency Under Oppression', *Journal of Philosophy*, 87 (1990), 500–7; Catriona Mackenzie, 'Responding to the Agency Dilemma: Autonomy, Adaptive Preferences, and Internalized Oppression', in Marina A. L. Oshana (ed.), *Personal Autonomy and Social Oppression: Philosophical Perspectives* (New York, Routledge, 2014), pp. 48–67.

[69] Erickson, 'Out of Line'; Audre Lorde, *Uses of the Erotic: The Erotic as Power* (Tucson, AZ, Kore Press, 2000); Carol S. Vance (ed.), *Pleasure and Danger: Exploring Female Sexuality* (Boston, MA, Routledge and Kegan Paul, 1984); Tuana, 'Coming to Understand'; Tristan Taormino *et al.* (eds), *The Feminist Porn Book*.

[70] Amber Hollibaugh, 'Desire for the Future: Radical Hope in Passion and Pleasure', in Carol S. Vance (ed.), *Pleasure and Danger: Exploring Female Sexuality* (Boston, MA, Routledge and Kegan Paul, 1984), pp. 401–10.

## Relationality and adult obligations to consenting children

In the preceding sections, I have frequently referred to ways in which other people and social institutions affect a child's ability to develop and exercise the capacity to consent. This is not accidental, since in my view consent is relational.[71] Although we look to individual children for consent, children do not grow into sexual agency alone. Nor do they flourish that way. Relationships are developmentally important for children, and they affect their lived experiences, well-being, and behaviours.[72] In addition to helping children grow and develop as persons, parents, educators, friends, community members, internet resources, and structural features of social environments (including laws, policies, institutions, norms, stereotypes, and social support systems) play a role in determining children's ability to give consent. Whatever one thinks about whether persons or consent are constitutively relational, it is clear that children depend on others for the support, information, education, capacity building, and social environments that enable them to develop and effectively use the ability to consent.

What then might the relational nature of consent indicate about adults' obligations to children? These obligations will be role related and may differ for parents, educators, medical professionals, law enforcement and legal professionals, legislators, and so on. In role-appropriate capacities, adults have at least three general types of responsibility that also apply to childhood sexuality. First, they must protect and promote children's well-being, interests, and some adults (for example, parents) must ensure childhood access to goods, including sexual goods, that enable flourishing. Second, adults must enable children to develop autonomy and to act as agents, including as sexual agents. Third, adults must uphold children's choice rights, and other rights, if and when they exist, even in the face of adult discomfort. Sometimes, those rights will conflict with children's interests.[73] In such cases, adults must decide whether to protect rights or interests and sometimes, although not always, rights should prevail. A full account of how to properly fulfil these responsibilities in relation to sexuality is beyond the scope of this chapter. However, a number of practical obligations suggest themselves.

[71] See Judith Butler, 'Sexual Consent: Some Thoughts on Psychoanalysis and Law', *Columbia Journal of Gender and the Law*, 21 (2011), 405–29; see also Popova, *Sexual Consent*; Ellie Anderson, 'Women in Philosophy: The Limits of Consent in Sexual Ethics', *Blog of the APA*, 24 April 2019. https://blog.apaonline.org/2019/04/24/women-in-philosophy-the-limits-of-consent-in-sexual-ethics/ (accessed 15 July 2025).

[72] S. B. Johnson, R. W. Blum, and J. N. Giedd, 'Adolescent Maturity and the Brain: The Promise and Pitfalls of Neuroscience Research in Adolescent Health Policy', *Journal of Adolescent Health*, 45 (2009), 216–21 at 219.

[73] Samantha Brennan, 'Children's Choices or Children's Interests: Which Do Their Rights Protect?', in David Archard and Colin M. Macleod (eds), *The Moral and Political Status of Children* (Oxford, Oxford University Press, 2003), pp. 53–69.

In order to ensure children's well-being and to promote their developing agency, adults have an obligation to provide them with comprehensive, sex-positive sex education. That education should teach them about consent and it should give children supportive opportunities to think about their own desires, risks, sexual and gender identity, relationships, and values. Similarly, adults must secure children's access to sexual healthcare where that care includes access to contraception and does not penalise children for sexual activity. Next, both to support well-being and to avoid undermining children's emerging and developing agency, adults must treat children's consent and non-consent as if they have moral weight and normative force, even in cases where it is not wrong to override a child's positive consent (though not their refusal). At the same time, adults must not infringe on children's choice rights and that will sometimes mean acknowledging children's rights to make bad sexual decisions. Interestingly, there is also an obligation to help the children exercise their rights and to develop as rights bearers. Children, in part, learn how to respect the rights of others when adults respect their rights, including to consent or withhold consent. There are likely other obligations not considered here and the topic bears further investigation. Finally, adults must create conditions in which children can disclose abuse and receive non-traumatising help while lessening the risk of abuse and exploitation in the first place.[74] This implies an obligation on the part of adults to actively work to recognise and end oppression. In this respect, Milena Popova believes consent has radical potential:

> When we move away from looking at consent as something that happens between individuals in a specific situation and start looking at it as something enmeshed in social structures, cultural practices, and complex operations of power, the radical potential of the idea of consent becomes really clear. This version of consent allows us to ask much bigger questions than who said yes and who said no. It allows us to start exploring the social and cultural forces that shape the options we have, how we see ourselves, how we are seen by others, right down to our very desires. It allows us to ask what the conditions are that we need to create for consent to be truly free, and truly meaningful. It allows us to start dismantling rape culture in favor of a culture of consent.[75]

Popova's vision hints also at the limits of consent. They are envisioning a society in which not only is sex uncoerced, but in which sex is good. Respecting consent helps to enable bodily autonomy, positive self-regarding attitudes, pleasure, and some degree of freedom for sexual exploration. But it cannot tell children, or anyone else, how to make sexual activity 'good' in either the practical or moral sense, nor to ensure that it will not be harmful. Instead, it can tell us how to enable sex that is not *wrong*, at least in one way, in that it does not involve a certain kind of violation.

[74] Anna Margrete Flåm and Eli Haugstvedt, 'Test Balloons? Small Signs of Big Events: A Qualitative Study on Circumstances Facilitating Adults' Awareness of Children's First Signs of Sexual Abuse', *Child Abuse and Neglect*, 37 (2013), 633–42.

[75] Popova, *Sexual Consent*, pp. 10–11.

What else might we need to know to enable good sex then? This question is especially significant in the context of sex education where discussions of consent are necessary, but where an over-focus on consent can distract from other important abilities. Among other things, children need to learn interpersonal and relationship skills, emotional awareness, and how to become aware of their reasons for agreeing to sexual activity so they can evaluate those reasons, likely with help from adults. Just because children are *capable* of consenting or *permitted* to consent does not mean they always *should* do so. Further, Quill Kukla offers a critique of limiting understandings of sexual exchanges to the model of requesting and accepting or refusing sex, suggesting instead that people learn other forms of sexual communication, such as inviting and offering.[76] Similarly, Dorothy Alison argues that in order to have good sex, indeed non-oppressive sex, we must be able to speak openly about our desires, pleasures, but also violations, without shame.[77] Thinking of sexuality through the lens of communication and negotiation can enhance consent and may assist with sexual flourishing, including for children. We can conclude, then, that sexual consent has its limits even if it is an essential component of morally and pragmatically good sex, and even as an essential component of well-being, autonomy, rights, and sexual flourishing for children.

## Conclusion

Throughout this chapter, I have explored reasons to think that children sometimes can and sometimes cannot validly consent to sexual activity. I began by offering a working definition of sexual consent. In the section 'Sufficiently informed consent in childhood', I discussed sufficiently informed consent in childhood, exploring both information and understanding requirements on valid consent. That discussion suggests that young children cannot give valid consent outside of their developmental stage while older children's lack of experience does not necessarily invalidate their consent. I also concluded that constructed information deficits can illegitimately interfere with children's ability to give valid consent, implying an adult responsibility to care not only for children but for the information environments within which they live and develop. In the section 'What's so special about sexuality in childhood?', I argued that sexuality can be a site of agency and well-being for children. If so, then although sexual activity can be risky, it can also be risky to deny that children can validly consent to sexual activity when they are uncoerced, sufficiently informed, capable of understanding what they are being asked to do, and otherwise competent. Considering risk prompted discussion of

[76] Quill Kukla, 'Sex Talks', *Aeon*, 4 February 2019. https://aeon.co/essays/consent-and-refusal-are-not-the-only-talking-points-in-sex (accessed 15 July 2025).

[77] Dorothy Alison, 'Public Silence, Private Terror', in Dorothy Alison (ed.), *Skin: Talking About Sex, Class and Literature* (New York, Firebrand Books, 1994), pp. 101–19.

the effects of oppression on childhood sexual consent in 'Oppression and consent'. There I argued that oppression can both hinder children as they develop the capacity to consent and make children's valid consent ineffectual when it does exist. If so, then adults must work to end oppression as part of their responsibility to support children's well-being and developing agency, including sexual agency. Finally, I reviewed the ways in which consent, including childhood sexual consent, is relational, drawing out some of the implications of that view before pointing to limits on consent as a tool for making sexual activity good.

This chapter provides an opportunity to begin conversations about childhood sexual consent. It opens up but does not resolve questions about how children gain the ability to consent, to whom they can and cannot consent, the value of sexuality in childhood, adult obligations to children as developing sexual agents, and adult responses to children's consensual sexual choices. Some topics I have not discussed at all. For example, intercultural consent in childhood, neurodivergent consent in childhood, childhood consent to sexual practices that may be considered deviant, the impact of developing as a consenting agent in an abusive household, gender identity as it relates to consent including in childhood, and so on. This is a beginning. More remains to be explored.

# Part II

# Children's Consent and Other Parties

# 5

# Children and Consent: Best Interests, Parents, and a Child's Views

DAVID ARCHARD

Medical procedures on adults require their permissive consent. Such procedures are wrongful unless adults give their permission to them. They do so through the exercise of their normative power of consent. If adults are unable to grant such permission, doctors may judge either that such permission would have been given had the person been able to respond or that what is envisaged is what is best for the individual. In these circumstances, in short, doctors may either rely on hypothetical rather than actual consent or simply act in the best interest of the adult. They may, of course, rely on both. However, the significant problems in judging what would have been agreed to in the absence of any explicit prior statement of wishes may mean that best interests alone is their guide as to what they should do.

Children are, in general, presumed incapable of giving or withholding consent. However, the presumption can be defeated by a demonstration of competence. Thus, older children may be able to show that they are competent to consent. In contrast, adults are presumed competent, and their incompetence must be demonstrated. In both cases—demonstrated and presumed competence—that may not suffice for their consent to be decisive. We may judge that consent, even if competently given and necessary for permission is not sufficient, either morally or legally, to be decisive in the relevant matter.

Incompetent adults may also have made known their wishes before they became incompetent. These can be appealed to when deciding what to do. The incompetence of children extends through their childhood, or until such point as they are judged competent in respect of some matter. Prior wishes would thus not have the role they do for adults. In the case of children, we choose for them, and their consent can thus be given by a proxy. Parents are those adults who, normally, are believed best placed to fulfil the role of proxy consenters. However, they should choose for their children with a view to what is in the latter's best interests.

*Proceedings of the British Academy*, **279**, 105–120, © Authors 2025.

These three paragraphs briefly and necessarily crudely summarise a familiar orthodoxy, one that is recognisable as informing and underpinning the statute and case law within England governing the medical treatment of children. It is also an orthodoxy that has been widely endorsed as a liberal standard by practical moral philosophers. It is a consequence of what elsewhere I have called the 'basic view' of the different moral and political status enjoyed by children and adults.[1] A number of questions are broached and two are much discussed. What exactly should we understand by best interests? May parents choose what is sub-optimal but nevertheless not harmful?[2] However, in what follows I want to ask two different questions, ones that are not as frequently considered. What exactly is involved in giving parents a power of choice for their children? What role should the views of children have?

To anticipate my conclusions: the paramount moral consideration ought always to be what is best for the child. If that is so, the parents' power of choice is severely constrained. At the same time as being obligated to choose what is best for the child, there are significant non-instrumental reasons to value the child's views on self-regarding matters and to do so independently of the reasonable or prudential nature of those views. These should matter, be listened to, and be appropriately taken into account. In sum, the child has more of a voice and parents have less of a choice when it comes to deciding for children than is normally assumed within the orthodox view.

In prospect: I criticise the idea that children could give hypothetical consent, and then respond to the arguments of Allen Buchanan and Dan Brock,[3] representative of a view generally subscribed to, that purport to show why parents have the privileged position that identifies them as proxy consenters for their children. I then provide non-instrumental reasons why children's views on decisions affecting their interests should be listened to, before considering what it means to give those views an appropriate weight.

I should note that my immediate focus for consideration of the issues is medical decision-making. It is an area much written about, one in which there have been many important legal judgments and statutory provisions, and one in which the

[1] David Archard, 'Children, Adults, Autonomy and Well-Being', in Alexander Bagattini and Colin Macleod (eds), *The Nature of Children's Well Being: Theory and Practice* (Dordrecht, Springer, 2015), pp. 3–14.

[2] On difficulties in understanding what best interests might mean, see Robert H. Mnookin, 'Foster Care: In Whose Best Interests?', in O. O'Neill and W. Ruddick (eds), *Having Children: Philosophical and Legal Reflections on Parenthood* (Oxford, Oxford University Press, 1979), pp. 179–213 and Jon Elster, 'Solomonic Judgments: Against the Best Interests of the Child', *University of Chicago Law Review*, 54 (1987), pp. 1–45. On the idea of a parental right to make non-harmful but sub-optimal choices of a child, see Lynn H. Gillam, 'The Zone of Parental Discretion: An Ethical Tool for Dealing with Disagreement Between Parents and Doctors About Medical Treatment for a Child', *Clinical Ethics*, 11 (2016), 1–8 and D. Wilkinson and J. Savulescu, *Ethics, Conflict and Medical Treatment for Children: From Disagreement to Dissensus* (London, Elsevier, 2019).

[3] Allen E. Buchanan and Dan W. Brock, *Deciding for Others: The Ethics of Surrogate Decision Making* (Cambridge, Cambridge University Press, 1989).

arguments of Buchanan and Brock have a certain authority. This is not to deny that there are other areas in which children have views that matter. I will allude to some of these in what follows.

## Proxy consent

The normative power of consent is grounded in a competence. This, following Buchanan and Brock, is decision-relative and variable. In other words, what is needed to be able to give or to withhold consent will differ according to the nature of the matter in respect of which consent is required. Roughly, the more complex and serious the matter the greater the relevant competence that is required. Although this allows that we may distinguish children according to the degrees of competence required in decision-making about different kinds of matter (children have to be older to be able to consent to more difficult matters), we should nevertheless operate with a general presumption of a child's incompetence. Below whatever age we choose to fix the boundary of childhood, children are assumed not able to give or withhold their consent. Herein lies the critical contrast with adults.

Where an individual cannot consent, we may allow another—a proxy—to consent on their behalf. Buchanan and Brock argue that a proxy (or surrogate) may either choose what she judges to be best for the individual or choose as the individual herself would choose if competent and aware of all the relevant features of the situation. The question of how we might authorise or nominate someone to be a proxy is to be distinguished from that of how that proxy should proceed. Thus, a competent adult might identify someone as the person to make choices for them as and when they themselves are not competent to do so. Having been chosen in this manner to be a surrogate that person can then either choose as they consider the nominating adult would herself choose or choose what they judge to be in the best interests of the now incompetent adult.

An individual might both nominate someone to be their proxy and indicate how they would wish the proxy to choose for them when they are no longer competent. However, the two instructions that could be given are distinct and need to be distinguished. If someone manages only to name and authorise their proxy before they cease to be competent, the issue arises of how that proxy should exercise the delegated power of choice. That issue does not arise if the person has specified in advance how they would wish their proxy to choose on their behalf.

The case of children is different from that of the adult in both regards. First, a child who is incompetent to consent is incompetent to authorise a proxy consenter. In whatever manner one exactly characterises the competence required of the normative power to consent, it will be closely matched to that required of the power to authorise another as one's proxy. If I am unable to agree to something then, fairly obviously, I am unable to agree that someone else shall be the person to agree on my behalf. To be able to understand what it might be to act as my proxy, I must at least properly understand what it is that the proxy is doing, namely, agreeing to something for me.

Second, there is no relevant counterfactual in the case of a child that is both sensible and gives us a proper analogue of what works in the case of the adult. To quote Buchanan and Brock, 'the substituted judgment principle [the alternative to a best interests principle] states that a surrogate is to choose as the patient would choose if the patient were competent and aware of the medical options and of the facts about his or her condition, including the fact that he or she is incompetent'.[4]

We are asked to imagine what a particular adult who is now incompetent would choose if competent and aware both of what needs to be decided and of her own incompetence. The most obvious case of such incompetence is unconsciousness. So, Buchanan and Brock ask us to think of what a patient might choose if she were to 'miraculously awake' from a coma for a few moments before relapsing into her comatose state.

Could not a child be imagined as awakening from the state of childish incapacity so as to be able, if only for the duration of a miraculous instant, to choose? No, since the miracle in question required for a child to be choosing as if competent is of a very different order to that of an adult wakening from a coma. It would have to be a case of a child becoming an adult and then choosing as such an adult before reverting to their state of childish incompetence. A child choosing if competent to do so is no longer a child. An adult who becomes incompetent to choose because of slipping into a coma remains an adult throughout. Indeed, in imagining what such a person would choose if 'miraculously awake' we can appeal to the settled beliefs and desires of that person before she became unconscious. In the case of the child, no such appeal is possible.

We can, of course, envisage a child in an adult's body. The 1988 'fantasy' comedy *Big* is about a young boy wishing 'to be big' and being transformed overnight into an adult.[5] Or rather, and more precisely, he is given an adult body. The comedy precisely derives from the incongruity of the childlike enthusiasm, views, wishes, and outlook of a 12-year-old being enacted and voiced by what appears to others as a fully grown man. This is a case of a child, nonetheless, who inhabits an adult body. What is needed in the current context of hypothetical choice is a child acquiring the beliefs, dispositions, values, and general outlook of their adult self. That is a miracle way beyond that of the comatose adult coming awake for an instant and it is, strictly speaking, unimaginable.

## Parents and best interests

If the child cannot choose for themselves, who should choose for them? Buchanan and Brock offer two 'obvious and compelling' reasons in favour of giving parents (or the broader family) the powers of surrogate decision-making in respect of an

[4] Buchanan and Brock, *Deciding for Others*, p. 94.

[5] *Big*, dir. by Penny Marshall (20th Century Fox, 1988). https://en.wikipedia.org/wiki/Big_(film)

incompetent child. Such decision-making, note, is guided by the best interests principle. The two reasons are that parents are those 'most knowledgeable' about the child's good and also those 'most concerned' about the child's good.[6] The reasons are thus epistemic and motivational: parents are those who know better than others what is best for their child and who are best disposed to do what is best for their child.

These reasons are not as obvious as they might at first appear, and they need not be as compelling as Buchanan and Brock urge. In respect of the epistemic reason, there is an important distinction to be made between knowing one's child and knowing what is best for one's child. It is easy to conflate the two. Doubtless, parents who live with their children and who undertake their quotidian care have an exceptionally close and familiar relation with them. They will know better than others what their children like and do not like, their beliefs, moods, unique traits, quirks of character, preferences, and fears. That does not mean that they know what is best for those children, even if they start from a position of greater knowledge of their children than everyone else.

In the first place, this is because a judgment of what is best for a child is a normative judgment, whereas the exceptional epistemic position a parent occupies need only be in respect of factual judgments. There is a familiar justificatory gap between facts and normative judgments. Facts must be conjoined with general normative principles to yield particular normative judgments. Thus, a parent may know what makes their child happy. But what makes their child happy need not be what is best for them.

Second, what parents do know about their child may simply not extend to everything relevant to a judgment of what is good for them. For instance, parents might well know better than anyone else what their child likes. Yet, what a child likes need not tell us everything we need to know to judge what is best for the child. What and who pleases a child, what food they enjoy eating, what activities they prefer, may be what conduces to their good. But we need to know more to know that this is indeed the case. A parent need not know what food regimen is best for their health, what educational programme best fosters their cognitive development, and what medical procedures and treatments best promote their health. Finally, to know what is in the child's best interests is to know what actions (and failures to act) yield which outcomes that are optimal. One could know a child very well, one could even correctly identify what are the best outcomes for a child, and yet not be best placed to know what is needed to bring about those outcomes.

The motivational reason is clearly defeasible. The vast majority of parents are moved to do what they think is best for their children; they will act in ways that sometimes display an extraordinary degree of selflessness and indeed self-sacrifice. Parents would and do die for the children's sake. However, once again, and as with the epistemic reason, an important distinction should be made. Doing what is believed to be best is not the same as doing what is, in fact, best. This is so however

[6] Buchanan and Brock, *Deciding for Others*, p. 136.

strongly the belief is held and however much it is grounded in deep knowledge of one's child (as opposed to knowledge of what is best for the child). Moreover, some parents—thankfully a small but, nevertheless, not insignificant number—are not moved to do what they believe best; some—very few but still not a negligible proportion—will abuse, maltreat, harm, and on occasion kill their children.

In sum, Buchanan's and Brock's 'compelling and obvious' reasons for giving the power of surrogate choice or consent to parents may seem to be obvious but are not compelling. They are not overwhelmingly persuasive and certainly not undeniable. Moreover, Buchanan and Brock recognise and clearly state one further significant qualifying consideration. The argument from the epistemic and motivational reasons, they add:

> accords to parents *no* independent interest or right to decide for their children and to enforce their choice when the choice may *not* best serve their children's welfare. Instead, it makes the parents' claim to decide wholly dependent on their tendency to decide more closely in accordance with their children's welfare.[7]

This consideration is well stated. However, the final sentence of the cited passage is worth unpacking. As earlier quoted, Buchanan and Brock believe that parents are those adults 'most knowledgeable' about and 'most concerned' to promote their child's good. That double claim has already been criticised. Here, their argument is that those who should choose for children are those whose 'tendency' is to choose what is good for children. Moreover, it is a tendency to choose 'in accordance' with a child's welfare. This is, strictly construed, less than choosing what is actually best. More importantly, parents' claim to be empowered to choose for their children is 'wholly dependent' on the tendency to choose what is good.

So, the significant consideration that Buchanan and Brock identify should be read as saying, 'Parents have only a tendency to choose what is good for their children and only have the right to choose if they exhibit that tendency.' What follows is that if others have a greater tendency to choose what is good for the child, then they should be the child's proxy choosers.

Now, of course, the claim that most parents tend to choose what is good for their children is plausible. It is relatively easy to find everyday confirmation of it. Yet it is a considerably weaker claim than one that asserts that parents *are* the most knowledgeable and the most concerned choosers for their own children. A tendency to do something is not an unfailing ability to do it. It is certainly not an ability all who exhibit the tendency will use. At most the claim is that most parents will tend to do what is best, but cannot be assumed always to do so.

Moreover, the weaker claim gets some plausibility from being conflated with two quite different claims. The first is that even if parents are not the best people to rear their children, it is best if we act on the presumption that they are. The 'we' in question is society and its state. Thus, it is perfectly possible to think that what

[7] Buchanan and Brock, *Deciding for Others*, p. 233.

is best for children is to act—that is, formulate our laws and policies in respect of children—as if their parents are the best placed to choose for them. Acting on this presumption does not mean that the presumption—that parents *are* best placed to choose for their children—is not defeasible; nor that we might show it to be mistaken in some circumstances or for some kinds of choices.

The second claim to identify and distinguish from the one that parents choose what is good or best for their children is as follows. Parents may be better as parents if *they* act on the presumption that they are. In general, though not always, we are better at doing things if we think that we are indeed good at doing those things. Parenting is arguably such a case. Yet, once again, even if this is generally or normally the case, we should allow that it is mistaken in some circumstances or for some categories of choice.

A final clarification is in order about the claim of Buchanan and Brock. They assert that parents have no independent interest or right to decide for their children. However, it is at least arguable that they have an interest in being the persons who discharge a fiduciary role of care, that is, in making decisions for the child solely in the light of what is best for the child. Harry Brighouse and Adam Swift give an admirably clear expression to this claim:

> The rights that parents have over their children are indeed justified by appeal to children's interests—parents should have just those rights that it is in children's interests for them to have. But parenting relationships—and hence the family itself—are justified in part by the fact that adults have an interest in playing that fiduciary role.[8]

This is important to state. The bare assertion made by Buchanan and Brock is that parents only have a claim to choose for their children if they (normally or on the whole) choose what is good or best for them. Stated in this basic fashion it is not obvious whether, and why, parents have any interest in making that claim. Brighouse and Swift make it apparent that parents might be argued to have an interest in doing what they stake a claim to do, namely, to choose for their children. This is so even if that interest is one in playing the fiduciary role of doing what is good or best for the child.

The bottom line is that those choices—and most especially that of consenting or not—that children are not competent to make should be made by designated proxy choosers. These proxies choose not what the child would agree to if competent to do so, inasmuch as this counterfactual hypothetical cannot be meaningfully construed. We cannot imagine any sense in which a child might choose as if they were not a child. Rather, the proxy chooses what is in the child's best interests. Parents are proxies insofar as they do so choose. They can have an interest in exercising such a role. Yet, that interest is one in discharging the duty of doing the best for one's child. In sum, the choices made for children

[8] Harry Brighouse and Adam Swift, *Family Values: The Ethics of Parent–Child Relationships* (Princeton, NJ, Princeton University Press, 2014), p. 54.

are justified in the final analysis by what is best for them, even if those adults who choose for them have an interest in choosing.

## Children's views and adult choices

But what then should we say concerning what children themselves want and express a view about? This surely matters. But how exactly should we take account of their views?[9] In answering this question, I give effect to two restrictions. The first is that I am considering only children capable of expressing a view. I do not, as do some defenders of a children's voice,[10] include children whose non-linguistic behaviour may reveal preferences; nor do I take any observable statements of emotional dispositions (sadness, happiness, fear) as the implicit voicing of views. There is a difference between the behavioural expression of a preference for one thing over another or of a feeling towards that thing and the formulation and articulation of a view about that thing. A very young child who turns its mouth away from food proffered on a spoon or smiles when offered it is not stating a view with a propositional form, 'This is food I would rather not have'. I am thus excluding infants and considering only children roughly above eight years of age.[11]

Second, the views expressed by children considered in the present context are on self-regarding matters, those that may be said to affect the child alone, and in respect of which adults, under a familiar liberal principle of individual liberty,[12] should enjoy unconstrained choice.

The United Nations Convention on the Rights of the Child's Article 12 is the classic statement of the putative right of children to be heard on matters affecting their own interests, these views being given a weight proportionate to the age and maturity of the child.[13] I shall take this Article as an important reference point. But what follows is not an analysis of this right as formulated.[14] Rather, it is an exploration of what it should mean to take account of the views of any child on self-regarding matters.

[9] I have been greatly influenced in my thinking about this matter by conversations and ongoing work with Suzanne Uniacke.

[10] For instance, Priscilla Alderson, *Children's Consent to Surgery* (London, Open University Press, 1993).

[11] Norway, in incorporating the United Nations Convention on the Rights of the Child into domestic law, construes the 'capable of expressing a view' in Article 12 as applying to those over this age.

[12] J. S. Mill, *On Liberty* (1859) is the canonical statement and defence of this principle, in S. Collini (ed.), *On Liberty and Other Writings* (Cambridge, Cambridge University Press, 1989).

[13] Article 12(1): 'States Parties shall assure to the child who is capable of forming his or her own views the right to express those views freely in all matters affecting the child, the views of the child being given due weight in accordance with the age and maturity of the child.' https://downloads.unicef.org.uk/wp-content/uploads/2016/08/unicef-convention-rights-child-uncrc.pdf (accessed 25 July 2025).

[14] For such analysis see my and Suzanne Uniacke's 'The Child's Right to a Voice', *Res Publica*, 27 (2021), 521–36.

Finally, the famous *Gillick* judgment is not discussed here.[15] It accords the mature minor—judged as such by the maturity of the child in its views on a self-regarding matter—the same right to make choices as an adult. It does not offer a judgment of how the immature minor's views should be taken into account. It does not deny that children's views should be heard. But it does not go far as to accord to the minor a right to have those views heard and accorded an appropriate weight.

With these restrictions in place, the first thing to say is that, for the purposes of effecting a contrast, it is odd to set side by side an adult's power of choice and a child's right to express a view. We examine each in turn. In this section, we consider the relation of an adult's views to their powers of choice; in the next we consider why we should listen to children.

First, we need to bear in mind the distinction between an adult's liberty to choose and their power to consent. The former is guaranteed by a principle such as that defended by J. S. Mill in *On Liberty*. This principle can be enshrined in law and policy (as Mill intended), but there is no guarantee that what is recognisably a liberal principle should be legally protected. Importantly, the principle, as Mill makes clear, is 'meant to apply only to human beings in the maturity of their faculties. We are not speaking of children.'[16]

The power to consent by contrast to the liberty to choose is a normative power, one 'the agent has … intentionally to shape the form of his moral world'.[17] Consent, for instance, releases the other to whom it is given of the obligation not to do what is consented to. Similarly, promising puts the promisor under an obligation to the promisee. Such normative powers do seem mysterious, and it is hard to explain how something an agent does—an exercise of will or a speech act or a behaviour—changes the moral world in the significant ways indicated.[18] How does the mere unforced utterance of the single word, 'Yes', release another from an enforceable obligation not to do something? Should we explain the power to consent by reference to a prior agreement that it should have that power, and how is *that* agreement to be understood?

Its mystery notwithstanding, such a power and its exercise are socially recognised and supported by conventions. In this manner, the power exists independently of and prior to any legal rule that recognises its exercise. One can be taken as giving consent to something even if no law gives effect to acts of consenting. However, both the protection of self-regarding choices and the recognition of the power of giving or withholding permissive consent apply only to agents 'in the maturity of their faculties'.

[15] *Gillick v West Norfolk and Wisbech AHA* [1986] AC 112 House of Lords.

[16] Mill, *Liberty*, ch. 1.

[17] Joseph Raz, 'Promises and Obligations', in J. Raz and P. M. S. Hacker (eds), *Law, Morality and Society. Essays in Honour of H. L. A. Hart* (Oxford, Clarendon Press, 1977), p. 228.

[18] M. H. Robins, *Promising, Intending, and Moral Autonomy* (Cambridge, Cambridge University Press, 1984).

An adult then has a power of choice in respect of self-regarding matters and whether to consent or not. However, it is not the case that adults express a view in either context and that this view is then accorded a certain weight. In respect of consent, it is standard to insist that wishing to φ does not amount to consenting to φ. Equally, I can consent to what I do not wish. I can consent, for instance, to a medical procedure I would rather not have and do not anticipate with pleasure.

In respect of self-regarding matters, someone may say something like, 'I intend to φ'. However, that is not the expression of a view about φ. It is a statement of intent. Moreover, an adult may choose to φ for any number of reasons and holding any number of views about φ-ing. If an adult says 'I want to φ', then this may indeed be taken as an expression of a view held by the adult as to its desirability. That view may explain why someone chooses to behave that way. However, it is not the case that expressing the view explains why the choice is to be respected and not constrained. It is certainly not the case that somehow, that view, weighted according to one's maturity as an adult, justifies the power or right of choice. Somebody has that power to choose because they are an adult.

In other words, it is important to distinguish the ground of the normative power to choose to do something or to consent and the status of any proposition the individual might entertain or express about the doing of that thing. Thus, one might think that individuals have a right to choose in self-regarding matters because their views about the desirability of what they choose are correct. On this account, adults have the right to choose because they are right to make the choices they do. They get it right as to what should be chosen. Although Mill appears to entertain this way of justifying personal liberty in self-regarding matters, he himself, and those sympathetic to his account, accept that individuals do not always get it right. Nevertheless, this does not fatally undermine the right to make choices.

Similarly, the normative power of consent does not rest on a view that individuals always or even invariably consent to what it is prudent for them to agree to. Consenting is a normative power that may be exercised in ways that are inimical to the interests of a person. Yet, the power is not diminished in consequence.

The failure to distinguish the ground of adult self-regarding liberty from the status of any views held or expressed by the adult is illustrated by an ambiguity in the term 'authoritative' which Harry Brighouse, in an influential article, uses to characterise the views of an adult.[19] He does so to provide a contrast with what he terms the 'consultative' status of a child's view. He intends that we should understand an adult's views as to self-regarding matters as determinative, whereas those of a child have instrumental value in assisting us to decide what should happen.

Here is the ambiguity. R. S. Peters distinguished two senses of authority.[20] 'An' authority is someone with epistemic privilege in respect of some matter. She

[19] Harry Brighouse, 'How Should Children Be Heard?', *Arizona Law Review*, 45 (2003), 691–711.

[20] R. S. Peters, 'Authority', *Proceedings of the Aristotelian Society*, Supp. Vol. 32 (1958), 207–24.

is someone who has knowledge in a domain that others lack. On the other hand, someone 'in' authority has, by virtue of her role or position or office, a right to issue commands that others are under an obligation to obey. A military commander is in authority according to army regulations; subordinates are duty bound to obey his commands. He need not be an authority on those matters—the best conduct of a battle, for instance—in respect of which he issues commands.

Here is the relevance of that distinction to Brighouse's characterisation of an adult's views. To describe their views as 'authoritative' might mean that they are epistemically in the best position to form them. Adults know better than anyone else what it is best for them to choose to do. So, an adult who says in respect of some self-regarding matter 'I wish to φ' speaks with authoritative knowledge of how and why φ is desirable, namely it is my wish and I know what I want. Yet such an expression of a wish is authoritative only in the sense the person making it is 'an' authority on what they want. The expression does not impose any duties on others to give them what they want.

On the other hand, to describe an adult's views as authoritative might mean that her views have—like a command—a normative status. They are to be seen as placing others under a duty to comply with what is said will be done. An adult who says in respect of a self-regarding matter 'I wish to φ' is authorised to do what they state that they wish to do. The utterance makes public the intention to φ and thereby places others under a duty not to interfere with the performance of φ. It does so only to the extent that someone has a right to φ, for instance if it is a self-regarding matter. Moreover, it is strictly speaking the freely chosen, intentional doing of φ, that obliges others not to prevent or hinder the performance of φ, not the expression of the wish to φ. The utterance is not authoritative; it is merely a statement of what the agent has the authority to do and can thereby compel compliance with its performance.

It should be clear from the earlier discussion that an adult's views are not authoritative in the first, epistemic, sense. Adults may normally and as a rule get some kinds of view about what is in their interests right; or, they may be more likely to get them right than others. But clearly adults' views on self-regarding matters are not always authoritative. Others with relevant competence—a doctor, for instance—are often better placed to make a wide range of authoritative judgments about what is best for another.

The views of an adult are not authoritative in the second sense. It is not the case that the expressed view as such puts others under an obligation to comply with what is expressed. Rather it is the case that the adult's *choice* is authoritative. It is the choosing to φ which must be respected. Her views are relevant only as an indication of what that choice might be or of why the choice is being made. After all, she might simply choose to φ without telling anyone that this is her choice. The choosing has authoritative status, not the expressed or unexpressed wish so to choose. Moreover, the choosing is to be respected even if the choice is unwise, that is even if the adult's views on why it makes sense for them to choose as they do fail to be authoritative in the first, epistemic sense. The agent's statement of why they make that choice may not show why the choice is sensible. But the choice should still be respected.

## Why do a child's views matter?

So, if an adult's choices are authoritative but not their views, why should we listen to those of children? Moreover, why having listened should we as adults take proper account of what is said? How—given what has been said—does a child's expression of views on self-regarding matters stand in relation to what an adult has the power to do? I will consider these questions in turn.

There are reasons of origin and of outcome that explain why we should listen to the views of the child. These are not instrumental reasons that see value in listening to the child because of, for instance, what we learn about what is, in fact, in the child's best interest or about what would be the costs of compelling the child, against her views, to do what we think is best. Such reasons are not insignificant. Indeed, a child's views as to what they would wish to see happen to them and why are a very good guide as to what the benefits might be of doing as they wish. And the manner in which a child might object to a proposed course of action is a reliable guide to the likely costs of defying their wishes.

Yet, the non-instrumental reasons for listening to a child are of a different kind. So, we should listen, first, because it is the view of someone capable of expressing a view because it is the view of a distinct person—this child—and no other person. It counts in this sense not for what is said but on account of who speaks. We should listen to the child because it is *their* view. Views have authorship even if they do not have authority. In hearing them, we acknowledge their author. It is in this sense that Mark Navin and Jason Wasserman insist that, '[t]he mere fact that a patient has a preference demonstrates that they possess a kind of personhood that deserves respect'.[21] We would disrespect an adult by discounting her preferences, however imprudent, and we disrespect a child by discounting her preferences in favour of a simple, unadorned, and unqualified judgement of what is prudent. Imagine that when asked a parent says of her child, 'This is what she wants and thinks'. We could still ask of the child, 'But what do *you* think?' and believe it important to ask because it is the child who answers and not the parent.

We should listen to the child, second, because it is a view about what happens to the person who expresses that view. Opinions on matters other than self-regarding ones perhaps matter only and to the extent that they get it right. Here in self-regarding cases, it matters that someone says what they want to happen

[21] Mark Christopher Navin and Jason Adam Wasserman, 'Capacity for Preferences and Pediatric Assent', *Hastings Center Report*, 49 (2019), 45–51.

*to them*; it is they who will bear the costs or enjoy the benefits of what is proposed. This makes a difference even if we can confidently assert that what someone says gets it wrong about what will benefit or harm them. Even if that is the case, the view someone takes on what they want gives us *a* reason, even if not a sufficient one, to take it into account. We should listen to them because it is *they* who will suffer or benefit as a result of what will be done.

Importantly in saying that the child's expression of a view gives us a reason to take it into account, it is not being said that its expression gives us a reason to think that the view is right (or more likely than first thought to be right). It is not that an adult need now doubt or be uncertain about what they believe is best for the child. Rather, its expression gives us a reason to think that the preference expressed by the view might be acted on—not a decisive reason but one that should be taken into account. It gives us a reason not to be sceptical about what is judged best for the child but to be cautious in acting on that judgment. We could confidently believe that we know what is best for the child and yet still think that we ought to hear what the child thinks. We would do so not in the expectation that a view contrary to our judgment of what is best thereby weakens our initial judgment but in the belief that it matters that what the child wants is not what we think best.

The critical point is that understanding why a child's expression of her views matters makes a difference to how those views are attended to, but that this difference is not to be understood as simply correcting a judgment of what is best for the child or of complying, or being more disposed to comply, with the child's wishes. Imagine, then, an exhausted parent under pressure who simply gives in to the child's repeated requests for something (to buy a certain toy or have a certain meal), not because that is best for the child or because she thinks it is important to hear the child. She does not want to hear any more from the child, and she does not think what the child wants is best. Compare that with the parent who is attentive to the child's views, takes pains to hear what is said, considers it carefully and refuses the request as not what is best.

Finally, we should note that some of a child's views about self-regarding matters play what could be called a constitutive role in their welfare or interests. This is true also of adults. Thus, for an individual who believes in a certain religion their life only goes well if they can live it in accord with their faith. The same will be true of other important commitments, such as to vegetarianism, or to the advancement of a political cause. In such cases, it is not possible to separate the view in question from a judgment of what is best for the individual, since what is in the person's interests is to be able to do what the view commends.

This kind of case raises interesting questions that bear further consideration. This cannot be done here. However, there is clearly a distinction between a 12-year-old vegetarian or one who refuses certain foods on religious grounds and a minor of the same age who prefers fast food to healthier options. There may also be cases where a child is judged to share the religious views of her parents such that what is in her interests is a decision as to medical treatment at odds with the recommendation of doctors. This is in her interests precisely because these are constituted by what she believes or can be taken to believe is demanded by her faith.[22]

## How should we hear the child's views?

How exactly should we take proper account of what a child says? How—in relation to self-regarding matters and to the normative power of consent—does the expression of a child's view stand in comparison to the making of a choice by an adult?

Children are excluded from the principle that protects choices and from the possibility of giving or withholding consent. They are disqualified because immaturity of their faculties means the absence or underdevelopment of those capacities that underpin both the principle of liberty and the normative power of consent. Children cannot make choices or give consent as adults can. The former lack what the latter have, namely, whatever it is that we judge is a sufficient 'maturity of faculties'.

However, here is a puzzling consideration. Consent is binary; it is either given or it is not.[23] Yet the maturity of faculties that grounds the normative power is acquired gradually and by degrees. Children are less mature in the relevant respects than adults and are not simply immature *simpliciter*. It is not as if adults acquire the grounds of the normative power all at once and on the morn of adulthood. That is so even if the social convention that ascribes such a power to adults and not to children treats the two groups as if that was the case.

Indeed, if we think of the faculties in terms of understanding—of what, for instance, it means to give agreement to something—very young children seem to be surprisingly capable. In one study, for instance, children as young as three were found to understand the normative implications of making and keeping promises.[24]

We can gauge the degree of maturity any child displays by evaluating the extent to which the views the child expresses on a self-regarding matter show understanding of the relevant issues and independence of judgment. To repeat, exercising the power of consent or of personal choice does not occupy the same normative space as the expression of a view. Nevertheless, the maturity of an agent who expresses a view is a useful proxy measure of the agent's capacity to consent or to choose.

[22] *Barts Health NHS Trust v Raqeeb* [2019] EWHC 2530 (Fam); *Raqeeb and Barts Health NHS Trust* [2019] EWHC 2531 (Admin); the case is critically reviewed in D. Archard, J. Brierley, and E. Cave, 'Making Decisions for Children: Accommodating Parental Choice in Best Interests Determinations', *Medical Law Review*, 28 (2020), 183–96.

[23] Buchanan and Brock, *Deciding for Others*, ch. 1.

[24] Patricia Kanngiessera, Bahar Köymenc, and Michael Tomasellob, 'Young Children Mostly Keep, and Expect Others to Keep, Their Promises', *Journal of Experimental Child Psychology*, 159 (2017), 140–58.

That still leaves it problematic how exactly such a measure of maturity might be reflected in the degree of choice permitted or the extent of consent recognised. How precisely could a child have *some* choice or *some* power of consent? Of course, we can allow that the scope of choice or of consent—*what* is consented to or chosen—can vary in its extent. We might thus allow that a child could exercise choice on this issue but not on that other one. We might make such a distinction because we judge the latter to be a more complex matter than the former, requiring as a consequence a greater degree of understanding. That makes perfect sense. What does not and is puzzling is how in respect of some single issue—one which is binary between choosing or not choosing some course of action—the degree or normative strength of the choice might vary. How exactly, for instance, could a child somehow have more choice than another on this matter but less than an adult? The same puzzlement would be provoked by the thought that a child has a greater power of consent to something than another.

Article 12 of the UNCRC speaks of 'the views of the child being given due weight in accordance with the age and maturity of the child'. This is deceptively simple and attractive. Yet, it invites difficult questions of how we estimate what is 'due weight' and how we could give that weighting practical effect.[25]

Such difficulties as there undoubtedly are in making sense of all of this should not cause us to relinquish the idea that children—in virtue of not being as mature as adults rather than simply immature—ought to have some measure of control over what happens to them in self-regarding matters. That they should have this control corrects the simple binary contrast of the 'basic view', whereby adult choices have determinative weight and the expressed preferences of children need not have any.

## Conclusion

In sum, the fact that children lack the capacity deemed essential for the giving or withholding of consent allows, even if it does not straightforwardly entail, that others can consent on their behalf. Parents are presumed to be the surrogate or proxy consenters for their children. But they have no such status simply in virtue of being parents. If they do so act, they should choose what they judge is best for a child. They should do so without it being granted that they are always the better judges of what is best.

Children cannot consent but their views on what they want in respect of those self-regarding matters for which the consent of adults must be sought do, nevertheless, count. They count not, or not principally or only, for instrumental reasons

[25] These matters are considered further in D. Archard and S. Uniacke, 'The Child's Right to a Voice', 531–34.

but because they are the views of the child about what happens to the child. How exactly they should be counted is a difficult matter. Nevertheless, count they should. Doing what is in the best interests of a child is important. Indeed, it should be at the heart of how we as adults treat children. However, promoting their best interests does not tell the whole story of what the child is owed. Hearing their voice is just as important.

# 6

# The Interaction of Children's Capacity Regimes and Parental and Judicial Powers: A 'Strictly' Legal View

SIR JONATHAN MONTGOMERY

IN THIS CHAPTER, I summarise the conception of children's rights to which the common law committed itself in the *Gillick* decision. I then consider the way in which some of the legal rights that are deployed to operationalise this conception are specified. In this, I draw on an understanding of the structure of legal rights that conceives them as constituted by correlative claims and obligations, and that stresses the importance of being precise about the nature of the rights in question.[1] I revisit earlier analysis in which I suggested we gain understanding from our recognition that patients' rights to control over their bodies are constituted by the combination of a claim-right not to be assaulted with a power to relieve doctors of their obligation to refrain from touching them.[2]

The legal protection of autonomy, rather than merely bodily integrity, requires us to understand not merely the nature of the rights that are deployed but also their combination. If autonomy can be understood in terms of the ownership of one's life, then we can build on jurisprudential analysis of the concept of 'ownership', which reminds us that it is constituted as a 'bundle' of rights and duties.[3] We can think about the legal concept of the 'autonomous patient' as shorthand for the possessor of a bundle of rights and obligations that constitute the desired legal status for the recipient of healthcare. I cannot elaborate the range of these rights here, but I aim to show that their value turns primarily on the nature and scope of the duties owed to patients by others. Further, the existence of these rights is not determined mainly by whether the patient is regarded as possessing legal capacity for decision-making.

[1] W. N. Hohfeld, *Fundamental Legal Conceptions* (New Haven, CT, Yale University Press, 1919).

[2] J. Montgomery, 'Children as Property?' *Modern Law Review*, 51 (1988), 323–42 at 332–3.

[3] T. Honore, *Making Law Bind* (Oxford, Oxford University Press, 1987), ch. 8.

*Proceedings of the British Academy*, **279**, 121–135, © Authors 2025.

Just as not all users of property hold the full incidents of ownership, many patients will not be entitled to, or be able to exercise, all the rights that we might ideally contemplate. This suggests that whether young people possess the legal status of having legal capacity to consent and (perhaps) veto treatment is of less significance than the wider obligations of those who deal with them. Examining these obligations also enables an assessment of how valuable young people are likely to find their legal rights to consent in actually pursuing the lives that they wish to lead.

## Capacity and the allocation of power

In *Gillick*, the House of Lords rejected a parent's claim that guidance published by the Department of Health and Social Care according to which doctors could sometimes give contraceptive treatment and advice to minors under the age of 16 was unlawful. The central ruling was that a young person with 'sufficient understanding and intelligence to enable him or her to understand fully what is proposed' could give a valid consent to the treatment and that when this was available no other consent was required to make the treatment lawful.[4] The House of Lords overturned the Court of Appeal's approach, which was based on the rights and obligations of adults rather than those of young patients. That analysis was that doctors who gave advice on contraception, contraceptive treatment, or abortion treatment, to a girl under 16 would 'infringe the legal rights of the parent or guardian' which included 'the right to control the manner in which and the place at which the child spends his or her time'.

The *Gillick* decision has been read by some as a vindication of children's rights and by others as a triumph for medicalisation. On the former view, the legal recognition that children can access health services without the knowledge and permission of their parents promotes and respects their autonomy.[5] Through the intervention of law, power is transferred from parents to children. Medical power is an incidental feature, but the assumption is that it is autonomy enhancing, since parental control is a more comprehensive intrusion into young people's autonomous lives than the discretion exercised by doctors on particular issues. From the latter perspective, the power shifts from law to medicine; parental power may be reduced, but children are not empowered, since they are at the mercy of doctors.[6] On both views, the extent to which the promise of *Gillick* to enhance children's rights will be realised is dependent on the actions of those around them.

Being able to act is not just a matter of competence to decide or something that just resides within the mind of the young person, as the phrasing of the *Gillick* test suggests. It depends on the rights and obligations that are placed on those around them.

[4] *Gillick v West Norfolk AHA* [1986]1 AC 112, 189.

[5] J. Eekelaar, 'The Emergence of Children's Rights', *Oxford Journal of Legal Studies*, 6 (1986), 161–82.

[6] J. Miola, *Medical Ethics and Medical Law: A Symbiotic Relationship* (Oxford, Hart, 2007), ch. 5.

We consider here the clinic, where clinicians and parents are the main players. The focus would be different in education, or work, or leisure activities. With this in mind, it can be seen that the test for *Gillick* competence is less of a step towards children's autonomy than it first appears. While children may be found competent, the degree of control this provides is limited because of the structure of legal rights and duties that make up the juridical construction of the position of patients.

From this perspective, the most significant element of the *Gillick* decision was the confirmation that parental rights were rooted in children's interests rather than family privacy.[7] Parental claims for non-interference by the state were justified by the presumption that their care was generally better than that offered by outsiders. The implication of this is that parental choices should be overridden when that presumption is rebutted; typically, upon the adjudication that decisions were not being made in the interests of the child. In general terms, this is where they place the child at significant risk of harm due to their failing to parent to a reasonable level (the child protection case).[8] In relation to specific issues, this is where the parental decision is found not to be in the 'best interests' of the child.[9] In all judicial contexts, the wishes and feelings of the child patient are important but not determinative.[10] Thus, the law privileges children's welfare rights over their autonomy when a conflict is perceived.[11]

## Rights and powers: why consent and refusal raise different legal issues

At law, consent permits treatment, but withholding it does not necessarily prevent it. First, there may be circumstances where consent is not a prerequisite for the legality of treatment. As a general principle where the physical intrusion is merely the sort of contact that is 'generally acceptable in the ordinary conduct of life', then it is considered to be so minimal as not to constitute a battery for which a justification is required.[12] The House of Lords has said that this is unlikely to include medical treatment,[13] but it may include elements of nursing care and perhaps elements of routine health surveillance.[14]

[7] J. Montgomery, 'Children as Property?'.

[8] See e.g. s 31 Children Act 1989.

[9] *Fixsler v Manchester University NHS Foundation Trust* [2021] EWCA Civ 1018.

[10] S 1(3)(a) Children Act 1989 and discussion below in the section 'Weak rights: the supervisory jurisdiction of the courts'.

[11] P. Alderson and J. Montgomery, *Health Care Choices: Making Decisions With Children* (London, Institute for Public Policy Research, 1996).

[12] *Collins v Wilcock* [1984] 1 WLR 1172 (DC) 1177 (Robert Goff LJ).

[13] *F v W Berkshire HA* [1989] 2 All ER 545, 564.

[14] R. Lavery, 'Routine Medical Treatment of Children', *Journal of Social Welfare Law*, 12 (1990), 375–84.

Second, consent is only one of the defences to the trespass action for unlawful contact. An alternative defence such as 'necessity' might be available. In *Gillick*, it was suggested that this might justify emergency treatment without contacting a person with parental responsibility. The scope of such a doctrine is uncertain, but it could, in principle, be invoked to support compulsory treatment (e.g. blood transfusions to save lives) obviating the need for consent.[15] The lower English courts flirted with this approach in relation to court-authorised caesarean sections until it was disapproved for that context by the Court of Appeal.[16] There is also some support for it in the jurisprudence of the European Court of Human Rights that rejects the claim that compulsory medical interventions can be regarded as inhuman and degrading under Article 3 of the Convention if circumstances make it of therapeutic necessity.[17]

Third, where a legally effective consent may be sought from another person, then no one consent-giver will have a veto. Consent is 'enabling' but not determinative. This was the point made by Lord Donaldson in *Re R* when he explained the 'concurrent consent' doctrine:

> A right of determination is wider than a right to consent. The parents can only have a right of determination if either the child has no right to consent, that is, is not a keyholder, or the parents hold a master key which could nullify the child's consent ... In a case in which the 'Gillick competent' child refuses treatment, but the parents consent, that consent enables treatment to be undertaken lawfully, but in no way determines that the child shall be so treated. In a case in which the positions are reversed, it is the child's consent which is the enabling factor and again the parents' refusal of consent is not determinative ... The failure or refusal of the 'Gillick competent' child is a very important factor in the doctor's decision whether or not to treat, but does not prevent the necessary consent being obtained from another competent source. [18]

[15] See *Re S* [1994] 2 FLR 416, 420 (although this was not part of the ruling in the case) and the discussion in P. Skegg, *Law, Ethics and Medicine* (Oxford, Oxford University Press, 1984), pp. 107–10. More recently, the existence of such 'emergency' powers has been accepted by Arbuthnot J, although its scope in cases where wishes were known was doubted by the Court of Appeal in *E v Northern Care Alliance NHS Foundation Trust; F v Somerset NHS Foundation Trust* [2021] EWCA 1888 [23]–[24].

[16] *Re MB* [1997] 2 FCR 541, *St George's Healthcare NHS Trust v S* [1998] 2 FCR 685.

[17] *Herczegfalvy v Austria* (1992) 15 EHRR 437; *Nevmerzhitsky v Ukraine* (2006) 43 EHRR 32; *Aggerholm v Denmark* (45439/18) [2020] ECHR 628; *YP v Russia* (2023) 76 EHRR 27. For analysis of the relevance for English law, see *NHS Trust v X (No 2)* [2021] EWHC 65 (Fam).

[18] *Re R* [1992] Fam 1, 23–4. In the later decision of *Re W* [1993] Fam 64, 78 he altered the metaphor, although it is not obvious that it is different in substance: 'On reflection I regret my use ... of the keyholder analogy, because keys can lock as well as unlock. I now prefer the analogy of the legal "flak jacket" which protects the doctor from claims by the litigious whether he acquires it from his patient who may be a minor over the age of 16, or a "*Gillick*-competent" child under that age or from another person having parental responsibilities which include a right to consent to treatment of the minor. Anyone who gives him a flak jacket (i.e. consent) may take it back, but the doctor only needs one and so long as he continues to have one he has the legal right to proceed.'

Refusal of consent will be determinative only if there is a single consent-giver, as is the case for adults. In those circumstances, the person with the power to give or withhold consent has a veto. The law provides control not through an assessment of the competence of the patient to understand what they are deciding but through the extent to which others have (or lack) legally effective powers.[19] This is a feature of the basic structure of child law. Concurrent consents are the norm in child cases because there will usually be more than one parent with legal authority, which can generally be exercised independently under s 2(7) of the Children Act 1989. This means that the validity of concurrent consent does not flow from a policy position on young people's autonomy rights but rather provides the context for it.

The giving of consent may also fail to be determinative in the sense that Lord Donaldson discusses. There may be obligations on other actors that constrain their discretion to offer the treatments that a patient chooses, for example, in legal limitations to the permissibility of abortions.[20] Mrs Gillick contended that there was such a constraint on family planning advice for those under 16 on the basis that it would constitute a criminal offence. This was firmly rejected by the House of Lords, although it had been accepted in the Court of Appeal.

Even the provision of legally permissible treatment may be discretionary. In different ways, these points show that capacity to give a valid consent is linked only indirectly to the legal right to control what happens to your body. The power to consent extends only to accepting or rejecting treatment that is offered. There may also be process limitations, such as obligatory court referrals for non-therapeutic sterilisation operations or cases with differences of medical opinion, that limit young patients' practical autonomy by making their choices vulnerable to judicial assessment that trumps their own.[21] Focus on the concurrent consent doctrine diverts attention from these other significant questions.

In the next sections of this chapter, I suggest three aspects of the law that should be the main focus of attention for those wishing to enhance young people's autonomy rights. First, that such rights based on competence are fragile because they are vulnerable to factual assessments driven more by prejudice than objective evaluation. This is something that affects both adults and children, but where prejudice may be more likely to affect the latter (along with other vulnerable populations). Second, that the status as a 'competent' decision-maker is of limited value in the absence of rights to secure the desired treatment (another thing that also affects both adults and children). Third, that the rights that the law appears to confer on

[19] Also, through the refusal to recognise a different type of legal power—that to control the patient. In the Court of Appeal in *Gillick*, Fox LJ thought this was among the rights that the law granted parents, but this was rejected by the House of Lords: *Gillick* 142H–143A, 145D–E. See further below in the section 'Limited rights: why the value of capacity may be low'.

[20] *Re X* [2014] EWHC 1871 (Fam) discussing the interaction of Gillick competence and the Abortion Act 1967. See also *R (AB) v Secretary of State for Health* [2017] UKSC 41 [94] on how the abortion legislation constrains patients' choices (Lady Hale).

[21] *Re B* [1987] 2 All ER 206; *A Teaching Hospitals NHS Trust v DV* [2021] EWHC 1037 (Fam).

competent young people are weakened by the supervisory jurisdiction of the courts. These issues are more significant for the scope of young people's autonomy than the law relating to consent.

## Fragile rights: the vulnerability of children to adults' assessment of capacity

The assessment of *Gillick* competence is said to be patient and decision specific. It operates on a binary basis. In relation to each decision, the child patient is either competent or incompetent. Once assessed, legal consequences flow automatically as to the legal validity of the child's consent. This apparent neatness obscures elements that make the application of the law much messier than this suggests. We have already considered the way in which concurrent consents complicate the matter. We will examine later how the views of children influence judicial decision-making, whether or not they are 'competent' under the *Gillick* test. In this section, we consider the fragility of legal rights that depend on factual assessment. The right to consent may appear to be a strong one at the level of doctrine, but if it is only available at the whim of those around you, it is easily destroyed.

There is ample evidence that those assessing competence make assumptions, perhaps even apply prejudices.[22] The following observation by Lord Templeman in *Gillick* perhaps says more about him than the young women who might contemplate seeking medical advice:

> I doubt whether a girl under the age of 16 is capable of a balanced judgment to embark on frequent, regular or casual sexual intercourse fortified by the illusion that medical science can protect her in mind and body and ignoring the danger of leaping from childhood to adulthood without the difficult formative transitional experiences of adolescence. There are many things which a girl under 16 needs to practise but sex is not one of them.[23]

The model of rational decision-making that dominates the capacity test, as explained in *Gillick*, means that patients' emotional responses can be used to justify declaring them incompetent.[24] Faith-based reasons have also been used to demonstrate lack of understanding. Hoping for a miracle has sometimes been taken as an indication of lack of *Gillick* competence and reliance on the support of faith leaders as evidence of undue influence compromising decisions.[25] These are

[22] See, for example, the empirical work of P. Alderson, *Children's Consent to Surgery* (Buckingham, Open University Press, 1993) and Alderson and Montgomery, *Health Care Choices*, pp. 10–14.

[23] [1986] 1 AC 112, 201C.

[24] See e.g. *Re M* [1999] 2 FLR 1097, 1100–1, discussed in D. Archard and M. Skivenes, 'Balancing a Child's Best Interests and a Child's Views', *International Journal of Children's Rights*, 17 (2009), 1–21.

[25] *Re T* [1992] 2 FLR 458, 473; *Re S* [1994] 2 FLR 1065. Discussed in J. Montgomery, 'Health Care Law for a Multi-Faith Society', in J. Murphy (ed.), *Ethnic Minorities, Their Families and the Law* (Oxford, Hart Publishing, 2000), pp. 161–79.

patterns of judicial practice rather than legal norms. In other cases, young people have been found *Gillick* competent despite their views being 'entrenched in line with his religious orthodoxy'.[26]

Nevertheless, recent litigation over puberty blockers suggests that in court the legal competence of young patients can still be highly dependent on the sympathy of judges for their choices. This can be seen in the litigation brought by Keira Bell, referred to in the judgments as Quincy Bell, against the Tavistock Clinic in relation to its approach to prescribing puberty blockers (PBs). As the case was brought by way of judicial review, there was no finding of fact on Keira Bell's competence.[27] However, the three judges in the Divisional Court felt able to conclude that it was:

> highly unlikely that a child aged 13 or under would ever be *Gillick* competent to give consent to being treated with PBs. In respect of children aged 14 and 15, we are also very doubtful that a child of this age could understand the long-term risks and consequences of treatment in such a way as to have sufficient understanding to give consent.[28]

The evidence on which this conclusion was reached is not explained. Indeed, the court noted that there were a number of statements from patients, including two aged 12 and 13 when they commenced PBs, who were strongly supportive of their treatment.[29]

On appeal it became apparent that the guidance that the Divisional Court offered was not based on submission by counsel.[30] The Court of Appeal considered that some of the factual findings were 'on the basis of impression'.[31] It suggested that the basis of the Divisional Court's conclusion on the ages at which competence was likely was based on evidence from a single professor who was quoted as referring to all those under 18 (and therefore giving evidence that was inconsistent with the court's findings).[32] The Court of Appeal commented on the failure to follow due process in relation to this material: 'none of it complied with the rules regarding expert evidence and a good deal of it is argumentative and adversarial'.[33] In effect, they suggested, the ruling 'would require the clinicians to suspend or at least to temper their clinical judgement and defer to what amounts to the clinical judgement of the court on which key features should inform an assessment of Gillick competence'.[34]

[26] *NHS Trust v CX* [2019] EWHC 3033 (Fam) [19]. See also *DV* [2021] EWHC 1037 (Fam).

[27] The defendants submitted that she was *Gillick* competent in relation to her decision to take PBs and that her decision was made after at least 10 consultations on the basis of the 'fullest possible information' *Bell v Tavistock and Portman NHS Foundation Trust* [2020] EWHC 3274 (Admin) [84].

[28] *Bell v Tavistock* (HC) [2020] EWHC 3274 (Admin) [145].

[29] *Bell v Tavistock* (HC) [84]–[88].

[30] *Bell v Tavistock* (HC); *Bell v Tavistock and Portman NHS Foundation Trust* [2021] EWCA Civ 1363 [11].

[31] *Bell v Tavistock* (CA) [33].

[32] *Bell v Tavistock* (CA) [37], noting paras [45]–[46] of the lower court's judgment.

[33] *Bell v Tavistock* (CA) [38].

[34] *Bell v Tavistock* (CA) [75].

In the judgment of the Court of Appeal, 'the court was not in a position to generalise about the capability of persons of different ages to understand what is necessary for them to be competent to consent to the administration of puberty blockers'.[35] To do so was contrary to the ruling in *Gillick* that it was for doctors not judges to decide on the capacity of particular patients under the age of 16 to consent to treatment.[36] This interpretation of *Gillick*, which is consistent with the explicit provision in Scots law,[37] supports the argument that the decision constitutes a medicalisation of legal rights. The unpredictability of judicial capacity assessments suggests that such medicalisation may be at least as protective of capacity rights as a more legalistic approach. However, this all shows little about what practical benefits young people gain if they are found to be competent. This is the concern of the next section.

## Limited rights: why the value of capacity may be low

The *value* of being found *Gillick* competent to young people wishing to shape their own lives depends mainly on the adequacy of the range of options that are available to them. Joseph Raz suggests that when people have choices within only a very limited range, they cannot be said to be autonomous.[38] This is why the duty of care in negligence requires doctors to explain reasonable alternatives to their proposed treatments.[39] *Gillick* competence determines *whether* a young person's decision 'counts' in law, but it does not explain *how* it counts.

This distinction can be demonstrated by the five points made by Lord Fraser as a summary of the law at the end of his speech in *Gillick*, which were adopted by the Department of Health and Social Services as guidance to the medical profession on when they might give family planning advice and treatment to girls under the age of 16. Only the first relates to capacity: 'that the girl (although under 16 years of age) will understand his advice'. The second relates to a social expectation: 'that he cannot persuade her to inform her parents or to allow him to inform the parents that she is seeking contraceptive advice'. This is unlikely to be amenable to legal enforcement, although it might fall within professional discipline. However, it indicates that the care offered to young women was expected by the judge to involve a degree of pressure to share with their parents the fact that they were engaged in sexual activities. This dilution of confidentiality might constitute a psychological

[35] *Bell v Tavistock* (CA) [85].

[36] *Bell v Tavistock* (CA) [76], [87], [94].

[37] Age of Legal Capacity (Scotland) Act 1991, s 2(4).

[38] J. Raz, *The Morality of Freedom* (Oxford, Oxford University Press, 1986), ch. 14, graphically illustrated by the examples of 'man in pit' (who can choose only when to eat and sleep) and the 'hounded woman' (who deploys her stamina, her ingenuity, and her willpower to a single task—escaping the carnivorous beast who hunts her).

[39] *Montgomery v Lanarkshire Health Board* [2015] UKSC 11, *McCulloch v Forth Valley Health Board* [2023] UKSC 26.

barrier to young people seeking medical advice and, in practice, have a significant impact on access to services.

Consequently, the implications of the *Gillick* decision for patient confidentiality were the subject of early academic commentary, which exposed the complexity of the idea of autonomy that the House of Lords had employed. Some argued that where child patients were found incompetent, it would be appropriate to inform parents of consultations.[40] Others suggested that privacy rights were acquired when children understood the principle of confidentiality, so that a patient could be *Gillick* incompetent in relation to one or more decisions but competent to assert their legal entitlement to confidentiality.[41] Official guidance supported the latter view,[42] which was upheld when challenged in the judicial review brought by Susan Axon.[43]

For the purpose of the argument being offered in this section, the crucial findings of Silber J in *Axon* were that parents were neither entitled to assert against doctors a right to be consulted, nor a right to be informed, about treatment that their children were seeking. In *Gillick*, the House of Lords had rejected an even stronger parental rights claim (which the Court of Appeal had upheld) that parents could assert a claim to control the child, with which doctors would be interfering.[44] These rulings show that the protection of children's autonomy comes at least as much from the way in which the rights of others are defined (and limited) as from judgments about children's competence. In *Gillick*, parents' proprietary claims over the persons of their children were rejected. In *Axon*, parents were denied rights to participation in decisions and to information about their children in circumstances when those rights would trump those children's privacy rights. The value to children of the right to consent is enhanced considerably by the rejection of overbearing parental power.

It would be legally coherent to find that a child was *Gillick* competent, so that their decisions could provide a 'flak jacket' to doctors against suits for battery but simultaneously accept a parental right to know. However, it would reduce the value to young patients of being found competent. It can even be argued that accepting a parental right of control enforceable against doctors concurrently with the validity of child consent would be a legal mechanism to ensure shared decision-making between children, parents, and health professionals. This would perhaps be poor policy for standard treatments, where children's independence might be strongly promoted, but it would broadly match the policy pursued by the Tavistock Clinic. They were clear that PBs should be prescribed only when all parties are agreed,

[40] I. Kennedy, *Treat Me Right* (Oxford, Oxford University Press, 1988), pp. 111–17.

[41] J. Montgomery, 'Confidentiality and the Immature Minor', *Family Law*, 101 (1987), 101–4.

[42] Department of Health 'Best Practice Guidance for Doctors and other Health Professionals on the Provision of Advice and Treatment to Young People under 16 on Contraception, Sexual and Reproductive Health', 2004 gateway reference No. 3382.

[43] *R (Axon) v Secretary of State for Health* [2006] EWHC 37 (Admin).

[44] *Gillick* [1986] 1 AC 112. See Lord Fraser at 171 rejecting the positions of Parker LJ at 124 and 138 and Fox LJ at 143. For a fuller analysis, see J. Montgomery, 'Children as Property?', 333–6.

giving an effective veto to parents, clinicians, and the patient.[45] The implementation of such a shared decision-making structure could be achieved either by recognising a right of parental control (as rejected in *Gillick*) or by a doctrine that does not permit concurrent consents to be exercised unilaterally (as with male circumcision).[46] In neither approach would *Gillick* competence be a determinative factor.

The value of the right to consent can also be reduced by the way in which the legal obligations of clinicians are defined and enforced. The final three points of guidance offered by Lord Fraser in *Gillick* relate to best interest decision-making. They were, and the gendering is probably significant, that:

> (3) that she is very likely to begin or to continue having sexual intercourse with or without contraceptive treatment; (4) that unless she receives contraceptive advice or treatment her physical or mental health or both are likely to suffer; (5) that her best interests require him to give her contraceptive advice, treatment or both without the parental consent.[47]

These points of guidance would seem to be legally enforceable only through negligence claims,[48] and only insofar as doctors might be judged as having stepped outside responsible professional practice if they ignore them. What does the most to determine the capability of young women to control their pregnancy risk in practice is not the test for capacity but these latter guidance points. These will constrain the freedoms even of those judged to be *Gillick* competent, demonstrating how this element of autonomous capability is independent of the recognition of the validity of consents.

This point is reinforced by the lack of an enforceable right in English law to specific treatments. The leading case is *R (Burke) v GMC* in which the Court of Appeal rejected the suggestion that patients are legally entitled to treatments of their choosing and stated that 'the right to choose is no more than a reflection of the fact that it is the doctor's duty to provide a treatment that he considers to be in the interests of the patient and that the patient is prepared to accept'.[49] The constraining factor is the way in which the duty to treat is defined. This is usually by reference to responsible medical practice, and the courts have proved reluctant to require clinicians to provide treatment that they regard as clinically inappropriate.[50]

[45] *AB v CD* [2021] EWHC 741 (Fam).

[46] *Re J (A Minor) (Prohibited Steps Order: Circumcision)* [2000] 1 FLR 571.

[47] *Gillick* [1986] 1 AC 112, 174D–E.

[48] The third point might be thought to have legal significance as a defence to the criminal offence of aiding and abetting unlawful sexual intercourse on the basis that it suggests that lawful medical care might be limited to circumstances in which it did not, in fact, encourage the offence, see Lord Scarman 191A–B. Lord Brandon explained why such an argument was not acceptable at 197D–F. The majority view was that 'the bona fide exercise … of clinical judgment must be complete negation of the guilty mind which is an essential ingredient of aiding and abetting the commission of unlawful sexual intercourse' Lord Scarman at 190G (see also Lord Fraser 174H–175A, Lord Bridge 194E–H). Lord Fraser himself places the point in the section of his speech dealing with parents' rights and duties not that of examining criminal liability.

[49] *R (Burke) v General Medical Council* [2005] EWCA Civ 1003, [51].

[50] *Airedale NHS Trust v Bland* [1993] 1 FLR 1026, *Aintree University Hospitals NHS Foundation Trust v James* [2013] UKSC 67.

This section has shown how the value to young people of 'passing' the test for *Gillick* competence may, in fact, be limited and that it is necessary to examine the legal obligations and rights of others in order to assess the extent to which the law promotes their autonomy. There is an additional suggestion in *Gillick* that legal rules might have a limited contribution to make. Lord Scarman observed that:

> The truth may well be that the rights of parents and children in this sensitive area are better protected by the professional standards of the medical profession than by 'a priori' legal lines of division between capacity and lack of capacity to consent since any such general dividing line is sure to produce in some cases injustice, hardship, and injury to health.[51]

His words raise two concerns about the role of law. The first is that medical ethics rather than legal rules might provide better protection for the rights in question.[52] The second is that a rules-based approach might lead to injustice in individual cases and that a more discretionary approach might be more attractive; one that focused on the facts of the case rather than the application of abstract rules.[53] This has been taken up by the courts in their oversight role of individual disputes and as the next section shows, *Gillick* competence does not play a significant role in such cases.

## Weak rights: the supervisory jurisdiction of the courts

I turn now to consider cases where the courts determine specific disputes over the healthcare of young people. In this context the autonomy rights that the law grants turn out to be weak ones. The choices that young people make can be overridden by judges, whose statutory obligation is to determine questions according to the principle that 'the child's welfare shall be … the paramount consideration'. The 'ascertainable wishes and feelings of the child' are explicitly identified as a relevant consideration, but only as one of a number of other factors, and they are to be considered 'in the light of [the child's] age and understanding'.[54] In the 1990s, the Court of Appeal held that the courts have jurisdiction to override the decisions of a *Gillick* competent child,[55] even over the age of 16 when a statutory presumption

[51] *Gillick* [1986] 1 AC 112, 191C–D.

[52] For discussion, see J. Miola, *Medical Ethics and Medical Law: A Symbiotic Relationship* (Oxford, Hart, 2007); C. Foster and J. Miola, 'Who's in Charge? The Relationship Between Medical Law, Medical Ethics and Medical Morality', *Medical Law Review*, 23 (2015), 505–30; J. Montgomery, 'Law and the Demoralisation of Medicine', *Legal Studies*, 26 (2006), 185–210.

[53] For discussion of this resistance to rules in the context of withdrawal of treatment cases during the 1990s, see J. Montgomery, 'Time for a Paradigm Shift? Medical Law in Transition', *Current Legal Problems*, 53 (2000), 363–408 at 402–5.

[54] Children Act 1989, s 1. For those between 16 and 18, see *NHS Trust v X (No 2)* [2021] EWHC 65 (Fam) holding that the same test applies under the inherent jurisdiction even though the case was considered under the High Court's inherent jurisdiction not the Children Act 1989.

[55] *Re R (A Minor)(Wardship: Consent to Treatment)* [1992] Fam 11.

of competence applies.[56] While it can be argued that this doctrine was not central to the reasoning in these rulings, it is now treated as established law. The Court of Appeal has recently upheld two High Court judgments that considered but overrode the decisions of two Jehovah's Witnesses, aged 16 and 17 respectively, to refuse blood transfusions.[57]

The formal weakness of the right to make decisions would matter less if judicial reasoning were in practice sympathetic to the autonomy of young people, even when their decisions are not considered ideal. Analysis of this issue is necessarily complicated by the fact-specific nature of the court rulings and the fact that only the most difficult cases will be brought before a judge. However, there are reasons to think that young people's autonomy is valued little for its own sake. Instead, the views expressed by children are deployed to inform a welfare decision that aims to reflect the value system considered to be implicit in the law rather than that of the young person. The judge is expected to make an 'objective' assessment in which the young person's views are significant but not determinative.[58] This is seen most clearly in cases which turn on the weight of the presumption in favour of life when it appears that the patient values her life differently to the adults who bring the matter to court. These cases demonstrate the weakness of the autonomy rights conferred by the law and the irrelevance of the test for competence.

*Plymouth Hospitals NHS Trust v YZ* proceeds without determining *Gillick* competence at all. A girl aged 14 had been taken to the Emergency Department after saying that she had taken an overdose, probably including paracetamol. Blood testing was required to establish the risks, which might have been fatal. The girl would initially agree to this but then withdraw her consent at the last minute. The hospital sought a ruling that she was not *Gillick* competent and that treatment could be given. The judge found that the evidence on *Gillick* competence was equivocal but did not resolve the issue. Instead, he permitted the treatment on a 'best interest' test.[59] There was, by implication, no need to determine whether the girl's decisions were autonomous. More commonly, judges acknowledge the child patient's views but override them. Thus, in a later case of paracetamol overdose where the young woman of 16 had been found by the treating clinicians to be *Gillick* competent, MacDonald J said 'Whilst it would appear that D's wishes are clearly not to have treatment, I am satisfied that those wishes are antithetic to her best interests in circumstances where the treatment proposed is designed to prevent damage to D's

[56] *Re W (A Minor) (Medical Treatment: Court's Jurisdiction)* [1993] Fam 64.

[57] *E v Northern Care Alliance NHSFT* [2021] EWCA Civ 1888. In neither case was the transfusion required, but it had been authorised if it proved necessary. See also *An NHS Trust v D* [2021] EWHC 2676 (Fam); *NHS Trust v X (No 2)* [2021] EWHC 65 (Fam) [59]-[61]; *CX* [2019] EWHC 3033 (Fam); *University Hospitals Plymouth NHS Trust v B (A Minor)* [2019] EWHC 1670 (Fam); *Plymouth Hospitals NHS Trust v YZ* [2017] EWHC 2211 (Fam); *Re P (A Child)* [2014] EWHC 1650 (Fam).

[58] *NHS Trust v X (No 2)* [2021] EWHC 65 (Fam).

[59] *YZ* [2017] EWHC 2211 (Fam). The case was heard out-of-hours by email and telephone due to the urgency.

liver and, in the extreme, save her life.'[60] It is very difficult to see what weight, if any, was placed on her views, even though they were clear and she had been found to be *Gillick* competent.

Court decisions from the 1990s on the choices made by young Jehovah's Witnesses demonstrated the judges' reluctance to accept religious choices that do not prolong children's lives.[61] More recent challenges on human rights grounds have also been unsuccessful. In two decisions involving successive treatments of a 15-year-old baptised Jehovah's Witness identified as *X*, Gwynneth Knowles J and Munby J authorised the giving of a blood transfusion against the young woman's wishes.[62] Munby J did list the case for a further full hearing to consider whether 'following the enactment of the Human Rights Act 1998 and other developments in the law, the consent to or refusal of medical treatment by a capacitous/*Gillick* competent minor under the age of 18 should be determinative'. However, after reviewing the arguments, he rejected the suggestion that human rights law required the views of a *Gillick* competent person to determine the outcome and upheld the jurisdiction of the courts to make welfare assessments, taking the patient's views into account.[63]

This is not to say that the wishes of young Jehovah's Witnesses never prevail. In *A Teaching Hospitals NHS Trust v DV*, the court approved a declaration that surgery could go ahead without the patient needing to worry about a transfusion. The declaration stated that it was lawful 'that the treating clinicians will not take steps towards providing him with a transfusion of whole blood, be that red cells, white cells, plasma and platelets, against his wishes'.[64] The court noted that DV had thought about the issues carefully, and his wishes were founded in deeply held core religious values. His parents and the treating clinicians all considered him to be *Gillick* competent and that it would be damaging to his welfare to go against his beliefs. Yet, it was the threat to welfare, rather than respect for autonomy, that determined the outcome. This was made explicit in *Re J (Blood Transfusion: Older Child: Jehovah's Witnesses)* where it was held that it was 'in J's best interests for his own decision to refuse the administration of blood or blood products in surgery to prevail' and the court refused permission for their administration on that welfarist basis.[65]

Occasionally, the courts have suggested that there might be circumstances where it would be wrong to override the choices that young people make. Concerning abortions, Munby J has said that he found it:

> hard to conceive of any case where such a drastic form of order – such an immensely invasive procedure – could be appropriate in the case of a mother who does not want

[60] *NHS Trust v D* [2021] EWHC 2676 (Fam).

[61] *Re L* [1998] 2 FLR 810; Re S [1994] 2 FLR 1065; *Re E* [1993] 1 FLR 386. Discussed in Montgomery, 'Health Care Law for a Multi-Faith Society'.

[62] *Barking, Havering and Redbridge University Hospitals NHS Trust v X (A Child)* [2020] EWHC 1630 (Fam); *Re X* [2020] EWHC 3003 (Fam).

[63] *NHS Trust v X* (No 2) [2020] EWHC 65 (Fam) [10].

[64] [2021] EWHC 1037 (Fam) [4].

[65] [2024] EWHC 1034 (Fam).

> a termination, unless there was powerful evidence that allowing the pregnancy to continue would put the mother's life or long-term health at very grave risk. Conversely, it would be a very strong thing indeed, if the mother wants a termination, to require her to continue with an unwanted pregnancy even though the conditions in s 1 of the 1967 Act are satisfied.[66]

Note that this conclusion was determined by the judge's assessment of the likely significance of the procedure and was independent of the question of capacity to decide as judged by the test for *Gillick* competence. In the event, the girl decided to accept a termination, which therefore proceeded on the basis of her consent, so the discussion of proceeding without consent did not need to be resolved.

It seems clear therefore that, despite recent challenges from the Jehovah's Witness community, it remains established law that the courts are not bound to accept the decision of a *Gillick* competent child as to whether proposed treatment is in their interests, as the 'paramount consideration' under the Children Act 1989, s 1. Thus, the rights that are accrued when people reach such competence prove weak in the face of judicial power to make independent evaluations of what treatment should be permitted.

## Conclusion

The analysis has shown that the role played by *Gillick* competence is not particularly significant in protecting young people's autonomy in court. Judges' perceptions of welfare routinely trump the values of patients. We have also seen that being assessed as competent does not give young patients the power to determine what treatment is given by health professionals in the clinic.

It is also clear that young people are vulnerable to the way competency assessments are made. This task has been delegated to clinicians. Some regard this as undermining legal regulation,[67] but when the possibility of bias in judicial evaluations is taken into account it may seem acceptable as a lesser risk to young people that their views will not be treated with respect. We have seen that such delegation has been approved by the Court of Appeal as the proper interpretation of *Gillick* and also by the Scottish Legislature.[68]

The *Gillick* decision demonstrated an understanding of parents' rights that is based on the interests of children. It suggested that there was a connection between

[66] *Re X* [2014] EWHC 1871 (Fam) [9]–[10], see also [12].

[67] J. Miola, 'Medical Law and Medical Ethics: Complementary or Corrosive?', *Medical Law International*, 6 (2004), 251–74.

[68] *Bell v Tavistock* (CA) [76], [87], [94]; Age of Legal Capacity (Scotland) Act 1991, s 2(4).

the test for capacity and promoting autonomy. However, if we want to translate strong children's autonomy rights into the law, then the priority is not to align philosophical and legal concepts of decision-making capacity but to create the bundle of duties in others that better correspond to the substance of the choices we believe that young people should be entitled to make. Such a bundle of rights, powers and duties is the legal form that self-ownership of young lives needs to take.

# 7

# A Future-Orientated View of Autonomy

EMMA CAVE*

THE FUNDAMENTAL QUESTION at the heart of this chapter is: how ought we to reconcile the obligation to respect the child's competent choices to consent to and/or refuse treatment and the obligation to promote their best interests? By a child here I mean an individual under 16 years of age. I focus on the circumstances in which in England and Wales a child's decision will not be determinative notwithstanding a finding that they satisfy the test for competence set out in *Gillick v West Norfolk and Wisbech Health Authority (Gillick)*,[1] because the decision is considered by others to be inimical to the child's best interests. In such cases, as we shall see, though the child's decision is not determinative, it is given weight. This right is protected by article 12 of the UN Convention on the Rights of the Child, which requires that a 'child who is capable of forming his or her own views' has 'the right to express those views freely in all matters affecting the child, the views of the child being given due weight in accordance with the age and maturity of the child'.

I draw upon two recent English judicial decisions in particular: *Re X (A Child) (No 2)* (*X*)[2], where Sir James Munby confirmed that a competent child's treatment refusal might be overridden by the court if prolonging life is considered to be in the child's best interests, and *Bell v The Tavistock and Portman NHS Foundation Trust* (*Bell*)[3], which is a judicial review of a policy on the treatment of children with gender dysphoria. *X* reiterated the power of the court to protect the lives of competent children, while the Court of Appeal in *Bell* rescued *Gillick* from treatment-specific restrictions imposed by the Divisional Court and reasserted the clinician's role in assessing competence.

* Emma Cave was a member of the Advisory Forum to the Independent review of gender identity services for children and young people. Views expressed in this article are solely the author's and do not seek to reflect or represent the views of the Review or the Advisory Forum.

[1] [1986] AC 112 (HL).

[2] [2021] EWHC 65 (Fam).

[3] [2020] EWHC 3274 (Admin); [2021] EWCA Civ 1363.

*Proceedings of the British Academy*, **279**, 136–152, © Authors 2025.

The Court of Appeal in *Bell* asserted that treatment refusal cases like *X* are 'quite different' to the judicial review of policies on child consent and declined to make comparisons between the two.[4] Nevertheless, this chapter will suggest a strong connection between the cases insofar as both recognise the qualified nature of competent decisions made by children, one by virtue of a judicial power to override competent decisions and the other by sanctioning a policy requirement of dual consent from both the competent child and parent.[5] The latter has been given little attention in the literature. In both instances, notwithstanding the child's decision being *Gillick* competent, the child is not permitted to consent independently.

Children's competent views can also be rendered non-determinative by the medical application of the flexible threshold for competence set out in *Gillick* and through legislative age-centred controls. Together, these four methods of qualifying the independent value given to children's competent views demonstrate a prioritisation of children's future autonomy over their current autonomy. As Nolan LJ said in *Re W*: '[T]he present state of the law is that an individual who has reached the age of 18 is free to do with his life what he wishes, but it is the duty of the court to ensure so far as it can that children survive to attain that age.'[6]

This chapter considers the existing and novel legal mechanisms used in England and Wales to achieve this goal and turns in the final section to their normative implications.

## Current and future autonomy

In 1986, John Eekelaar argued that the immediate decisions of children might be overridden where a failure to do so would prevent them from developing into functionally autonomous agents. Eekelaar set out a hierarchy of children's basic, developmental and autonomy rights so that autonomy interests take precedence only when the basic and developmental interests are not harmed as a consequence.[7] Similarly, Michael Freeman argued that children should be protected from their own choices where complying with them would remove the opportunity 'to mature to a rationally autonomous adulthood … capable of deciding on [their] own system of ends as free and rational beings'.[8]

In *Gillick*,[9] Mrs Gillick successfully argued in the Court of Appeal that she had a right to veto contraceptive treatment being given to her daughter. Parental

[4] [2021] EWCA Civ 1363 [82].

[5] 'Parent' is used as a shorthand for person with parental responsibility within the meaning of the Children Act 1989, s 3.

[6] *Re W (A Minor) (Medical Treatment: Courts Jurisdiction)* [1993] Fam 64, 94.

[7] J Eekelaar, 'The Emergence of Children's Rights', *Oxford Journal of Legal Studies*, 6 (1986), 161–82 at 161, 170–1.

[8] M. D. A. Freeman, *The Rights and Wrongs of Children* (Cambridge, Cambridge University Press, 1983), p. 57.

[9] [1986] AC 112 (HL).

consent was needed not because the child lacked the ability to consent but because the parent had the power to make the decision. Eekelaar argued that this decision 'effectively annihilates any scope for the legal recognition of autonomy interests in children'.[10] The House of Lords in a three:two decision came to a different conclusion, but the judges in the majority differed in their reasoning. For Lord Scarman, once a child has sufficient understanding and maturity, the power of parents 'yields' to the child's autonomy rights. He said: '… as a matter of law the parental right to determine whether or not their minor child below the age of 16 will have medical treatment terminates if and when the child achieved a sufficient understanding and intelligence to enable him or her to understand fully what is proposed'.[11]

Eekelaar argued that the implication for competent children is that the question 'can no longer be: what is in the best interest of the child? It must be, has the child capacity to make his own decisions'.[12] Lord Fraser was more reticent and focussed on the coincidence of the decision made by the child and their best interests. Lord Bridge agreed with both Lord Scarman and Lord Fraser. The resulting picture is confusing. There is support for children making their own decisions where they have the requisite autonomy but also emphasis on limiting the options available to the child to those that are welfare-enhancing.

For Eekelaar, squaring autonomy and basic/developmental interests relies on a robust application of the test for capacity: 'This recognition of the autonomy interests of children can be reconciled with their basic and developmental interests only through the empirical application of the concept of the acquisition of full capacity.'[13]

A competency test was set out in *Gillick* but was and remains vague.[14] Even if it was sufficiently robust to recognise autonomous decisions, many would reject the argument that children should be given 'that most dangerous but most precious of rights: the right to make their own mistakes'.[15] Section 1(1) of the Children Act 1989 makes the child's welfare the court's paramount consideration in cases involving the upbringing of the child and clinical professional guidance makes the child's best interests the overarching guiding principle in medical decision-making.[16] The courts have recognised that in matters relating to the upbringing of the child, acting in the child's best interests will sometimes require that their competent decision is vetoed.[17] So while adults with capacity can make a decision that is contrary to their best interests, even if it will result in their death,[18] some decisions made by competent children can be overridden in their best interests.

[10] Eekelaar, 'The Emergence of Children's Rights', 180.
[11] [1986] AC 112, 188. Cited in *Re D (A Child)* [2019] UKSC 42 [23] (Lady Hale).
[12] Eekelaar, 'The Emergence of Children's Rights', 181.
[13] Eekelaar, 'The Emergence of Children's Rights', 181.
[14] E. Cave, 'Goodbye Gillick? Identifying and Resolving Problems with the Concept of Child Competence', *Legal Studies*, 34 (2014), 103–22
[15] Eekelaar, 'The Emergence of Children's Rights', 182.
[16] General Medical Council, *0–18 years: Guidance for all Doctors* (2007, updated 2018).
[17] *Re R (A Minor) (Wardship: Consent to Treatment)* [1992] Fam 11; *X* [2021] EWHC 65 (Fam).
[18] *Ms B v An NHS Hospital Trust* [2002] EWHC 429 (Fam).

In 1994, Eekelaar argued that the best interests test accommodates 'dynamic self-determinism' that was intended to incorporate basic, developmental and autonomy interests to ensure that by adulthood the person is capable of making autonomous choices.[19] It allows the child, in suitable cases, to determine what their own best interests are. On this model, however, self-determinism can be disapplied, even in relation to a competent decision, if the decision is contrary to the child's physical or mental self-interest:

> The rationale for such a restriction is that the *purpose* of dynamic self-determinism is to bring a child to the threshold of adulthood with the maximum opportunities to form and pursue life-goals which reflect as closely as possible an autonomous choice. Life and, on the whole, health are essential preconditions for the exercise of such choice.[20]

Eekelaar found a way to balance the protection of autonomy—by reference to article 12(1) of the UN Convention on the Rights of the Child—and the 'primary consideration' of the child's best interests under article 3—that mitigated the danger that paternalism will minimise or ignore the view of the child in a manner that is incompatible with their rights.[21]

Joel Feinberg's earlier work also recognises the importance of ensuring that children are protected to an extent that allows them to develop their potential.[22] Feinberg distinguishes rights held by autonomous adults, held by both adults and children, and held by children alone. The latter category includes 'rights-in-trust' that can be breached by not holding future options open until the child 'is a fully formed self-determining adult capable of deciding among them'.[23] It is not clear that legal competence would of itself be sufficient to protect the child's right 'to reach maturity with as many open options, opportunities, and advantages as possible'.[24] Dena Davis has applied the concept of the open future in the field of reproduction. She argues:

> These rights [i.e. autonomy rights] can be violated by adults now, in ways that cut off the possibility that the child, when it achieves adulthood, can exercise them. A striking example is the right to reproduce. A young child cannot physically exercise that right, and a teenager might lack the legal and moral grounds on which to assert such a right. But clearly the child, when he or she attains adulthood, will have that right, and therefore the child now has the right not to be sterilized, so that the child may exercise that right in the future.[25]

[19] J. Eekelaar, 'The Interests of the Child and the Child's Wishes: The Role of Dynamic Self-Determinism', *International Journal of Law, Policy and the Family*, 8 (1994), 42–61.

[20] Eekelaar, 'The Interests of the Child', 53.

[21] Eekelaar, 'The Interests of the Child', 221–35.

[22] J. Feinberg, 'The Child's Right to an Open Future', in W. Aiken and H. LaFollette (eds), *Whose Child?* (Totowa, NJ, Rowman & Littlefield, 1980), 124–53.

[23] Feinberg, 'The Child's Right', 125.

[24] Feinberg, 'The Child's Right', 130.

[25] D. Davis, 'Genetic Dilemmas and the Child's Right to an Open Future', *Hastings Center Report*, 27 (1997), 7–15.

There are thus two basic models that might dictate the relationship between a child's competent choice and a determination of the outcome on the basis of the principle of best interests. In one, the child's competent choice is determinative at which point their best interests are not for others to determine. Their choice is overridden only where they currently lack the requisite autonomy to decide because they have not reached the legal threshold of competence. This approach appeals to will (or choice) theorists,[26] who argue that the function of rights is to secure an agent's ability to choose between options. On this account, having a right means that the rights holder can control the performance of a duty. Where children are not autonomous agents, will theorists might consider that parents or others can make decisions on the child's behalf, as their representatives.[27]

Alternatively, the child's current autonomous choices are given weight but might be vetoed if the choice would cause them grave harm in favour of them reaching adulthood and being able to exercise choices at that point. This model appeals to interest (or benefit) theorists who claim that rights protect the individual's significant interests, including their welfare interests. For interest theorists,[28] having a right means the rights holder benefits from the performance of an enforced duty designed to protect their interests. It will become apparent in the next sections describing four mechanisms currently in operation to limit the determinative nature of children's competent decisions that the interest theory better describes the law relating to the medical treatment of children.

## Legislative age-centred controls

How children's views are considered in treatment decisions about them is strongly influenced by the law. An obvious way this might be achieved is through legislation imposing age-related restrictions on the medical procedures that children can undergo. For example, the Human Tissue Act 2004 defines children as those under 18 and sets out special requirements for them to be able to donate tissue and organs. Another example is the Botulinum Toxin and Cosmetic Fillers (Children) Act 2021, which makes it a criminal offence in England to administer cosmetic fillers and botulinum toxin for under-18-year-olds or to make arrangements for or book appointments to provide them, unless they are approved by a doctor. The basis of the Act is that under-18-year-olds lack the maturity to give valid consent to the procedures in the absence of a medical or psychological assessment. There are anomalies in the protections afforded to minors in that 16- and 17-year-olds are

[26] Notably H. L. A. Hart, *Essays on Bentham* (Oxford, Clarendon Press, 1982), 168.

[27] David Archard, 'Children, Adults, Best Interests and Rights', *Medical Law International*, 13 (2013), 55–74.

[28] Notably J. Raz, *The Morality of Freedom* (Oxford, Oxford University Press, 1998), pp. 80–90; J. Raz, 'Legal Rights', *Oxford Journal of Legal Studies*, 4 (1984), 1–21.

sometimes incorporated within the definition of 'child' and sometimes afforded privileges normally applied to adults. Section 8 of the Family Law Reform Act 1969 allows (*pro tanto*) persons of 16 and 17 to consent to medical treatment on the same footing as adults and the Mental Capacity Act 2005 assumes they have capacity. The Medicines for Human Use (Clinical Trials) Regulations 2004 sets out the consent requirements for clinical trials of 'Investigational Medicinal Products'. The Regulations require the consent of a parent or someone with parental responsibility and the involvement of children under the age of 16 in the decision-making process wherever possible.

Statute in England and Wales does not operate a one size fits all approach to minors, but the point pertinent to this chapter is that legislation can and does impose additional requirements and safeguards to protect children under the age of 16, even if they are assessed on the common law *Gillick* test as competent to provide consent to the medical procedure in question.[29]

## Judicial powers of override

The landmark 1986 decision of *Gillick* set out a threshold approach in relation to children under the age of 16, whereby *Gillick* competent children's views would potentially have determinative value once they reach a threshold: 'a minor's capacity to make his or her own decision depends upon the minor having sufficient understanding and intelligence to make the decision'.[30]

At this point, according to Lord Scarman, the rights of parents to decide 'yields to the child's right to make his own decisions'.[31] The court, too, might recognise a child's competent decision as authoritative, even if it is contrary to the child's best interests. In *An NHS Trust v A, B, C*, for example, a Trust sought a declaration that either 13-year-old A was competent to consent to termination of pregnancy, or was incompetent in which case termination was in her best interests. Mostyn J said:

> It is implicit in [*Gillick*] that provided the child, under the age of 16, has sufficient understanding and intelligence, she can then be lawfully prescribed with contraception even if the result of that would lead her to take steps which are wholly contrary to her best interests. So, the question of best interests does not really inform the primary decision I have to make which is whether she has the necessary capacity.[32]

There are, however, important judicial limitations imposed on the competent child's right to make a determinative choice. The court in *Re R* recognised parental and judicial powers to veto children's competent decisions in order to protect

29 [1986] AC 112.
30 *Gillick* [1986] AC 112, 188B (Lord Scarman).
31 *Gillick* [1986] AC 112, 186.
32 [2014] EWHC 1445 (Fam).

their best interests, at least where the child's decision poses a serious threat to their life or health.[33] In *AB v CD* Lieven J recognised that parents can consent if a competent child does not or cannot make a decision (if, for example, they are overwhelmed) but opined that parents cannot override the wishes of the child: 'The very essence of *Gillick* is, in my view, that a parent's right to consent or "determine" treatment cannot trump or overbear the decision of the child.'[34]

In *X* Sir James Munby accepted that 15-year-old X was *Gillick* competent.[35] Sir James considered whether *Re R* and *Re W* (which broadly mirrors the *Re R* ruling in relation to 16–17-year-olds)[36] remain good law. While in *Gillick* Lord Scarman recognised that the parental right to consent would yield to a competent child,[37] Lord Donaldson in *Re R* found that the right to determine whether the child is treated is wider than the right to consent: parents and the court and the child hold the powers concurrently.[38] Lord Scarman had referred to the termination of the parental right to 'determine whether or not their minor … will have medical treatment',[39] but Lord Donaldson and Balcombe LJ considered that Lord Scarman did not mean to give the child an exclusive right to consent in these circumstances.[40]

In *Re R* the power of veto was ascribed to both the court and parents, but in *X* the focus was exclusively on the court's powers. X is a Jehovah's Witness with sickle cell syndrome which has in the past and is likely in future to urgently require the administration of blood products to avert the risk of serious harm or death. X was 'mature and wise beyond her years' and was considered *Gillick* competent.[41] The NHS Trust sought an order that 'top-up' blood transfusions would be lawful for a two-year rolling period that lasted until X's 18th birthday. Sir James denied the rolling order which would give clinicians too much power and risk insufficient account being taken of the pertinent facts at the relevant time. But Sir James held that the court's powers of veto survive social and legal developments in children's rights. For Sir James, the child's voice remains highly relevant and will include the impact on the child of their views not being taken into account.[42] There is a suggestion that where the child is competent, her view might also have independent value. But the independent value is qualified, so that there will be some circumstances where the competent child's view is not determinative.[43] The relevance of the best

[33] *Re R* [1992] Fam 11.
[34] [2021] EWHC 741 (Fam) [67]. Supported in *Bell v Tavistock & Portman NHS Foundation Trust* [2021] EWCA Civ 1363 [48].
[35] [2021] EWHC 65 (Fam). Permission to appeal was denied. Approved in *E & F (Minors): Blood Transfusion* [2021] EWCA Civ 1888 [59].
[36] *Re R* [1992] Fam 11 and *Re W* [1993] Fam 64.
[37] [1986] AC 112, 188–9.
[38] *Re R* [1992] Fam 11, 24.
[39] *Gillick* [1986] AC 112, 188–9.
[40] *Re W*, 84 (Lord Donaldson), 87 (Balcombe LJ).
[41] [2021] EWHC 65 (Fam) [4].
[42] [2021] EWHC 65 (Fam) [25]. And see *DV (A Child)* [2021] EWHC 1037 (Fam).
[43] [2021] EWHC 65 (Fam) [30].

interests test renders the weight accorded to the competent child's views case- and fact-specific.[44]

Human rights arguments that suggested a threshold be drawn beyond which a competent decision is authoritative were rejected. While human rights-based arguments have persuaded judges to amend the common law to protect adult and child autonomy rights in *Hewer v Bryant*, *Gillick*, *Montgomery v Lanarkshire Health Board (Montgomery)*, and *Re D*,[45] Sir James opined that in this case any change to the legal 'conventional wisdom' must be made by Parliament.[46]

## Manipulating the threshold for competence

In the past, some cases have set a high threshold for understanding,[47] that many adults could not achieve. In *Re E (A Minor)*, Ward J authorised a blood transfusion of a 15-year-old Jehovah's Witness. It was held that E:

> did not have any sufficient comprehension of the pain he has yet to suffer, of the fear that he will be undergoing, of the distress not only occasioned by that fear but also—and importantly—the distress he will inevitably suffer as he, a loving son, helplessly watches his parents' and his family's distress ... I find that he has no realization of the full implications which lie before him as to the process of dying. He may have some concept of the fact that he will die, but as to the manner of his death and to the extent of his and his family's suffering I find he has not the ability to turn his mind to it nor the will to do so.[48]

It has been suggested that an alternative threshold might be appropriate that swaps full understanding for *sufficiency* of maturity and understanding. In an adoption case, *Re S*,[49] Cobb J applied aspects of the Mental Capacity Act 2005 test, which broadly applies from the age of 16, to determine competence in an under-16-year-old. This position found favour with the Divisional Court in *Bell*[50] but was not considered helpful 'in this case' by the Court of Appeal.[51] It was scorned by Sir James Munby in *X* who contrasted the adult and child tests: 'In the first, one is ... in the realm of psychiatry. ... In the other ... rather that of child and adolescent

[44] [2021] EWHC 65 (Fam) [24].

[45] *Hewer v Bryant* [1970] 1 QB 357, *Gillick* [1986] AC 112, *Montgomery v Lanarkshire Health Board* [2015] UKSC 12, *Re D (A Child)* [2019] UKSC 42: See E. Cave, 'Confirmation of the High Court's Power to Override a Child's Treatment Decision: A NHS Trust v X (In the Matter of X (A Child) (No. 2)) [2021] EWHC 65 (Fam)', *Medical Law Review*, 29 (2021), 537–46.

[46] [2021] EWHC 65 (Fam) [161].

[47] For example, *Re M (Medical Treatment: Consent)* [1999] 2 FLR 1097.

[48] *Re E (A minor) (Wardship: Medical Treatment)* [1993] 1 FLR 386. See C. Bridge, 'Religious Beliefs and Teenage Refusal of Medical Treatment', *Modern Law Review*, 62 (1999), 585–94.

[49] *Re S (Child as Parent: Adoption Consent)* [2017] EWHC 2729 (Fam).

[50] [2020] EWHC 3274 (Admin) [126], [131].

[51] [2021] EWCA Civ 1363 [83].

psychology.'[52] It seems unlikely that the courts will further develop an analogous position with the 2005 Act to limit the propensity to raise the threshold where the child's decision would result in their serious harm. However there has, in recent cases such as *X*,[53] been a refreshing willingness to acknowledge the *Gillick* competency of mature minors and rely instead on the court's powers of veto to prevent harm. This is a more honest and transparent approach that has in mind the young person's reception of the judgment. And, yet, there will inevitably be cases on the threshold of competence where experts find the ambiguous *Gillick* test unhelpful or disagree on its application.

The Divisional Court decision in *Bell*, though later overruled, sought to provide guidance for doctors as to what would be required to demonstrate the requisite understanding, maturity and intelligence for children seeking medical intervention for gender dysphoria. *Bell* was a judicial review of National Health Service (NHS) protocols prescribing gonadotrophin-releasing hormone agonists (referred to in the judgments as 'puberty blockers', which in the interest of clarity will be the term used in this chapter) to children under the age of 18 experiencing issues with their gender identity. The first respondent, the Tavistock and Portman NHS Foundation Trust, operated a national specialised Gender Identity Development Service (GIDS) for children and young people, and their families. The first claimant, Quincy (Keira) Bell, was assigned female gender at birth and was prescribed puberty blocking drugs at 15 and went on to take what were referred to in the judgments as 'cross-sex hormones' before then regretting this course of action. The second claimant, Mrs A, was the mother of a 15-year-old child with autism and experiencing gender dysphoria who was concerned that puberty blockers would be prescribed. As I discuss further below, the policy of the GIDS was not to treat without parental support, so Mrs A's involvement was 'largely theoretical'.[54] In the Divisional Court, Sharp P, Lewis LJ and Lieven J held that the *Gillick* test would apply to each child in a treatment and person-specific manner,[55] but that in the context of treatment for gender dysphoria, competence would require compliance with eight factors:

> It follows that to achieve *Gillick* competence the child or young person would have to understand not simply the implications of taking PBs [puberty blockers] but those of progressing to cross-sex hormones. The relevant information therefore that a child would have to understand, retain and weigh up in order to have the requisite competence in relation to PBs, would be as follows: (i) the immediate consequences of the treatment in physical and psychological terms; (ii) the fact that the vast majority of patients taking PBs go on to CSH [cross sex hormones] and therefore that s/he is on a

[52] [2021] EWHC 65 (Fam) [73].

[53] [2021] EWHC 65 (Fam) [2]; *E & F (Minors: Blood Transfusion)* [2021] EWCA Civ 1888 [3]. Contrast *Mercy Hospitals Victoria v D1* [2018] VSC 519 in the Victoria Supreme Court where 17-year-old D1 was found to be immature and to lack the requisite understanding to refuse blood products.

[54] [2020] EWHC 3274 (Admin) [89].

[55] [2020] EWHC 3274 (Admin) [145].

> pathway to much greater medical interventions; (iii) the relationship between taking CSH and subsequent surgery, with the implications of such surgery; (iv) the fact that CSH may well lead to a loss of fertility; (v) the impact of CSH on sexual function; (vi) the impact that taking this step on this treatment pathway may have on future and life-long relationships; (vii) the unknown physical consequences of taking PBs; and (viii) the fact that the evidence base for this treatment is as yet highly uncertain.[56]

The Divisional Court set a very high threshold for competence, concluding that:

> It is highly unlikely that a child aged 13 or under would be competent to give consent to the administration of puberty blockers. It is doubtful that a child aged 14 or 15 could understand and weigh the long-term risks and consequences of the administration of puberty blockers.[57]

The court did not consider whether parents could consent on the child's behalf as it was not considered relevant on the facts given that the Tavistock's policy was to act on the child's valid and informed consent with support from the parent and clinician. A few months later, however, in *AB v CD*[58] Lieven J considered whether AB and CD, the parents of XY, could consent on XY's behalf to the administration of puberty blockers. Lieven J held that 'whether or not XY is *Gillick* competent to make a decision about PBs [puberty blockers], her parents retain the parental right to consent to that treatment'.[59] So long as XY agreed, and provided she could not give valid consent—whether because she was incompetent or because she was overwhelmed or disinclined to make a decision—her parents were in law able to do so on her behalf.

Returning to *Bell* in the Divisional Court, the conclusion was that in most cases a best interests determination by the court would be necessary. There, the views of the incompetent child would be taken into account, but the choice of the child would not necessarily be upheld. Andrew Grubb commented in relation to a case from the 1990s that a high threshold imposed in the case of a Jehovah's Witness minor refusing life-sustaining treatment would make it 'very difficult if not impossible for a teenager ever to be legally competent … The court's approach is not directly related to the question of the child's maturity … Rather, it is a device patently intended to justify a finding of incompetence.'[60]

There is much that distinguishes *Bell* from the treatment refusal cases Grubb referred to, but a comparable outcome is that the courts in both cases raised the threshold for competence to a level that would prevent most minors from making a determinative decision.

The Tavistock's appeal was allowed in June 2021. Lord Burnett of Maldon CJ gave the leading judgment holding that the Divisional Court had 'placed an

[56] [2020] EWHC 3274 (Admin) [138].
[57] [2020] EWHC 3274 (Admin) [51].
[58] [2021] EWHC 741 (Fam).
[59] [2021] EWHC 741 (Fam) [69].
[60] A Grubb, 'Commentary on *Re L* (Medical Treatment: Gillick Competency)', *Medical Law Review*, 7 (1999), 58–92 at 60.

improper restriction on the *Gillick* test of competence'.[61] He said: 'The declaration would require the clinicians to suspend or at least to temper their clinical judgement and defer to what amounts to the clinical judgement of the court.'[62] Instead, *Gillick* competence should be assessed by clinicians on the facts[63] and, except in cases of dispute, there would be no need to seek the court's determination of best interests in each case.[64]

The high and prescriptive threshold was abandoned in favour of the flexible standard set out in *Gillick*. In theory, this opened the way for the competent decisions of children with gender dysphoria to be determinative. However, in practice certain barriers apply. One such barrier remains the flexibility of the *Gillick* competence test, which can lead to the threshold being elevated by clinicians or the court to protect the child's welfare. While the Divisional Court had set out a court-imposed specific application of *Gillick* in the context of referral for gender dysphoria, the reassertion of the clinician's role in assessing competence by the Court of Appeal does not *necessarily* mean the standard applied will be lower in any given case. The threshold for competence is responsive to the seriousness of the decision and its potential to conflict with a future-orientated view of autonomy.

## Dual consent

So far, I have identified three ways in which a child's current decision might be vetoed to protect their future autonomy interests: legislative age-related criteria, judicial veto, and the adaptability of the criteria for competence. I have argued that all three are current and relevant. In this section the potential for policy restrictions on the ability of minors to make determinative decisions is considered in light of the Court of Appeal decision in *Bell*. Though the potential for policy restrictions on the powers of children competent to decide to make a determinative decision has long existed, their impact has only recently come to light.

There is recognition in *Bell* that, theoretically, a *Gillick* competent child would be able to give sole authority for treatment. Indeed, in *AB*, Lieven J said that clinicians 'proceeded before *Bell* on the basis that XY was *Gillick* competent in respect to the decision to take puberty blockers and therefore it was not necessary to ask whether the parents could also consent'.[65]

The GIDS policy was to require the competent consent of the child and referral would not proceed on the basis of parental consent alone.[66] Nor would it proceed for children under the age of 15 without 'parental support (or that of their guardian

[61] [2021] EWCA Civ 1363 [94].
[62] [2021] EWCA Civ 1363 [74].
[63] [2021] EWCA Civ 1363 [88].
[64] [2021] EWCA Civ 1363 [89].
[65] [2021] EWHC 741 (Fam) [49].
[66] [2020] EWHC 3274 (Admin), [47].

or social services where appropriate)'.[67] The Court of Appeal in *Bell* translates this requirement as one of dual consent. It says: 'The policy and practice under consideration in this case requires *the informed consent* of both child and parents before Tavistock refers to the Trusts, again before either Trust prescribes puberty blockers and once more before prescription of cross-sex hormones.'[68]

The policy requiring parental support was not at issue in *Bell*. Nonetheless, it is possible to draw a distinction between recognition in *AB* that the competent child provides the legal consent notwithstanding the policy requirement for parental support, and recognition in *Bell* that the GIDS policy requires valid consent of both parent and child. It is questionable whether the service specification in force at the time went this far. It listed as separate factors that might influence the complexity and length of an assessment for referral of a child approaching puberty the 'client's capacity to understand and consent' and 'family conflict ... about how to proceed'.[69] With regard to criteria for referral it listed as a criterion that 'there is support from the family/carers' and said 'Clients under the age of 16 should be assessed regarding their ability to give informed consent and whether they have appropriate autonomy to make decisions.'[70]

A recognition of the need for dual consent goes beyond this. Whereas the service specification separates out the competent child's ability to provide valid consent and the policy consideration of familial support which has been shown to enhance the chances of successful treatment,[71] the Court of Appeal tacitly accepts a requirement for valid and informed consent from both the parent(s) and the competent child. In practical terms both positions accept that a child's competent consent is not sufficient for referral without parental agreement. However, there is an important difference between a qualification on the independent value of the child's view as a clinical consideration and one providing a legal function. Support as a clinical consideration can exist on a continuum. Valid and informed consent, however, must reach the standards set out in law and professional guidance.[72]

'Valid consent' can protect a healthcare professional whose touching of the patient during treatment would otherwise be unlawful from a claim in battery. Consent is not the only lawful justification for treatment, but when it applies it requires that the person consenting has mental capacity, makes a voluntary decision and does so on the basis of basic information.[73] 'Informed consent' additionally imposes a requirement to disclose material risks about reasonable treatment

[67] [2020] EWHC 3274 (Admin) [40].
[68] [2021] EWCA Civ 1363 [83] and see [5]. (My italics.)
[69] NHS England, *NHS Standard Contract for GIDS for Children and Adolescents*, Schedule 2 (E13/S(Hss)/3: 2020), p. 24.
[70] NHS England, *NHS Standard Contract*, pp. 30–1.
[71] NHS England, *NHS Standard Contract*, p. 8.
[72] See E. Cave, 'Valid Consent to Medical Treatment', *Journal Medical Ethics*, 47 (2021), 1–4.
[73] *Chatterton v Gerson* [1981] QB 432.

alternatives in order to comply with the law of negligence.[74] In the quote above,[75] the Court of Appeal in *Bell* required the dual 'informed consent' of parent and child rather than informed consent of the child and support of the parent. This raises interesting legal questions as to the standard of information disclosure required in respect of the child and parent in cases of dual consent.

The Supreme Court in the case of *Montgomery* in 2015 protected adult patient choice, recognising that 'An adult person of sound mind is entitled to decide which, if any, of the available forms of treatment to undergo, and her consent must be obtained before treatment interfering with her bodily integrity is undertaken.'[76] This does not apply in a straightforward manner to children who, as we have seen, are not necessarily so entitled: the court can overrule their consent and refusal, policy can dictate that their competent consent is not sufficient and give parents an effective veto on their ability to consent to treatment, and clinicians have scope to determine the threshold for competence.[77] Where there is potential for the child's competent decision to be non-determinative, the legal relevance of consent is suited less to protecting their choice, responsibility, and autonomy rights, which are the focus in adult cases, and more on protecting clinicians from a claim in trespass. There is therefore a mismatch between the legal restriction on the competent child being able to make a determinative decision and the requirement that their dual consent should be informed, insofar as the purpose of informed consent in adult cases is to promote choice, autonomy, and responsibility.

There is further evidence of poor fit between dual consent and the law governing informed consent in that the Divisional Court in *Bell* recognised that the child need not understand all the information on material risks and reasonable alternatives that is required to be set out in light of *Montgomery* in order for the child to be considered competent. This matter was not addressed by the Court of Appeal. If the Divisional Court is right, then children will need to be given the basic information required to consent to trespass as set out in *Chatterton v Gerson*,[78] and also additional information required to demonstrate their understanding so as to satisfy *Gillick*, but this should not necessarily include all the matters required for an informed consent as set out in relation to adults in the case of *Montgomery*. And yet, to limit potential liability in negligence a clinician might be required to disclose material risks, which would comprise making disclosures even when clinicians believe that the child will not understand some of the information and might be frightened by it. A tension therefore exists between the duty to disclose material risks to consenting patients and the assertion that material risks do not necessarily need to be understood in order for a child to be found to have *Gillick* competence.

74 *Montgomery v Lanarkshire* [2015] UKSC 11.

75 [2021] EWCA Civ 1363 [83].

76 [2015] UKSC 11 [87].

77 See E. Cave and C. Purshouse, 'Think of the Children: Liability for Non-Disclosure of Information Post-Montgomery', *Medical Law Review*, 28 (2020), 270–92.

78 [1981] QB 432.

What emerges is a complex picture in which the courts assert the right of the child to give informed consent but limit the choice and responsibility that flows from it.

## The relevance of the child's view in best interests decisions

We have seen that there are various mechanisms by which a child's competent view can be vetoed in their best interests. What role does their view have in the assessment of best interests? In the case of adults who lack capacity, the Mental Capacity Act 2005 requires an assessment of their best interests under section 4.[79] The individual's wishes and feelings will be taken into consideration but will 'not necessarily be the deciding factor'.[80] However, influenced by the UN Convention on the Rights of Persons with Disabilities, the Court of Protection jurisprudence has evolved to make the consideration of the patient's point of view central to the decision. In *Aintree University Hospital NHS Foundation Trust v James* Lade Hale said, 'Insofar as it is possible to ascertain the patient's wishes and feelings, his beliefs and values or the things which were important to him, it is those which should be taken into account because they are a component in making the choice which is right for him as an individual human being.'[81]

The evolution has brought the Court of Protection close to a rebuttable presumption that the patient's wishes and feelings should be upheld.[82]

In *E & F* the Court of Appeal alleged that the best interests assessment has been applied 'in a broadly consistent manner' across the High Court with respect to children and the Court of Protection with respect to those over 16.[83] With respect to both adults and children, the Court of Appeal recommends an assessment 'from the individual's point of view', but recognises that factors differ when applied to individuals of different ages. In cases involving young people, the two 'transcendent factors' are 'the preservation of life and personal autonomy'.[84] On the one hand, one might expect that the individual viewpoint of a *Gillick* competent child would be particularly strong given that it is contemporaneously autonomous. But on the other hand, the status of children requires that their view is undermined if accepting it would put their lives at risk. Sir Andrew McFarlane recognised that 'once a young person becomes an adult, decisions about whether to accept or reject medical

[79] On the similarities and differences between standards of capacity for adults and children, see Donnelly and Lyons in this volume.

[80] Mental Capacity Act 2005 Code of Practice (2007) para 5.38.

[81] [2013] UKSC 67 [45].

[82] See A. Ruck Keene and C. Auckland 'More Presumptions Please? Wishes, Feelings and Best Interests Decision-Making', *Elder Law Journal*, 5 (2015), 293–301.

[83] [2021] EWCA Civ 1888 [48] (Sir Andrew McFarlane). Note this case pertained to minors over the age of 16 whose decisions are also subject to veto.

[84] *E & F (Minors: Blood Transfusion)* [2021] EWCA Civ 1888 [53]. See also [71] (Sir Andrew McFarlane).

treatment become theirs absolutely, but before that age the court must act upon its objective assessment of the young person's best interests, even where this conflicts with sincere and considered views.'[85]

Thus, while there are similarities in the overarching principles applied to determine the best interests of children and adults lacking capacity, there is a stark contrast between the near presumption that the adult's best interests are represented by their past and present will and preferences and the emphasis on protecting children's future autonomy. Children can therefore be overruled in the four ways outlined above so that their autonomous decision is not determinative and additionally, when others decide on their behalf, their view will not necessarily carry the same weight that an incapacitous adult's decision would.

## Conclusion

In this chapter, I started by setting out two ways to reconcile commitment to the child's competent views and their best interests in decisions about their medical treatment. In the first form, the test for competence serves as a threshold, beyond which children will be able to decide. The ascension of human rights and the protection of individual autonomy in cases relating to adults would seem to favour the will conception. In *Montgomery* for example, the Supreme Court departed from previous case law[86] in order to better protect the autonomy rights of adult patients.

In the second form, decisions that could gravely impact on a child's health, notwithstanding that they may be competent, can be overridden if they conflict with the child's best interests. This position is compatible with Eekelaar's dynamic self-determinism which can be disapplied to protect the child's life and health. It is also relevant to the protection of the child's open future. This is not to say that autonomy is not valued in such cases, but while children's views have weight, the value can be qualified via a range of legal and policy mechanisms if their choice would deny them a healthy future.

Some have tried to conceive of ways to strengthen the test for competence so that it would be sufficiently robust to allow competent decisions to be relied upon in the child's best interests as true expressions of their autonomous choice.[87] But in *X*, Sir James considered one such argument a 'conceptually problematic' 'will-o'-the-wisp', too focussed on academic opinion and insufficiently suited to the 'pragmatic world of the court room'.[88] According to this opinion, however the

[85] [2021] EWCA Civ 1888 [73].

[86] *Sidaway v Board of Governors of the Bethlem Royal Hospital* [1985] AC 871 (HL).

[87] V. Chico and L. Hagger, 'The Mental Capacity Act 2005 and Mature Minors: A Missed Opportunity?', *Journal of Social Welfare and Family Law*, 33 (2011), 157–68; A. McFarlane, 'Mental Capacity: One Standard for All Ages', *The Family in Law*, 41 (2011), 479–85; E. Cave, 'Goodbye Gillick?'.

[88] [2021] EWHC 65 (Fam) [70], [71] and [60].

tests may be adapted, there might still be cases where the best interests of the child are served by the courts vetoing their autonomous current decision. According to *Re W* which was confirmed in *X*, this is the legal position and any change is a matter for Parliament.[89]

The judiciary have been keen to mark as special those cases where the court is asked to approve life-sustaining treatment children refuse.[90] But is this the exception to the rule or one of several exceptions? The threshold test retains importance and relevance in other treatment cases. In line with Lord Scarman's approach in *Gillick*, competent children able to make a treatment decision should generally have that decision upheld. However, there are three additional ways identified in this chapter in which either the threshold can be raised or reaching it will not give children a determinative choice.

First, statute can outline special cases where the capacity of children to consent is limited. Parliament might choose to do so, for instance, if the risk inherent in a procedure is particularly high. In such cases, the common law *Gillick* threshold can be disapplied. Second, the nature of the *Gillick* test lends itself to commensurate application by clinicians so that the threshold can be adapted to the gravity of the decision. Insofar as the threshold's application cannot be accurately predicted, this weakens the link between a threshold and determinative choice. Third, policy considerations can be applied to particular treatments or interventions which restrict the value of the child's competent choice. In *Bell* the Court of Appeal accepted and amplified the potential for dual consent, qualifying the independent value assigned to the child's competent decision.

With regard to dual consent requirements, children seeking to make authoritative decisions might seek to challenge policies that limit their ability to do so through a declaratory hearing or judicial review, but the tacit support for the requirement of parental approval for treatment and the application of the label 'informed consent' by the Court of Appeal might limit their chances of success. The decision as to which treatments should be available thereby incorporates the option to restrict the value of competent children's choices and 'Such policy decisions are for the National Health Service, the medical profession and its regulators and Government and Parliament.'[91]

Moreover, in relation to judicial review the bar is set high: 'a policy will be unlawful if it misdirects officials as to their legal obligations'.[92] Normally then, one will need to show that the policy sanctions unlawful conduct.

Consequently, while in clinical practice independent value will often be assigned to children's competent decisions, the law recognises the validity of limits imposed

[89] *Re W* [1993] Fam 64, 87 (Balcombe LJ); [2021] EWHC 65 (Fam) [162].

[90] See, for example, *Bell v Tavistock* [2021] EWCA Civ 1363 [82]; *Re D (A Child)* [2019] UKSC 42 [50].

[91] [2021] EWCA Civ 1363, [3].

[92] *R (A) v Secretary of State for the Home Department* [2021] UKSC 37 [44] and summarised at para [84], as cited in [2021] EWCA Civ 1363 [54].

by Parliament in age-related restrictions on uptake of certain medical treatment; by the courts in the case of restricting choices about life sustaining treatment; by policy makers and thus parents through requirements for dual consent or parental agreement; and through clinicians in their application of the threshold for *Gillick* competence.

This chapter has set out to clarify a complex legal landscape and advance a novel framework for understanding the scope of children's medical treatment decisions. To conclude, it is worth briefly considering normative implications. In terms of negative consequences, notwithstanding the flexibility inherent in the *Gillick* threshold, a link to a right to make a determinative choice once the threshold is reached has the benefit of clarity, which is beneficial for clinicians and families alike. While statutory limitations and the court's powers to override competent decisions that threaten life have been closely debated and analysed in terms of their human rights implications, the same is not necessarily true of policy exceptions. Some children will be surprised that having reached the threshold for competence they cannot necessarily, subject to the exceptions set out in *X*, make an authoritative decision. There is value in making clear to clinicians, professional bodies, children, and their families the alternative routes to balancing children's competent views and their best interests.

Policy restrictions on the authority of competent children, such as the requirement for dual consent, can have several benefits. Most obviously, restrictions on competent choices that would result in physical or mental harm can protect children's future autonomy. But conversely, by blurring the threshold approach so that the independent value ascribed to competent choices is qualified, policy makers are given greater scope to move from denial of treatment or a requirement that all cases come before the court to determine best interests, to one that accommodates the views of potential individual child recipients and potentially allows more timely access to treatment. If competent children can assess the risks and decide in conjunction with their parents, the responsibility for the decision is shared. In *Montgomery*, Lords Kerr and Reed recognised that by providing informed consent, adult patients accept 'responsibility for the taking of risks affecting their own lives, and living with the consequences of their choices'.[93] In circumstances where policy dictates that the responsibility is too great to bear alone, the ability to restrict a child's authority and share the responsibility for their decision might therefore have the effect of making a risk-laden or controversial treatment more accessible.

[93] [2015] UKSC 12 [81].

# 8

# Medical Treatment Refusals by Teenagers and the Law: Justice That Is More Caring?

JO BRIDGEMAN

THIS CHAPTER FOCUSES upon the limited body of reported case law concerned with the refusal of teenagers to consent to recommended medical treatment, drawing on the insights of Carol Gilligan's ethics of care to argue for reasoning in such cases that integrates care with justice. As of June 2025, there are 20 reported cases concerned with the refusal by teenagers—a child aged between the ages of 13 and 17[1]—to consent to recommended medical treatment[2] and four reported cases concerning the legality of the termination of a teenager's pregnancy.[3] In nine cases, the refusal is to the administration of blood in their treatment by teenagers who are

[1] This chapter is concerned with children aged 13–17 who have the ability to express a view about their medical treatment and are not rendered unable to do so by disability, e.g. *A Local Authority and An NHS Trust v MC, FC, C* [2017] EWHC 370 (Fam), or their medical condition, e.g. *A Hospital NHS Trust v LP and TP* [2019] EWHC 2989.

[2] Please see list of cases at the end of the chapter. This number excludes *Bell v Tavistock and Portman NHS Foundation Trust* [2020] EWHC 3274, an application for *judicial review* of the practice of prescribing puberty blocking drugs to children under the age of 18. Also excluded is the case that followed *AB v CD* [2021] EWHC 741, which concerned an application, in light of *Bell*, by *parents* that they could consent to the administration of puberty blockers to their 15-year-old child, who had been assigned male at birth but identified as female. For consideration of the issues raised by these cases see, Kirsty Moreton, 'A Backwards-Step for *Gillick*: Trans Children's Inability to Consent to Treatment for Gender Dysphoria—*Quincy Bell & Mrs A v The Tavistock and Portman NHS Foundation Trust and Ors* [2020] EWHC 3274 (Admin)', *Medical Law Review*, 29 (2021), 699–715; Hannah Hirst, 'The Legal Rights and Wrongs of Puberty Blocking in England', *Child and Family Law Quarterly*, 33 (2021), 115–42; Hillary Chua, 'Consent to Treatment for Transgender Youth: The Next Chapter—*Bell & Anor v The Tavistock and Portman NHS Foundation Trust & Ors*', *Modern Law Review*, 86 (2023), 214–25.

[3] *Re P (A Minor)* [1986] 1 FLR 272, *Re B (Wardship: Abortion)* [1991] 2 FLR 426, *An NHS Trust v A, B, C* [2014] EWHC 1445, *Re X (A Child)* [2014] EWHC 1871. Non-therapeutic sterilisation and parental disputes on the issue of vaccination are also excluded.

*Proceedings of the British Academy*, **279**, 153–167, © Authors 2025.

Jehovah's Witnesses.[4] In the analysis that follows, I first explain the insights from Carol Gilligan's *In a Different Voice* of particular relevance to the cases concerning refusals by teenagers to consent to recommended medical treatment. I then demonstrate the reasoning, through the ethics of justice, in the judgments of the court. Relational reasoning used by some of the teenagers to explain their decisions is then identified and I argue that 14-year-old JA explained his decision in terms of both justice and care.[5] My argument is that in their reasoning judges should give consideration to relationships and interdependency, recognising the realities of vulnerability and hurt for the individual in a relationship as well as seeking a fair outcome through the prioritisation of competing values and conflicting rights. Judgements about the future medical treatment of a teenager should be reasoned in an approach that integrates justice and care.

## In a Different Voice

The insights from Carol Gilligan's *In a Different Voice* on developmental psychology are clearly relevant to judicial responses to the refusals by teenagers to consent to recommended medical treatment. Following *Gillick*, a developmental view of childhood is adopted in which the acquisition of decision-making responsibilities depends upon increasing levels of capacity; that is, a child is able to take responsibility for making their own decisions when he or she 'reaches a sufficient understanding and intelligence to be capable of making up his own mind on the matter requiring decision'.[6] As Lord Scarman emphasised in *Gillick*, the level of knowledge and understanding that will be 'sufficient' changes with the nature of the decision and must in all cases demonstrate a 'wise choice'.[7] More recently, in his judgment in *Re X (A Child) (No 2)*,[8] Sir James Munby observed that 'Gillick competence ... is tied to the normal development over time of the typical child and teenager'.[9] But, the judges appear to view psychological maturity in terms of hierarchical, abstract, reasoning, for example, prioritising the protection of life

[4] In other cases, children who had been brought up according to the tenets of the faith have been rendered unable to express their views by their condition. In *M Children's Hospital NHS Foundation Trust v Y* [2014] EWHC 2651, 13-and-a-half-year-old T dipped into unconsciousness, he had responded to the consultant's explanation of the treatment with a thumbs up, but given his critical condition it was not possible to ascertain further from him his wishes and feelings. *LP and TP* [2019] EWHC 2989, concerned 13-year-old P who was in an induced coma due to multiple serious injuries sustained in a road traffic accident. MacDonald J afforded respect to P's views, noted his parents' evidence that he shared their beliefs but that P was too young to be formally admitted as a Jehovah's Witness: [21(i)], [21(iv)].

[5] *Re JA* [2014] EWHC 1135.

[6] *Gillick v West Norfolk and Wisbech AHA* [1986] AC 112, 186.

[7] *Gillick* 188.

[8] *Re X (A Child) (No 2)* [2021] EWHC 65.

[9] *Re X (A Child) (No 2)* [73].

over self-determination. This approach is consistent with the highest developmental stage identified by Lawrence Kohlberg in his stage sequence of moral development from fairness based on individual need, through fairness based in societal conventions to a principled understanding through equality and reciprocity.[10] Lawrence Kohlberg considered the highest stage of moral development to be in a 'reflective understanding of human rights', emphasising the individual, separation, freedom from interference by others, rights, justice, and fairness.[11] The reasoning of judges giving consent to medical treatment refused by teenagers through this abstract, principled, approach is demonstrated below.

As Carol Gilligan observed, Lawrence Kohlberg's theory of moral development was derived from his studies of boys/men over a period of 20 years. In his stage sequence of moral development, women appear to be morally deficient, failing to reach the higher stages. Yet, Carol Gilligan argued, rather than this revealing a problem in women's moral development, instead it indicated a problem with theory.[12] The problem being that theories about human experience had derived from studies that excluded the voices of women and their experiences of life.[13] In *In a Different Voice*, Carol Gilligan analysed the findings from three studies carried out in the 10 years prior to the book's publication in 1982 that listened to people talking about self and morality and experiences of conflict and choice, including the voices, experiences and lives of women and girls. The college student study which asked about understandings of morality identified a common theme in the responses of the female participants of a desire not to hurt others and the hope that morality could enable conflicts to be resolved without causing hurt to others or the self,[14] in which 'moral judgement is orientated towards issues of responsibility and care'.[15] But further, that while there were two different starting points, of justice and care, over time the men and women in the study integrated both in the resolution of moral conflict.[16] The abortion study interviewed women considering the termination of a confirmed pregnancy shortly after the decision of the Supreme Court of the United States in *Roe v Wade* gave constitutional protection to the right of the pregnant woman to decide whether to undergo a termination in the first trimester.[17] The study, which was concerned with the different ways in which women think about dilemmas in their lives, identified the resolution of the issue in terms which recognised connection and interdependency between self and other requiring

[10] Carol Gilligan, *In a Different Voice: Psychological Theory and Women's Development* (Cambridge, MA, Harvard University Press, 1993 [1982]), p. 27.

[11] Gilligan, *In a Different Voice*, pp. 19–20.

[12] Gilligan, *In a Different Voice*, pp. 1–2.

[13] Gilligan, *In a Different Voice*, p. xiii.

[14] Gilligan, *In a Different Voice*, p. 65.

[15] Gilligan, *In a Different Voice*, p. 99.

[16] Gilligan, *In a Different Voice*, p. 167.

[17] *Roe v Wade* 410 US 113 (1973), which was overturned by the US Supreme Court in *Dobbs v Jackson Women's Health Organization* (2022) 597 US 215 (2022).

care and a concern not to hurt both the other and the self.[18] The hypotheses from these two studies were then explored in the rights and responsibilities study of men and women across all ages on self and morality and moral conflict and choice.[19] Through this research, Carol Gilligan observed two distinct ways of speaking about moral problems and the relationship between the self and others which she labelled the 'ethics of justice' and the 'ethics of care'.

The third study, the rights and responsibilities study, is of particular relevance to decisions to give consent to medical treatment refused by teenagers. The rights and responsibilities study was based around the 'Heinz dilemma' exploring resolution in a conflict of moral norms.[20] The question asked was, should Heinz steal from the pharmacist the drug that could save his wife's life but which he could not afford to buy? Eleven-year-old Jake was clear in his view that Heinz should steal the drug. Jake reasoned through a hierarchy of values in the abstract to determine an impersonal conflict of claims objectively employing an idea of fairness.[21] Jake prioritised the right to life above the right to property. Amy, at the same age, demonstrated different reasoning. Amy was concerned with relationships extending over time, recognising Heinz's 'wife's continuing need for her husband and the husband's continuing concern for his wife'. She sought a solution that would 'sustain rather than sever connection'.[22] Amy reasoned in terms of connection, responsibility for one another, and the need for a response.[23] The dilemma for Amy depended on the preservation of networks of care. For Amy, communication was the mode through which to resolve the conflict.[24] Perhaps Heinz and the chemist could come to some agreement about payment; perhaps the chemist would change his mind if he better understood the position; perhaps someone else could help Heinz and his wife. On Kohlberg's scale, Amy's responses are considered less mature for appearing not to think systematically about morality or law but seeking to resolve the problem by 'activating the network by communication'.[25] But, Carol Gilligan argued, Amy can be understood as reasoning in terms of a:

> world of relationships and psychological truths where an awareness of the connection between people gives rise to a recognition of responsibility for one another, a perception of the need for response. Seen in this light, her understanding of morality as arising from the recognition of relationship, her belief in communication as a mode of conflict resolution, and her conviction that the solution to the dilemma will follow from its compelling representation seem to be far from naïve or cognitively immature.[26]

[18] Gilligan, *In a Different Voice*, p. 74.
[19] Gilligan, *In a Different Voice*, pp. 2–3, explained further below.
[20] Gilligan, *In a Different Voice*, p. 25.
[21] Gilligan, *In a Different Voice*, p. 32.
[22] Gilligan, *In a Different Voice*, p. 28.
[23] Gilligan, *In a Different Voice*, pp. 28, 30.
[24] Gilligan, *In a Different Voice*, p. 30.
[25] Gilligan, *In a Different Voice*, pp. 30–1.
[26] Gilligan, *In a Different Voice*, p. 30.

Amy's reasoning captures the ethics of care, Jake's the ethics of justice. This was an observation of both an orientation, towards care and responsiveness or rights and rules, and a method, a contextual or an abstract mode of determination.[27]

When asked about responsibility, Jake started from the responsibility to himself then considered his responsibility to others from whom he was separate but with whom he had a relationship. Responsibility took the form of limitation, 'a restraint of aggression', appreciating that his actions could affect others and those of others affect him. Equal respect for rules therefore protected individual autonomy.[28] In contrast, Amy emphasised the importance of the context for the exercise of responsibility to others. For Amy, responsibility depended on relationships and response, finding the solution that caused the least hurt to the self and others. Jake reasoned in terms of conflicting rights; Amy in terms of responsibility as response, an act of care.[29]

Carol Gilligan noted, however, that the interviewer repeated the questions conveying to Amy that what she was saying about the Heinz dilemma was not being heard or that her answers were not the right ones. Amy maintained her reasoning while becoming more guarded in her answers.[30] The interviewer struggled to understand Amy's responses as Amy had reframed the question, answering a different question to the one posed. Rather than decide whether Heinz *should* steal the drug, Amy was concerned with the question whether the response to the dilemma should be *stealing*, that is, she assumed action was needed and questioned the form that action should take.[31] Her concern was to find a different solution, one that preserved relationships. The interviewer did not hear the reframed question or the reasoning Amy employed as she sought a better solution to the problem Heinz faced.[32] Asked the same question at 15, Amy shifted between prioritisation of life over property and seeing that as threatening to relationships and distanced from reality.[33]

Although the different voice was discerned through studies which included the reasoning of girls and women, Carol Gilligan did not claim to have identified a gendered difference. It is not a feminine voice. Rather, the ethics of justice and ethics of care provide different starting points, modes of reasoning, and orientations. Carol Gilligan concluded that we all reason through rights and responsibilities at different times, although one orientation or mode tends to dominate. Furthermore, she did not argue that abstract rights reasoning should be replaced with reasoning through relationships and responsibility, but that there should be an integration of the ethics of care and of justice. The ethic of responsibility, placing the self in the context of relationships and responding through the activity of care, she argued, is

[27] Gilligan, *In a Different Voice*, p. 19.
[28] Gilligan, *In a Different Voice*, p. 37.
[29] Gilligan, *In a Different Voice*, p. 38.
[30] Gilligan, *In a Different Voice*, p. 29.
[31] Gilligan, *In a Different Voice*, p. 31.
[32] Gilligan, *In a Different Voice*, p. 31.
[33] Gilligan, *In a Different Voice*, p. xxii.

transformed by recognition of justice in rights. A rights-based approach challenges the idea of selflessness as a virtue and understanding rights transforms understandings of care and relationships. The starting point of responsibility and care, recognising differing needs and concerned with not hurting others is complicated by the recognition of the need to be true to the self, while the starting point of equality, rights, and justice, involves balancing the claims of the other and the self, transformed through understandings of relationships and care.[34] Reasoning that integrates justice and care involves reconstructing hypothetical dilemmas in real terms, seeking to understand the actual consequences for the individual. Specifically, an integrated mode of reasoning seeks to understand the causes of suffering and anticipate which actions are likely to cause hurt to determine from an assessment of vulnerability and hurt where greater responsibility lies. Therefore, understandings of responsibility and choice require judgement that is contextual in a dialogue between fairness and care.[35]

As Carol Gilligan herself suggested in a 1995 article, the reframing of psychology to recognise two distinct voices fundamentally changes the way in which we see the world and provides the basis for a different philosophy, political theory, and legal theory.[36] Drawing on these insights, I now demonstrate the abstract hierarchical reasoning adopted in judgments concerned with consent to medical treatment refused by teenagers.

## Hierarchical reasoning

The approach of the courts to cases concerning the refusal by teenagers to consent to medical treatment was determined in the 1990s cases of *Re R* and *Re W*.[37] This approach was recently confirmed by Sir James Munby in *Re X (A Child) (No 2)* notwithstanding changes in the intervening 30 years resulting from the Mental Capacity Act 2005, the Human Rights Act 1998, and the shift in medical law generally from medical paternalism to greater respect for patient autonomy.[38] The legal principles established in *Re R* and *Re W* that Sir James Munby concluded remained valid included that the court will give careful attention to the wishes of a child old enough to 'express sensible views' as one factor in determination of their best interests. The analysis that follows suggests that whether the views of the older child are heard by the court and whether they are judged 'sensible' depends upon their alignment with dominant norms. In all cases, whether the child is under

[34] Gilligan, *In a Different Voice*, p. 164.

[35] Gilligan, *In a Different Voice*, p. 174.

[36] Gilligan, *In a Different Voice*, p. 22.

[37] *Re R (A Minor) (Wardship: Medical Treatment)* [1992] 1 FLR 190; *Re W (A Minor) (Medical Treatment: Court's Jurisdiction)* [1993] Fam 64.

[38] *Re X (A Child) (No 2)* [2021] EWHC 65.

or over 16,[39] *Gillick* competent or not, in the care of the state or not, the duty of the court is to protect the welfare of the child. In all cases, whether the child is assessed to be *Gillick* competent or not, whether the presumption of capacity in s 8 of the Family Law Reform Act 1969 has been rebutted or not, whether the child lacks capacity as defined in sections 2(1) and 3(1) of the Mental Capacity Act 2005 or not,[40] the duty of the judge is to determine the best interests of the child. Those cases also established that, irrespective of competence or capacity, the child's decision could be overridden by consent given by any holder of parental responsibility, including the local authority, or the court according to their judgement of the welfare of the child. But, as did Jake in his resolution of the Heinz dilemma, the reasoning adopted in the judgments in cases concerned with the refusals of teenagers to recommended medical treatment involves abstract, hierarchical reasoning which prioritises competing values.

The first case, decided before but reported after *Re R* and *Re W*, concerned the refusal of A, aged 15 and three-quarters, to the administration of blood in the treatment of leukaemia as he and his family were 'devoted and strongly devout members of the Jehovah's Witness belief'.[41] Establishing the framework for decision-making, Ward J stated that the law 'echoes the libertarian philosophy of John Stuart Mill' starting from the 'fundamental principle that adults of full capacity have freedom of choice'. The judge quoted from Lord Scarman in *Sidaway*:

> The right of self-determination, the description applied by some to what is no more and no less than the right of a patient to determine for himself whether he will or will not accept the doctor's advice, is vividly illustrated where the treatment recommended is surgery. A doctor who operates without the consent of his patient is, save in cases of emergency or mental disability, guilty of a civil wrong of trespass to the person. He is also guilty of the criminal offence of assault. The existence of the patient's right to make his own decision may be seen as a basic human right protected by the common law.[42]

However, as A was neither an adult nor within the scope of the Family Law Reform Act 1969, Ward J then referred to Lord Scarman's speech in *Gillick* that parental rights yield to the rights of the child to decide once the child has a 'sufficient understanding and intelligence to be capable of making up his own mind on the matter requiring a decision'.[43] But the case did not turn on whether A had sufficient

[39] The age at which the Family Law Reform Act 1969 which creates a presumption of capacity to consent to medical treatment and the Mental Capacity Act 2005 setting out law which applies to patients who lack capacity both apply.

[40] *Re X (A Child) (No 2)* [76].

[41] *Re E* [1993] 1 FLR, 386, 388.

[42] *Re E* 390, quoting *Sidaway v Board of Governors of the Bethlehem Royal Hospital and the Maudsley Hospital* [1985] AC 871, 882. It is notable that Lord Scarman's rights-based approach was not then being adopted in provision of information cases and was not adopted until the Supreme Court decision in *Montgomery v Lanarkshire Health Board* [2015] UKSC 11.

[43] *Re E* 390 quoting *Gillick v West Norfolk and Wisbech Area Health Authority and Another* [1986] AC 112, 186.

intelligence and understanding to override his parents' rights, as the responsibility of the judge was, in the exercise of the inherent jurisdiction of the court, to decide upon A's medical treatment with his welfare as the paramount consideration.[44]

In determination of A's welfare, the judge said that A's wishes were very important and weighed heavily in the assessment. In particular, given the fundamental right of adults to exercise choice and A's proximity to adulthood, weight was given to A's understanding that as a consequence of his religious convictions he was refusing medical treatment that might save his life. However, within the framework of choice, Ward J described A's decision as a 'considered wish to choose for oneself to die' and expressed the view that A was making a 'choice of death'. In the view of the judge, this choice was not in A's best interests given that 'life is precious'.[45] The judge stated that he had 'endeavoured to pay every respect and give great weight to the religious principles which underlie the family's decision and also to the fundamental human right to decide things for oneself', but concluded that, objectively, A's welfare required that he should be administered with the drugs and the necessary blood and blood products. In Ward J's judgment, greater weight had to be given to protection of A's life than his religious beliefs. In abstract reasoning in which the weight of competing values was assessed, life was prioritised over conviction.

As Sir James Munby expressed it in the more recent case of X, in which he authorised the administration of blood to 15-and-a-half-year-old X in the treatment of sickle cell disease, while overriding X's 'strongly held religious beliefs' was significant, objectively, protection of X's life or prevention of serious harm outweighed her beliefs.[46] The judge agreed with Counsel for CAFCASS that 'preserving the lives of children until adulthood is a legitimate aim'.[47] The conclusion on X's welfare that prioritised life over conviction outweighed respect for X's autonomy. However, the welfare determination to give consent was reached without consideration of relationships or understanding of responsibilities to self and others. Protection of life and prevention of serious harm was prioritised without consideration of the hurt caused in the experience of a failure of response.

In the 1990s case of *Re W* Mr Munby QC, appearing on behalf of the Official Solicitor as *amicus curiae*, argued that in extraordinary cases, such as sterilisation, abortion, organ donation, or when a child has refused treatment necessary to prolong or save his or her life or avoid the risk of serious and irreparable harm, the court should give proper weight to the wishes of the child but decide according to its assessment of the best interests of the child. Consequently, he argued that the judge should consent to W's transfer, against her wishes, to a different centre for the treatment of anorexia given that W was at risk of irreparable harm.[48] Nolan LJ

[44] *Re E*.

[45] *Re E* 393.

[46] *Re X* [2020] EWHC 3003 [15].

[47] *Re X (A Child) (No 2)* [2021] EWHC 65 [134].

[48] *Re W* 69–71.

stressed that the responsibility of the court in the exercise of its inherent jurisdiction is in all cases to determine the best interests of the child.[49] This required the court to consider all of the factors in the welfare checklist and, alongside her wishes, of particular importance in this case was the risk of harm to W. W's wish was to stay where she was and not to be moved to a specialist treatment centre. The court considered the risk of harm to W to be a 'serious and imminent', 'grave and irreversible risk of mental or physical harm'.[50] Hierarchical reasoning prioritised the prevention of serious harm to W over her experiences, views, and wishes. I now bring W's relational reasoning to consideration of her decision and then demonstrate the recognition of the inevitability of hurt in the relational reasoning of the teenagers in *Re E* and *Re M*.

## Relational reasoning

Sixteen-year-old W was an orphan whose testamentary guardian had been unable to care for her and her siblings. As a consequence, W and her siblings were in the care of the local authority. Over the past seven years the children had been cared for by three sets of foster parents. The first was a temporary arrangement. In the second placement, W had been bullied and not been given the protection she required. In the third the foster mother had undergone treatment for breast cancer.[51] At the time of the application by the local authority to court, W was being cared for in a specialist residential unit for children and adolescents. The foster family with whom she had been living when admitted had decided that they would not be able to care for her when she was discharged. The judge noted W's wish to be cared for within a family when discharged. However, for her treatment, rather than be moved to a specialist treatment centre, she wished to remain in the unit where she currently was. W explained that she knew the staff in this unit and had two friends, described by Thorpe J as 'quasi-family bonding'. The unit was also near to her brother and sister and the proposed foster parents.[52] W expressed her desire to remain where she was in terms of her relationships, in terms of a concern to maintain those relationships she had and a desire for future caring relationships. Despite the loss of relationships which had not enabled W to care for herself, W can be heard to have expressed a desire to hold on to the restorative possibilities of care in those relationships she maintained and in the possibilities of future relationships. Of significance to W was the hurt she would experience if she were transferred to a different unit where she would feel all alone, removed from those she cared about. The issue then becomes that of W's treatment and her response to those treating her in the context

[49] *Re W* 92.
[50] *Re W* 94.
[51] *Re W* 72.
[52] *Re W* 83.

of her desire to preserve relationships important to herself and the possibility of care for herself and others in the future. That is, W articulated her vulnerability and the hurt that she had, was, and could, experience in relational rather than individualistic terms.

In the case of *Re E*, considered above, while noting that, at 15 and three-quarters, A was nearing the age at which his views would be determinative, Ward J expressed the view that A's 'volition' had been 'conditioned' by the 'strong and powerful' influences of the teachings of the faith.[53] This included a wish to honour his parents as the 'Bible exhorts him' to and secure their love and respect. Inevitably, all thinking is developed under influences, including the idea that the preservation of life outweighs respect for strongly held beliefs. The judge's approach to the influence of the faith generally and A's parents specifically was premised upon a conception of the need for rules to limit the harm that can be caused through the influence of individuals who are primarily separate rather than appreciating connections arising from both relationships and beliefs. The alternative is to recognise that the self is formed in the context of social and personal relationships.

Furthermore, Ward J expressed the view that 'teenagers often express views with vehemence and conviction—all the vehemence and conviction of youth! Those of us who have passed beyond callow youth can all remember the convictions we have loudly proclaimed which now we find somewhat embarrassing.'[54]

Consequently, the judge thought that there was a possibility that in the future A's strongly held religious convictions might diminish or he may reject them.[55] Yet, this was A's authentic expression of his beliefs and, as Johnson J observed in the subsequent case of *Re P*, A adhered to his views into adulthood and, upon reaching the age of 18, he refused further blood products and died.[56] The moral conflict for A arose from the medical condition from which he suffered which required the administration of blood in its treatment contrary to his established beliefs, all alternatives having been tried without success. Either decision, to refuse or to accept the administration of blood, would inevitably cause hurt to A and his family. The judge emphasised the imagined harm of the experience of death and the effect upon A of realising the distress of his family but not the social and personal realities of A's life in the context of the beliefs that he shared with his family.

In *Re M*, M had heart failure and had been told two days before the court hearing that a transplant was the only option, but despite explanations, advice, and counselling would not give her consent.[57] In his judgment, Johnson J referred to the notes of the solicitor instructed by the Official Solicitor to find out M's

[53] *Re E* 393.
[54] *Re E* 393.
[55] *Re E* 393.
[56] *Re P (Medical Treatment: Best Interests)* [2003] EWHC 2327 [8].
[57] *Re M (Medical Treatment: Consent)* [1999] 2 FLR 1097, 1099.

wishes and feelings. While concerned to appear to hear her views, M's relational reasoning seemed not to have been understood. M had said that she did not want a transplant, but knew that if she did not, she would die. She did not want to die, but she would rather die 'with 15 years of my own heart' than have the transplant.[58] To the judge this was inconsistent; if preservation of life and the harm caused by a heart transplant were in conflict one had to prevail and surely that was the preservation of life. However, M explained that, 'If I had someone else's heart, I would be different from anybody else ... I would feel different with someone else's heart, that's a good enough reason not to have a heart transplant, even if it saved my life.'[59]

M adopted relational rather than individualistic reasoning recognising that she had responsibilities to both herself and to her family which meant that she was faced with a decision in which it was inevitable that someone would get hurt, herself or her family. M explained: 'I feel selfish. If I had the transplant I wouldn't be happy. If I were to die my family would be sad.'[60] M addressed but was not able to resolve the conflicting responsibilities and the question of who was most vulnerable and may be most hurt, reasoning from her parents' perspective while retaining her own. M explained that if she had a child her age she would 'go with whatever is best—what they want—I would not let them die'.[61] The judge interpreted M's views as demonstrating that she was 'overwhelmed' by the situation she was in given the swift deterioration from being a healthy active young woman to being at risk of death so that she had not 'been able to come to terms with her situation'. The judge employed abstract hierarchical reasoning prioritising life over the harm of a heart transplant viewed in terms of the physical and mental consequences for M as an individual. M's complex relational reasoning through which she sought to balance the needs and interests of herself and others was replaced by the more simple ordering of competing values. I argue in the next section that in the case of *Re JA*, rather than adopt abstract reasoning, considerations of justice and of care are integrated.[62]

## Integrating justice and care

Fourteen-year-old J had the 'spectre of serious illness' hanging over him as his parents, who were both HIV positive, had refused to agree to him being tested.[63] His parents had rejected mainstream medical treatment of their HIV believing that their

[58] *Re M (Medical Treatment: Consent)* 1100.
[59] *Re M (Medical Treatment: Consent)* 1100.
[60] *Re M (Medical Treatment: Consent)* 1100.
[61] *Re M (Medical Treatment: Consent)* 1100.
[62] *Re JA* [2014] EWHC 1135.
[63] *Re JA* [5].

health had been adversely affected by anti-retroviral therapy (ART).[64] Baker J considered that J had demonstrated, in his written statement, an understanding of HIV and the consequences of a positive diagnosis.[65] J expressed his decision to refuse testing to determine his HIV status and treatment if he tested positive in relational terms. He explained that he had listened to, but did not agree with, the views of the Trust's lead consultant for children with HIV. His main concern, informed by the views of his parents, was fear as to how medication might affect him, physically and emotionally.[66] J told the judge that while he agreed that he had been influenced by his parents, he thought that this was less so than when he was younger as other people had also influenced his thinking. He also told the judge that future decisions about his treatment would be influenced by other important relationships in his life, saying:

> I can't say that I'm never ever going to change my view, I know there's a possibility I will. When I grow up other people might influence my decisions. Like at university or even sixth form college. My partner—she could have different views and we might talk about it and I might go on to medication. I'm not saying that my view won't change.[67]

J was able to explain to the judge that communication with others in his web of relationships had and would continue to inform decisions he made about his care. His reasoning was informed by consideration of his self in the context of relationships both personal and with professionals, present and future.

Recognising the possible effect of a positive diagnosis on relationships within the context of discriminatory attitudes to HIV, J expressed his concern about his friends finding out his status and as a consequence rejecting him. This meant that he did not want special treatment at school or to take too much time off school to attend clinic.[68] His relationships with his friends were important to him, and he was aware of how these could be adversely affected. But he recognised that professionals did need to know his status to ensure that he received the care he needed. He acknowledged that he might need psychological therapy in the future and, having tested positive, agreed that his GP and emergency services should be aware of his diagnosis.[69] J therefore situated his decision about his medical care in the context of his self and his relationships.

But J was also able to explain his position in terms of dominant norms, although contextualising these based on the evidence and information provided to him. He explained to the judge that he had balanced the risks and, at that time, considered the risks of taking the medication to be higher than the risks of the virus. He also expressed the wish for more evidence. He told the judge that he did not have the

[64] *Re JA* [5]–[7].
[65] *Re JA* [60].
[66] *Re JA* [60].
[67] *Re JA* [60].
[68] *Re JA* [62].
[69] *Re JA* [64].

proof to enable him to accept the truth of his positive test. The judge asked J why he did not believe that he had sufficient proof of his HIV status given that J had had the test, the test had been analysed in the laboratory, and the result provided to him. J explained that 'I don't feel like a piece of paper is enough. I like to see what is going on' in the laboratory.[70] Presenting his decision in terms of risks, evidence, and information, J said he wanted more information from the consultant, other specialists, and people with a positive status so he could talk about his decision and find out how others had experienced the side effects of taking the medication. He told the judge that he would make decisions about his future treatment balancing of the risks and informed by experience.[71]

Baker J considered that J lacked *Gillick* competence to make decisions about having the test to determine his HIV status and, once tested to be positive, to receive ART, authorising both in J's best interests. However, the judge gave J some responsibility for his care as the best way through which to secure his co-operation and ensure the greater benefits from the wider treatments required. The judge held that J had *Gillick* competence to make his own decisions with respect to monitoring, blood tests, chest x-rays, psychotherapy, and peer support to which, by the time of the final judgment, J was agreed. The judge sought both to ensure the testing and treatment necessary to save J's life and also to minimise hurt through a response that recognised J's vulnerabilities.

## Conclusion

The dominant mode of reasoning in cases concerned with consent to medical treatment refused by teenagers is through hierarchical ordering of competing values. Judges can, but often do not seem to, hear explanations for the decision by teenagers expressed in terms of relationships, responsibilities, and care and the vulnerabilities and hurt in the resolution of moral conflict. An approach to cases concerned with the medical treatment of teenagers that integrated the ethics of justice and ethics of care would attend to the expression of the different voice. As a mode of reasoning, it would require consideration of the dilemma in real terms, seeking to understand it in terms of the actual consequences for the individual.[72] Integration of rights and responsibilities would mean that decisions about the medical treatment of teenagers would seek to find different solutions to the simple prioritisation of competing values, solutions informed through seeking to understand vulnerabilities and hurt for the individual in relationships. The result could be resolutions to the dilemma presented by teenagers who have refused their consent to

[70] *Re JA* [62].
[71] *Re JA* [63].
[72] Gilligan, *In a Different Voice*, pp. 100–1.

recommended medical treatment that are more responsive to the actual realities of their lives. Integration of the ethics of care with the ethics of justice may lead to justice that is more caring.

## Teenage refusal of medical treatment cases

What follows is a list, as of June 2025, of cases of refusal of consent to medical treatment by teenagers aged 13 years or older and able to express their wishes.

*Re E (A Minor) (Wardship: Medical Treatment)* [1993] 1 FLR 386: 15 years, male, administration of blood in treatment of leukaemia

*Re R (A Minor) (Wardship: Medical Treatment)* [1992] 1 FLR 190: 15 years, female, administration of drugs for psychotic state

*Re W (A Minor) (Medical Treatment: Court's Jurisdiction)* [1993] Fam 64: 16 years, female, treatment for anorexia

*Re S (A Minor) (Medical Treatment)* [1994] 2 FLR 1065: 15 years, female, administration of blood in treatment of beta minor thalassemia

*Re L (Medical Treatment: Gillick Competency)* [1998] 2 FLR 810: 14 years, female, administration of blood in treatment of severe burns

*Re M (Medical Treatment: Consent)* [1999] 2 FLR 1097: 15 years, female, heart transplant

*Re P (Medical Treatment: Best Interests)* [2003] EWHC 2327: 16 years, male, administration of blood in treatment of hypermobility syndrome

*An NHS Foundation Trust v A, M, and P* [2014] EWHC 920: 15 years, female, treatment of vomiting no organic cause or malignant pathology

*Re JA (A Minor)* [2014] EWHC 1135: 14 years, male, test and treat HIV

*An NHS Foundation Hospital v P* [2014] EWHC 1650: 17 years, female, antidote for paracetamol overdose

*Plymouth Hospitals NHS Trust v YZ* [2017] EWHC 2211: 14 years, female, test and treat suspected paracetamol overdose

*University Hospitals Plymouth NHS Trust v B (A Minor)* [2019] EWHC 1670: 16 years, female, administration of insulin in treatment of diabetes

*An NHS Trust v CX* [2019] EWHC 3033: 14 years, male, administration of blood in treatment of lymphatic cancer

*Re GW* [2021] EWHC 2105: 17 years, female, MS & self-harming

*Barking, Havering and Redbridge University Hospitals NHS Trust v X* [2020] EWHC 1630; *Re X* [2020] EWHC 3003; *Re X (A Child) (No 2)* [2021] EWHC 65: 15 years, female administration of blood in treatment of sickle cell

*An NHS Trust v D (A Minor)* [2021] EWHC 2676: 16 years, female, test and treat suspected paracetamol overdose

*A Teaching Hospitals NHS Trust v DV* [2021] EWHC 1037: 17 years, male, administration of blood in the treatment of cancer

*E & F (Minors: Blood Transfusion)* [2021] EWCA Civ 1888; appeal by E, girl, 16 years 8 months at time of decision of Theis J in May 2012 declaring lawful administration of blood if necessary during procedure to remove appendix; F, boy, 17 years 5 months at the time of the decision of Judd J declaring lawful the administration of blood if required due to haemorrhage following accident

*Y NHS Foundation Trust v AN* [2024] EWHC 805: 16 years 4 months, female, wanted more time to come to terms with diagnosis of acute leukaemia

*Re J (Blood Transfusion: Older Child: Jehovah's Witnesses)* [2024] EWHC 1034: 17 years 7 months, male, refusal of blood if required in the event of emergency during surgery to remove obstruction in the ureter leading from left kidney

# 9

# Consent to Medical Treatment for Trans Youth in Australia

STEPH JOWETT*

THE AUSTRALIAN LEGAL framework for consent to medical treatment for trans youth has long occupied a controversial and shifting landscape. It sits alongside advancing medical knowledge about gender diversity,[1] the lived experience of trans young people,[2] and the politicisation of trans lives in Australia and abroad.[3] The Australian legal experience is noteworthy in that the body of case law on the medical treatment of trans youth has developed over two decades, with significant changes to the legal framework.[4] Viewed as a whole, the jurisprudence is haphazard, inconsistent, and continually changing. Australian law presents a portrait of the shortcomings of case law responses to complex medico-socio-political phenomena and the harms attendant on the adjudication of individuals' bodies;[5] it offers a body of knowledge

* I would like to thank the editors of *Consenting Children* and an anonymous reviewer whose feedback has helped me to improve this contribution.

[1] Jenifer K. McGuire and Quinlyn J. Morrow, 'Pathways of Gender Development', in Michelle Forcier, Gerrit van Schalkwyk and Jack L. Turban (eds), *Pediatric Gender Identity* (New York, Springer, 2020), pp. 33–46.

[2] Clare Bartholomaeus, Damien W. Riggs and Annie Pullen Sansfaçon, 'Expanding and Improving Trans Affirming Care in Australia: Experiences with Healthcare Professionals among Transgender Young People and Their Parents', *Health Sociology Review*, 30 (2021), 58–71.

[3] Josh Taylor, 'How Children Became the Target in a Rightwing Culture War over Gender', *The Guardian*, 24 August 2019. https://www.theguardian.com/society/2019/aug/24/how-children-became-the-target-in-a-rightwing-culture-war-over-gender (accessed 23 December 2024); Florence Ashley and Sergio Domínguez, 'Transgender Healthcare Does Not Stop at the Doorstep of the Clinic', *American Journal of Medicine*, 134 (2020), 158–60.

[4] For a comprehensive historical review of these cases, see Steph Jowett, *Consent for Medical Treatment of Trans Youth* (Cambridge, Cambridge University Press, 2022).

[5] Fiona Kelly, '"The Court Process Is Slow but Biology Is Fast": Assessing the Impact of the Family Court Approval Process on Transgender Children and Their Families', *Australian Journal of Family Law*, 30 (2016), 112–28.

*Proceedings of the British Academy*, **279**, 168–191, © Authors 2025.

of which law and policy makers in comparable jurisdictions should take heed when crafting regulation in this area.

Trans individuals identify as having a gender that is incongruent with their sex assigned at birth. They may be distinguished from individuals who are cisgendered, being those whose gender is congruent with their sex assigned at birth.[6] I use trans as an umbrella term for people with a non-cis gender modality;[7] however, individuals may self-identify as trans, non-binary, genderqueer, agender (genderless), or employ other terms. The prevalence of youth in Australia identifying as trans is approximately 2.3 per cent.[8] While gender norms and expressions, and the extent to which gender dysphoria occurs, are culturally dependent, this is not inconsistent with data from other countries.[9] Further, approximately 8 per cent of trans youth in Australia report having a non-binary gender.[10]

Gender dysphoria—a clinical diagnosis in the *DSM-5*—is experienced by a subset of trans individuals; it manifests in clinically significant distress associated with the incongruence between their gender and sex assigned at birth.[11] Medical treatment to explore or affirm the gender of such individuals is available in Australia. However, the barriers to affirming gender, medical and non-medical, remain especially high for minors.

Since 2004, trans young people in Australia, their families, and clinicians have encountered legal barriers to giving lawful consent to or to gaining authorisation for treatment. The legal framework primarily comprises a patchwork of decisions by single judges of the Family Court, alongside two Full Court decisions in *Re: Jamie* and *Re: Kelvin*.[12] The shifting case law sits alongside relatively static legislation governing the age of majority, as well as the powers of parents and the Family Court of Australia, as laid out in the Family Law Act 1975 (Cth).

[6] Charlotte Chuck Tate, Cris P. Youssef, and Jay N. Bettergarcia, 'Integrating the Study of Transgender Spectrum and Cisgender Experiences of Self-Categorization from a Personality Perspective', *Review of General Psychology*, 18 (2014), 302–12 at 302.

[7] Florence Ashley, '"Trans" Is My Gender Modality: A Modest Terminological Proposal', in Laura Erickson-Schroth (ed.), *Trans Bodies, Trans Selves*, 2nd edn (New York, Oxford University Press, 2022).

[8] Christopher M. Fisher *et al.*, *6th National Survey of Australian Secondary Students and Sexual Health 2018* (Melbourne, Australian Research Centre in Sex, Health and Society, La Trobe University, 2019), p. 113.

[9] John Shields *et al.*, 'Estimating Population Size and Demographic Characteristics of Lesbian, Gay, Bisexual, and Transgender Youth in Middle School', *Journal of Adolescent Health*, 52 (2013), 248–50.

[10] Ada S. Cheung *et al.*, 'Non-Binary and Binary Gender Identity in Australian Trans and Gender Diverse Individuals', *Archives of Sexual Behavior*, 49 (2020), 2673–81.

[11] American Psychiatric Association, *Diagnostic and Statistical Manual of Mental Disorders*, 5th edn (Washington, DC, American Psychiatric Publishing, 2013).

[12] *Re: Jamie* (2013) 50 Fam LR 369; *Re: Kelvin* (2017) 57 Fam LR 503. The Family Court is a federal court which heard family law matters in all states and territories of Australia except for Western Australia which has a separate Family Court. Single judges of the Court hear applications at first instance and the Full Court comprising multiple members of the bench hears appeals from single judges of the Court. In 2021, it merged with the Federal Circuit Court to become The Federal Circuit and Family Court of Australia.

In this chapter, I argue that the legal framework, historical and contemporary, is underpinned by cisgenderism. Cisgenderism 'unlike "transphobia" … describes a prejudicial ideology, rather than an individual attitude, that is systemic, multi-level and reflected in authoritative cultural discourses'.[13] More demanding laws that (without clear justification) apply only to trans youth seeking vital gender-affirming healthcare is cisgenderism; these additional legal requirements discriminate against trans individuals and contribute to trans stigma. These laws have not furthered the well-being of trans young people. Rather, as a barrier to accessing care, they have become a source of harm.[14] Consent laws dictating who provides consent to gender affirming care, and the process for obtaining it, should reflect medical realities and facilitate timely access to clinically recommended treatment.[15] Further, laws bearing on adolescent decision-making should reflect the evolving capacities of young people and the exercise of their bodily autonomy;[16] especially where it surrounds a choice central to a person's sense of self and long-term well-being. At present, the law does not further either of these ends.

In the next section, I outline—by reference to current clinical guidelines—the relevant medical treatment sought by trans youth in Australia for context. I then consider the legal barriers to such treatment shaped by case law over time. I explain and evaluate the nature and development of authorities establishing the legal parameters for consent to each stage of treatment—either curtailing or enabling consent by youth or their legal guardians. The case law highlights the dynamic and complicated legal framework that trans youth, families, lawyers, and doctors have had to navigate. The early decisions analysed restricted the decision-making of trans youth and their guardians by requiring court approval of puberty blockers, gender-affirming hormones and surgical interventions, or judicial assessment of *Gillick* competence for those treatments.[17] More recent decisions have retreated from gatekeeping in many decisions concerning puberty blockers and gender-affirming hormones. However, one of the latest decisions reverses this trend in significant ways, regressing the law for all forms of treatment in cases of dispute.[18] My analysis also exposes the current absence of Full Court authority on the principles governing consent to surgical interventions. I conclude that the Australian legal framework has failed to keep pace with medical knowledge and standards of best practice.

[13] Y. Gavriel Ansara and Peter Hegarty, 'Cisgenderism in Psychology: Pathologising and Misgendering Children from 1999 to 2008', *Psychology & Sexuality*, 3 (2012), 137–60 at 143.

[14] See Kelly, *The Court Process Is Slow*.

[15] On the incongruence of the law with medical knowledge, see Jowett, *Medical Treatment of Trans Youth*.

[16] Steph Jowett, Georgina Dimopoulos and Fiona Kelly, 'Reforming the Law on Consent to Medical Treatment for Trans Youth: A Renewed Call for Legislative Intervention', *Laws*, 11 (2022), 56 at 9–11.

[17] *Gillick* competence refers to legal competence attained at common law when a young person 'achieves a sufficient understanding and intelligence to enable him or her to understand fully what is proposed': *Gillick v West Norfolk and Wisbech Area Health Authority* [1986] AC 112, 189.

[18] See discussion below of *Re: Imogen (No 6)* [2020] FamCA 761.

It requires the discriminatory and harmful process of court oversight of medical decision-making by and for some trans youth.

## Medical treatment of trans youth in Australia

Medical treatment of trans young people has been available in Australia since 2003.[19] The treatment approach has been similar to that in Europe and North America and, more recently, the United Kingdom. International guidelines for treating trans youth have been available since the 2006 'Dutch protocol'.[20] Since 2018, clinicians in Australia have had clinical guidelines specific to youth in the Australian context.[21] The *Australian Standards of Care and Treatment Guidelines for Trans and Gender Diverse Children and Adolescents* ('the *Australian Guidelines*') were developed to respond to particular challenges in providing care to trans youth in Australia. These include the degree of cultural and linguistic diversity in Australia and large geographical distances between cities and rural and regional areas.[22] The *Guidelines* were based upon a consensus of Australian clinicians working in the area, previously published standards of care and treatment guidance, position statements, and data from non-randomised clinical studies and observational studies. The *Australian Guidelines* are endorsed by the Australian Professional Association for Trans Health (AUSPath), the national body for professionals involved in the health, rights, and well-being of all trans people.

The *Australian Guidelines* broadly adopt a gender-affirming approach that is individualised.[23] Interventions to align gender expression or identity with sex assigned at birth are considered unethical,[24] and are illegal in many Australian states under laws criminalising suppression practices or conversion therapy.[25] Recommended medical treatment comprises three distinct, yet commonly overlapping, treatment stages: pubertal suppression (stage 1); gender-affirming treatment using oestrogen or testosterone (stage 2); and gender-affirming surgical interventions (stage 3). The

[19] Michelle Telfer, Michelle Tollit, and Debi Feldman, 'Transformation of Health-Care and Legal Systems for the Transgender Population: The Need for Change in Australia', *Journal of Paediatrics and Child Health*, 51 (2015), 1051–3.

[20] H. A. Delemarre-Van De Waal and P. T. Cohen-Kettenis, 'Clinical Management of Gender Identity Disorder in Adolescents: A Protocol on Psychological and Paediatric Endocrinology Aspects', *European Journal of Endocrinology*, 155 (2006) S131–7.

[21] Michelle Telfer *et al.*, *Australian Standards of Care and Treatment Guidelines for Trans and Gender Diverse Children and Adolescents*, Version 1.3 (Melbourne, Royal Children's Hospital Melbourne, 2021).

[22] Michelle M. Telfer *et al.*, 'Australian Standards of Care and Treatment Guidelines for Transgender and Gender Diverse Children and Adolescents', *The Medical Journal of Australia*, 209 (2018), 132–6.

[23] Telfer *et al.*, *Australian Standards*, v 1.3.

[24] WPATH, 'Standards of Care for the Health of Transsexual, Transgender and Gender Nonconforming People, Version 8', *International Journal Transgender Health*, 23 (2022), S1–S258.

[25] See *Public Health Act 2005* (Qld), s 213H; *Change or Suppression (Conversion) Practices Prohibition Act 2021* (Vic); *Sexuality and Gender Identity Conversion Practices Act 2020* (ACT).

language of 'staged' treatment, referring to the different types of treatment available for adolescents, is predominantly utilised in Australian legal judgments and the legal literature rather than the *Australian Guidelines* themselves. While the language of stages connotes a linear trajectory with a defined endpoint, the *Australian Guidelines* emphasise that there is no defined treatment trajectory. Trans individuals may seek some, all, or none of these 'stages'; treatment is inherently individualised. This is particularly so for those who identify as non-binary.

According to the *Australian Guidelines*, the young person must be diagnosed with gender dysphoria under *DSM-5*, while meeting other clinical criteria, to receive treatment.[26] Stage 1, pubertal suppression, involves the administration of gonadotrophin-releasing hormone (GnRH) analogues to suppress or block the advance of natal puberty. This is not recommended until the individual's pubertal development has reached a prescribed threshold (Tanner stage 2). The effects are largely reversible. The administration of gender-affirming hormones, testosterone, or oestrogen (stage 2) carries a more significant number of irreversible effects. The *Australian Guidelines* note that there is no age threshold for the commencement of gender-affirming hormones; older international clinical guidelines mandated a minimum of age 12 as a threshold requirement.[27] Chest surgery on transmasculine youth (stage 3) is permitted, where clinically indicated, on trans young people in Australia, albeit rarely.[28] However, genital surgery is not currently recommended before adulthood under the *Australian Guidelines* for '[d]ecisions regarding an individual adolescent's best interest and ability to consent for genital surgery are more complex than that of chest reconstructive surgery'.[29]

It is essential to keep in mind that outcomes for trans youth treated with variations of the three-staged protocol are positive.[30] There is evidence that medical treatment in adolescence, rather than just psychological support, improves the psychological functioning and well-being of trans youth.[31] Taking puberty blockers, where desired by individuals, is associated with reduced lifetime suicide ideation in trans and gender diverse youth.[32] Similarly, access to gender-affirming hormones

[26] Telfer *et al.*, *Australian Standards*, v 1.3.

[27] Telfer *et al.*, *Australian Standards*, v 1.3; WPATH 'Standards of Care'.

[28] Telfer *et al.*, *Australian Standards*, v 1.3; See e.g. *Re: Alex* (2009) 42 Fam LR 645; *Re: Leo* [2015] FamCA 50; *Re: Lincoln (No 2)* [2016] FamCA 1071; *Re: Quinn* [2016] FamCA 617; *Re: Tony* [2016] FamCA 936.

[29] Telfer *et al.*, *Australian Standards*, v 1.3, p. 25.

[30] Anna I. R. van der Miesen *et al.*, 'Psychological Functioning in Transgender Adolescents Before and After Gender-Affirmative Care Compared With Cisgender General Population Peers', *Journal of Adolescent Health*, 66 (2020), 699–704.

[31] Annelou L. C. de Vries *et al.*, 'Young Adult Psychological Outcome After Puberty Suppression and Gender Reassignment', *Pediatrics*, 134 (2014), 696–704; Rosalia Costa *et al.*, 'Psychological Support, Puberty Suppression, and Psychosocial Functioning in Adolescents with Gender Dysphoria', *Journal of Sexual Medicine*, 12 (2015), 2206–14.

[32] Jack L. Turban *et al.*, 'Pubertal Suppression for Transgender Youth and Risk of Suicidal Ideation', *Pediatrics*, 145 (2020), e20191725.

in adolescence leads to improved mental health outcomes, including lower odds of suicidal ideation and severe psychological distress in adulthood, compared with those who desired but were unable to access the treatment.[33] These are welcome findings for a cohort that exhibit high levels of distress. A 2016, nationally representative, Australian study found that among 859 trans youth aged 14 to 25 years of age, 79.7 per cent had self-harmed, 82.4 per cent had suicidal thoughts, and 48.1 per cent had attempted suicide at some point in their life.[34] The only empirically supported treatment that resolves this distress is gender-affirming medical care.[35] Opting not to provide medical treatment is not a neutral course of action; neither is delaying treatment until adulthood. In the case of puberty blockers—especially—the timing of treatment is crucial to abate irreversible, unwanted, and distressing pubertal development. In the absence of treatment, or the presence of delayed treatment, continuation and possible worsening of psychosocial distress is likely, and the risk of an adolescent self-harming or attempting suicide is not appropriately addressed.

There is currently a limited evidence base behind gender-affirming interventions in adolescence, particularly as to the long-term consequences of puberty blockers.[36] As such, early treatment of gender dysphoria in adolescence has been criticised and labelled as 'experimental', a label which Simona Giordano and Søren Holm convincingly argue is misplaced.[37] In part, criticism stems from the lack of randomised controlled trials, comparing the relative outcomes of treating and not treating youth with gender dysphoria. Such trials are neither feasible, nor ethical in this context.[38] Further, uncertainty over medium and long-term effects of a treatment does not mean it is experimental; this is the case, for example, for many approved drugs used 'off label' or in paediatrics. In these circumstances, whether a medical intervention is clinically appropriate is determined by a probabilistic calculation of likely risks and benefits to the patient.[39] Concerns that stem from desistance studies showing

[33] Jack L. Turban *et al.*, 'Access to Gender-Affirming Hormones during Adolescence and Mental Health Outcomes among Transgender Adults', *PLoS ONE*, 17 (2022), e0261039.

[34] Penelope Strauss *et al.*, 'Associations Between Negative Life Experiences and the Mental Health of Trans and Gender Diverse Young People in Australia: Findings from Trans Pathways', *Psychological Medicine*, 50 (2020), 808–17.

[35] Marcus A Hidalgo *et al.*, 'The Gender Affirmative Model: What We Know and What We Aim to Learn', *Human Development*, 56 (2013), 285–90.

[36] Ken C. Pang *et al.*, 'Everyone Agrees Transgender Children Require More Science', *Medical Journal of Australia*, 211 (2019), 142. In the United Kingdom, domestic prescription of puberty-suppressing hormones to minors for gender dysphoria has been largely prohibited by a combination of the Medicines (Gonadotrophin Releasing Hormone Analogues) (Restrictions on Private Sales and Supplies) Order 2024 and greylisting under the Part XVIIIB of the NHS Drug Tariff, during the period which the PATHWAYS trial takes place to establish the evidence base on the management of gender incongruence in this population: https://fundingawards.nihr.ac.uk/award/NIHR167530 (accessed 13 July 2025).

[37] Simona Giordano and Søren Holm, 'Is Puberty Delaying Treatment "Experimental Treatment"?', *International Journal of Transgender Health*, 21 (2020), 113–21.

[38] Giordano and Holm 'Puberty Delaying Treatment'.

[39] Giordano and Holm 'Puberty Delaying Treatment', 116.

that a high rate of pre-pubertal trans youth grow up to be cisgender adults are clinically irrelevant to the choice of treatment approach for pubertal youth; desistance research fails to offer sound reasons to deny or delay gender-affirming care to this cohort.[40] In recognition of the need for greater evidence, longitudinal studies of trans youth have begun in many jurisdictions, and are likely to provide significant data to inform clinical practice.[41] This chapter proceeds from the view that current concerns over the evidence base do not warrant greater control over gender-affirming medical care than applies to other types of medical treatment.

## The Australian legal framework for consent to treatment for trans youth

In Australia, legally valid consent to medical treatment is required to negate civil or criminal liability. Those under the age of 18 in Australia are considered minors and are presumed to lack decision-making capacity in respect of medical decisions.[42] Since the 1992 decision of the High Court in *Marion's Case*,[43] however, the doctrine of *Gillick* competence has formed a part of Australian law.[44] Young people under the age of 18 who demonstrate the understanding and intelligence required by the *Gillick* test may provide valid consent for their own assessment and treatment.[45] Where youth cannot provide consent, parents and guardians routinely provide consent on behalf of minors in their care. This is an incident of parental responsibility under the Family Law Act 1975 (Cth), as well as common and criminal law insofar as parents and guardians have a duty to provide the necessaries of life to children in their care, including healthcare.[46]

In the case of trans youth seeking treatment for gender dysphoria, considerably different requirements apply to valid consent compared to the general Australian

[40] Florence Ashley, 'The Clinical Irrelevance of "Desistance" Research for Transgender and Gender Creative Youth', *Psychology of Sexual Orientation and Gender Diversity*, 9 (2022), 387–97.

[41] See M. A. Tollit *et al.*, 'What Are the Health Outcomes of Trans and Gender Diverse Young People in Australia? Study Protocol for the Trans20 Longitudinal Cohort Study', *BMJ Open*, 9 (2019), e032151; Kristina R. Olson and Selin Gülgöz, 'Early Findings from the TransYouth Project: Gender Development in Transgender Children', *Child Development Perspectives*, 12 (2018), 93–7.

[42] *Age of Majority Act 1974* (ACT), s 5; *Minors (Property and Contracts) Act 1970* (NSW), s 9; *Age of Majority Act 1974* (NT), s 4; *Law Reform Act 1995* (Qld), s 17; *Age of Majority (Reduction) Act 1970* (SA), s 3; *Age of Majority Act 1973* (Tas), s 3; *Age of Majority Act 1977* (Vic), s 3; *Age of Majority Act 1972* (WA), s 5. In South Australia, young people aged 16 years of age and over may consent to medical treatment 'as validly and effectively as an adult': *Consent to Medical Treatment and Palliative Care Act 1995* (SA), ss 3(a)(i), 4, 6.

[43] *Secretary, Department of Health & Community Services v JWB and SMB (Marion's Case)* (1992) 175 CLR 218.

[44] *Gillick*; *Marion's Case* 237.

[45] South Australia has codified a version of the *Gillick* test for those under 16 years of age: *Consent to Medical Treatment and Palliative Care Act 1995*, s 12(b)(i).

[46] *Marion's Case* 235 (Mason CJ, Dawson, Toohey, and Gaudron JJ).

regime for medical consent. These flow from a body of case law developed from 1992 onwards carving out a category of 'special medical procedures' that lies outside the bounds of treatment to which legal guardians in Australia can provide valid consent. Special medical procedures sit alongside the more general limitation that parents and guardians cannot consent to illegal procedures or those not in the best interests of the child. This special category was fashioned in response to the non-therapeutic sterilisation of intellectually disabled children. The Australian High Court in *Marion's Case*—which concerned the non-therapeutic sterilisation of an intellectually impaired child—took the view that a procedural safeguard was necessary to prevent parents exercising their ability to consent to non-therapeutic sterilisation procedures to the long-term detriment of young people, against a backdrop of discriminatory treatment of women and intellectually disabled people. The procedural safeguard being that parents must apply to a court for authorisation of treatment.

In *Marion's Case*, the Australian High Court held that where some or all of a set of factors were present, a court would consider that type of treatment a special medical procedure, for which treatment could not be performed without court approval, the relevant factors being:

- The procedure is non-therapeutic in nature;
- The procedure is major, irreversible, and invasive;
- There is a significant risk of the wrong decision being made, 'either as to a child's present or future capacity to consent or about what are the best interests of a child who cannot consent',[47] emanating from the complexity of the question of consent, the medicalisation of a decision that is not purely medical, and the potential conflict between the interests of the child and family members involved;[48] and
- Grave consequences would flow were a wrong decision made.

When these criteria are met, they render the relevant treatment a 'special case' as a class.[49]

The judiciary has relied on at least some of these factors in subsequent cases to identify further special medical procedures, including—at various points in time—the hormonal and surgical treatment of gender dysphoria. In the 2004 case of *Re: Alex*,[50] a single judge of the Family Court found hormonal treatment for a trans young person to be a special medical procedure. The next sub-section explores this key judgment, as well as several others. Early decisions restricted the decision-making of trans youth and their guardians by requiring court approval of stage

[47] *Marion's Case 250.*
[48] *Marion's Case 250–252.*
[49] *Marion's Case 250.*
[50] *Re: Alex (Hormonal Treatment for Gender Dysphoria)* (2004) 31 Fam LR 503.

1 or stage 2 treatment or judicial assessment of *Gillick* competence. More recent decisions have removed this gatekeeping function from most decisions about stage 1 and stage 2 treatment for *some* trans youth who have full parental support. The analysis indicates a current absence of clear legal authority on the principles governing consent to stage 3 treatment, as well as where there is a dispute or controversy over treatment.

## Legal status of treatment for gender dysphoria as a medical intervention

Treatment for trans youth has been treated as 'special' in Australia since the case of *Re: Alex* in 2004.[51] *Re: Alex* was the first case before an Australian court to consider the law in respect of consent to gender-affirming treatment for trans youth. Nicholson CJ, noted that, at the time, the application was a 'novel' one.[52] It was proposed that Alex, aged 10, receive a combination of progesterone and oestrogen to suppress menstruation— in essence, the contraceptive pill, though labelled as stage 1 treatment.[53] It was further proposed that when Alex reached 16 years of age, he commence taking pubertal blockers (also stage 1 treatment) and testosterone to encourage masculinisation of his body (stage 2 treatment).[54]

By reference to the High Court's decision in *Marion's Case* and the principles developed therein, Nicholson CJ ruled that the proposed treatment, both stage 1 and stage 2, constituted a 'special medical procedure'.[55] His Honour considered the relevant principles to define a special medical procedure as: (1) 'invasive, permanent and irreversible'; and (2) 'not for the purpose of curing a malfunction or disease'.[56]

Nicholson CJ accepted the evidence before the court that although stage 1 treatment (the contraceptive pill and pubertal blockers) had reversible effects, stage 2 (testosterone) carried irreversible effects.[57] Accepting the submission that his Honour should treat both stages of treatment as a 'single treatment plan', Nicholson CJ concluded that the proposed treatment was, as a whole, irreversible.[58]

Nicholson CJ then ruled on whether the treatment (both stage 1 and stage 2) was for the purpose of '[curing] a disease or [correcting] a malfunction'[59] and, thus, therapeutic. His Honour held that 'therapeutic' treatment, as defined by the High Court *Marion's Case*, was confined to the treatment of physiological conditions,

[51] *Re: Alex.*
[52] *Re: Alex* [180].
[53] *Re: Alex* [19]–[20], [112]–[117].
[54] *Re: Alex* [19], [21].
[55] *Re: Alex* [196].
[56] *Re: Alex* [153].
[57] *Re: Alex* [181], [183].
[58] *Re: Alex* [188].
[59] *Re: Alex* [190].

namely, 'disease in or malfunctioning of organs'.[60] Since the treatment was for gender identity disorder, a psychiatric condition in the *DSM-IV*,[61] without conclusive evidence that it had physiological underpinnings, the proposed hormonal treatment did not meet the criteria for being therapeutic.[62] Accordingly, Nicholson CJ found that the treatment amounted to a special medical procedure and required court authorisation.[63]

The conclusion that treatment for a psychiatric condition is not therapeutic is absurd by medical standards and indeed the problematic nature of a test based upon a therapeutic/non-therapeutic distinction was foreshadowed by one of the judges in the minority in *Marion's Case*. There, Deane J noted that the distinction between what is therapeutic or non-therapeutic is far 'from precise and, particularly where psychiatric illness is involved, may be all but meaningless'.[64] Legal interpretation aside, as Kerridge, Lowe and Stewart aptly note, the categorisation of treatment for gender dysphoria as non-therapeutic, 'sends a message that these illnesses are not real and devastating'.[65] Nevertheless, *Re: Alex* was the authoritative case in this area in Australia for nearly a decade. It resulted in over 10 applications to the Family Court for approval of treatment of trans youth before the law changed. In every case, single judges of the Family Court authorised treatment.

In 2013, Nicholson CJ's ruling in *Re: Alex* received Full Court scrutiny in *Re: Jamie.*[66] The majority of the Court—Bryant CJ, Finn and Strickland JJ—held that, since gender dysphoria is a psychiatric condition in the *DSM-5*,[67] treatment was therapeutic as it was to treat a 'malfunction or disease'.[68] This was despite it not being possible to determine the cause of diverse gender identity conclusively.[69] Unlike Nicholson CJ, their Honours declined to limit the observations of the majority in respect of therapeutic treatments in *Marion's Case* to physical disease.[70] As such, stage 1 treatment was held not to be a special medical procedure.[71] This conclusion was also supported by the observation that gender dysphoria is neither 'novel' nor 'as unusual as it presented itself in 2003 when *Re: Alex* was decided'.[72]

[60] *Re: Alex* [195].

[61] American Psychiatric Association, *Diagnostic and Statistical Manual of Mental Disorders*, 4th edn (Washington, DC, American Psychiatric Publishing, 1994).

[62] *Re: Alex* [195]–[196].

[63] *Re: Alex* [196].

[64] *Marion's Case* 296 (Deane J).

[65] Ian Kerridge, Michael Lowe, and Cameron Stewart, *Ethics and Law for the Health Professions*, 3rd edn (Annandale, NSW, Federation Press, 2009), p. 493.

[66] *Re: Jamie* (2013) 50 Fam LR 369.

[67] The relevant DSM diagnosis had been revised between the time when submissions were received and the judgment was released.

[68] *Re: Jamie* [91].

[69] *Re: Jamie* [95].

[70] *Re: Jamie* [97] (Bryant CJ), [176] (Finn J), [193] (Strickland J).

[71] *Re: Jamie* [98].

[72] *Re: Jamie* [99].

Among arguments presented to the Court that the treatment should still be considered a special medical procedure were that there was a significant risk of making the wrong decision because the 'procedures to treat it/respond to it are experimental', 'ethically complex and contentious', and that 'there are differing professional opinions as to how a child or adolescent should be treated for gender identity disorder'.[73] The Court's view was that 'the evidence ... was overwhelmingly indicative of the treatment being a common treatment' and, that 'many conditions result in different views about what treatment should be given'. The possibility of there being multiple treatment options did not, provided they are not invasive, permanent, and irreversible, render a treatment as one requiring court approval.[74] Bryant CJ conceded that there might be cases in the future that require the Court's authorisation due to the 'evolving state of medical knowledge', but for the reasons above, stage 1 treatment did not.[75]

Accordingly, the Court held that treatment of gender dysphoria was 'not a special medical procedure that displaces the parental responsibility of [Jamie's parents] to decide upon the appropriate treatment for their child. Properly advised and informed, parents are in a position to make such decisions'.[76] On that basis, the Court unanimously ruled that 'absent controversy' or where a child is capable of making their own decision, stage 1 treatment fell within the ambit of procedures to which parents could consent.[77] However, where there was a dispute about stage 1 (or indeed stage 2) treatment, an application to the Court was necessary.[78]

Regarding stage 2 treatment, however, the Court ruled differently. Despite finding that stage 2 treatment is also therapeutic, the Court viewed the irreversible nature of the treatment to create a significant risk that the wrong decision would be made about a child's capacity or best interests. This risk, combined with the (supposedly) 'grave consequences of a wrong decision', required that it remain a special medical procedure.[79] Court oversight remained appropriate and treatment could not be authorised by parental consent.[80] Judicial assessment of *Gillick* competence or best interests would be necessary. This aspect of the *Re: Jamie* decision has attracted significant criticism, insofar as commentators have read *Marion's Case* to make the therapeutic/non-therapeutic criterion a threshold distinction, such that other criteria including reversibility of effects are inapplicable if treatment is determined to be therapeutic—no court application need be required.[81]

73 *Re: Jamie* [101].

74 *Re: Jamie* [102], [105].

75 *Re: Jamie* [106].

76 *Re: Jamie* [107].

77 *Re: Jamie* [108], [140] (Bryant CJ), [179] (Finn J), [194] (Strickland J).

78 *Re: Jamie* [140].

79 *Re: Jamie* [140] (Bryant CJ), [182] (Finn J), [195] (Strickland J).

80 *Re: Jamie* [140] (Bryant CJ).

81 Felicity Bell, 'Children with Gender Dysphoria and the Jurisdiction of the Family Court', *UNSW Law Journal*, 38 (2015), 426–54 at 440–1; Kerridge, Lowe and Stewart, *Ethics and Law*, pp. 480–90; Malcolm K. Smith, 'The Boundaries of Parental Decision-Making and the Requirement to Obtain Court Approval for "Special Medical Procedures"', *Queensland Lawyer*, 33 (2013), 182–7 at 186–7.

Five years after the *Re: Jamie* decision, the Full Court of the Family Court took the opportunity to revisit the law in respect of stage 2 treatment in *Re: Kelvin*.[82] With regards to whether stage 2 treatment remained a special medical procedure, the majority of the court concluded that it did not; it falls within the scope of medical decisions that parents are permitted to make. In reaching this view, their central consideration was whether the existing law was 'able to effectively reflect the current state of medical knowledge'.[83]

The Court observed that it was 'readily apparent that the judicial understanding of Gender Dysphoria and its treatment [had] fallen behind the advances in medical science'.[84] These advances included: the revisions of the diagnosis between *DSM-IV* and *DSM-5*; development of the *Australian Guidelines*; evidence of outcomes of those treated at the Melbourne paediatric gender clinic; and increased knowledge regarding the risks of non-treatment. These factors were said to render it beyond dispute that 'the state of medical knowledge has evolved since the decision in *Re Jamie*' and the risks of making a wrong decision with grave consequences had lowered.[85] Accordingly, stage 2 treatment for gender dysphoria 'can no longer be considered a medical procedure for which consent lies outside the bounds of parental authority and requires the imprimatur of the Court'.[86] However, of importance to later judgments, the majority noted that their ruling did not address the need for court authorisation where there is a 'genuine dispute or controversy' as to whether treatment should be administered.[87]

The form, at law, of the majority in *Re: Kelvin*'s departure from *Re: Jamie* was that there were legally relevant factual differences; it was unnecessary to rule that *Re: Jamie* was 'plainly wrong'.[88] The minority of the Court took a different view on the reasons: there were significant issues of interpretation in *Re: Jamie* that rendered it necessary to correct the record. In the minority's view, 'the principles that emerge from *Marion's Case* when applied to *Re: Jamie* should have resulted in the conclusion that in relation to stage 2 treatment for Gender Dysphoria the court has no role to play unless there is a dispute about consent or treatment'.[89] In particular, one of the erroneous interpretations in *Re: Jamie* stemmed from a lack of recognition that *Marion's Case* does not 'stand for the proposition that consent to a therapeutic procedure which has grave or irreversible consequences is outside the scope of parental power or outside the consent of a competent child'.[90]

[82] *Re: Kelvin* [2017] FamCA 78.
[83] *Re: Kelvin* [152].
[84] *Re: Kelvin.*
[85] *Re: Kelvin* [159].
[86] *Re: Kelvin* [164].
[87] *Re: Kelvin* [167].
[88] *Re: Kelvin* [171]–[177].
[89] *Re: Kelvin* [189].
[90] *Re: Kelvin.*

The effect of not ruling *Re: Jamie* to have been wrongly decided was that it created a situation in which *Re: Kelvin* and *Re: Jamie* seemingly existed in parallel.[91] The implications are significant, since the breadth of coverage of the decisions is different.

The Court in *Re: Jamie* did not address the status of stage 3 treatment and in *Re: Kelvin* explicitly noted that its conclusions did not apply to stage 3 treatment. At the time of writing, there remains no Full Court consideration of the legal principles applicable to gender-affirming surgery. Single judges of the Family Court have tended to equate the law on stage 3 treatment with the law on stage 2 treatment, given the importance that reversibility has assumed in the case law.[92] Since *Re: Kelvin*, however, which removed many legal requirements for stage 2 treatment, single judges have been in conflict as to whether the same can be said for stage 3 treatment.[93] That is, whether, in accordance with *Re: Jamie*, judicial assessment of *Gillick* competence is required.[94] Or whether, following *Re: Kelvin*, 'where treating practitioners have agreed that the subject child is *Gillick* competent, where it is agreed that the proposed treatment is therapeutic and where there is no controversy, no application to the Family Court is necessary before Stage 3 treatment for Gender Dysphoria can proceed'.[95]

The significant ambiguity as to the legal principles applicable to surgical treatment of trans youth in Australia—due to differences in what Full Court judgments cover—demonstrates the trouble with regulating this area of medicine through common law. Clarification of the law is needed.

## Competence and court authorisation

As well as considering the scope of parental consent, trans youth cases have also considered whether the child is competent to consent to treatment themselves. In *Re: Alex*, before dealing with the ambit of parental consent, Nicholson CJ considered the question of whether Alex could consent to the treatment himself.

The expert evidence presented in *Re: Alex* was inconclusive on whether Alex was *Gillick* competent to consent to stage 1 and 2 treatment. His Honour noted that while one of the reports 'suggest[ed] Alex may in fact have *Gillick* capacity or may reach that standard soon … nonetheless it [was the expert's] view that the decision should be in the court's hands'.[96] In Nicholson CJ's view, the evidence did not conclusively establish that Alex was competent to consent to the proposed treatment.[97]

91 Stephanie Jowett and Fiona Kelly, '*Re Imogen*: A Step in the Wrong Direction', *Australian Journal of Family Law*, 32 (2021), 31–56.

92 See e.g. *Re: Leo* [11].

93 *Re: Matthew* [2018] FamCA 161; *Re: LG* [2017] FCWA 179.

94 *RE: LG* [14].

95 *Re: Matthew* [1].

96 *Re: Alex* [165].

97 *Re: Alex* [168].

His Honour noted that 'it is one thing for a child or young person to have a general understanding of what is proposed and its effect but it is quite another to conclude that he/she has sufficient maturity to fully understand the grave nature and effects of the proposed treatment'.[98] In the context of gender-affirmation, Nicholson CJ opined *in dicta* that he had 'doubts about the correctness of the proposition' that 'if this Court finds that the child has achieved "a sufficient understanding and intelligence" to enable the child "to understand fully what is proposed", then this Court has no further role in this matter'.[99] His Honour proffered that:

> there is a considerable difference between a child or young person deciding to use contraceptives as in Gillick and a child or young person determining upon a course that will 'change' his/her sex. It is highly questionable whether a 13 year old could ever be regarded as having the capacity for the latter, and this situation may well continue until the young person reaches maturity.[100]

In *Re: Jamie*, in the context of stage 2 treatment (only), Bryant CJ emphasised the importance of enabling adolescent autonomy:

> it would be contrary to the *Convention on the Rights of the Child*, and to the autonomous decision-making to which a *Gillick* competent child is entitled, to hold that there is a particular class of treatment, namely stage two treatment for childhood gender identity disorder, that disentitles autonomous decision-making by the child, whereas no other medical procedure does.[101]

However, it was her Honour's view that due to the irreversible nature of stage 2 treatment, the *court* should determine *Gillick* competence rather than the child's treating doctors.[102]

The nature of stage 2 treatment was said to impart a 'significant risk of making the wrong decision as to a child's capacity to consent' and carry particularly grave consequences were a wrong decision made.[103] These concerns were listed in *Marion's Case* in the context of a child with intellectual disability where—especially against the background of the eugenics movement—they may be considered valid. However, the Court in *Re: Jamie* did not explain why a trans youth's competence might be especially difficult to discern or why there is a significantly increased risk of them making the wrong decision about gender-affirming care, compared to other types of decisions children and young people make. The risk assessment was not positioned with respect to any medical literature on gender-affirming care or adolescent decision-making capacity.

The Court was cognisant of the impact this requirement would have, noting that it could seem harsh to require court applications considering the expense, stress,

[98] *Re: Alex* [168].
[99] *Re: Alex* [172]–[173].
[100] *Re: Alex* [173].
[101] *Re: Jamie* [134].
[102] *Re: Jamie* [137] (Bryant CJ).
[103] *Re: Jamie* [137].

and possible delay it may cause 'particularly when the court may ultimately reach the same decision which the child and her parents had already reached with the child's doctors'.[104] Nevertheless, the Court considered themselves bound by the decision in *Marion's Case*.[105]

In the five years between *Re: Jamie* and *Re: Kelvin*, the former stood as the authoritative case. The Family Court heard more than 30 cases in which judges ruled on the competence of trans youth. Judges in later cases also applied the approach to stage 2 treatment from *Re: Jamie* to stage 3 treatment and, accordingly, young people were found *Gillick* competent by the Court to provide their own consent to chest reconstructive surgery.[106] However, the requirement for Court assessment of *Gillick* competence for stage 2 treatment emerging from the *Re: Jamie* judgment was novel and lacking a clear and convincing rationale for characterising or treating mature trans youth seeking gender-affirming treatment differently in competence assessments than their cis-peers seeking other treatment. Plausibly, *Re: Jamie* exemplifies the discriminatory approach taken towards trans youth in the Australian case law.

Following the *Re: Jamie* decision, dissatisfaction with the law grew, with judicial and academic critique targeting the legal reasoning in the judgment, as well as its legally disruptive and harmful impacts.[107] Family Court Judges spoke in the media and in their judgments of the need for law reform, either through legislative intervention or another Full Court referral, or even a High Court decision.[108] The opportunity arose in the case of *Re: Kelvin*.[109]

In *Re: Kelvin*, the Court was asked to rule on a stated case which confined them to the question of whether there was a need to apply to the Family Court for a determination of *Gillick* competence in circumstances where: (1) stage 2 treatment for gender dysphoria is proposed; (2) the child consents to the treatment; (3) the treating medical practitioners agree that the child is *Gillick* competent to give that consent; and (4) the parents of the child do not object to the treatment. The

[104] *Re: Jamie* [138] (Bryant CJ), [185]–[186] (Finn J).

[105] *Re: Jamie* [138] (Bryant CJ).

[106] See e.g. *Re: Leo*; *Re: Quinn*; *Re: Lincoln (No. 2)*. In respect of stage 1 treatment, as a result of the *Re: Jamie* judgment, parents can consent on minors' behalf without the need for a court application. There is little case law on this issue. However, in *Re: Ryan* [2017] FamCA 821 [6], the judge briefly addressed the law on *Gillick* competence and consent to stage 1 treatment, observing that an application to determine competence by a court was unnecessary since, unlike stage 2 treatment, it is not irreversible. The question arose in *Re: Ryan* because assessment of competence regarding stage 2 treatment was also sought and there was dispute between the parents.

[107] The Hon Justice Steven Strickland, 'To Treat or Not to Treat: Legal Responses to Transgender Young People Revisited' Association of Family and Conciliation Courts Australian Chapter Conference (2015); *Re: Martin* [2015] FamCA 1189 [38] (Bennett J); *Re: Lucas* [2016] FamCA 1129 [72]–[73] (Tree J); Fiona Kelly, 'Australian Children Living With Gender Dysphoria: Does the Family Court Have a Role to Play?', *Journal of Law and Medicine*, 22 (2014), 105–20; Bell, 'Children with Gender Dysphoria'; Katherine France, 'Let Me Be Me: Parental Responsibility, Gillick Competence, and Transgender Minors' Access to Hormone Treatments', *Family Law Review*, 4 (2014), 227–48.

[108] Justice Strickland, 'To Treat or Not to Treat'; *Re Martin* (Bennett J).

[109] *Re: Kelvin*.

majority interpretation of the *Re: Jamie* judgment was that the factors that had led stage 2 treatment to be deemed a 'special case' in *Re: Jamie* had made it appropriate for the Court to determine *Gillick* competence at that point in time. Accordingly, their Honours held that the facts presented to them, notably the changes in medical knowledge, alleviated their concerns regarding stage 2 and the need to retain court approval of such treatment and allowed them to find there was 'no longer a basis for the Court to determine *Gillick* competence'.[110] That is, in circumstances where the young person, their parents and their medical team were in agreement about treatment, it was no longer necessary to apply for Family Court determination of competence. The minority also reached that outcome. However, as above, they felt it would be appropriate to rule *Re: Jamie* wrongly decided, on the basis that *Marion's Case* is not authority for 'a freestanding obligation to obtain a court finding that a child is *Gillick* competent before his or her consent can be given effect'.[111]

While the *Re: Kelvin* judgment was heralded as a victory for its removal of the requirement to go to court for most adolescents,[112] it has begun to be criticised for its shortcomings in terms of children's rights,[113] and other aspects of clinical care for trans youth that are not covered in the judgment. It has also become increasingly clear that the narrow coverage of the judgment creates practical issues.

By failing to rule that *Re: Jamie* was plainly wrong, the Court in *Re: Kelvin* created the situation in which both judgments remain authoritative. This poses problems for ascertaining the applicable legal principles for stage 3 treatment and for *Gillick* competence when there is a dispute in respect of any stage of treatment. As will be discussed below in relation to *Re: Imogen*,[114] where a parent is unsupportive of treatment, the agency of a *Gillick* competent youth is compromised. Regarding stage 3 treatment, in *Re: LG*, Duncanson J held that *Re: Jamie* rather than *Re: Kelvin* remained the appropriate authority.[115] On this view, court assessment of *Gillick* competence is required for surgery to be lawful. This is despite *Re: Jamie* also being silent on the law in respect of stage 3 treatment. By contrast, Rees J in *Re: Matthew* held that the reasoning in *Re: Kelvin* could be extended to stage 3 treatment; judicial assessment of *Gillick* competence is no longer required.[116] Another recent case regarding stage 3 treatment, *Re: Ryan*, arose in circumstances of parental dispute.[117] Cleary J did not opine on whether, in the absence of a dispute, a court application was necessary for stage 3 treatment. However, her Honour's *dicta* are

110 *Re: Kelvin* [182].

111 *Re: Kelvin* [189].

112 Michelle Telfer *et al.*, 'Transgender Adolescents and Legal Reform: How Improved Access to Healthcare Was Achieved through Medical, Legal and Community Collaboration', *Journal of Paediatrics and Child Health*, 54 (2018), 1096–9.

113 Georgina Dimopoulos, 'Rethinking *Re Kelvin*: A Children's Rights Perspective', *UNSW Law Journal*, 44 (2021), 637–72.

114 *Re: Imogen (No 6)*.

115 *Re: Matthew* [45]–[46].

116 *Re: LG* [14].

117 *Re: Ryan* [2019] FamCA 112.

suggestive of agreement with Rees J in *Re: Matthew*.[118] In *Re: Imogen*, Watts J held that if all parties agree, 'the law is the same for stage 3 treatment [as it is for stage 2 treatment] and there is no necessity for this Court to determine whether the subject child is *Gillick* competent before stage 3 treatment for Gender Dysphoria can proceed', citing Rees J in *Re: Matthew*.[119] However, arguably, in a situation where all parties agree, there is conflicting authority on whether a court must determine *Gillick* competence before stage 3 treatment can commence. While the weight of judicial opinion favours the *Re: Kelvin* approach to *Gillick* competence in surgical cases, the lack of clarity in the law is undesirable.

## The status of conflict or controversy

The current legal principles in this area converge when there is an absence of unanimity among parents, doctors involved with treatment, and the child, regardless of whether it is stage 1, 2, or 3 treatment under consideration. Alongside the absence of Full Court *dicta* on stage 3 treatment, there is an absence of proper consideration by the Full Court of the impact of dispute and controversy.

The Court in *Re: Jamie* makes cursory reference to controversy altering the lawful process of obtaining consent but does not elucidate what this means in practical terms. The Court observed that '[i]f there is a dispute about whether treatment should be provided (in respect of either stage one or stage two), and what form treatment should take, it is appropriate for this to be determined by the court'.[120] This position was supported by the Australian Human Rights Commission who intervened.[121] However, the three judgments produced by the Full Court in *Re: Jamie* contained differing references to the impact of a dispute and what the pathway to treatment would be.

In the subsequent decision of *Re: Elliott*,[122] Tree J argued that the *Re: Jamie* judgment establishes a role for the court where there is a dispute over *Gillick* competence, but the Court espoused two, potentially three, conflicting answers to the nature of that role. The approach favoured by Bryant CJ in *Re: Jamie* was a best interests assessment with 'significant weight to the views of the child in accordance with his or her age or maturity',[123] rather than an assessment of competence.[124] Finn J, by contrast, held that '[i]f the court was completely satisfied of the child's capacity to consent to stage two treatment, it would be unnecessary for it to have to authorise the treatment' unless 'the court had any doubt about that capacity'.[125]

118 *Re: Ryan* [23]–[24] (Cleary J).
119 *Re: Imogen (No 6)* [34].
120 *Re: Jamie* [140] (Bryant CJ).
121 *Re: Jamie* [46], [56].
122 *Re: Elliott* [2017] FamCA 1008 [14]–[18].
123 *Re: Jamie* [140] (Bryant CJ).
124 *Re: Jamie* [140] (Bryant CJ).
125 *Re: Jamie* [188] (Finn J).

Strickland J did not directly address the issue, though Tree J notes that 'his Honour may have propounded a third test, because there he indicated that court authorisation would not be required "where the child is able to give consent to the proposed treatment"'.[126] As Tree J points out, '[p]lainly these approaches are not consistent'.[127] This conflict in the *Re: Jamie* judgments was left unresolved by the Full Court in *Re: Kelvin* because the framing of the stated case excluded situations where there was dispute. The question of law presented to the Court was to clarify the need for judicial competence assessments in circumstances where 'the parents of the child do not object to the treatment'. The judgment did not directly address the law where a *Gillick* competent child seeks treatment and where one or more individuals with parental responsibility object.

It was quite unclear following *Re: Kelvin* what legal principles applied where the child's doctor assessed the child to be *Gillick* competent, but one or both parents did not support treatment. Did a passive lack of support amount to a 'dispute' or 'controversy', or was a disputing parent required to confront medical practitioners or bring a court application? *Re: Jamie* and *Re: Kelvin* created uncertainty through their cursory and contradictory references to controversy and dispute, and the failure to elaborate on what circumstances would constitute a dispute or controversy necessitating court oversight, and indeed what that oversight might look like.

Dispute between parents was the basis of the 2019 case of *Re: Ryan*. However, the judge assessed the young person as *Gillick* competent and did not consider the law in any further detail. The applicable legal principles in cases of dispute were addressed by a single judge of the Family Court in *Re: Imogen* in 2020.[128] *Re: Imogen* was squarely focused on the conflict in opinions between parents as to the validity of the young person's gender identity and diagnosis and, consequently, the appropriate treatment and competence to consent to that treatment.

In *Re: Imogen*, Watts J interpreted the authorities such that for all cases of treatment of trans youth, for all three stages of treatment, the consent of all persons with parental responsibility must be gained. In the absence of all parents providing consent, court involvement is a mandatory step in gaining authorisation for treatment. The binary of full parent support versus anything short of it has created a framework that nullifies the effect of *Gillick* competence assessments. That is, even where a young person is clinically assessed as *Gillick* competent, the consent of all parents is needed in addition to the young person's to negate the need for court involvement. If a parent does not provide consent to treatment, whether as a result of lack of contact or involvement in the child's life, through express disapproval, or disputing the young person's competence, diagnosis or proposed treatment, court involvement is required.[129]

[126] *Re: Jamie* [195] (Strickland J).
[127] *Re: Elliott* [16].
[128] *Re: Imogen (No 6)*.
[129] *Re: Imogen (No. 6)*[35].

In circumstances where a court application is made, depending on which aspects are in dispute, the court may undertake an assessment of the adolescent's *Gillick* competence, perform a best interests assessment, or do both. If the only aspect in dispute is *Gillick* competence, Watts J noted that the court need only make that assessment, in line with the Court's approach in *Re: Jamie.*[130] However, if dispute surrounds the diagnosis of gender dysphoria or the proposed treatment, in whole or in part, Watts J opined that a best interests assessment must be undertaken by the judge.[131] The requirement for a best interests assessment is not removed if a competence assessment is also undertaken, and the former will be determinative.[132]

The combined effect of these requirements is to render the practical effect of a *Gillick* competence assessment by clinicians meaningless for the purposes of gaining lawful authority for treatment. It also undermines the ability of supportive parents to provide consent, opening the door for unsupportive parents—who could be uninvolved or represent a harm to the child—to interfere and to bar their child's timely access to therapeutic treatment. Where a parent is unable to be located, the issue may be intractable in the absence of going to court. The interpretation of the legal principles by Watts J in *Re: Imogen*, particularly in equating the absence of consent by a parent with controversy or dispute, has resulted in a large-scale shift in the legal framework and, correspondingly, the consent process for all treatment decisions in this area. Further, in imposing the requirement for all parents to consent in all cases—even where an adolescent is assessed as competent—and a best interests assessment to potentially override even the wishes of an adolescent judicially assessed as *Gillick* competent, adolescent autonomy and legal capacity is severely undercut.

The potential for harm as a result of the *Re: Imogen* requirements cannot be overstated. The case has led treating medical practitioners to require that all parents consent, resulting in applications to the Family Court and the Supreme Court of Queensland where this has not been possible to obtain or where a parent is of the view that it would be harmful for the other parent to be involved.[133] In one case, a trans adolescent forced to make contact with their estranged father to obtain the latter's consent to stage 2 treatment led to a reply that was 'far from friendly or loving', espousing unscientific and transphobic views. This prompted an 'immediate and near fatal' response from the adolescent who demonstrated determination to 'jump from a cliff' and presumably would have but for being prevented access to said cliff by an unwilling ticket seller.[134]

In these cases before the Family Court, Watts J's interpretation of dispute in *Re: Imogen* has, so far, remained uncritiqued. However, in the recent decision of *Re A*

[130] *Re: Imogen (No. 6)* [35].
[131] *Re: Imogen (No. 6)* [35].
[132] *Re: Imogen (No. 6)* [35].
[133] *Re a Declaration Regarding Medical Treatment for 'A'* [2020] QSC 389; *Re: Rowan* [2022] FedCFamC1F 134 [19]; *Re: Jesse* [2021] FedCFamC1F 42 [39]; *Re: Addison* [2021] FamCA 253 [2]; *Re: Kelly* [2022] FedCFamC1F 380.
[134] *Re: Ash* [2021] FedCFamC1F 100 [9]–[11].

by the Queensland Supreme Court, Boddice J was critical of the statements regarding the impact of controversy or conflict on *Gillick* in *Re: Jamie* and *Re: Imogen.* His Honour opined that:

> if the child is *Gillick* competent, then subject to some *obiter dicta* in … [*Re: Jamie*], that really should be the end of the matter. It is then a situation where the child, if giving consent to that treatment, is to receive the treatment notwithstanding the views of one or more of the child's parents.[135]

> [o]nce it is concluded that the child is *Gillick* competent, the question must be asked why it is that a child who is almost 17 years of age, is *Gillick* competent and is firm in the view of what treatment they would like, should be denied the opportunity to do so without the consent of both parents. Such a conclusion would be inconsistent with the human rights of the child and a recognition of the importance of *Gillick* competence and its effect as a matter of law.[136]

His Honour was prepared to rule that *Re: Jamie* and *Re: Imogen* wrongly stated the law, and decline to follow them on this basis; however, he considered this unnecessary, the conclusions stated by the Full Court in *Re: Jamie* were merely *obiter dicta.*[137] The decision was made under the state supreme court's *parens patriae* jurisdiction rather than the statutory welfare jurisdiction of the Family Court. The latter is the venue for these applications in the overwhelming majority of these cases. At the time of writing, no cases before state supreme courts or the Family Court have dealt with the differing views of Watts J and Boddice J, leaving the legal principles uncertain in respect of parental consent.

I agree with Boddice J's approach and argue that it should be followed as it accords with the spirit of *Gillick*, the interpretation and application of *Gillick* in other contexts, and children's rights. Without a clear anchor to special medical procedure principles, or restrictions on consent to children's healthcare in other contexts, the *Re: Imogen* requirement for all parents' consent in all cases gatekeeps treatment from trans youth seeking gender-affirming care in a way that has not been applied to cis-youth in any other context. *Re: Imogen* appears to be novel and discriminatory move against trans youth.

## Lessons and a way forward

This chapter has presented a case study of the Australian legal experience of medical treatment for trans youth. It reveals a legal framework that has continually shifted, imposing, removing, and re-imposing immensely burdensome requirements to gaining valid consent or lawful authorisation to treatment. Differences in

[135] *Re A* [2022] QSC 159 [15].
[136] *Re A* [24].
[137] *Re A* [27].

the scope and breadth of questions considered in various judgments have resulted in an incoherent patchwork of findings and associated reasoning. The imposition of legal barriers to gender-affirming treatment without clear justification is a clear case of cisgenderism and discrimination. A Full Court judgment has not addressed crucial aspects of this area of law, including the law on stage 3 treatment and what circumstances constitute a dispute or controversy necessitating court approval.[138]

Much of the case law in this area, stretching back two decades, has pre-dated the intense social and political discourse on trans and non-binary identities which has come to bear on this area of healthcare in recent years. Australian cases have historically involved evidence from treating medical practitioners and family that are supportive of treatment, with opposing voices largely absent. The 2020 case of *Re: Imogen* was noted to be the first case in which a judge would evaluate evidence—introduced by a parent unsupportive of treatment—'critical of the pro-trans "affirmative" treatment model'.[139] There, Watts J ruled that treatment focused on psychotherapy and the withholding of hormones was 'risky and unproven' and that gender-affirming care is 'consistent with the current approach to treatment for Gender Dysphoria, currently accepted by the majority of the medical profession'.[140] With the law still uncertain, and unsupportive parents given significant agency to undermine the provision of care to their trans child, it may be that as further applications come to court, the Australian jurisprudence is further influenced by contemporary social and political discourse on gender-affirming care.

The utility of legal barriers to gender-affirming treatment placed by Australian judges is dubious at best. Despite over 100 cases coming before the Family Court, the requirement for court oversight and approval has resulted in a ruling that

[138] It has also been pointed out by Parkinson that current guidance doesn't extend to clarifying the legality of providing care through a general physician, rather than involving multidisciplinary assessment (the informed consent model). Additionally, he suggests that treatment of non-binary youth could be characterised as more 'novel' than treatment for those with a binary gender identity and fall outside the scope of parental consent as 'it is very likely that the courts would regard this treatment as either non-therapeutic (ie, cosmetic) or experimental'. Neither of these arguments have been subject to court treatment. Given the focus by the courts on a psychiatric diagnosis and the *Australian Guidelines* accepted by the courts to treat this support an individualised approach, the suggestion that the law to date applies only to binary trans youth is questionable. 'Novelty' of treatment has not been the decisive characteristic in the body of case law to date. See Patrick Parkinson, 'Adolescent Gender Dysphoria and the Informed Consent Model of Care', *Journal of Law and Medicine*, 28 (2021), 734–44.

[139] Bernard Lane, 'Gender Critics Get Day in Court', *The Australian* (Canberra), 29 June 2020.

[140] *Re: Imogen (No 6)* [224], [226]. In an earlier proceeding concerning Imogen, an organisation with unorthodox views on healthcare for trans youth sought to intervene in the proceedings and introduce evidence that Imogen was suffering from 'rapid onset gender dysphoria', which posits that gender dysphoria arises in some cases from 'social contagion': *Re: Imogen (No. 4)* [2020] FamCA 396 [14]. This theory is, as Ashley observes, 'best understood as an attempt to circumvent existing research demonstrating the importance of gender affirmation, relying on scientific-sounding language to achieve respectability': Florence Ashley, 'A Critical Commentary on "Rapid-Onset Gender Dysphoria"', *The Sociological Review Monographs*, 68 (2020), 779–99. The views of the organisation were not forensically scrutinised and their application to intervene was dismissed by the judge.

authorised treatment in all but one case.[141] When this argument was presented to the Full Court in *Re: Kelvin*, they were quick to point out that 'a requirement for court involvement, may in itself serve as a filter of the types of case where stage 2 treatment is recommended and undertaken'.[142] However, rather than this requirement acting to filter out cases where treatment was clinically unnecessary, it is more likely that the 'types of cases' filtered out were those of young people with less support or resources. Accordingly, we must ask the question of whether court involvement serves any purpose other than to assuage cisgendered concerns? It is likely that systematic legal barriers to trans medicine have prevented some youth from accessing treatment due to the expense, time, and support required to gain legal authorisation. These factors are separate and entirely unrelated to the supposed rationales for legal hurdles, which are to prevent gender affirmation that is not 'genuine' or which may be later regretted by a child as they mature. In sum, legal barriers are either ineffectual at achieving their aims or unnecessary insofar as their aims are achieved by clinical processes. Further, they create significant—supposedly unintended—barriers to treatment.

The implications of this unnecessary legal framework for trans young people, their families and doctors are immense. The requirement to seek court approval creates significant barriers to treatment and results in significant harm to trans youth and families.[143] The harm is not concordant with the aim of this body of law, that is, to prevent harm to and improve the well-being of young people. These barriers have likely deterred or delayed many trans youth in Australia from accessing necessary therapeutic treatment.

For youth without parental support and appropriate resources, the historical and extant barriers created by the law render vital gender-affirming healthcare practically inaccessible. Court processes involve a significant expense to families, clinicians, and the broader healthcare system. They involve the financial costs of court fees, solicitor and barrister fees, time taken to attend legal proceedings, delay to treatment and other opportunity costs. These are significant. It also cannot be ignored that requirements to gain court approval have a harmful psychological impact. As Cameron Stewart,[144] Georgina Dimopoulos, and Michelle Taylor-Sands argue,[145] this is an example of 'nomoigenesis' or sickness created by the law.

Australian laws that require a court application before gender-affirming treatment also have a normative impact. The legal requirement implies that being trans is illegal, wrong, or needs justification to cisgendered judges. Cisgenderism permeates the Australian law in this area as gender-affirming treatment continually attracts

141 In one case, the application was dismissed due to a missing psychiatrists report in relation to *Gillick* competence: *Re: Jan* [2016] FamCA 1171.

142 *Re: Kelvin* [119].

143 Kelly, *The Court Process Is Slow*.

144 Cameron Stewart, 'Cracks in the Lintel of Consent', in Ian Freckelton and Kerry Petersen (eds), *Tensions and Traumas in Health Law* (Annandale, NSW, Federation Press, 2017), pp. 214–33.

145 Georgina Dimopoulos and Michelle Taylor-Sands, '*Re Imogen*: The Role of the Family Court of Australia in Disputes over Gender Dysphoria Treatment', Monash Bioethics Review, 39 (2021), 42–66.

different rules from Family Court judges than those which apply to other types of medical interventions for young people. This approach frames cisgendered people as normal and their medical treatments as valid, while trans youth are 'othered' and the necessity of their treatment questioned, discriminating against them on this basis.[146] These laws stem from a view that only gender which is fixed, long-lasting and aligned with sex assigned at birth is valid and normal and, by requiring legal assessment, being trans is not. Australian case law that has acted to gatekeep gender-affirming treatment, and continues to do so for some trans youth, relies on historic tropes of trans youth as uncertain or confused and is based on normative hierarchies that devalue trans lives and that see desistence in trans identities as the best outcome. The adjudication of trans bodies by cisgendered individuals is inherently problematic. The case law fails to account for, and adequately consider, the lived experience of trans youth. Nevertheless, this fragile, cisgendered, ever-changing legal framework must potentially be navigated by trans youth, families, and clinicians in accessing different types of medical treatment if they fall within the gaps of *Re: Kelvin.*

The Australian legal framework in this area is in urgent need of reform. Such reform would need to cover the field such that the patchwork coverage in judgments stops, and judges are not continually tasked with revising the law to keep pace with medicine. I have written on the stakeholder concerns in this space and various options for law reform elsewhere.[147] We argue that a rights-based approach must underpin reform in this area, recognising and respecting 'the evolving autonomy and agency of trans young people to make decisions about their bodies and identities', as opposed to the paternalistic cisgendered approach which has dominated the case law to date.[148] We suggest that the optimal solution for reform, which best takes account of stakeholder concerns, as well as relative benefits and risks of differing approaches, is three-pronged:

1. A statutory presumption of capacity that treats the decisions of those aged 16 years and over the same as those of adults;
2. A decision-specific statutory test for competence that overcomes the practical challenges attending the *Gillick* test and clarifies the role of parents once a young person is deemed competent; and
3. A statutory provision that specifically clarifies that the law pertaining to access to gender-affirming healthcare is not different to that pertaining to other forms of healthcare.[149]

These proposals are not revolutionary. They have been implemented in other jurisdictions and in relation to other kinds of healthcare. Notably, the statutory

[146] Ansara and Hegarty, 'Cisgenderism in Psychology', 141.
[147] Jowett, Dimopoulos, and Kelly, 'Reforming the Law'.
[148] Jowett, Dimopoulos, and Kelly, 'Reforming the Law', 9.
[149] Jowett, Dimopoulos, and Kelly, 'Reforming the Law', 18.

presumption of capacity at age 16 would align Australia with the law in England and Wales.[150] A specific provision that clarifies the law on consent to gender-affirming care is arguably required by the continuing jurisprudence that paints it as special and requiring tighter controls.[151] As has been argued elsewhere,[152] legislative intervention would be ideal. However, sufficient political appetite has yet to be generated. Whatever approach is taken to reform in this area, the trans child's voice should be at the centre of such efforts.

As has been demonstrated in this chapter, current Australian consent laws applicable to gender-affirming care of trans youth are woefully inadequate. Implicitly cisgendered and discriminatory in their requirements, they serve to create harm and perpetuate inequities rather than protecting young people. Undoubtedly in unjustifiably curtailing access to recommended medical treatment, the law does not support the well-being of trans young people in Australia. Consent laws should address the breadth of treatment that is clinically necessary and be grounded in accurate interpretations of medical literature.[153] They should reflect respect for children's rights and not discriminate on the basis of gender modality.

The Australian experience in this area to date has been one which places the child's voice below the interests of adults.[154] Other jurisdictions should be reticent to do the same. *Gillick*, and children's rights instruments, demand that the voices of mature trans young people be considered on a par with those of their parents and other adults.[155] As Bryant CJ remarked in *Re: Jamie*, 'one might think that, of all the medical treatments that might arise, treatment for something as personal and essential as the perception of one's gender and sexuality would be the very exemplar of when the rights of the *Gillick* competent child should be given full effect'.[156]

150 Family Law Reform Act 1969 (England and Wales), s 8. See also Mental Capacity Act 2005 (England and Wales), s 2(5).

151 Jowett, Dimopoulos, and Kelly, 'Reforming the Law', 18.

152 Jowett and Kelly, '*Re Imogen*'.

153 See Jowett, *Medical Treatment of Trans Youth.*

154 Dimopoulos, '*Rethinking Re Kelvin*'.

155 Dimopoulos, '*Rethinking Re Kelvin*'.

156 *Re: Jamie* [135] (Bryant CJ).

10

# On Sharing the Normative Power of Consent

PETER SCHABER

BETTY, WHO IS 13 years of age, validly refuses to undergo treatment that would save her life. Betty's refusal is valid because she has decision-making capacity, is adequately informed, and she acts voluntarily. According to the law governing medical treatment decisions in England and Wales, valid consent is normally required for treatment to be lawful. This is true as much for minors as it is for adults, but in the case of minors, legal power to consent to treatment may be possessed or shared by others.[1] Children aged 15 years and younger are presumed to lack the normative power to consent to medical treatment. Treatment decisions are taken on their behalf by those who exercise parental responsibility. However, these minors may acquire the legal power to consent to medical treatment if it has been confirmed that they possess the requisite decision-making capacity. Children 16- and 17-year-olds are rebuttably presumed to possess the normative and legal power to consent to treatment.[2] Thus a competent minor's consent will, other things equal, make the provision of medical treatment lawful. However, a minor's possession of the normative power to consent to treatment does not extinguish the normative—and legal—power to consent to treatment on an adolescent's behalf held by those who exercise parental responsibility. As Anthony Skelton, Lisa Forsberg, and Isra Black observe, '[r]ather, parents and the courts retain the power to consent concurrently with the adolescent'.[3] Parents or the courts, therefore, have the normative power to consent to treatment that adolescents validly refuse.[4] Whereas decisions of competent adults regarding their own treatment is 'normatively determinative',[5] an adolescent's

[1] For a detailed outline of the law governing children's medical treatment in England and Wales, see Anthony Skelton, Lisa Forsberg, and Isra Black, 'Overriding Adolescent Refusals of Treatment', *Journal of Ethics and Social Philosophy*, 20 (2021), 221–47.

[2] The presumption will be rebutted, other things equal, if a minor is found to lack decision-making capacity.

[3] Skelton *et al.*, 'Overriding Adolescent Refusals of Treatment', 224.

[4] Skelton *et al.*, 'Overriding Adolescent Refusals of Treatment', 224.

[5] Skelton *et al.*, 'Overriding Adolescent Refusals of Treatment', 221.

*Proceedings of the British Academy*, **279**, 192–204, © Authors 2025.

refusal is not treated as normatively determinative in law. So, Betty's refusal does not settle the matter of whether she receives life-saving treatment. Her parents or the courts may intervene and consent, overriding her refusal of treatment.

Neil Manson describes the situation above as one where the normative and legal power of consent is *shared* between adolescents and other parties. As he puts it: '(T)here is an intermediate, transitional period where the adolescent shares the normative power to permit her own treatment.'[6] A child who lacks decision-making capacity has no normative and legal power to consent; adults with capacity have, other things equal, an unshared normative and legal power to consent to treatment; and adolescents with capacity, other things equal, share their normative and legal power to consent to medical treatment with others. But what does it mean to share the legal power to consent with others? And how could the sharing of adolescents' normative and legal power to consent with others be justified? I shall treat these two questions in this chapter. I will argue that the limited power to refuse arguably serves the adolescent's interest to be protected from being severely harmed. The (shared) normative power to consent serves a normative control interest adolescents arguably (also) have. The limitation of their normative power to refuse is justified in cases where the interest in having normative control the full power of consent serves is outweighed by the interest to be protected from being severely harmed. If Betty validly refuses to consent to a minor medical treatment, no one should step in and overturn her refusal. In the life-saving treatment case, however, parents or the courts should have the normative power to consent to the medical treatment and thereby make it permissible. Adolescents sharing their normative power to consent with parents or courts when the choice made is greatly contrary to the adolescent's interest. These other parties should not share normative powers with adolescents with regard to decisions whose impact is relatively minor.

The chapter has four sections. The first section explains the concept of normative powers. The second section proposes an understanding of what it means to share a normative power with others. The third section discusses the question of whether the English legal regime on adolescent consent involves shared normative powers and whether—as Manson thinks—an asymmetry between the adolescent's consent being normatively determinative and the adolescent's refusal to consent not being normatively determinative can be defended. The fourth section addresses the justification for adolescents sharing their normative power to consent with others.

## Normative powers

Before discussing the question of what it means to share a normative power, we need to be clear about what it means to have a normative power. I'll focus here on consent as a paradigm case of a normative power.

[6] N. Manson, 'Transitional Paternalism: How Shared Normative Powers Give Rise to the Asymmetry of Adolescent Consent', *Bioethics*, 29 (2015), 66–73 at 70.

Normative powers are powers to bring about normative changes.[7] More precisely, it is the exercise of a normative power that brings about a normative change. If A consents to a medical treatment, A exercises the normative power of consent. A thereby makes permissible a treatment that would otherwise have been impermissible. It is A's act of consent that creates the normative change. It does so if it meets the practical requirements of being adequately informed, voluntary, and given by a competent person.[8] The consenter is properly informed if she knows the relevant facts and her consent is not based on mistaken beliefs. Consent is voluntary if it is not brought about by deception, coercion, or manipulation. The consenter is competent to consent if she is able to understand the relevant information, and to apply it to herself, to reason with the information, and to express a choice. (Much more needs to be said about these validity requirements. This is just to give a rough idea of their content.)

Consent is the exercise of a normative power, one might say, if it creates the normative change of making permissible an act that would otherwise be impermissible. It must be noted here that the change brought about by consent does not have to consist in making an act all things considered permissible. An act that harms third parties, for instance, remains impermissible, even if it is first-personally consented to. The normative change brought about by consent in this case consists in making it the case that the consenter is not wronged by the act. The consenter is not wronged because the consent-receiver acts with her valid consent. She would be wronged if that other person acted without her valid consent. However, the act is wrong, but not as an act performed without valid consent; rather as an act inflicting harm upon third parties. Morally effective consent involves eliminating the wronging the act would have been if not consented to by the consenter. If no wronging of a third party is involved and no one else has a normative power over the act in question, consent makes the act permissible. This is, for instance, the case when adults consent to medical treatment (provided their consent is valid).

Note here that valid consent is only morally effective if the duty the consent refers to is a consent-sensitive duty. Consent-sensitive duties are conditional duties. They do not have the form (1) 'You ought not do x to A'; they rather have the form (2) 'You ought not do x to A if A does not consent to you doing x to her'. If you consent to a consent-insensitive duty no moral change is created. For instance, if one has consent-insensitive duty not to exploit people, a party's consent to an exploitative transaction can't be morally effective.[9]

[7] See R. Chang, 'Do We Have Normative Powers?', *Proceedings of the Aristotelian Society*, Supplementary Volume, 94 (2020), 275–300; D. Owens, *Shaping the Normative Landscape* (Oxford, Oxford University Press, 2012), pp. 127–9; and V. Tadros, 'Appropriate Normative Powers', *Proceedings of the Aristotelian Society*, Supplementary Volume, 94 (2020), 301–26.

[8] E. Bullock, 'Valid Consent', in A. Müller and P. Schaber (eds), *The Routledge Handbook the Ethics of Consent* (London, Routledge, 2018), pp. 85–94.

[9] See P. Schaber, 'The Volenti Maxim', *The Journal of Ethics*, 24 (2020), 79–89 at 86; also V. Tadros, *Wrongs and Crimes* (Oxford, Oxford University Press, 2016), p. 20.

Exercises of normative powers are acts that bring about normative changes. But more needs to be said to clarify the concept of a normative power. Many acts create normative changes without being the exercises of normative powers. We are able to change the normative landscape by—among other things—harming, benefiting, threatening people.[10] Take the case of harming. By harming another person, I change the situation so that I am bound by the duty to make amends. Yet, harming another person is not an exercise of a normative power. It is the impact my harming has on the well-being of the victim that brings about the normative change by creating a duty to make amends. The normative change is brought about indirectly. It is ultimately grounded in a further fact, a fact about the victim's well-being, not in the act of harming itself. The normative change brought about by the exercise of a normative power of consent, on the other hand, is ultimately grounded in the act of consent itself, not in a further fact.

The normative change created by the exercise of a normative power such as the normative power to consent is not brought about by chance. It is the result of an act that is based on an intention to bring about the normative change. As Victor Tadros puts it: '[T]he exercise of a normative power is a distinctive kind of intentional activity, where one directly alters the rights and duties of oneself and others.'[11] The rights and duties are altered by the act itself, or as Tadros writes: '[T]he execution of the power itself generates the relationship between duty holder and right holder …'[12] The exercise of a normative power of consent is an act that aims at changing the rights and duties of the consenter and the consent-receiver. And it is an exercise of the normative power to consent if and only if the consent-giver intends to create a normative change between consenter and consent-receiver.

Thus, one could define the exercise of a normative power in the following way: '(NP). An act is an exercise of a normative power if it is performed with the intention to bring about a certain normative change and the normative change is brought about by the act itself.'

However, this definition of normative powers faces a difficulty. It is still too broad and covers cases that should not be understood as exercises of normative power. Consider this example: Brenda is doing Kate a favour. Brenda does not do Kate a favour because she is concerned about Kate's well-being. Rather, Brenda does Kate a favour because Brenda wants to create a duty of gratitude. Assume that what Brenda does for Kate creates such a duty of gratitude. It is thus the act of doing a favour itself that created the normative change, an act that is based on the intention to bring about a certain normative change. This fits the description of the exercise of a normative power. Yet, Brenda's doing Kate a favour is not the exercise of a normative power.

[10] For other examples of this kind, see J. Raz, 'Normative Powers', in U. Heuer (ed.), *The Roots of Normativity* (Oxford, Oxford University Press, 2022), 162–78.

[11] Tadros, 'Appropriate Normative Powers', 313.

[12] Tadros, 'Appropriate Normative Powers', 314.

How does doing a favour differ from the exercise of a normative power like giving consent such that the latter unlike the former is an exercise of a normative power? What we have in mind when we talk of exercises of normative powers is something acts of consenting, making requests and promises, and giving orders have in common, and other ways of creating normative changes lack. Consider the 'doing Kate a favour' example again. Doing Kate a favour might be based on many different intentions. Brenda might want to promote Kate's well-being, or do something for her own reputation, or create a duty of gratitude, and other things more. The intention to create a normative change is not constitutive of the act performed by Brenda being an act of doing a favour. By contrast, the intention to create a normative change is constitutive for an act to be an act of consent. Consent is given with the intention of creating a certain normative change. When Brenda consents to Kate's doing x Brenda wants to make it the case that she is not wronged by Kate doing x. As David Owens puts it: 'I propose … to reserve "consent to φ-ing" for cases where you (intentionally) communicate the intention of hereby making it the case that someone would not wrong you by φ-ing.'[13]

An act is an exercise of a normative power if and only if the communicated intention to create a normative change is constitutive of the type of act it is. Let me explain. Consider the case of Mary consenting to lend John her phone. She might do so for various reasons. She might want to do him a favour or she might want to show him that she is a generous person. These are motivating reasons to give consent. Mary would, however, not consent to John taking her phone if she did not want to release him from his duty not to take her phone. Consent is about releasing another person from a duty. What Mary does can be taken as an act of consent only if she communicates that she wants to release him from a duty he has towards her. Otherwise, it would not be consent. To consent to John's taking her phone is for Jill to communicate that she does not want to be wronged by John's doing so. Whether Mary wants to be wronged by John is not an open question for him once he takes her act as an act of consent. She might, of course, communicate this intention without really having it. However, if John takes her communicative act as consent he believes that she wants to permit him to take her phone. Whether she wants to do him a favour by consenting to him taking her phone is on the other hand an open question. She might consent to John for this and other reasons. However, in saying 'Mary consents to lending John her phone because she does not want to be wronged by him' we refer to the fact she communicates her intention to release John from his duty not to use her phone. This is what constitutes consent. Thus, the exercise of a normative power should be understood in the following way (NP*):

> (NP*). An act is an exercise of a normative power if the agent communicates the intention to bring about a certain normative change and would not be the particular type of act if this intention to bring about the particular normative change was not communicated and the normative change is brought about by the act itself.

[13] Owens, *Shaping*, p. 166.

It is constitutive for the act performed by Mary to be an act of consent that she communicates that she wants to release John from his duty not to take her phone. In contrast, Brenda's doing Kate a favour could be based on different intentions. Brenda might want to create a duty of gratitude. But it would count as an act of doing Kate a favour even if it was based on a completely different intention. Many acts change the normative situation directly. And they might even do it intentionally without being an exercise of a normative power. As long as the communication of the intention to change the normative situation is not constitutive for the act being a certain type of act (like consenting, promising, or requesting), it is not an exercise of a normative power. It is the exercise of a normative power if this is the case. An act is the exercise of certain normative power if the agent communicates the intention to create a particular normative change: for consent, the intention not to be wronged by the act consented to, for promises to be under an obligation to keep the promise, and for requests to create a reason for the request-receiver to do as requested.

## Sharing normative powers

Individuals have normative powers and, as Manson puts it, they 'can have normative powers that are shared with others'.[14] But what does it mean to share normative powers with others? Here is a proposal about how this should be understood: '(SNP). A and B share a normative power x if they are both able to bring about the same normative change by performing the same type of act.'

This holds for two different types of shared normative power situations: (1) When two or more people have full normative powers and (2) when the relevant normative power is jointly shared such that only collective exercise of the normative power brings about the normative change. Here is an example of the first type of shared normative power (1): Jay and Paul jointly own a car. They both can make it permissible for third parties to use the car by consenting. Susan may not use the car if neither Jay nor Paul consents to Susan using it. However, if Jay consents to Susan using the car Susan may use it. If Paul consents to Susan using the car Susan may also use it. Jay and Paul share the normative power to consent because they both can make it permissible for third parties to use their car by giving their consent. If Jay consents to Susan using the car and Paul refuses consent, it would be permissible for Susan to use the car because either Jay or Paul can make it permissible to use their car.

Here is an example of the second type of shared normative power (2): John is allowed to borrow the car Jill owns with Christine, Jack, and Sibyl only if the three also consent to John borrowing the car. If Jill has given her consent but Christine, Jack, and Sibyl have not been asked yet, John is not allowed to take the car. The

[14] Manson, 'Transitional Paternalism', 69.

other three must give their consent to make this permissible. Jill's consent thus does not make it permissible. Yet, her consent does make a moral difference. If John took the car he would commit a wrong, but he would not wrong Jill. By giving consent, Jill has waived her right and therefore is not wronged by John's taking the car. John would wrong Christine, Jack, and Sibyl. The moral change Jill's consent brings about consists in making it the case that she is not wronged by John's taking the car. Jill cannot release John from his duties he has towards the three other owners of the car. Jill can make it the case that only she is not wronged by John. She makes this the case by consenting. If Jill consents to John taking the car, Jill is not wronged by John's taking the car, even if the other three do not consent to it. But her consent can't make it the case that one of the three others is not wronged by John doing so.

Christine, Jack, Jill, and Sibyl share the normative power to make it permissible for John to take the car by jointly consenting to him doing so. The four, together, have the right to give permission. None of them, however, has the normative power individually to lend or sell the car. But individually, they have a right to release another person from a duty they have towards them that they do not share with the others.

## Sharing the normative power to consent to medical treatment

Let us consider again the case of Betty. She does not give consent to life-saving treatment. Her parents step in, consent to the treatment, thereby waiving her right not to receive treatment. Does Betty share her normative power to consent with her parents? The parents' consent makes the treatment in question legally permissible. Betty is not wronged by the treatment if her parent's consent waives her right.

Her parents' consent has the power to waive her right not to receive medical treatment. Her consent is also able to waive this right. If she consents to the medical treatment, the treatment is permissible. This fits the definition of what it means to share a normative power. Parents as well as adolescents are able to create the same normative change (making an impermissible act permissible) by the same type of act, namely, by giving their consent. Betty's consent makes the treatment permissible and her parents' consent makes the treatment permissible.

Manson thinks that intervention when the adolescents refuse consent is more likely to be justified in the refusal than in the consent case and that the normative power to consent thus rather be shared in the refusal than in the consent case. 'The fact that an agent has refused a treatment which seems to be in her best, vital, interest should be a prompt for closer investigation' and might be a good reason to overrule the refusal to consent.[15] Take the case of a refusal of life-saving treatment. Parents or courts need to have the legal power to override such a refusal to prevent the adolescent from being severely harmed. To prevent this from happening,

[15] Manson, 'Transitional Paternalism', 69.

parents or courts should have the legal power to override the adolescent's refusal to consent. Thus, Manson writes, 'in the adolescent case, the child's own decision about her treatment is overridden in her best interests'.[16]

This is on Manson's view the reason why there should be a transitional period where the adolescent shares her normative power with her parents or the courts. It is preceded by a period where they have no normative power to consent and is (expected to be) followed by a period where they have unshared normative power. This transitional paternalistic period is in the best interests of the adolescent: '[a]dolescence is a period where there is a gradual expansion of autonomy, more and more options become open … new powers are acquired …'.[17] But with the gradual expansion of autonomy and new autonomy powers comes the risk of harm. It is this risk of harm that gives us reasons not to respect adolescents' decisions fully in a 'small set of decision-making contexts: that is, ones where the refusal would be severely harmful'.[18] Manson concedes that harm might also obtain in the consent case; however, this seems to be less likely to be the case.

If one took Manson's view to be a defence of a strict asymmetry between refusal and consent,[19] one would face the following difficulty. If the protection from being severely harmed is a reason to override a refusal to consent to treatment, it is at the same time a reason to override the adolescent's consent. Thus Manson's justification of paternalistic intervention is not a justification of the asymmetry between refusal to consent and consent. The reference to the child's best interests would only justify the asymmetry if only refusals to consent posed a risk of severe harm. This, however, is not the case. Consent can also pose the risk of severe harm. Consider a case of an adolescent seeking cosmetic breast enlargement. Were there a case of a physician offering an adolescent such an intervention and the adolescent consented, we might expect consent in the same way as cases of refusal to consent not to be normatively determinative. Thus, if transitional paternalism is about protecting adolescents' fundamental interests, it ought to apply to consent as well as to refusals to consent. (Though this position has not, as yet, manifested in legal doctrine.) As Skelton, Forsberg, and Black put it: 'We would stress that it need not, of course, be the case that consent is prudentially unproblematic all things considered … we might envisage cases in which the converse is true.'[20]

Since physicians are obliged to offer only treatments that are in the best interest of the patient, the case for paternalistic interference in adolescents' exercise of

[16] Manson, 'Transitional Paternalism', 70.

[17] Manson, 'Transitional Paternalism', 72. A similar justification of the asymmetry between the right to consent and the right to refuse to consent can be found in F. Tucker, 'Developing Autonomy and Transitional Paternalism', *Bioethics*, 30 (2016), 759–66 at 766: 'Transitional paternalism … offers guiding principles that can protect and promote adolescents' fundamental interests …'

[18] Manson, 'Transitional Paternalism', 72.

[19] An interpretation Manson would quite likely not be happy with.

[20] Skelton *et al.*, 'Overriding Adolescent Refusals of Treatment', 240.

consent may be rare.[21] Yet, it is not impossible. And if intervention by parents or courts is about protecting adolescents from being severely harmed, an adolescent's consent perhaps ought to be as provisional in the case of consenting as it is in the case of them refusing to give consent. Then adolescents would share the power of consent (and refusal) with parents and the courts.

I suggest here that it would be easier to justify intervening in the consent case than in the refusal case. If Betty does not consent to the life-saving treatment and her parents intervene and consent, treatment will be undertaken without her consent and presumably also against her will. (Consenting to an act and wanting the act to be performed are not the same. You can consent to an act and hope that the consent-receiver will not perform it. You can want someone to do something without consenting to her doing it.) If, on the other hand, Betty consents to a medical treatment, yet her parents step in and override her consent, nothing will be done without Betty's consent. It will be true that something Betty wants done will not be done. But if something she consented to is not done, nothing is done to her without her consent. The medical treatment simply would not be undertaken.

Intervening in the refusal case would lead to an act performed without an adolescent's consent. This is harder to justify. Stronger reasons must speak in favour of intervening when adolescents refuse to consent than when they consent to medical treatment. Why is this the case? If Betty consented, but received no treatment, the physician would not act according to her will, but would also not perform an act without her consent. The physician is in any case free not to undertake the treatment. In the consent case, one has to justify not acting according to Betty's will and compelling her to remain in some state. In the refusal case, one has to justify not acting according to Betty's will and in addition performing an act without her consent. The latter has two potentially problematic features, the former only one. This makes it more difficult to justify the latter than the former. This is not due to higher costs brought about by the latter, it is due to the fact that the latter has not just one but two wrong-making features, (1) 'acting against Betty's will' and (2) 'acting without Betty's consent'.

## Should the normative power to consent be shared?

According to the doctrine we are discussing here, adolescents have the power to change the normative situation by giving consent. However, their power to consent is conditional on their parents or the courts not overriding their refusal (or possibly their consent). The question is whether a moral justification can be found for this form of sharing the normative power with others.

[21] As David Wendler puts it: 'The principle that physicians should always act in the best interests of the patient is widely endorsed.' See D. Wendler, 'Are Physicians Obligated Always to Act in the Patient's Best Interest?', *Journal of Medical Ethics*, 36 (2010), 66–70 at 66.

Rob Lawlor thinks that the position faces a serious difficulty. It 'relies on deception, letting adolescents believe that they have a choice when, in reality, they do not'.[22] Take the case of the 13-year-old Brenda who consents to a life-saving treatment. Her consent makes a treatment permissible that would otherwise have been impermissible. She chose consent over refusal to consent. However, if she had chosen refusal over consent, her parents would have stepped in and permitted the treatment. Lawlor thinks that Brenda might have thought that she was free to consent. But, in fact, she had no choice. Her refusal would have been overridden by her parents.

Does Brenda have no choice? Her consent is provisional. But she is able to make a medical treatment permissible. She has the choice between consenting and not consenting to the treatment. Her consent might in both cases be overruled. But this does not mean that she has no choice. It means only that she does not have the final word with regard to whether the medical treatment is permissible or not. Brenda has a choice as far as she is able to make the treatment permissible. She may consent to the treatment and neither parents nor courts may step in. Brenda would bring about the normative change. Brenda therefore has a choice. She can freely choose to consent. This is what she does if she decides to consent even if she has no genuine option to refuse consent. But can it be justified that she does not have the full power to consent?

Skelton, Forsberg, and Black develop a justification of the legal doctrine in question by backing it with a substantive theory of welfare. They argue that the doctrine may be accounted for if one focuses on the unique features of the well-being of adolescents.[23] The fact that what is good for adolescents differs from what is good for adults may, on Skelton *et al.*'s view, provide us with a justification of the differential treatment of adolescents. Subjective experience plays a different role in the well-being of an adolescent and adult. They write:

> It seems that much less of what makes an adult's life go well is due to the possession of objective goods, though such goods may be in part what an adult cares about ... By contrast, it is plausible that what is good for a young child lies in part in the possession of so-called 'objective' goods, things good for an individual regardless of her subjective attitudes toward them ... Adolescents occupy a middle position between young children ... and typical adults ...[24]

Subjective considerations as well objective goods matter for adolescents. As the adolescent ages 'her well-being becomes increasingly based on subjective considerations or the passage of events meeting her expectations or aligning with her values'.[25] Still, important aspects of her well-being will remain objective. Skelton

[22] R. Lawlor, 'Ambiguities and Asymmetries in Consent and Refusal: Reply to Manson', *Bioethics*, 30 (2016), 353–7 at 355.

[23] Skelton *et al.*, 'Overriding Adolescent Refusals of Treatment'.

[24] Skelton *et al.*, 'Overriding Adolescent Refusals of Treatment', 236.

[25] Skelton *et al.*, 'Overriding Adolescent Refusals of Treatment', 237.

*et al.* argue that, among other things, shielding adolescents from taking full responsibility for their actions may be objectively good for them.[26] They take this 'shielding' to be 'a variety of freedom: freedom from making certain kinds of decisions in the absence of a safety net of scrutiny and possible limitation on action'.[27] This, on Skelton *et al.*'s view, may imply the freedom from having the full power to refuse to consent to medical treatment. It is objectively good for adolescents not to possess the unlimited power to refuse to consent. Thus, they conclude that their 'welfarist view' may support the concurrent consent doctrine.[28]

Does the fact that it is objectively good for adolescents to be shielded from taking full responsibility for their actions justify the sharing of the normative power to consent between the adolescent and other parties? The question is whether there is an interest of the adolescent that is served by the normative power to share their normative power to consent. Skelton *et al.* argue that it might be objectively good to have such a limited power to consent. The question is how the different interests that are at stake here are to be weighed against each other. Limiting the normative power to consent is justified only if the interests served by the full power to consent are outweighed by the interests served by having only a limited power to consent.

The power of consent serves a control interest over what others do to us. David Owens holds that there are different reasons for a person to have an interest in controlling what happens to her.[29] First, the fact that someone decides to undergo medical treatment is a good sign that it is also in her interest to do so. Second, in addition, it is often the case that something is in the interest of a person *because* she has decided to do it: 'The fact that I have chosen to φ may actually make it the case that φ-ing is in my interests rather than merely indicate that this is so.'[30] Finally, our decisions also have a social dimension. Owens gives this example: 'Often it is not embarrassing to be observed naked (…) provided one has chosen to be so observed.'[31]

Tadros also argues that our interest in controlling what others do to us plays a central role in explaining why we have the normative power of consent: '(T)he idea that we value having control over our lives, including, importantly, control over the actions of others who would interfere with us, is central to explaining these wrongs.'[32] And he adds: 'We value having this control, and other people respecting our control, simply in itself. When we are subject to consent-sensitive duties, and we respect those duties, we are independent of each other, just in the sense that we can restrict bodily interference by others.'[33]

[26] It has to be noted that this is on their view not the only prudential good and also not the only prudential good at play in these decisions.

[27] Skelton *et al.*, 'Overriding Adolescent Refusals of Treatment', 237.

[28] Skelton *et al.*, 'Overriding Adolescent Refusals of Treatment', 237.

[29] Owens, *Shaping*, p. 166.

[30] Owens, *Shaping*, p. 167.

[31] Owens, *Shaping*, p. 167.

[32] Tadros, *Wrongs and Crimes*, p. 222.

[33] Tadros, *Wrongs and Crimes*, p. 222.

Recall that A has a consent-sensitive duty towards B not to do x if A is obliged not to do x unless B consents to A doing x. We value having control over our consent-sensitive duties for various reasons. Having this control serves the different interests Owens mentions.

The main interest consent serves is what Owens calls a normative interest.[34] The full power of consent adults have serves an interest in having normative control over the actions that would interfere with our lives. It is the interest in being able to decide what others may or may not do to us. Having such a normative interest explains how it could be good to allow another person to perform an act even if that is not in the interest of the consent-giver: it is good for her so far as it is controlled by her. And this is in the interest the normative power of consent serves: it enables us to control what others may do or not do to us.

Adults have this interest in having normative control. But do adolescents have such an interest, too? Due to the gradual expansion of their autonomy, they also have such a normative interest. This is an interest the power to consent the adolescents have serves. It is also a reason why they have this power. Children do not have such a control interest because they are not capable of exerting control that is in their interest, and this is why they do not have the power to consent to medical treatment.

Adolescents have an interest in having normative control and arguably an interest in being shielded from taking full responsibility for some of their actions. Their normative power to consent serves their interest in having normative control. That their consent can be overridden by their parents or by the courts serves their welfare interest. Their consent is justifiably overridden if it is in their best interest. The intervention might serve what is objectively good for them, but it is only justified if the welfare interest served by the intervention is more weighty than the control interest it thwarts. That is to say, the sharing of the normative power is justified only if having normative control over what others do to us and other people respecting this control is not as valuable for adolescents as it is for adults, and in particular if it is of less value for adolescents than not being shielded from taking full responsibility in cases where basic interests are at stake. This is what justifies the sharing of the normative power to consent between adolescents and their parents or the courts. The given view of well-being shows that the control interests of adolescents are in certain cases outweighed by their interests to be protected from being severely harmed. Intervention is justified in cases where the interest in being protected from being severely harmed outweighs the interest in having normative control. It is justified when a life-saving treatment is at stake. It is also likely justified when the adolescent would, without treatment, suffer from a permanent loss of limb or disfigurement. It might, on the other hand, not be justified if the adolescent refused to consent to knee surgery, preferring physiotherapy as an alternative treatment. Shared normative power is justified when the control interest an individual has is

[34] Owens, *Shaping*, p. 6.

less important than the welfare interest they have in being shielded or protected from the full effects or consequences of their medical decisions.

## Conclusion

Thirteen-year-old Betty validly refuses to consent to a life-saving treatment. If she had the full normative power to consent, the treatment would be impermissible. According to the legal doctrine I have discussed in this paper, adolescents have the limited normative power to give provisional consent. They share the normative power to consent with others. People share a normative power if they are able to create the same type of normative change by the same type of act. This is what adolescents, parents and courts are able to do with regard to medical treatments. By consenting they can make a particular medical treatment permissible. The adolescent's consent is provisional, while the consent of the parents or the courts is normatively determinative. However, all parties are able to bring about the same normative change. The limited power of consent arguably serves the adolescents' interest to be protected from being severely harmed. The normative power to consent serves a control interest adolescents arguably also have. The limitation of their normative power of consent is justified in cases where the interest in having normative control the full power of consent serves is outweighed by the interest in being protected from being severely harmed. If Betty validly refused to consent to a minor medical treatment no one could step in and overturn her refusal. In the life-saving treatment case, however, parents or the courts have the normative power to consent to the medical treatment and make it thereby permissible.

11

# Treating Adolescents Differently

ANTHONY SKELTON, ISRA BLACK, AND LISA FORSBERG*

CONSIDER THE FOLLOWING two cases.

> *Sam's blood transfusion.* Sam is 16 years of age. Sam is rushed to hospital after being hit by a car on the way to school. She sustains serious, life-threatening injuries and loses a lot of blood. Her physician concludes that she needs a blood transfusion to survive. The physician asks for Sam's consent to this course of treatment. Sam understands and appreciates her medical options. She consents to the blood transfusion on grounds that it is best for her given her values. Sam is deemed to possess the decision-making capacity to decide on her medical treatment.
>
> *Hilary's blood transfusion.* Hilary is 16 years of age. Hilary has Crohn's disease. He is admitted to hospital with lower gastrointestinal bleeding. According to the physician in charge of Hilary's care, the bleeding poses a significant threat to his health and life. His physician concludes that a blood transfusion is necessary to survive. Hilary understands and appreciates his medical options. He refuses the blood transfusion on grounds that it fails to cohere with his values. Hilary is deemed to possess the capacity to decide on his medical treatment.

It is plausible that Sam's consent has the power to permit the blood transfusion offered by her physician and that no one else need provide consent on her behalf. Sam's consent would be considered normatively (and legally) determinative. It is equally plausible that Hilary's refusal would *not*, however, be normatively (or legally) determinative. His refusal might justifiably be overridden by consent to the blood transfusion provided by either a parent or a court; these parties would *share* (with Hilary) the power to consent to his treatment and thereby render it (morally and legally) permissible for a physician to provide it.

In the case of adolescents, consent and refusal (in these kinds of situations) are, then, plausibly treated *asymmetrically*. By contrast, in the case of adults and young

* Each author contributed equally to writing this chapter. Thanks to Guy Fletcher for helpful comments on a previous version.

*Proceedings of the British Academy*, **279**, 205–228, © Authors 2025.

children, consent and refusal are treated *symmetrically*. Were Hilary and Sam younger and unable to demonstrate decision-making capacity, neither their consent nor their refusal would be normatively or legally determinative in the above cases. Consent or refusal in this case would fall to the natural or legal person exercising parental responsibility. Were Hilary and Sam aged 18 years, their choices in the above cases would be treated as normatively and legally determinative, whether they consent or refuse.

An asymmetry of the sort described above cannot merely be asserted or considered a brute normative fact. In Hilary's case, an adolescent's *valid* refusal is overridden, and an invasive medical intervention is imposed on them for their own good, even though the procedure contravenes their most fundamental and reflectively considered convictions. Such paternalistic treatment would, if carried out on an adult with capacity, constitute a grave insult, if not a serious legal wrong. Hence, the asymmetrical treatment of consent and refusal in the case of minors with capacity requires justification.

In previous work, we developed a philosophical justification of the 'concurrent consents' doctrine in English law, which would yield the results we found plausible in the medical treatment cases of Sam and Hilary, respectively.[1] For ease of reference, this doctrine is that in the case of adolescents whereas consent is treated as normatively (and legally) determinative, refusal is not always treated as normatively (or legally) determinative. Our defence of differential and paternalistic treatment of adolescents—compared to adults and younger children—rests on a distinct conception of adolescent well-being vis-à-vis these other welfare subjects.

In this chapter, we extend our treatment of adolescent decision-making. We consider the question of what justifies the differential treatment of adolescents more generally. We clarify our (well-being-based) view and defend its commitments regarding the nature of well-being over the life course.

This chapter has five sections. In the first section, we clarify our focus. In the second section, we reject two popular justifications for the differential and paternalistic treatment of adolescents. In the third section, we articulate a theory of what is fundamentally and non-instrumentally prudentially good for adolescents. This theory of well-being explains why adolescents may share normative powers (including asymmetrically) with other parties. In the fourth section, we evaluate our well-being-based approach to the differential treatment of adolescents through critical comparison with two recent attempts to support the differential and paternalistic treatment of adolescents. In the fifth section, we deflect the objection that our view is flawed since it assumes (and inherits the shortcomings of) variabilism about well-being.

[1] Anthony Skelton, Lisa Forsberg, and Isra Black, 'Overriding Adolescent Refusals of Treatment', *Journal of Ethics and Social Philosophy*, 20 (2021), 221–47.

## Preliminaries

It is important to clarify two things at the outset. First, the cases of Sam and Hilary above concern medical decision-making. It would be a mistake, however, to think that the intuitions and asymmetry above about the normative determinacy of consent and refusal are not operative in other domains, for example, the family or work. Second, asymmetry in the normative determinacy of consent and refusal, respectively, need not always cut in the same direction. In the case of the 'concurrent consents' doctrine, it is consent that is normatively (and legally) determinative, whereas refusal is not. We may, however, envisage situations that invert the consent–refusal asymmetry. Consider the following examples illustrative of these two clarifications.

> *Teen Marriage*. Alex is 16 years of age. Alex has been in a relationship with her partner for two years. The relationship is supported by both sets of parents. Recently, Alex's partner—who has just turned 18 years of age—proposed marriage. Alex is in love and can foresee a long and happy marriage. She understands and appreciates the implications of marriage. She has agreed to the proposal as the best expression of her values. Alex has the capacity to marry.

> *Paper Round*. Lindsay is 13 years old. Lindsay is looking to make more money to save for a new bike. He applies to the local newsagent for a paper round. Lindsay understands and appreciates what the work entails (including early mornings, physical exertion, and customer care). Lindsay sees this job as the best means to the end of a new bike.

In *Teen Marriage*, it is plausible that Alex's consent to marry would not be normatively determinative. Rather, her parents or an official (or court) would have a say in whether her wishes should prevail.[2] However, were Alex to refuse her partner's proposal, it is plausible that her decision would be determinative—otherwise, we would be on the terrain of forced marriage.[3] For *Paper Round*, the situation may be legally complex,[4] but morally, the newsagent might plausibly require Lindsay's parents' approval of the paper round job. Whereas in the situation in which Lindsay's parents had arranged with the newsagent the offer of a paper round, it seems that his refusal to work would be normatively determinative.

[2] See e.g. French Civil Code, Titre V: Du mariage. In France, marriageable age is 18 years (article 144), but the State procurator [procureur de la République] in the relevant locality may dispense of this requirement for serious reasons [motifs graves]. However, even with official dispensation, parental consent (or the consent of one parent in the case of disagreement) is required (article 148).

[3] See e.g. French Civil Code, article 146: 'There is no marriage without first-personal consent' [*Il n'y a pas de mariage, lorsqu'il n'y a point de consentement*].

[4] For example, in English law, contracts made by minors are generally voidable and parents are usually unable to contract on behalf of their children.

## Two popular views rejected

What might be said in favour of treating adolescents differentially and paternalistically—by giving their consents and refusals asymmetrical normative power, according to their perceived better interests? There are a range of views on the justification of differential (and paternalistic) treatment. We shall briefly consider and reject two views prior to subjecting our own view to critical discussion in the fourth section.

The first view focuses on the situational vulnerability of adolescents during the transition between childhood, on the one hand, and adulthood, on the other hand.[5] Adolescence is a period in which individuals are attempting to assert themselves in accordance with their values yet remain vulnerable—for example, because their values are provisional, or their decisions are more prone to risky behaviour or regret, or they are more susceptible to peer pressure—which, in turn, elicits reliance on and responsibility on the part of others. This vulnerability would justify the (transitional) paternalism expressed in differential treatment. Vulnerability works to justify the asymmetry in normative powers across consent and refusal, since the adolescents in question possess the capacity to choose among various courses of action.

However, vulnerability alone cannot justify differential treatment. First, some adults are vulnerable (not necessarily for the same reasons,[6] but) in the same manner as at least some adolescents—including the elderly, the severely ill, the disabled, and marginalised members of society—many of whom may well possess the capacity to take medical and other kinds of decisions. Yet, we do not typically think that we may treat vulnerable adults' decisions as akin to those of adolescents. Rather, we ought to respect the former's autonomy or agency and work with these capacities to help an individual deliberate towards a choice aligning with their perceived interests, recognising that the final decision is up to them.[7] To treat them otherwise—by imposing asymmetrical normative powers on the relevant choices—would be to fail to respect their status. If this is true, vulnerability alone cannot provide the answer to why differential treatment is permissible in the case of adolescents.

The second view says that the main justification for differential treatment of adolescents is the severity of the potential outcomes of deciding one way

[5] See e.g. Johannes Giesinger, 'Vulnerability and Autonomy: Children and Adults', *Ethics and Social Welfare*, 13 (2019), 216–29.

[6] Giesinger, 'Vulnerability', 5; cf. Emma Cave and Hannah Cave, 'Skeleton Keys to Hospital Doors: Adolescent Adults who Refuse Life-Sustaining Medical Treatment', *Modern Law Review*, 86 (2023), 984–1010.

[7] For example, the 'vulnerability' jurisdiction of the English High Court operates on the basis that the court's powers are, at least in the first instance, there to be 'facilitative' of an individual's autonomy: *L v J* [2010] EWHC 2665 (Fam). And while the Court of Appeal in *A Local Authority v DL* [2012] EWCA Civ 253 held that the High Court's inherent powers go beyond 'providing interim relief designed to permit the vulnerable individual the "space" to make decisions for themselves', it is clear that the Court will not routinely impose (and has not imposed) a decision on individuals who have or may come to have the capacity decisions for themselves.

rather than another (for example, in the cases of Sam and Hilary).[8] Here, the idea is that when consenting or refusing to do something has significant costs to the adolescent making the decision, it is justified to consider the consent or refusal—whatever the case may be—as not normatively determinative. That is, it is capable of being overridden by the consent or the refusal of another party capable of (and empowered to provide) valid consent or refusal—for example, a parent or court.

While intuitively appealing, this view (again) cannot account for the differential treatment of (valid) adult and adolescent decisions. There are cases in which adults validly refuse to accept or to do certain things and in so doing visit significant (even irreversible) costs on themselves.[9] In many such cases—especially, but not uniquely, in medicine—we respect the adult's choice, despite the fact that the decision is hard to fathom or reckless or deadly. The question is why respect such a decision when made by an adult but not when made by an adolescent?

Further, as the case of *Paper Round* suggests, we might be happy to endorse sharing of normative powers in the case of adolescents when the stakes are relatively low. In Lindsay's case, the difference between the possible outcomes does not seem especially great, and in any case, it would be relatively easy to retreat from any of the options chosen. Therefore, the potential severity of outcomes cannot provide a justification for treating adolescents differently across all cases in which asymmetrically shared normative powers may be in play.

There has to be some feature of the decision-making context, then, that is present in the case of adolescents but lacking in the case of adults that clarifies why it makes sense to treat them differently, and this feature must be supplementary to vulnerability or the risk of significant harm.

## A theory of adolescent well-being

In 'Overriding Adolescent Refusals of Treatment',[10] we offered a well-being-based justification for the concurrent consents doctrine in English Law. We argued that it is the unique features of adolescent well-being that justify the asymmetry in the normative power of adolescent consent to and refusal of medical treatment. We submit that our approach might be invoked in defence of differential and paternalistic treatment of adolescents more generally.

A theory of well-being tells us how well or poorly things are going for an individual both at a time and across time. It provides an account of what makes something fundamentally, non-instrumentally *prudentially* good for (bad for) an

[8] See e.g. Nigel Lowe and Satvinder Juss, 'Medical Treatment: Pragmatism and the Search for Principle', *Modern Law Review*, 56 (1993), 865–72.

[9] See e.g. *Re C (Adult: Refusal of Treatment)* [1994] 1 WLR 290 (Fam).

[10] Skelton, Forsberg, and Black, 'Overriding'.

individual and to what degree.[11] Some prudential goods that make one better off may fall into the category of so-called 'subjective' prudential goods, while others may fall into the category of so-called 'objective' prudential goods.[12] The former are non-instrumentally good (bad) for the individual because and in so far as that individual has a favourable (unfavourable) attitude toward them (e.g. a desire or aversion), while the latter are non-instumentally good (bad) for an individual regardless of whether they have a favourable (unfavourable) attitude toward them. Were, for example, autonomy an objective non-instrumental prudential good, its possession or exercise would be non-instrumentally good for an individual even if that individual did not value or want it.

A theory of well-being is subjective if it makes an individual's well-being depend at least in part on that individual's 'set of attitudes or concerns'.[13] A theory of well-being is objective if it denies this dependence.[14]

On our conception of adolescent well-being, an adolescent individual's well-being comprises a distinctive plurality of (objective and subjective) goods, including happiness, autonomy, supportive and caring relationships, and—most important to our defence of the differential treatment of adolescents—what we call 'shielding'. Shielding is the non-instrumental prudential good of being protected from the full effect of one's decisions or possessing a variety of freedom from making certain kinds of decisions in the absence of a safety net. Appeal to the non-instrumental prudential good of shielding helps us articulate what is plausible in our intuitive judgements about the cases we have considered, as well as the asymmetrical sharing of normative powers.

If we take the blood transfusions of Sam and Hilary in tandem, we can see how the non-instrumental prudential good of shielding comes into play and how it may have asymmetrical application respecting the normative powers of interested parties. In the case of Sam, the choice to receive a blood transfusion aligns not only with her own values but also with what her physician (discharging their own professional duty of care) expects would be best. Here, we might think that the demands of the prudential value of shielding are met by the structural features of the scenario; there is no need to safeguard Sam from the full force of her decision given her choice to consent. This is because in medical contexts, the offer of treatment in accordance with the physician's duty of care ought to reflect, other things equal, a professional judgement as to the patient's best interests.[15] There is, then, a kind of antecedent safety net inherent in the medical domain. This ex ante safety net

[11] Guy Fletcher, *The Philosophy of Well-Being: An Introduction* (New York, Routledge, 2016); Ben Bradley, *Well-Being* (Cambridge, Polity Press, 2015); James Griffin, *Well-Being: Its Meaning, Measurement, and Moral Importance* (Oxford, Clarendon Press, 1986).

[12] For helpful discussion of the distinction between subjective and objective theories, see, L. W. Sumner, *Welfare, Happiness, and Ethics* (Oxford, Clarendon Press, 1996), pp. 26–44; Fletcher, *Well-Being*, pp. 65–75; and Eden Lin, 'Well-Being, Part 2: Theories of Well-Being', *Philosophy Compass*, 17 (2022), 1–23.

[13] Sumner, *Welfare*, p. 81; also pp. 38, 42, 82, 163FN29.

[14] Sumner, *Welfare*, pp. 38, 43.

[15] See e.g. *R (Burke) v General Medical Council* [2005] EWCA Civ 1003.

explains why Sam's consent may well be normatively (morally or legally) determinative, and why there is no need for another party (such as parents or a court) to second-guess her choice.

In the case of Hilary—who, recall, is refusing a blood transfusion—his choice coheres with his own values, but it conflicts with what his physician expects would be best. Here, the prudential value of shielding demands more of us because the refusal of life-prolonging treatment is out of step with the safety margin built into the offer of treatment. As such, we might expect Hilary's refusal not to be normatively (morally or legally) determinative and require the scrutiny of another authoritative party (for example, a parent). It seems reasonable, given shielding, that the decision would not be Hilary's alone to make.

In the case of *Teen Marriage*, given the risks of marriage in general (including relationship breakdown)—risks that may be amplified by marriage at a young age[16]—it is perhaps unsurprising that Alex's first-personal consent to marriage would be subject to further layers of approval (by officials and parents). Conversely, there is no real risk in Alex not getting married at a young age, and indeed there is risk in outsourcing consent to marriage to another party. As such, we can think of the value of shielding as providing a safety net for the choice to consent, whereas the best mode of protecting Alex's well-being (especially the element relating to autonomy) gives her refusal decisive force. As in the medical treatment cases above, shielding explains why consent or refusal might not be determinative and why the sharing of normative powers may be asymmetrical across the options.

*Paper Round* is less clear cut (in part because the stakes are lower). In *Paper Round*, assuming that the newsagent is interested in Lindsay's welfare (if only instrumentally), it seems correct to require parental approval of employment, since this may bring to light any reasons why Lindsay should not deliver newspapers. It might be good for Lindsay to be free from making the decision alone, that is, to be shielded from the full effects of taking on a job, which may include opportunity costs like less time for study, family, friends, and hobbies. Again, shielding affords Lindsay a choice, but not without a safety net. Whereas similar to the case of *Teen Marriage*, Lindsay's refusal of work can be safely allocated to him alone, and indeed there are good protective reasons to think that the refusal ought to be first-personal alone. The discussion of the cases reveals how the prudential value of shielding might yield shared normative powers—through its connection to freedom more broadly, which also comprises an adolescent's well-being. Recall that shielding is a variety of freedom (to take decisions) comprising a safeguarding backstop (to have those decisions scrutinised by a trustworthy party). Being free from making certain decisions in the absence of a safety net involves such decisions being shared with others in supportive and caring relationships (the possession of which is itself non-derivatively prudentially good for adolescents).

[16] Philip N. Cohen, 'How We Really Can Study Divorce Using Just Five Questions and a Giant Sample' (2015) https://familyinequality.wordpress.com/2015/07/22/how-we-really-can-study-divorce/ (accessed 13 July 2025).

Let us now turn to consider how decision-making power might be shared between adolescents and those with whom they have caring and supportive relationships in particular domains of life.

One option would be to place decision-making in some domain (e.g. education) beyond the scope of adolescents' decision-making authority altogether—call this the 'restricted scope' option.[17] There is, in this case, a domain in which neither an adolescent's consent nor their refusal is definitive. A second option would be to give adolescents full decision-making authority in the relevant domain—call this the 'unconstrained power' option. In this case, an adolescents' consent and refusal are treated like an adult's in a particular domain. A third option is to give adolescents some decision-authority in a particular domain but subject their choices in this domain to review—call this the 'constrained power' option.[18] This option is the one in which the asymmetries discussed above take place and that—crucially—our view supports.

We might envisage that each of these options instantiates the plural goods comprising adolescent well-being to different degrees. Take the value of autonomy. The unconstrained power option exemplifies this value the most, the restricted scope option the least (or perhaps not at all), and the constrained power option somewhat (to the extent that the adolescent's decisions are afforded 'consideration respect', but not 'compliance respect').[19] There may be sound prudential reasons to opt for the restricted scope option, ceding autonomy for other values. Likewise, there may be sound prudential reasons not to select the unconstrained power option. Too much autonomy may be risky.

The constrained power option breaks the dichotomy between the choice of maximal autonomy and none at all. Importantly, attention to the flavour of freedom allows for nuance in the specification of the constrained power option. In some cases, concern for an adolescent's overall prudential good requires us to attenuate individual autonomy. We might impose review of an adolescent's decision-making in a particular context across all the options available to the agent. In such a case, we opt for symmetrical shielding. However, it may not always be necessary (and it may be counterproductive) for autonomy always to give way to shielding and vice versa. It is plausible that we might opt for an asymmetrical mix of autonomy and shielding for a particular domain of decision-making—for example, when the

[17] Neil C. Manson, 'Transitional Paternalism: How Shared Normative Powers Give Rise to the Asymmetry of Adolescent Consent and Refusal', *Bioethics*, 29 (2015), 66–73 at 71. See also Tamar Schapiro, 'What Is a Child?', *Ethics*, 109 (1999), 715–38 at 734: 'we can imagine agents at an intermediate stage—agents who have established their authority over some of the constitutionally essential domains but not over others … many of the people we conventionally call children … can be thought of as falling into this intermediate category; they have adult status with respect to some domains of discretion, but not others'.

[18] Manson, 'Transitional', 71.

[19] Suzanne Uniacke, 'Respect for Autonomy in Medical Ethics', in David Archard, Monique Deveaux, Neil Manson, and Daniel Weinstock (eds), *Reading Onora O'Neill* (London, Routledge, 2013), pp. 94–110.

risks attached to a particular option are low or when there is value in the adolescent's decision having full normative power (and entailing, other things equal, full responsibility). Thus, in the medical domain, the ex ante safety net afforded by the physician's duty of care lowers the risk of consent to treatment and provides a good opportunity to practise the exercise of autonomy.[20]

While concerning *Teen Marriage*, permitting consent without further review might jeopardise the goods comprising adolescent well-being other than autonomy, whereas allowing refusal to be decisive seems to pose little threat to non-freedom related non-instrumental prudential goods, and more protective of freedom overall than imposing symmetrical shielding across the options (which would expose adolescents to forced marriage). Shared normative powers and the asymmetry in the normative power of the options available to the agent emerge as a function of the value of shielding among other non-instrumental prudential goods.

A final, clarificatory point flows from our characterisation of shielding as a variety of freedom distinct from the value of autonomy. Not all circumstances of constrained (and shared) normative powers involve shielding. Consider the following example.

> *Communal Cottage*. Charlie, Sam, and Vivian own a cottage in common. They agree that any one or more of them may use the cottage, but all of them must agree each instance of use. If one dissents, no one may use the cottage.

In *Communal Cottage*, the sharing of normative powers and the limitation of each of party's decision-making authority is a result of the exercise of autonomy: the use agreement. This is not necessarily the explanation for sharing of normative powers when shielding is in play. It is the non-instrumental prudential value of the adolescent's exercise of decision-making authority paired with the insurance of another party's review that gives rise to the allocation of decision-making authority to, for example, parents or officials. An adolescent need not agree to share normative powers in order to possess the freedom that comes from being shielded.

## Two rival views rejected

In the previous section, we articulated a theory of adolescent well-being, comprising a plurality of items considered non-instrumentally prudentially good for adolescents, including shielding—or freedom from making certain kinds of decisions

[20] See Skelton, Forsberg, and Black, 'Overriding', 238–9, where we argue that 'the rule according to which consents always have the power to render treatment permissible is justified by the fact that it involves promoting instrumentally beneficial exercises of autonomy without the threat of serious costs'. What Schapiro, 'Child', 736 argues with regard to the value of exercising autonomy within restricted domains of discretion might also hold for situations in which an adolescent is asymmetrically shielded, '[t]he aim here is not simply to give them practice at decision making, as if decision making were a skill. Instead, it is to put them in a position where they are forced to come up with provisional principles of deliberation, principles whose applicability is likely to extend beyond the limits of the questions at hand.'

in the absence of a safety net of scrutiny—autonomy, caring and supportive relationships, among others. Shielding, considered among other non-instrumental prudential goods, explains why in certain decision-making contexts, adolescents may share normative powers with others, including asymmetrically across the options available.

We now turn to assessing how our view fares in explaining the differential (and paternalistic) treatment of adolescents and adults. We do this by way of comparison of our view with two recent rival accounts of differential treatment defended by Andrew Franklin-Hall and Monica Betzler.[21]

Franklin-Hall argues that the differential treatment of adolescents and adults arises from the application of two different conceptions of competence (or capacity) that ground the individual's decision-making authority—the decision-based conception and the abilities-based conception, respectively.[22] These competing conceptions of capacity capture two distinct values protected by autonomy: authenticity and agency.[23] 'Whereas *authenticity* is the value of choosing in a way that expresses or conforms to one's enduring values, *agency* is the value of being able to make one's own choice, to exercise one's will, especially over one's own life and affairs.'[24]

According to Franklin-Hall, the decision-based conception protects the value of authenticity, whereas the abilities-based conception protects the value of agency.[25] On the one hand, the decision-based conception grounds an individual's decision-making authority in the ability to understand and appreciate information relevant to a decision *and* to make a choice coherent with their own values. As Franklin-Hall observes, '[c]ompetence, therefore, is tied to subjective rationality'.[26] On the other hand, the abilities-based conception grounds an individual's decision-making authority just when he is '*capable* of making an autonomous decision in the … [decision-based] sense, even if his decision is not at all consistent with what is important to him'.[27]

> What matters, therefore, is not the character of the actual decision, but certain properties of the decision-maker at the time of the decision, namely, that one possesses, to a sufficient degree, the epistemic and deliberative abilities for understanding and appreciating the information relevant to the decision, for effectively comparing the pros and

[21] Andrew Franklin-Hall, 'Competence for Minors in Medical Decision-Making: A Life-Stage Approach', in this volume; Monika Betzler, 'The Moral Significance of Adolescence', *Journal of Applied Philosophy*, 39 (2021), 547–61.

[22] Franklin-Hall, 'Competence', 34.

[23] Franklin-Hall, 'Competence', 35. See Daniel Brudney and John Lantos, 'Agency and Authenticity: Which Value Grounds Patient Choice?', *Theoretical Medicine and Bioethics*, 32 (2011), 217–27.

[24] Franklin-Hall, 'Competence', 35–6 (original emphasis).

[25] Franklin-Hall, 'Competence', 36.

[26] Franklin-Hall, 'Competence', 34; see Isra Black, 'Asymmetry of Adolescent Decision-Making Capacity and Rational Choice' in this volume for a defence of this kind of view.

[27] Franklin-Hall, 'Competence', 34 (original emphasis).

> cons of different courses of action, for evaluating those options in the light of one's enduring values, for resisting contrary inclinations, and so on ....[28]

Franklin-Hall claims that for adults, the abilities-based conception of capacity is the appropriate standard. Adults possess a '*robust* right to autonomy',[29] which blocks the withdrawal of decision-making authority on grounds that an individual is failing to make the better choice from the point of view of their own values.[30] Rather (and in virtue of the status of adults as 'reasoning agents in a relation of basic practical equality'),[31] 'we ... [may] interfere only when we cannot sufficiently attribute the choice to the person's agency—it was not really *her choice* at all'.[32]

For adolescents, Franklin-Hall proposes that we accept an attenuated decision-based conception of capacity, for two reasons. First, endorsing the abilities-based standard applicable to adults would yield results that are 'hard to accept' in adolescents, that is, we may be unwilling to accept 'extremely harmful ... and subjectively unreasonable' decisions on the latter's part.[33] Second, employing a decision-based conception of capacity while tempering its rigour during adolescence is an element of the instrumentally beneficial endeavour of instilling in young people the capacities and insight necessary for successful 'life-authorship'.[34] On Franklin-Hall's view, each individual has a right to life-authorship, a right to manage their life according to their choices. It is consistent with respecting this right that adolescents may be treated paternalistically even beyond the point at which they develop the abilities constitutive of agency, provided it is made clear that their right to life-authorship will be respected in the not-too-distant future.

We have two sets of objections to Franklin-Hall's account of the differential treatment of adults and adolescents. The first set of objections targets the merits and plausibility of the abilities-based conception of capacity. For one, it is not clear that the abilities-based conception requires deployment of the relevant agential properties by an agent making a decision to a degree that plausibly meets Franklin-Hall's own criterion that—to ground decision-making authority—an individual's choice must be sufficiently attributable to their agency. It seems important not only that agents have the *ability* to reason through to a choice consistent with what they value, but that to some extent they *do*.[35]

According to Franklin-Hall, in order to have capacity on the abilities-based conception, it is not necessary that, but merely possible for, an individual to use the reasons given by deliberation over the relevant courses of action to choose

28 Franklin-Hall, 'Competence', 34.
29 Franklin-Hall, 'Competence', 31 (original emphasis).
30 Franklin-Hall, 'Competence', 31.
31 Franklin-Hall, 'Competence', 37.
32 Franklin-Hall, 'Competence', 37 (original emphasis).
33 Franklin-Hall, 'Competence', 41.
34 Franklin-Hall, 'Competence', 42.
35 See Catriona Mackenzie, 'Three Dimensions of Autonomy: A Relational Analysis', in Andrea Veltman and Mark Piper (eds), *Autonomy, Oppression, and Gender* (Oxford, Oxford University Press, 2014), pp. 15–41.

between the available options. One *need not*, but *may* use the epistemic and deliberative abilities Franklin-Hall articulates in support of one's decision. One may well choose the most valued option (given one's credences regarding the options and their expected outcomes and one's subjective values), but one might equally ignore one's subjectively rational reasons for action and choose on entirely different grounds. Understood in this way, the robust right to autonomy that Franklin-Hall suggests that adults possess is a function of a somewhat undemanding threshold for agency. On Franklin-Hall's view, for adults it suffices to have the status of reasoning agent to hold decision-making authority. There is a divorce between one's status as a reasoning agent, and one's being an agent making reasoned choices. The issue is that by distinguishing reasoning agent status from action on reasons—and making the former what matters for decision-making capacity and authority—Franklin-Hall thins out the attributability of a choice to an agent. We might agree that insofar as you are a reasoning agent, the choices you make are attributable to you—they are the issue of your will. But they may be to a flimsy degree only; the choices are yours, but to the extent that you set aside your subjectively rational reasons for action, not much of your will—your inventory of values and modes of thought—need feature in your decision-making. We might doubt, *pace* Franklin-Hall, whether this conception of agency is sufficient to ground the robust respect for adult decision-making authority he envisages.

Franklin-Hall asks whether the agent's choice was 'her choice *at all*'.[36] But that may be the wrong question, for it allows for a gap between an individual's synchronic possession of the properties commensurate with agency and meaningful exercise of *their* will. The right enquiry, we suggest, is 'whether the agent's choice is her choice *enough*?'. Hence, we expect translation of the agent's will into their choices. The *sufficiency* of attributable agency depends on the connection between the reasons for action deliberation yields (in the presence of sufficient abilities)—reasons informed by what the agent values or cares about at the relevant time (which may, but need not be *authentic* concerns)—and the reasons on which the agent acts. To do so rests a robust—albeit not necessarily decisive—right to autonomy on more secure agential footings than Franklin-Hall's abilities-based conception of capacity.

For another, Franklin-Hall suggests that the abilities-based conception is reflected in our social practices. But the example—of former Apple CEO Steve Jobs—he offers to support this claim is of dubious value. Following his pancreatic cancer diagnosis, Jobs declined standard (and potentially successful) treatment in favour of self-help and alternative remedies—much to the consternation of friends and family.[37] Despite this opprobrium and the apparent inconsistency of Jobs' behaviour with his enduring values, no one seriously doubted his capacity to decide. Franklin-Hall takes this as evidence that our social practices give adults

[36] Franklin-Hall, 'Competence', 37 (original emphasis).
[37] Franklin-Hall, 'Competence', 38–9.

final decision-making authority, even when their decisions are subjectively irrational and extremely harmful.

But Jobs' case can be explained in more plausible ways. First, if we hold a sufficiency (decision-based) conception of capacity, an individual need only offer some subjectively rational reasons (rather than a full or coherent set) in order to have decision-making authority.[38] As such, Jobs' dislike of 'the idea of his body being "opened" ' may have sufficed to ground his decision-making authority. Second, it is not implausible that Jobs may have benefitted from (or fallen prey to) the deference accorded to privileged white men. Stories do not abound of unprivileged people, for example, women and racial minorities of any gender, demonstrating capacity merely on the abilities-based conception. Our social practices do not seem to reflect the abilities-based conception in respect of all adults;[39] and—as we have argued—neither does the abilities-based capacity exemplify the ideal of agency.

Putting Jobs' case aside in the spirit of charity, Franklin-Hall may be correct that adults enjoy a 'robust right to autonomy' as a matter of social practice, whereas adolescents do not. But it need not always be the case that the agent's decision-making authority takes for its grounding their decision-making capacity. Perhaps decision-making authority has its own, independent value.[40] Or, more practical considerations—for example, the stakes of the decision (or of its context) and the difficulty of interference to withdraw decision-making authority—may be in play. *Pace* Franklin-Hall, invoking different operative conceptions of capacity may not be the most plausible route to explaining the differential treatment of adults and adolescents.

Our second set of objections to Franklin-Hall's account of the justification for treating adults and adolescents differently targets his argument for accepting the decision-based conception of capacity for adolescents, albeit tempered by the postponement of the adolescent's 'ability to enter into certain adult paths' because of the instrumental benefits that attend on having extended preparation for adulthood and the stage of life at which the postponement occurs.[41] Our worry is that Franklin-Hall allows the concept of postponement to bear too much normative weight. That a decision is susceptible to deferral into adulthood does not seem to be a morally relevant feature rendering paternalistic treatment of adolescents (im) permissible.

[38] See *Re SB (A Patient) (Capacity to Consent to Termination)* [2013] EWHC 1417 (COP).

[39] There is clear evidence, at least in England and Wales, that the test of decision-making capacity is applied with uneven rigour. As Marie Fox and Jaime Lindsey observe, for example, '[pregnant] women's decisions are more likely to be overridden on the basis of incompetence [than men]': Marie Fox and Jaime Lindsey, 'Health Law, Medicine and Ethics: Are Women More Likely to Have Their Healthcare Decisions Overruled?', in Rosemary Auchmuty (ed.), *Great Debates in Gender and Law* (New York, Bloomsbury Publishing, 2018), pp. 121–5 at 123–4. See also Zaina Mahmoud and Elizabeth Chloe Romanis, 'On Gestation and Motherhood', *Medical Law Review*, 31 (2023), 109–40.

[40] Isra Black, Lisa Forsberg, and Anthony Skelton, 'Transformative Choice and Decision-Making Capacity', *Law Quarterly Review*, 139 (2023), 654–80 at 679.

[41] Franklin-Hall, 'Competence', 43.

To illustrate, consider Franklin-Hall's discussion of '*forced, momentous choices*', that is, 'important decisions that arise ... that cannot be postponed without effectively deciding the matter one way or another'.[42] The cases of Sam and Hilary above seem good examples. Franklin-Hall argues that an adolescent's subjectively rational decision ought to prevail, even if it is (objectively) harmful. Thus, both Sam and Hilary's medical decisions would prevail, notwithstanding that in Hilary's case his refusal of treatment entails death. We might reasonably disagree with Franklin-Hall that adolescent decisions ought to be normatively determinative when faced with forced, momentous choices. The outcome he would recommend—arising from his unmoderated commitment to the decision-based account of competence for adolescents in the case of forced, momentous choice—in Hilary's case is hard to swallow on the evidence available to us. (Though it would not be in the case of adults.) There seem to be grounds for paternalistic intervention that Franklin-Hall's view cannot accommodate. Recall that Franklin-Hall rejects the abilities-based view for adolescents on grounds that it would have implications that we would be unwilling to accept. Yet his own view of how we should treat adolescents' decisions has implications we would be unwilling to accept and so we should reject it, too.

We think that appeal to the distinctness of adolescent well-being and the prudential value of shielding is superior to Franklin-Hall's competence and life-stage account in three ways. First, shielding is agnostic as to the operative conception of capacity and does not commit us to thinking that there are different standards of capacity that adults and adolescents must meet to ground their decision-making authority. Second, shielding provides an explanation for the asymmetry in the normative determinacy of different adolescent choices (for a set of options). Third, shielding delivers the right verdicts on when paternalism towards adolescents is justified in hard cases, without undermining our considered judgements about the authority of autonomous adults.

Monica Betzler argues that 'the aim of adolescence is to develop autonomy'.[43] This aim grounds the differential treatment of adolescents and adults: whereas adolescents *need* autonomy-supporting relationships, adults do not. As Betzler puts it: 'what marks the relevant distinction between adolescents and adults is that the former, but not the latter, need to have autonomy-supporting relationships if they are to become skilled autonomous agents. Adolescents would not be able to develop their autonomous capacities if they did not receive such relational support.'[44]

Betzler argues that, in the usual run of things, the type of stance towards adolescents characteristic of autonomy-support—the 'Relational View'—will recommend against paternalism; such measures amount to a 'relational wrong', which impedes development of autonomy.[45] However, Betzler does not exclude paternalistic intervention in the lives of adolescents in some cases, for example, when

[42] Franklin-Hall, 'Competence', 44 (original emphasis).
[43] Betzler, 'Significance', 9.
[44] Betzler, 'Significance', 6.
[45] Betzler, 'Significance', 9.

they commit 'acts of extreme self-harm or seriously [endanger] their lives [broadly, construed] in other ways' that cast doubt on the autonomous quality of the relevant decision.[46] Here, Betzler allows scope (at least) for the asymmetrical sharing of normative powers between adolescents and adults across the options available.[47] She concludes that provided cases of paternalistic interference 'remain infrequent and are well justified, they should not prevent an adolescent from becoming a skilled autonomous agent and so they do not affect the Relational View's commitment to autonomy support'.[48]

Concerning adults, Betzler concedes that close relationships may be valuable in developing or improving an individual's autonomous agency. However, 'we should be wary of treating adults as adolescents', since behaving in this way risks undermining equal respect between adults in favour of 'some kind of therapeutic relationship'.[49]

We have four objections to Betzler's account of the moral significance of adolescence and the justification for treating adolescents in ways different to adults. First, we might agree with Betzler that one of the aims of adolescence is to develop autonomy. But she writes as if the latter is the former's only aim. Another aim of adolescence might be to transition to the next phase of life without the practice or exercise of autonomy having led to serious misfortune or harm. This aim might temper autonomy-supporting measures that license risk-taking and mistake-making on the part of adolescents. And provide support for paternalism.[50] Likewise, there may be goods available in adolescence that are worth having irrespective of their impact on (and potentially in tension with) the development of autonomy.

Second, Betzler admits that paternalism is warranted in the case of adolescents when the stakes are high (such as in the cases of Sam and Hilary), *and* when their 'level of autonomy [is] … difficult to ascertain'.[51] This is not sufficient grounds for differentiating between the treatment of adults and adolescents, since there are cases with these features involving adults where we think interference is legitimate. (Although we might doubt whether intervention in the case of marginal autonomy is paternalistic.[52]) This seems to suggest that a deeper explanation is called for.

Third, Betzler's discussion of paternalism seems to leave room for intervention only when the stakes are high *and* the adolescent's autonomy is in doubt. This might seem under-capacious. In the cases we discuss above, the autonomy of our

[46] Betzler, 'Significance', 10.
[47] Betzler, 'Significance', 10.
[48] Betzler, 'Significance', 10–11.
[49] Betzler, 'Significance', 12.
[50] See *Re W (A Minor) (Medical Treatment: Court's Jurisdiction)* [1993] Fam 64 (CA) 81–2 (Lord Donaldson MR): 'Prudence does not involve avoiding all risk, but it does involve avoiding taking risks which, if they eventuate, may have irreparable consequences or which are disproportionate to the benefits which could accrue from taking them.'
[51] Betzler, 'Significance', 10.
[52] Betzler, 'Significance', FN3, writes that she adopts a capacious conception of paternalism. We suggest that an agent's being regarded as autonomous is a condition of paternalistic interference.

adolescents is not in doubt, yet we might think there are compelling grounds for parental or official intervention in at least some cases due to the potential harm that lies in letting an adolescent decide what to do. It is not only cases in which the stakes are high and autonomy is unclear that we think paternalism is warranted. Finally, we find it implausible that adults in close personal relationships may not need to relate to each other in autonomy-supporting ways. Further, we doubt that mutual engagement in this way necessarily or even probably undermines the moral equality of adults.

All of this is to say that our well-being-based account fares better than Betzler's in explaining the differential treatment of adults and adolescents. Attention to the prudential value of shielding is consistent with measures supportive of the development of autonomy. Our view allows for more capacious paternalistic intervention in cases in which the adolescent exercise of autonomy poses an all things considered threat to well-being (and as such is more plausible). We can accommodate the asymmetrical sharing of normative powers between adults and adolescents across the options available to the agent (an attractive feature of Betzler's view). And our account does not require us to take a stance on what makes for egalitarian relationships between adults.

## Defending invariabilism

Invariabilism is the view that the same theory of well-being is true for all welfare subjects (adults, children, newborns, non-human animals, and so on).[53] Variabilism is the view that invariabilism is false. According to variabilism, a theory of well-being may be true for adults but not for small children and vice versa. Our welfarist defence of differential and paternalistic treatment of adolescents is variabilist.

We hold that adolescent well-being consists in a distinctive plurality of (objective and subjective) non-instrumental prudential goods. Adult well-being comprises primarily subjective goods—for example, the satisfaction of informed preferences[54] or authentic happiness[55]—and young children's well-being comprises primarily objective goods. For children, while the satisfaction of (some) preferences is non-instrumentally good for them, there is, in addition, a range of other things that are non-instrumentally prudentially good for them, including unstructured play and

[53] Hedonism about well-being seems a good candidate for an invariabilist view, since it appears to fit all individuals plausibly thought to qualify as welfare subjects. Hedonism about well-being is the view that at bottom only pleasure is non-instrumentally prudentially good for an individual and only pain is non-instrumentally prudentially bad for an individual. For defence, see Roger Crisp, 'Hedonism Reconsidered', *Philosophy and Phenomenological Research*, 73 (2006), 619–45 and Sharron Hewitt, 'What Do Our Intuitions About the Experience Machine Really Tell Us About Hedonism?', *Philosophical Studies*, 151 (2010), 331–49.

[54] See e.g. David Sobel, 'Full Information Accounts of Well-Being', *Ethics*, 104 (1994), 784–810.

[55] Sumner, *Welfare*, pp. 138–83.

valuable, supportive relationships.[56] For adolescents, the relevant non-instrumental prudential goods include happiness, autonomy, supportive and caring relationships, and (of course) shielding. Subjective attitudes matter more to adolescent well-being than the same for a younger child's. Yet in at least in some cases, objective prudential goods matter more to adolescent well-being than they do to adult well-being.

Our variabilist view holds that well-being may consist in different non-instrumental prudential goods (bads) across adults, adolescents, and younger children. Even when the same goods (or kinds of goods) feature across welfare subjects, these may have differential prudential (dis)value. Indeed, our view is gradualist (more on which below) insofar as well-being moves from being more objective to being more subjective as one matures (albeit maturation is not linear with age and may not occur in all welfare subjects). As such, it speaks (directly) to the permissibility of differential treatment of adults, adolescents, and children. If adult well-being is more subjective—what is non-instrumentally prudentially good for them is a matter mainly of their subjective attitudes—and adolescent well-being more objective—not mainly a matter of their subjective attitudes —we might permissibly treat the latter in ways that leave the treatment of the former undisturbed.

The philosophical literature, to the extent that it takes typical adults to be the standard welfare subject against which to develop theories of well-being, tends to assume the truth of invariabilism. As such, the debate between variabilists and invariabilists is relatively new. We consider two recent defences of invariabilism.

Andrée-Anne Cormier and Mauro Rossi argue for a version of *generalism*: the invariabilist view that 'the same theory of well-being applies to both children and adults'.[57] Cormier and Rossi challenge variabilism in a number of ways. Here we focus on their thesis that opponents of generalism—variabilists—have difficulty accounting 'for the existence of a *fundamental* change in children's and adults' prudential standards'.[58] An individual's development from childhood, through adolescence, and into adulthood is typically progressive, albeit non-linear. As such, Cormier and Rossi contend that it is implausible to think that there is a 'tipping point' that shifts what is fundamentally, non-instrumentally prudentially good for a particular agent from what is fundamentally, non-instrumentally prudentially good for children to what is fundamentally, non-instrumentally prudentially good for

[56] Anthony Skelton, 'Utilitarianism, Welfare, Children', in Alexander Bagattini and Colin Macleod (eds), *The Nature of Children's Well-Being: Theory and Practice* (New York, Springer, 2015), pp. 85–103; Anthony Skelton, 'Children's Well-Being: A Philosophical Analysis', in Guy Fletcher (ed.), *The Routledge Handbook of Philosophy of Well-Being* (New York, Routledge, 2016), pp. 366–77; Anthony Skelton, 'Children and Wellbeing', in Anca Gheaus, Gideon Calder, and Jurgen De Wispelaere (eds), *The Routledge Handbook of the Philosophy of Childhood and Children* (New York, Routledge, 2018), pp. 90–100.

[57] Andrée-Anne Cormier and Mauro Rossi, 'Is Children's Wellbeing Different From Adults' Wellbeing?', *Canadian Journal of Philosophy*, 49 (2019), 1146–68 at 1146. It is unclear whether Cormier and Rossi are invariabilists as such. They do not, for example, defend invariabilism about human and non-human animal well-being.

[58] Cormier and Rossi, 'Different', 1156 (original emphasis).

adults.[59] Moreover, Cormier and Rossi deny gradualism about well-being over the life course. They argue that there is 'no non-*ad hoc* rationale for holding that some constituents of children's wellbeing cease to determine the individual's wellbeing when the individual moves from an area of indeterminate adulthood to an area of determinate adulthood'.[60]

We agree with Cormier and Rossi that there is no abrupt change in the nature of well-being as an individual matures. However, *pace* Cormier and Rossi, we hold that gradualism offers a promising approach to dealing with the worry about the transition between accounts of well-being over the life course.

In his discussion of the ethics of abortion, L. Wayne Sumner argues that a plausible view of the moral status of the foetus must be 'gradual, differential, and developmental'.[61] It is gradual if it allows for moral status to be acquired gradually over a period of time rather than at some specific point (e.g. conception or birth); a gradualist view of moral status sets 'not a threshold point, but a threshold period or stage' during which moral status is acquired.[62] It is differential insofar as the allocation of moral status it accords a foetus before and after the threshold period or stage is different (e.g. none before the threshold period and some or full status afterward); and developmental insofar as it grants significance to fact that a foetus develops during pregnancy.[63] The upshot of this approach is that '[a]n adequate view of the fetus promises a morally significant division between early abortions (before the threshold stage) and late abortions (after the threshold stage). It also promises borderline cases (during the threshold stage).'[64]

Sumner's account provides a plausible model for developing theories of well-being for individual welfare subjects over time. An appropriate theory will have to place weight on the fact that humans typically develop and change across childhood and adolescence. The fact that children's and adolescents' development is non-linear and variable across different capacities and domains of activity makes judgments about which life-stage theory of well-being is applicable to them less *ad hoc* and more *hard.* We might think that there are borderline cases where it is indeterminate whether an individual has passed the threshold stage from childhood to adolescence or from adolescence to adulthood. But this does entail that it will sometimes be clear that some of the prudential goods (bads) present in earlier stages of life (for example, the good of shielding for adolescents) have fallen away in significance.

Cormier and Rossi think that approaches of the sort we have articulated fail. Imagine, they say, that hedonism is the correct theory of well-being for children, while the correct theory of well-being for adults consists in the development of their

[59] Cormier and Rossi, 'Different', 1156–7.

[60] Cormier and Rossi, 'Different', 1157.

[61] L. W. Sumner, *Abortion and Moral Theory* (Princeton, NJ, Princeton University Press, 1981), p. 126.

[62] Sumner, *Abortion*, p. 125.

[63] Sumner, *Abortion*, p. 126.

[64] Sumner, *Abortion*, p. 126.

higher-level capacities. It follows from this set of views that once a child transitions to adulthood, their well-being will depend on the higher-level capacities not their capacity for pleasure. But, they ask, why should the translation to adulthood 'alter the prudential status of the capacity to experience pleasure and pain or of the experiences themselves?'[65] The opponent of generalism, they go on to say, must explain the change in the prudential value of pleasure (pain).

The right counter to Cormier and Rossi is to argue that we need not deny that pleasure (pain) may have a salient role in the well-being (ill-being) of an adult. The important point is that the development of a novel capacity (for rational reflection) may alter our view of the role in one's life of the prudential value of pleasure (pain), though it may be hard to say in the threshold stage between childhood and adulthood exactly to what this amounts. If it turns out that the satisfaction of informed preferences is what the well-being of adults consists in, for example, then the prudential value of pleasure will turn out to be a matter of what an individual wants or desires (contra hedonism). The onset of a new capacity for rational reflection on and adjudication of one's desires will provide an explanation of why the prudential value of pleasure (pain) has altered in adults and perhaps why in this transition an individual may go from high to low well-being.

Cormier and Rossi reject this kind of counter, by claiming that to hold that adult well-being consists in the prudential goods of childhood and goods specific to adulthood jointly would violate the principle according to which 'if the exercise of a fully developed capacity is intrinsically good for an individual (i.e. good in itself, in virtue of its internal properties), then the exercise of the same capacity is intrinsically good for that individual even when such a capacity is only partially developed'.[66]

It is not necessary for us to take a position on whether this principle is valid, though we have our doubts. It is plausible that adults, children, and adolescents share non-instrumental prudential goods in common (e.g. the prudential goods of pleasure and loving relationships). Yet to the extent that there are childhood-specific (or indeed adolescence-specific) prudential goods, Cormier and Rossi's principle does not rule them out. We might think that there are non-instrumental prudential goods specific to childhood or adolescence (but not adulthood) that compete with the development of certain capacities or the value of certain pleasures (pains) in childhood or adolescence. Shielding may be one of them.

Eden Lin argues that we should accept invariabilism for two main reasons.[67] First, Lin argues that we should favour invariabilism in virtue of its simplicity compared to variabilism. Second, Lin argues that 'there appear to be no significant reasons to favour variabilism'.[68]

[65] Cormier and Rossi, 'Different', 1157.

[66] Cormier and Rossi, 'Different', 1158.

[67] Eden Lin, 'Welfare Invariabilism', *Ethics*, 128 (2018), 320–45.

[68] Lin, 'Invariabilism', 334.

On simplicity, Lin says that invariabilism offers a simpler 'picture than the one available on variabilism, and the greater simplicity of a view is a reason to favor it':[69] 'According to variabilism, at least one theory is true of some subjects but false of others, and there could even turn out to be a large plurality of true theories, each of them true of different subjects. By contrast, according to invariabilism, welfare is "one size fits all".'[70]

Lin does not make too much of this reason to resist variabilism. Rightly so. Appeals to simplicity are not decisive. First, we might follow W. D. Ross in thinking that what matters most to developing a theory in ethics (including, we think, a theory of well-being) is what 'reflection on our ... convictions seems actually to reveal'. As Ross emphasises, '[l]oyalty to the facts is worth more than a symmetrical architectonic or a hastily reached simplicity'.[71]

If the more complicated picture seems to reflect the prudential facts more adequately, it is the one we ought to accept. At best, simplicity might provide a reason to favour one theory over another, if both seem *equally* loyal to the facts, *and* the former is simpler than the latter. Second, it is not clear how facts about simplicity affect or dictate facts about what has non-instrumental prudential *value*. Suppose one theory of well-being were to fit our prudential convictions more adequately than another, simpler theory of well-being. It is not clear how the latter's simplicity would by itself indicate that it is the better *theory of prudential value*. To think that it is, we would need to have concluded in advance of our search for a theory of well-being that a simpler theory of prudential value is a better theory. But we have not drawn this conclusion. On the contrary.

Lin's second argument against variabilism is that 'it is difficult, on reflection, to see what could explain why a theory of welfare might be true of some subjects but false of others'.[72] Lin concedes the variabilist intuition that 'it is natural to suppose that the many differences in the natures or capacities of welfare subjects could explain why different theories might be true of them'.[73] Thus, differences in nature and capacities of typical dogs and typical adult humans might explain differences in what is non-instrumentally, basically prudentially good (bad) for these subjects. A typical adult human possesses, for example, the capacity for higher-order contemplation and the appreciation of beauty (whereas dogs do not), which suggests that it might be non-instrumentally, basically prudentially good for a typical human adult but not for the typical dog to view paintings in the National Portrait Gallery. Lin argues, however, that the variabilist view is mistaken, for a number of reasons. We consider two of the reasons he offers.

Lin first seeks to undermine the argument that what is non-instrumentally, basically prudentially good for some subjects is not non-instrumentally, basically

[69] Lin, 'Invariabilism', 324.
[70] Lin, 'Invariabilism', 324.
[71] W. D. Ross, *The Right and the Good* (Oxford, Oxford University Press, 1930), p. 23.
[72] Lin, 'Invariabilism', 325.
[73] Lin, 'Invariabilism', 325.

prudentially good for others. Here, he targets what he terms the variabilists' 'Inaccessibility Strategy' (see the National Portrait Gallery example above):

> the observation that, among the kinds that might turn out to be basic goods for us, there are kinds that are *inaccessible* to certain welfare subjects, in the sense that those subjects lack the physical or psychological capacities that are needed to possess, or to otherwise be suitably related to, tokens of those kinds.[74]

Lin argues that the Inaccessibility Strategy fails for it relies on a false assumption:

> *Inaccessibility Excludes Goodness* [IEG]: If a subject *S* is incapable of possessing (or otherwise being suitably related to) tokens of a kind *K*, then *K* is not a basic good for *S*.[75]

To demonstrate the falsity of IEG, Lin relies on an analogy to moral requirements. He stipulates that Rossian pluralism holds that there is a prima facie duty not to lie. He imagines a moral agent for whom lying is impossible. Lin says that even for an agent with this nature, the prima facie duty not to lie would obtain in their case: 'Rossian pluralism merely implies that, for any acts of lying, if this agent were to perform those acts, each of them would be prima facie wrong. Lying—the kind—can be prima facie wrong for an agent, even if the agent is incapable of performing any action of that kind.'[76]

We might demur. It is hard for us to imagine an agent for whom lying is impossible. They would have a will and a psychological make up quite different from our own. They would be the kind of agent for whom certain temptations do not register or for whom certain goods lack the power to motivate. They would be the kind of an agent who would, for example, not tell a small lie to save someone they love from murder. Given their make-up, one might think of such an agent that it is simply not true that they have an obligation not to lie. In the same way, we think a foetus has no such obligation since they cannot lie. If the argument that there exists some invariable list of morally wrong act types fails, then it cannot be employed (analogically) to support the claim that IEG is false.

The failure of Lin's analogy may not be sufficient to impugn his rejection of IEG. Suppose Andie is anhedonic in the actual world. It does not follow that it would not be non-instrumentally good for her to (say) experience pleasure in some possible world where experiencing pleasure was accessible to her. Lin argues that this is all one needs to secure the point that pleasure is non-instrumentally good for Andie in the actual world. This latter claim just is the claim that pleasure would be good for Andie were she to experience it in some possible world (however remote).

On Lin's view, then, one may hold that (for example) the satisfaction of informed preferences is non-instrumentally good for a child in the actual world where they cannot form such preferences. For this claim amounts only to the claim

[74] Lin, 'Invariabilism', 324–5.

[75] Lin, 'Invariabilism', 325 (original emphasis).

[76] Lin, 'Invariabilism', 326.

that the satisfaction of such preferences would be non-instrumentally good for a child in a possible world (however remote) in which they had such preferences satisfied. This implies that there is a large inventory of possible items that might be non-instrumentally good for an individual (whether an adult, child, or dog). As long as there is a possible world in which something is accessible to an individual, it remains true that it may be non-instrumentally good for that individual in the actual world, however they are constituted.

We admit that this is one way to secure theoretical invariabilism. But it has the cost of making invariabilism irrelevant in practice, where our focus is on what makes individuals non-instrumentally better (worse) off in the actual world and nearby possible worlds. While variabilism might not be true in theory, it seems to us to yield identical implications to invariabilism in practice. All we need for our purposes is *practical* variabilism. Lin does not seem to reject this latter position, noting that the inaccessibility of a prudential good may exclude 'its practical relevance' to well-being assessments and attempts to promote well-being.[77]

In addition to arguing for the falsity of IEG, Lin attacks variabilism by rejecting the argument that 'Even if the same list of basic goods and bads is true of all welfare subjects, different theories could be true of different subjects because the basic prudential values of the tokens of some basic good or bad are fixed differently for different subjects.'[78]

Lin considers the view that pleasure might be of different prudential value for different welfare subjects (e.g. humans and dogs). He objects that there is no plausible explanation for such a view.[79] Suppose, he says, that the value of a pleasure for cognitively typical adults is a matter of its intensity, duration, and quality. The quality of a pleasure might be fixed by an intellectual capacity that adults possess but that children do not. So, in children the value of a pleasure would be fixed only by its intensity and duration—that is, its quantitative dimensions. For cognitively typical adults, then, the non-instrumental prudential value of pleasure would depend on both quantitative and qualitative considerations, whereas this would not be the case for children. This would be a form of variabilism, at least with respect the value of the goods constitutive of well-being.

Lin's reply to this putative argument for variabilism relies on the same (analogical, counterfactual) approach he employs to show that IEG is allegedly false, namely, that were the nature and capacities of welfare subjects relevantly similar to the 'benchmark' welfare subject (in some possible world), the degree to which what is non-instrumentally good for the former would be fixed in the same way as it is for the latter.

[77] Lin, 'Invariabilism', 327.
[78] Lin, 'Invariabilism', 333.
[79] Lin, 'Invariabilism', 333.

We think this a rather desperate way to secure invariabilism.[80] But we need not quarrel with it. Suppose we accept that the prudential value of whatever is non-instrumentally good is theoretically fixed for all welfare subjects. This still leaves us needing to determine the differences in non-instrumental goods in practice for various welfare subjects, for example, children, adolescents, and adults. Lin concedes that in practice what is non-instrumentally good for some welfare subjects is not non-instrumentally good for others. So, what may be good for children or adolescents in practice may not be good for adults and vice versa.

For our position about adolescent well-being to be viable we need only to defend practical variabilism. We might argue that even if it is true that certain prudential goods not currently accessible to non-human welfare subjects or younger children are non-instrumentally good for them in theory (or in some possible world), they are not applicable to them in their actual circumstances and thus irrelevant to them in current practice. We can ignore these inaccessible non-instrumental prudential goods and focus on the accessible non-instrumental prudential goods and their relative importance. We might determine their relative importance by appeal to something like the reflective equilibrium approach on which Lin relies for assessing the truth of certain counterfactuals about well-being.[81] So far as accessible goods go, even if their relevance is theoretically fixed, it may be that—practically—the relevant prudential goods matter more or less to different classes of welfare subject (for example, adults and adolescents, respectively).[82] In practice, even if not in theory, something like variabilism may hold.

## Conclusion

The differential and paternalistic treatment of adolescents requires justification. In this chapter, we argued that this treatment of adolescents rests on a distinct conception of well-being vis-à-vis these other welfare subjects. In the first section, we clarified our focus. In the second section, we rejected two popular justifications for the differential and paternalistic treatment of adolescents. In the third section, we articulated our theory of what is fundamentally and non-instrumentally prudentially good for adolescents, which included the prudential good of what we called shielding. This theory of well-being, we argued, explains why adolescents may be treated differentailly and paternalistically in numerous domains. In the fourth section, we argued that our well-being–based justification of differential treatment is superior to the justifications offered in recent work by Franklin-Hall and Betzler.

[80] This Morning, 'If My Grandmother Had Wheels She Would Have Been a Bike' (2016): https://www.youtube.com/watch?v=2G9ZGIOiPjY (accessed 13 July 2025).

[81] Lin, 'Invariabilism', 329. For an excellent discussion of reflective equilibrium, see T. M. Scanlon, 'Rawls on Justification', in S. Freeman (ed.), *The Cambridge Companion to Rawls* (Cambridge, Cambridge University Press, 2003), pp. 139–67.

[82] See Skelton, Forsberg, and Black, 'Overriding', 242–3.

In the final section, we defended our commitment to variabilism about well-being against recent attacks from Cormier and Rossi and Lin. We think our view of the justification of differential and paternalistic treatment of adolescents has attractive implications for a range of cases and holds up well in the face of philosophical criticism.

# 12

# Children and Ineffective Consent*

LISA FORSBERG

CHILDREN OCCUPY A curious place in our moral and legal practices, including in our consent practices. It is widely believed that differential treatment of children, often in the form of paternalistic non-consensual interference, is permitted in many cases, including in cases where children have similar capacities for autonomous action as competent adults. We take children's consent not to be necessary for a range of actions that parents and other adults undertake in their regard. We also often take children's consent not to be a sufficient justification for action when it would suffice for comparably autonomous adults. Consent is usually taken to affect our duties and how we may act towards the person giving consent, but consent given by children often does not seem to do so in the same way or to the same degree. Why is this?

This chapter explores how children's consent can in some sense be *ineffective* in terms of guiding consent-receivers' behaviour, using the legal 'concurrent consents doctrine'—which allows for children's consent to be supplanted by the consent of parents and courts—as its focus. I argue against views that hold that the way children's consent is sometimes ineffective in changing our duties is best explained by children's consent being invalid due to deficiencies in the consent-giver. These accounts fail because other parties' powers to consent to interventions that are contrary to children's welfare interests are also constrained, in the same way children's consent is constrained under the concurrent consents doctrine. When children's consent is ineffective, this fact is better explained by views that

* Thank you to Isra Black, Achas Burin, Ben Davies, Luke Davies, Gabriel De Marco, Tom Douglas, Viktor Ivankovic, Max Kiener, Robert Noggle, Peter Schaber, Anthony Skelton, and audiences at the Society for Applied Philosophy, the International Society for Utilitarian Studies 2023, the Joint Session 2023, and the European Congress on Analytic Philosophy 2023 conferences. The research was funded by a British Academy Postdoctoral Fellowship (award pf170028), the European Research Council (grant number 819757), and the Uehiro Foundation for Ethics and Education.

focus on how concern for children's well-being structures our duties, such that they are less consent-sensitive.[1]

The first section sets out the concurrent consents doctrine and explains how children's consent may be deprived of the effect consent is typically taken to have in English law. The second section considers views on which children's consent is ineffective in altering the duties and behaviour of consent-receivers because children's consent is defective on grounds of invalidity. The third section elaborates consent's role in guiding our reasons for action. The fourth section considers views on which consent is ineffective because its scope is constrained. The final section considers how our duties to children affect the effectiveness of their consent.

## Children and (concurrent) consent

Consent is a normative power that permits us to change the moral (and often legal) status of acts that others undertake in our regard. When valid, my consent renders actions that would, in the absence of my consent, have wronged me *pro tanto* permissible.[2] Seana Shiffrin describes the power of consent as follows:

> When an agent gives consent to another—to a doctor to perform an examination or to a worker to enter the agent's apartment—she transforms, in the way intended, the moral situation between the parties simply through the transmission of her will to do so. Prior to conferring consent, the agent's right to control her body, and her property, forbade touching or entering as forms of assault and trespass. Simply by expressing her will, the consenting agent morally transforms the situation as intended, thereby generating a permission for another. A new obligation arises too. The agent becomes obliged not to raise complaints that she otherwise could make about entry into her personal space and has a duty to inform the recipient if she wishes to revoke the permission.[3]

The power to consent or refuse is generally taken to be valuable because of its relation to our autonomy, and in particular our normative interests in exercising control over the *directed* duties others owe to us,[4] and in shaping our lives as we wish or in accordance with what we value.[5] As Massimo Renzo notes, we typically want our valid consents to guide others' behaviour towards us and take this to be part of the

[1] Consent-sensitive duties are duties an agent can be released from by another agent's consent: Victor Tadros, *Wrongs and Crimes* (New York, Oxford University Press, 2016), p. 201.

[2] *Pro tanto* because it may still be all-things-considered impermissible due to other considerations.

[3] Seana Valentine Shiffrin, 'Promising, Intimate Relationships, and Conventionalism', *The Philosophical Review*, 117 (2008), 481–524 at 500.

[4] For the distinction between directed and non-directed duties, see e.g. Gopal Sreenivasan, 'Duties and Their Direction', *Ethics* 120 (2010), 465–94: 'a duty is a directed duty if there is someone to whom it is owed; and … it is a nondirected duty if there is no one to whom it is owed'.

[5] Massimo Renzo, 'Defective Normative Powers: The Case of Consent', *Journal of Practical Ethics*, 10 (2022), 49–77 at 52. See also Joseph Raz, 'Voluntary Obligations and Normative Powers', *Aristotelian Society Supplement*, 46 (1972), 79–102.

story of what standard consent does: '[w]e normally hope to use consent as a way of *guiding* other people's behavior so that it does not wrong us'.[6] We want it to be the case not just that another party does or does not φ us, but also that they φ us *because* we consent to it, or do not φ us *because* we refuse our consent to φ. We want their conduct to be *sensitive* to our consent.

But when the consent-giver is a child, our conduct is not always sensitive—or as sensitive—to their consent. There are many arrangements, including legal arrangements, under which children's consent (refusal) is not treated as determinative, that is, capable of changing the duties others are under.

Under the so-called *concurrent consents doctrine* in English law, a minor's possession of the power to consent to and thereby permit medical treatment does not extinguish the power to consent to the same on the minor's behalf held by those who exercise parental responsibility (or by courts): 'parents and the courts retain the power to consent *concurrently* with the [minor]'.[7]

Children who are 15 or younger are presumed to lack decision-making capacity to consent to medical treatment; those who exercise parental responsibility have the authority to take medical treatment decisions on their behalf. Children under 16 who meet the standard of decision-making capacity set out in *Gillick* can give consent that (other things equal) has the power to permit their own medical treatment: 'a minor's capacity to make his or her own decision depends upon the minor having sufficient understanding and intelligence to make the decision'.[8]

Children who are 16 or 17 years old are rebuttably presumed to possess decision-making capacity to consent to treatment.[9] The consent by a minor with decision-making capacity will therefore, other things equal, make the provision of medical treatment lawful.

The upshot of the concurrent consents doctrine is that even if a child has capacity according to the relevant legal norms, parents and courts have the power to consent to and thereby permit interventions that minors validly refuse.[10] This makes

[6] Renzo, 'Defective Normative Powers', 59. Emphasis added. Renzo notes that the guiding function of consent is 'surprisingly neglected' in much recent philosophical literature on consent, which 'largely focuses on the idea that the point of consent is to affect the normative status of the conduct being consented to': 'Defective Normative Powers', 59. Indeed, some consent theorists—most notably David Owens, who thinks that the (sole) function of consent is to change whether a wrong is done to us—deny that consent has a guiding function: Owens, 'The Possibility of Consent', 407–8; Owens, 'Shaping the Normative Landscape', 172–6. See also John Gardner, 'The Opposite of Rape', *Oxford Journal of Legal Studies*, 38 (2018), 48–70 at 57. I will assume that we typically want consent to have a guiding function, since it seems that for the forms of consent we are interested in here, e.g. medical (in particular) and sexual consent, we do typically want consent to guide other people's behaviour towards us.

[7] Anthony Skelton, Lisa Forsberg, and Isra Black, 'Overriding Adolescent Refusals of Treatment', *Journal of Ethics and Social Philosophy*, 20 (2021), 221–47 at 224.

[8] *Gillick v West Norfolk and Wisbech Area Health Authority* [1986] AC 112, 188B (Lord Scarman).

[9] Family Law Reform Act 1969, s 8; Mental Capacity Act 2005, s 1(2). The presumption will be rebutted if a minor is found to lack decision-making capacity.

[10] See Skelton *et al.*, 'Overriding Adolescent Refusals of Treatment', 224. We see the concurrent consents doctrine in operation e.g. in *Re R (A Minor) (Wardship: Consent to Treatment)* [1992] Fam 11.

children's consent against the background of the concurrent consents doctrine different to consent by standard agents—adults with decision-making capacity—whose consents and refusals of medical interventions are normatively and legally determinative.[11]

The treatment of children's consent as non-decisive under the concurrent consents doctrine seems to accord with our intuitions about the power children's consent has in moral terms, and in particular the idea that children should be involved in decision-making concerning them,[12] but that their preferences and choices should not lead to serious harm.[13] Consider:

> *Elective Medical Procedure*. Celeste is 15 years old and worries about the shape of her labia, after a comment from one of her classmates. She consents to a labiaplasty procedure at a private clinic near her home.

We might think that we may treat Celeste's consent as non-decisive, either morally or legally; her consent would not justify us undertaking an act potentially harmful to her. But in like cases when an adult agent validly consents to this kind of bodily interference, their consent is normally taken to extinguish any duty others might have not to undertake the act that would result in the bodily interference. Consider the standard formulation, according to which consent changes the normative status of interference with others.

1. B owes a duty to A not to φ;
2. A can release B from this duty by consenting to B φing;
3. If B φs A without A's consent, B wrongs A; but if A consents, B does not wrong A.[14]

It is less clear when children's consent does what standard consent does in cases such as Celeste's, which is to render action on consent permissible vis-à-vis the consent-giver. When the consent-giver is a child, it is less clear that we are not wronging them when acting on their consent and in ways that are harmful to them. It is also less clear that we are wronging them by undertaking an act in respect of which they have refused consent when our so doing benefits them. We might say that children's consent does not guide the consent-receiver's conduct to the same degree as standard or adult consent. Children's consent does not seem to be

[11] *Ms B v An NHS Hospital Trust* [2002] EWHC 429 (Fam); Skelton *et al.*, 'Overriding Adolescent Refusals of Treatment', 221.

[12] See David Archard, 'Children and Consent: Best Interests, Parents, and a Child's Views', in this volume, pp. 105–21.

[13] Suzanne Uniacke, 'Respect for Autonomy in Medical Ethics', in David Archard, Monique Deveaux, Neil Manson, and Daniel Weinstock (eds), *Reading Onora O'Neill* (London, Routledge, 2013), pp. 94–110; Skelton *et al.*, 'Overriding Adolescent Refusals of Treatment'; Skelton, *et al.*, 'Treating Adolescents Differently', in this volume, pp. 205–28.

[14] This is a standard formulation. See e.g. Tadros, *Wrongs and Crimes*.

normatively and legally determinative in the same way as adult consent. In what follows, I consider why this may be.

## Ineffective because defective?

A standard view is that children's consent does not have the power to guide our behaviour because it is in some way defective. On one view, children's consent is defective to such an extent that it is altogether invalid. This is usually taken to be due to limitations in children's agency or autonomy—expressed through the notion of incapacity—which cause their consent to lack in qualities or properties that would typically provide consent with its normative force. Because children's consent lacks normative force, it fails to change our directed duties in the usual way.

This kind of view might seem intuitively and theoretically plausible. It seems intuitive that it is permissible or even required not to act on children's consent in cases such as *Elective Medical Procedure*, and this may be because Celeste's consent is defective. Theoretically, various explanations may be available for why children's consent/refusal is putatively defective. For example, Terrance McConnell notes that '[c]onsent involves giving permission, and that implies that the person giving permission has authority over the matter' in respect of which permission is given.[15] We might think that children never have the necessary authority to consent. They might not (yet) be the kinds of independent agents that have rights against interference giving rise to consent requirements; perhaps they hold the relevant rights 'in theory' but the rights are held 'in trust' until the child becomes a fully fledged agent capable of exercising them or a standard rights-holder;[16] if they are younger, perhaps they do not yet have the (full) concept of permission.

On the deficiency view, we do not act *on* children's consent, that is, act with their consent as providing a reason (not) to act. We might sometimes, of course, act *in accordance with* a child's consent: sometimes the child will consent to things that would have been done to them anyway, regardless of whether they 'consented to' or 'refused' it, and we might take their 'consent' or 'refusal' into account in a weaker sense, as an expression of their preferences when we determine how to act in their best interests. But we might think that these are not cases of *consent* proper by the child; rather it is something *consent-like* but weaker, that does not affect our reasons for action in the way consent normally would.[17] What we do when we seem to be (permissibly) acting (or not) in the presence of children's consent, then, is not really *acting on* their consent or responding to their consent directly. Rather, we

[15] Terrance McConnell, 'When Is Consent Required?', in Peter Schaber and Andreas Müller (eds), *The Routledge Handbook of the Ethics of Consent* (London, Routledge, 2018), pp. 75–84 at 76.

[16] Joel Feinberg, 'The Child's Right to an Open Future', in William Aiken and Hugh LaFollette (eds), *Whose Child? Children's Rights, Parental Authority, and State Power* (Totowa, NJ, Rowman and Littlefield, 1980), pp. 124–53.

[17] There may, of course, be other duties arising, for example, to consider the child's view/preferences.

are acting on other morally relevant considerations, for example, relating to their (current or future) well-being or acting prospectively, treating them *as if* they have capacities for consent, taking responsibility, etc, for the purposes of developing these capacities, regardless of whether they, in fact, do possess them. We are acting on considerations not directly related to or arising from, though sometimes coinciding with, their consent.

The above plausibly captures some of what we do when we act in response to children's consent, and this might provide an account of how we may act towards very young children. Some 'consents' given by children are clearly defective such that they are invalid. Very young children clearly do not have capacity validly to consent to or to refuse medical treatment, for example.

Yet some children will have capacity, at least in respect of some decisions. Amy Mullin and (separately) Paul Bou-Habib and Serena Olsaretti note that children often possess a meaningful degree of autonomy prior to adolescence. As Bou-Habib and Olsaretti note, 'persons develop intrapersonal capacities for autonomy gradually, and accordingly, they hold those capacities to increasing degrees'.[18] Mullin argues that children as young as three may sometimes possess some capacities central to autonomy, including abilities to engage in means-ends reasoning, appreciate value, have commitments, and 'a sufficient strength of will' to act in accordance with what they care about, at least to some degree.[19] By enjoying 'some local autonomy, and as they increasingly improve on such capacities, they acquire a gradually greater capacity for autonomy'.[20] Indeed, some children will have agential capacities that are on a par with standard agents (adults with decision-making capacity). Even if we think that a cut-off at, for example, 18 years of age tracks acquisition of the capacities commensurate with autonomy, few would claim that such a threshold tracks acquisition of the capacities perfectly. While we might find it intuitively compelling that we are not under a duty to act on a child's refusal of life-prolonging medical treatment or on Celeste's consent in *Elective Medical Procedure*, it does not seem like the right explanation is that their consent is necessarily defective and invalid.

Of course, children's consent might be defective on grounds other than capacity. Children usually have much more limited life experience than adults. This might explain why a child's consent is not robustly or sufficiently autonomous, even if their agential capacities are similar to adults. But not all children have less life experience than all adults. Some children have experienced war, fled to another country, lived in extreme poverty, have had to take very difficult decisions, lost

[18] Paul Bou-Habib and Serena Olsaretti, 'Autonomy and Children's Well-Being', in Alexander Bagattini and Colin Macleod (eds), *The Nature of Children's Well-Being* (New York, Springer, 2015), pp. 15–33 at 27.

[19] Amy Mullin, 'Children, Autonomy, and Care', *Journal of Social Philosophy*, 38 (2007), 536–53; Bou-Habib and Olsaretti, 'Autonomy and Children's Well-Being', 28.

[20] Bou-habib and Olsaretti, 'Autonomy and Children's Well-Being', 28. See also Mullin, 'Children, Autonomy, and Care' and Feinberg, 'The Child's Right to an Open Future'.

loved ones, and so on. And some adults have led protected lives, experienced few things, have limited interest in reflecting on their life choices, and so on. It is plausible that such adults could nevertheless give valid consent, but it seems hard to explain why they would be in a position to give a 'more autonomous' consent than a child with considerable life experience.

Children may also not (yet) have robust or settled values or stable preferences that guide their conduct in the way that is necessary for their decisions to consent or refuse particular forms of interference to be an instantiation of their autonomy, even if they have decision-making capacity. This could cause tokens of their consent to be defective and, we might think, less respect-worthy. But while this may often be the case, and may give us reason to provide a safety net for their action,[21] it is not obvious that children's values would always be so unsettled in comparison to adults that their consent would always be defective to the extent that it was *invalid*.

One might argue that a child's consent is defective (and invalid) because other parties retain the power to consent to the intervention in question, with their consents overriding or replacing the child's consent. But it seems hard to explain why a *child's* consent would be invalid because, under the concurrent consents doctrine, other parties retain the power to consent. The mere presence of another party with consenting power/authority cannot render a child's consent invalid, for if that were the case *all* consents given under the concurrent consents doctrine would be invalid, since it is true for consents given by parents and courts, too, that another party possesses the power to consent. Since no one seriously argues that the consents given by parents or courts are invalid because others have authority to consent, it seems odd to suggest that authority to consent held by other parties would so affect children's consent.

I have argued that children's consent is not necessarily ineffective because it is defective, but nevertheless it fails to guide or direct the consent-receiver's behaviour or conduct. As such, it is necessary to consider further children's consent and its reason-giving force.

## Children's consent and our reasons for action

Children's consent given against the background of the concurrent consents doctrine does not seem to have the guiding function in respect of the consent-receiver's behaviour that we would normally expect consent to have. A child's consent to $\varphi$ is only taken to be determinative if $\varphi$ is not (sufficiently) contrary to the child's best interests. Where her decision *is* (sufficiently) contrary to her interests, the child's consent (or possibly refusal) can be overridden or supplanted with a consent by

[21] Skelton *et al.*, 'Overriding Adolescent Refusals of Treatment'; Skelton, *et al.*, 'Treating Adolescents Differently'.

her parents or by the court. This state of affairs is not, however, because children's consent is necessarily defective.

Rather, children's consent does not play a fully directive role in our deliberations and reasons for action, compared to adults. Vis-à-vis the latter, ordinarily, 'we want consent to not only be present but also to play a central role in the consent-receiver's reasons for action'.[22] As Renzo observes:

> the point of consent is not simply to ensure that a given behavior does not wrong us but that it doesn't wrong us *in the right way*. Ideally, we want our consent to ensure that we are not wronged because our consent guides how others behave toward us, and not because we adjust our will to what is going to happen to us anyway ... Thus, at least when things go well, consent enables us to control whether what is done to us wrongs precisely by controlling what is done to us.[23]

This, Renzo notes, 'fits with the autonomy-based justification of consent': 'If the point of consent is to enhance our capacity to shape our life as we wish, we should care not only that those who happen to [φ us] have our permission but also that they would not [φ us] if they hadn't our permission.'[24]

For consent to play a proper role in an agent's practical deliberation or reasons for action it should generally be the case that, first, 'the agent would not have been willing to act in the absence of consent',[25] and second, that the agent cares about the consent playing *some* role in the explanation for why they acted'.[26] It seems that children's consent fails to play consent's standard role in the consent-receiver's deliberations and that that explains its ineffectiveness.

That is not to say that children's consent necessarily plays *no* role in guiding others' reasons for action. To help us see this, let us consider what Elise Woodard calls *moot consent*, where 'an agent *A* consents to *B* φing, but if *A* hadn't consented, *B* would have φ'd anyway'.[27]

Woodard gives the following example of moot consent:

> *Surgery.* Arnold consents to Dr. Brooks performing an invasive surgery. However, had Arnold not consented, the doctor would have performed the surgery anyway.

Say that Arnold is a child in England and Wales, and therefore subject to the concurrent consents doctrine. If Arnold validly refuses treatment, Dr Brooks might seek permission to proceed with the surgery anyway, on the basis of consent given by Arnold's parents or a court. However, if Arnold consents, it is *his consent* that features in Dr Brooks' reasons for action, because Arnold's consent is sufficient (other things equal) to render surgery lawful.[28]

[22] Elise Woodard, 'Mistreated Consent', unpublished manuscript. See also Renzo, 'Defective Normative Powers', 59.

[23] Renzo, 'Defective Normative Powers', 59.

[24] Renzo, 'Defective Normative Powers', 59.

[25] Woodard, 'Mistreated Consent'.

[26] Woodard, 'Mistreated Consent'.

[27] Woodard, 'Mistreated Consent'.

[28] Though not on its own; more on this in section that follows.

Arnold's case shows that children's consent against the background of the concurrent consents doctrine is unlike standard cases of moot consent. If Arnold consents, consent does seem to play its standard guiding function. If Arnold refuses, refusal nevertheless plays *some* role in Dr Brooks' deliberation about what to do, since he will have to look elsewhere for consent to perform the surgery. Consent or refusal does not play the *same* role in guiding a consent-receiver's behaviour for children as it does adults, but since it plays *some* role, rather than *no* role at all, children's consent under the concurrent consents doctrine is not completely moot.

Had Arnold been an adult refusing treatment, and Dr Brooks had performed surgery over his refusal, this would have been a case of moot consent, since there is nowhere else to look for consent to render the intervention permissible. Arnold's objection to Dr Brooks' action would be that consent did not properly feature in Dr Brooks' deliberation because refusal did not *fully* direct the latter's behaviour. Adult Arnold's complaint would be that consent or refusal failed to play its proper role within its *scope of application.*

To clarify what I mean by consent's role within its scope of application, a clinician does not act *merely* on a consent provided; her reasons for action also include the patient's best interests: that it would be all things considered good for the patient to have the treatment. This is standard in medical cases and not something that distinguishes cases involving children. Patient consent never provides the full reason for action in medical contexts. That the treatment is (in the treating clinician's professional judgement) in the patient's best interests is always *a* reason for action, and arguably the clinician's main reason for action, which together with patient consent is what renders treatment (morally and legally) permissible.[29] The notion that consent may not provide *full* justification for a consent-receiver's action is common to consent cases in general, not just medical ones: it is compatible with standard views that consent does not provide a reason for action. A's consent to B's φ-ing is not itself a reason for B to φ. Rather, A's consent to φ removes reasons B would otherwise have not to φ A.[30] A's consent *alters* B's reasons for action, A's

[29] In respect of children and decisions about medical interventions, best interests come in at several different stages. Best interests are present at the stage at which a doctor offers interventions, regardless of whether the patient is a child or an adult agent. Doctors' duties are such that they may only offer interventions that are within the range that they consider to be in the best interests of the patient. The offer of intervention x can be rejected or accepted by the patient if she is found to have decision-making capacity. In relation to children, there is a second way in which best interests come in: in determining whether we should use the concurrent consents doctrine to override the child's decision by acting on consent by a party with concurrently held consenting power to the treatment offered, because doing so would be in the best interests of the child.

[30] Woodard, 'Mistreated Consent'. See also Michelle Madden Dempsey, 'Victimless Conduct and the *Volenti* Maxim: How Consent Works', *Criminal Law and Philosophy*, 7 (2013), 11–27; Heidi Hurd, 'The Normative Force of Consent', in Peter Schaber and Andreas Müller (eds), *The Routledge Handbook of the Ethics of Consent* (London, Routledge, 2018), pp. 44–54.

consent does not *provide* them.[31] This, then, is compatible with consent playing *some* role in one's reasons for action.

In the concurrent consents case, a child's consent is sought first and if the child validly consents to medical treatment it is her consent that permits the treatment; no other party's consent is sought as additional authority. Children can consent without parental authority.[32] This distinguishes concurrent consent cases from parental consent cases simpliciter, such as parents consenting on behalf of a very young child. In the case of children's consent, then, it is not the case that a child's consent is always moot just because it is given against a background when others, too, have authority to consent to the same action. In many cases, the agent will be acting on the child's consent—in all cases where the conduct to which she consents is not (sufficiently) contrary to her best interests. Moreover, it is possible that a child's refusal will be treated as decisive also when it is contrary to her best interests, such as in the case of Hannah Jones' successful refusal of a potentially life-saving heart transplant or in the case of Joshua McAuley who successfully refused a blood transfusion following a car accident.[33]

I have suggested that children's consent plays *some* but not the *same* role as adult consent in in guiding the consent-receiver's reasons for action. In concurrent consent cases where the consent acted on is a consent by the parent(s) or the court, while *consent* plays a proper role in the consent-receiver's reasons for action, *the child's* consent does not. While consent plays (it seems) the right kind of role in our deliberations and reasons for actions in child Arnold's case in justifying the provision of treatment, we are largely indifferent to *whose* consent it is. But we might object that it should be the *child's consent* that plays the proper role in our reasons for action.

Unlike in the standard cases of moot consent, which involve the consent-receiver disregarding the interests of the consent-giver or subjecting them to her own—in ordinary concurrent consents cases, the consent-receiver is not indifferent to the child's interests or putting her own interests above those of the child. So while there seems to be something not quite right about how the child's consent features in the consent-receiver's reasons for action, it is not the case that she in acting

[31] As Woodard notes, 'it is natural and not uncommon to talk in terms of consent altering reasons for action'; Woodard, 'Mistreating Consent'. See also Govert den Hartogh, G., 'Can Consent Be Presumed?', *Journal of Applied Philosophy*, 28 (2011), 295–307; Neil Manson, 'Permissive Consent: A Robust Reason-Changing Account', *Philosophical Studies*, 173 (2016), 3317–34; Alan Wertheimer, *Consent to Sexual Relations* (Cambridge, Cambridge University Press, 2003).

[32] As Lord Scarman noted in *Gillick*, when children are *Gillick* competent in respect of a decision, the rights of parents to decide 'yields to the child's right to make his own decisions' in respect of that decision.

[33] Kirsty L. Moreton, 'Reflecting on "Hannah's Choice": Using the Ethics of Care to Justify Child Participation in End of Life Decision-Making', *Medical Law Review*, 8 (2020), 124–54; Press Association, 'Jehovah's Witness Teenager Dies After Refusing Blood Transfusion', *The Guardian*, 18 May 2010.

shows disregard for the consent-giver's interests.[34] This is significant because it means that the consent-giver is *less mistaken* about the consent-receiver's reasons for action than she would be in typical cases of moot consent (for example, in the context of sex). In medical cases where the concurrent consents doctrine operates, the consent-giver would usually assume that the consent-receiver acts in what they perceive to be the consent-giver's best interests in φ-ing to her, and she would usually be correct about this (although the consent-giver may think that the consent-receiver is wrong about whether φ is in her best interests).[35]

But even if the consent-receiver's not acting on children's consent in concurrent consents cases is well-intentioned, it might still be an expression of some inappropriate attitudes to consent or to the consent-giver, such as disrespect. It might seem that we are to some extent disrespectful towards children when we do not treat their consent as determinative. We seem to be treating children paternalistically, and paternalism of this kind often assumes defectiveness on the part of the agent. It might seem, then, that the way we act in respect of children's consent *does* assume that children are defective as agents or that their consent is defective. Can we explain not treating children's consent as decisive without assuming that they or their consent are defective? I will suggest a positive answer, but first some more general observations on how consent's scope of application may be constrained are warranted.

## Ineffective because constrained?

To see more clearly how children's consent can fail to be effective even when it is not invalid, it is helpful to consider other, more general, instances in which consent's transformative power is morally or legally limited, that is, where consent does not change a consent-receiver's directed duties.

It is widely accepted that an agent's consent is not always sufficient to waive their rights and render action on consent permissible (in terms of the consent-receiver's

[34] While in most cases involving moot consent (or other types of consent not acted on), we are normally right to infer bad motivations on the part of the agent acting in the absence of consent, this is not the case in children's consent cases against a background of the concurrent consents doctrine. When we do not act on children's consent in such cases, it is not because we put our own interests before those of the child. We act with good motivations—the child's interests—both in cases when we act on, and when we do not act on, children's consent. As Woodard notes, '[i]n some sense, agents who give moot consent get lucky: their will accorded with what was going to happen anyway': Woodard, 'Mistreated Consent'. But in cases involving children's consent the consenting child is perhaps not *merely* getting lucky; the agent acting in some way towards her does not do so *just* by, due to luck, doing what they were going to anyway. They are guided by considerations relating to the child's interests, even if whether the child gets what she wants will be a matter of luck, in some sense.

[35] While the child may be unaware of the fact that her consent is moot, she is less mistaken about the consent-receiver's reasons for action towards her more broadly and in particular about the consent-receiver's overall intentions being to benefit her.

directed duties). This is the case for standard, adult agents as well as for children. As well as the capacity and what might be described as 'authenticity' grounds discussed earlier, consent does not always have power to change directed duties that others are under, for example, when the consent given is invalid on other grounds, due to coercion, undue influence, or lack of relevant (consent-enabling) information. But consent may also lack the normative power to change directed duties others are under due to the *nature of the act consented to*, depriving the consent of its usual effect.

Consent's power to render acts *legally* permissible is constrained in many jurisdictions. In English law, A's consent to φ does not in itself furnish a defence against criminal liability where B's φ-ing causes ABH or greater injury (contrary to the Offences Against the Person Act 1861).[36] Certain acts, such as prize fights,[37] sadomasochistic violence,[38] killing on request,[39] some body modifications,[40] therefore remain unlawful, notwithstanding the valid consent of the party or parties directly involved.[41] In other jurisdictions, such as Germany and France, similar provisions exist that negate consent's legal effect to acts such as being killed and eaten,[42] and 'dwarf-tossing' for entertainment purposes.[43] There is some disagreement in the literature about what exactly happens to consent given in such cases and the correct terminology for describing it, but we might say that consent given in such cases is legally valid but legally ineffective.[44] This is because it is plausible that there is nothing intrinsically defective about the consent given that renders it invalid, but that it would, nevertheless, be wrong (vis-à-vis the consent-giver) for the consent-receiver to act on consent—the consent-receiver should not take consent as a reason for action. It is not always clear whether the consent is taken to be valid but ineffective, or invalid, or whether it is impossible to give valid consent in respect of the act in question. Some commentators (including Tadros) use the language of invalidity to talk about such consents.[45] But it seems that A's consent to φ could meet all the relevant conditions (in medical treatment, information, capacity, and voluntariness) for consent to be valid, and still be ineffective in releasing B from her duty not to φ to A.

[36] In law this might be because the act would constitute a public wrong. But the claim often does not seem to be merely that consent cannot render the act consented to all things considered permissible; it also seem to be a claim about consent's power being limited.

[37] *Donovan* (1934) 2 KB 498.

[38] *Brown (Anthony Joseph)* [1994] 1 AC 212 (HL).

[39] *R (Pretty) v Director of Public Prosecutions* [2001] UKHL 61.

[40] *BM* [2018] EWCA Crim 560. See Haroon Siddique, 'Body Modification Artist "Dr Evil" Admits GBH Against Customers', *The Guardian*, 12 February 2019.

[41] Lisa Forsberg, 'The Scope of the Medical Exception in Criminal Law', *Modern Law Review*, 88 (2025), 237–66.

[42] See e.g. Luke Harding, 'German Court Finds Cannibal Guilty of Murder', *The Guardian*, 10 May 2006.

[43] *Commune de Morsang-sur-Orge*, arrêt du 27 octobre 1995 (Conseil d'Etat, Assemblée).

[44] Isra Black, 'Asymmetry of Adolescent Decision-Making Capacity and Rational Choice', in this volume, pp. 48–77 at 51–2.

[45] Tadros, *Wrongs and Crimes*.

The idea that consent can be ineffective due to the act consented to is also relatively common in the philosophical literature. When A's consent to B's φ-ing is incompatible with some other duty that A is under (typically duties to self but potentially also duties to others),[46] this could affect the force of A's consent to φ. Tadros, for example, says that 'whether consent to harm is morally valid [...] depends in part on whether the person consenting violates a self-regarding duty in giving it'.[47] Perhaps the most widely accepted explanation of limitations on the normatively transformative power of standard agents' consent is something like this: we normally think that if A has consented to B's act φ, A's consent releases B from the directed duty she would otherwise be under not to φ in respect of A. But if A, in consenting to and thereby permitting B's φ-ing violates a duty to self, it may be that A's consent is not normatively transformative. We might also think that B might still act wrongly, even if A's consent to φ were normatively transformative, because B would be complicit in A's wrongdoing (consisting in her violating her duty to self).[48] We are under duties not to do certain things to ourselves (usually harm ourselves in certain ways). Therefore it may also be wrong to have others do these things to us (harm us in these ways); if it is impermissible for me to φ myself, my consenting to φ may not render it permissible for you to φ me.[49]

[46] McConnell, 'When Is Consent Required?', 82. See also discussions re inalienable rights, for example, Terrance McConnell, *Inalienable Rights: The Limits of Consent in Medicine and the Law* (New York, Oxford University Press, 2000); Hillel Steiner, 'Directed Duties and Inalienable Rights', *Ethics*, 123 (2013), 230–44; Pierfrancesco Biasetti, 'Infinite Regress and Hohfeld: A Comment on Hillel Steiner's "Directed Duties and Inalienable Rights"', *Ethics*, 126 (2015), 139–52.

[47] Tadros, *Wrongs and Crimes*.

[48] Luke Davies, 'Duties to Self and Being Used Merely as a Means', *Journal of Moral Philosophy* (2024) https://doi.org/10.1163/17455243-20244458.

[49] McConnell, 'When Is Consent Required?'. One might object that an alternative justification could be provided that focuses on the rights/interests of others, rather than our duties to the consent-giver or whether we wrong or harm her. Even though A can permissibly act on B's consent to A's destroying her property (McConnell describes rights over property as 'paradigmatically alienable'), and A may do so by various means, A may not permissibly set B's house on fire if doing so threatens the property of others. Although B would not be wronged if she has given valid consent, other parties might be. But this is just to say that B's valid consent to A's φ-ing makes A's φ-ing permissible qua not wronging B, it does not make A's φ-ing all things considered permissible. Considerations that determine whether B's φ-ing is all things permissible could certainly justify A's not acting on B's consent—and may indeed require it—but it seems that we can easily explain this without making any reference to limits to B's consent. Rendering an act all things considered permissible just is not something consent does, except where there are no other considerations bearing on the all things considered permissibility of the act in question. Obviously, consent does not alone guarantee permissibility *tout court*. But what we are interested in here is not all things considered permissibility but interpersonal wronging. See also Michelle Madden Dempsey, 'The Volenti Maxim', in Peter Schaber and Andreas Müller (eds), *The Routledge Handbook of the Ethics of Consent* (London, Routledge, 2018), pp. 187–98. Note also that our consent to 'φ only has the power to make it the case that we are not wronged by φ *in the way we would have been wronged had we not consented.* It gives us neither the power to make it the case that φ is not wrong all things considered, nor the power to make it the case that φ does not wrong us in other ways', since '[o]ur power only ranges over the consent-sensitive duties we are owed, not all the duties we are owed': Renzo, 'Defective Normative Powers', 56. See also Owens, 'Shaping the Normative Landscape', 181; Dempsey, 'Victimless Conduct and the Volenti Maxim'; Peter Schaber, 'The Volenti Maxim', *Journal of Ethics*, 24 (2019), 79–89.

Cases involving constrained consent seem to suggest that consent can be ineffective in altering the directed duties of others in the way it usually does, and that this can be the case without there being something intrinsically defective about the consent or the consent-giver to render consent invalid. In the legal examples outlined above, we see that consent to certain act-types is ruled out: valid consent is constrained or ineffective and acting on consent is impermissible. What is interesting, for the purposes of our discussion of children's consent, however, is that in these examples, consent's power is constrained regardless of whether the consent-giver is a child or an adult.

In the domain of medical interventions in which the concurrent consents doctrine operates, the relevant act-types are usually ruled-in—they are legally permissible—for both the consent-giver and the consent-receiver, if they are an adult, but not necessarily if they are a child. Consider the fairly typical case of a Jehovah's Witness who would require a blood transfusion to remain alive. In English law, it is lawful for a doctor to offer the transfusion, and an adult patient able to make a valid decision may consent to treatment or may refuse it.[50] Whereas a child Jehovah's Witness may consent to a blood transfusion, but more often than not will be unable to refuse it.[51] Further, it is lawful for a doctor to offer labiaplasty to adults and children, but whereas an adult's valid consent or refusal of the procedure will be legally effective, it is plausible that a child's valid consent to the intervention would be legally ineffective.[52] For children, therefore, valid consent (refusal) may be ineffective because it is constrained, but this is not because the act-type—here, a procedure that falls within the 'medical exception'[53]—is impermissible.

The case of general constrained consent is helpful for it allows us to identify what happens in medical decision-making cases in which children's consent is ineffective in virtue of the application of the concurrent consents doctrine. Children's valid consent may be ineffective because its normative power to alter the consent-receiver's directed duties is constrained. But the reason for children's consent's constrained power is not—unlike in the general cases—that the proposed interventions are impermissible as a type. The puzzle that confronts us is one of explaining why children's consent to *tokens* of these otherwise permissible act-types is ineffective in changing the directed duties of others.

[50] *Re T (Adult: Refusal of Treatment)* [1993] Fam 95 (CA Civ).

[51] See e.g. *Re P (Medical Treatment: Best Interests)* [2003] EWHC 2327 (Fam); Press Association, 'Jehovah's Witness Teenager Dies After Refusing Blood Transfusion'.

[52] For discussion of 'concurrent refusals', see Skelton *et al.*, 'Overriding Adolescent Refusals of Treatment', 240.

[53] Forsberg, 'The Scope of the Medical Exception'.

## Children and our duties towards them

I suggest that an alternative explanation for the ineffectiveness of children's consent in altering our duties or reasons for action is not defectiveness on the part of the agent or her consent. Rather, the explanation goes to how we relate normatively to children and in particular how concern for children's well-being structures our duties towards them.

We plausibly owe very onerous duties to children, in particular in respect of promoting their well-being. For example, we owe it to children to provide certain forms of care and consideration that we do not owe to adult agents. Some of what we owe children is due to partiality and caretaker roles we have in respect of them, for example, in virtue of being their parents. But we might owe children more in terms of care and consideration even when we lack any duties of partiality towards them, simply because they are children.[54] This might be described in terms of children having positive rights to certain things including certain basic goods, or due to their special vulnerability and dependence on adults in terms of meeting their basic needs.[55] Unlike others who may be vulnerable, such as older adults, children start life from a position of extreme vulnerability, as well as lacking the ability to make decisions about their own lives.[56] Vulnerability and dependence are often taken to justify paternalistic treatment of children. In respect of younger children, this is generally seen as relatively uncontroversial. But it is often thought that older children, too, including those who are able to give valid consent, may be (permissibly) paternalistically treated. Adolescents may be more vulnerable than adults, for example, because their values are more likely to be more provisional or less settled, or because they may be more prone to risky behaviour.[57] Their vulnerability may justify some paternalism towards them, but it cannot on its own explain why we may treat their consents/refusals as non-determinative, because other groups are vulnerable too, including some older adults, and we typically do not think that they may be paternalistically treated.[58]

One explanation, which I—together with Isra Black and Anthony Skelton—have proposed elsewhere, is that children may fare well differently to adults and

[54] Onora O'Neill, 'Children's Rights and Children's Lives', *Ethics*, 98 (1988), 445–63.

[55] Alexander Bagattini, 'Children's Well-Being and Vulnerability', *Ethics and Social Welfare*, 13 (2019), 211–15.

[56] See e.g. Robert Goodin, Protecting the Vulnerable: A Re-analysis of our Social Responsibilities (Chicago, University of Chicago Press, 1986); Catriona Mackenzie, Wendy Rogers, and Susan Dodds (eds), *Vulnerability: New Essays in Ethics and Feminist Philosophy* (New York, Oxford University Press, 2014).

[57] Skelton *et al.*, 'Treating Adolescents Differently', p. 208.

[58] Skelton *et al.*, 'Treating Adolescents Differently', p. 208. Though we arguably may have more onerous duties towards older adults in virtue of their vulnerability, compared to the typical adult, and we may have more onerous duties towards other adults who are particularly vulnerable, too.

that their well-being includes the good of 'shielding'—'the non-instrumental prudential good of being protected from the full effect of one's decisions or possessing a variety of freedom from making certain kinds of decisions in the absence of a safety net'.[59] If this account is correct, our duties to children—including children who have decision-making capacity—may include duties to promote their well-being that requires some degree of paternalism.[60] Even if we do not accept this account, it is plausible that we have onerous duties to promote children's well-being (however construed) and that this may sometimes require some degree of paternalism.

Crucially, this justification does not presuppose that children are defective as agents or that their consents or refusals are invalid. We can reject views according to which children's consent is invalid or defective, but nevertheless hold that children's consent does not affect our consent-sensitive duties in the same way standard consent does. We can see how this is the case by considering how our duties to act with concern for children's well-being *also* constrain the power of parental consent. For, as we have seen, it is true of parental consent too, that it cannot displace our duties to act so as to promote children's well-being. Parental consent, too, is only effective when the consent or refusal is not (sufficiently) contrary to the child's welfare interests.[61] This is the case even though parents are (usually) fully fledged autonomous moral agents and we typically have no concerns about their capacity to give valid consent.[62] In *Elective Medical Procedure*, Celeste's parents might not be able to consent to the procedure on Celeste's behalf, either. But in this case it is not because Celeste's parents' consent is taken to be defective due to factors such as limited agency or autonomy of the consent-giver.[63] This might suggest that the

[59] Skelton *et al.*, 'Treating Adolescents Differently', p. 210.

[60] Skelton *et al.*, 'Treating Adolescents Differently'.

[61] See e.g. *An NHS Trust v SR* [2012] EWHC 3842 (Fam), where a mother was unable to refuse the recommended course of cancer treatment in favour of 'alternative therapies'.

[62] As Montgomery notes, 'the most significant element of the *Gillick* decision was the confirmation that parental rights were rooted in children's interests rather than family privacy': Jonathan Montgomery, 'The Interaction of Children's Capacity Regimes and Parental and Judicial Powers: A "Strictly" Legal View', in this volume, pp. 121–35 at 123. See also Jonathan Montgomery, 'Children as Property?', *Modern Law Review*, 51 (1988), 323–42. He further observes that: 'The implication of this is that parental choices should be overridden when that presumption is rebutted; typically, upon the adjudication that decisions were not being made in the interests of the child. In general terms, this is where they place the child at significant risk of harm due to their failing to parent to a reasonable level (the child protection case). In relation to specific issues, this is where the parental decision is found not to be in the "best interests" of the child. In all judicial contexts, the wishes and feelings of the child patient are important but not determinative. Thus, the law privileges children's welfare rights over their autonomy when a conflict is perceived.' Montgomery, 'The Interaction of Children's Capacity Regimes and Parental and Judicial Powers', p. 123. See also Priscilla Alderson and Jonathan Montgomery, *Health Care Choices: Making Decisions with Children* (London, IPPR, 1996).

[63] It is unclear whether parents are required to have (as in being assessed for) capacity in the ordinary run of things, but it is generally assumed that they do have capacity.

ineffectiveness is located in the consent-receiver's duties rather than in (deficiencies in) the consent-giver's consent.

We might think that the duties we have to promote children's welfare constrain our reasons to act on their consent, when the action consented to is sufficiently detrimental to their other interests, especially their welfare interests. Tadros and others believe that 'the primary function of duties is to constrain our practical reasoning'.[64] This means that: 'If you have a duty not to φ, that means that in deliberating about how to act, φ-ing is in some important sense not an option. It would be inappropriate for you to see yourself as free to φ, even if there are respects in which φ-ing would be valuable.'[65]

It is plausible that acting (sufficiently seriously) contrary to a child's interest should not be an option, especially to parents, but also to adults in general. It is also plausible that this duty is more important, and would therefore not be completely extinguished, even if the child were able to give valid consent to the act that was contrary to their interests, and that the same would be true for the consent of their parents.[66] We might think that the duty we have to act with concern for children's welfare interests would be so strong that it would not be fully consent-sensitive. Our duty to promote children's well-being would give us reasons different to those given by adult well-being. This concern for a child's well-being constrains our duties such that they do not change *completely* in response to children's consent, *even when* the child is sufficiently autonomous to give valid consent. While an adult agent's refusal of bodily interference completely extinguishes any directed duty the consent-receiver might have to undertake the act involving the bodily interference, duties to act may not be completely extinguished when the refusal is given by a child.[67] We might think, then, that due to the nature of our duties to safeguard children's well-being, a non-decisive role *is* the proper role for children's consent to play in our deliberations.

This is also plausible if we think about what makes *consent* valuable. If we accept that what makes consent valuable appeals to the value of autonomy, that '[b]eing able to control the consent-sensitive duties that others owe us is valuable because it increases our capacity to exercise our self-determining agency and shape our life as we wish',[68] it may be valuable for children to have the power to consent. And this is true even if it is against the background of the concurrent consents doctrine where children's consent is not determinative in respect of whether φ is undertaken. It may be a valuable for a child to 'practise' exercising her autonomy

[64] Though this is not the only function of duties, see e.g. Tadros, *Wrongs and Crimes*, 218.

[65] Renzo, 'Defective Normative Powers', 55.

[66] This might, for example, be the case in respect of procedures such as female genital mutilation and hymenoplasty.

[67] The claim is not just that it is all things considered impermissible to act on a child's valid consent when this involves harming them. It might be, all things considered, impermissible to act on an adult's valid consent, too. The claim is about interpersonal wronging.

[68] Renzo, 'Defective Normative Powers', 52.

(for example, for instrumental, forward-looking reasons).[69] If we accept the criticism according to which children's values are less settled, this may reduce the value to them (at that point in time) of having full power to shape their life. And it seems plausible that for children to have the full power to change others' duties towards them such that they would no longer be under a duty to act to promote the child's well-being would not be especially valuable to children.

At the same time, it might be valuable for a child to have the power to determine whether they are wronged by some act undertaken in respect of them.[70] If part of what makes it valuable for adults to have the normative power of consent is to be able to control when others wrong us, and it is valuable for adults because of the way having this power relates to their autonomy, it seems plausible that it would be valuable for children to have the power to determine whether they are wronged *pro tanto* by some act, too, because of the way it would relate to their autonomy.[71] Children's consent in concurrent consent cases would realise this value—allowing them to shape their life in this way—even if when their consent did not guide others' behaviour.

Of course, determining our duties in respect of children involves considering the harms and wrongs that flow from acting contrary to their consent/refusal (disrespect, dignitary harm, etc.).[72] Even if our not acting on a child's consent does not express inadequate regard for the consent-giver's interests, it might express insufficient regard for her will. Our duties to children change in nature and scope as children mature and develop, and while concern for their well-being remains a primary consideration, *how* we promote their well-being changes as they become increasingly autonomous, and so on. We might also think that there are some decisions that are so central to children's autonomy that in respect of them our duties *are* fully consent-sensitive.[73]

Structurally, views that locate limits in the effectiveness of children's consent in the consent-receiver's duties rather than in deficiencies in the child as an agent or in her consent seem better able to capture what happens in concurrent consents cases. Duties construed in this way better track the relevant values (children's autonomy and well-being), compared to views that hold children's consent to be defective (even when they have decision-making capacity) and their consent therefore to be invalid and thus ineffective in changing our duties. It is also intuitively plausible that we have duties to children to act in their best interests, and that they are not completely altered by children's consent even if the consent given is valid. It seems

[69] See e.g. Skelton *et al.*, 'Overriding Adolescent Refusals of Treatment'; Emma Cave, 'A Future-Orientated View of Autonomy', in this volume, pp. 136–52.

[70] And to mark dissent to whatever was imposed on them.

[71] Indeed, as we have noted before, some consent theorists think that having the power to determine whether someone else's act wrongs you is the primary or only value of consent.

[72] Tom Dougherty, 'Affirmative Consent and Due Diligence'.

[73] See Andrew Franklin-Hall, 'On Becoming an Adult: Autonomy and the Moral Relevance of Life's Stages', *The Philosophical Quarterly*, 63 (2013), 223–47 for discussion of 'forced momentous choices'. See also Skelton *et al.*, 'Overriding Adolescent Refusals of Treatment'.

plausible that autonomy is not all that matters, and that concern for others' welfare should play *some* role in our *duties* towards others.[74]

Of course, we would need to say more than I am able to do here about exactly how our duties to children are different from our duties to adults in order fully to determine the plausibility of this view.[75] For now the claim is just that it is more plausible to locate the 'ineffectiveness' of children's consent in our duties and reasons for action than in the (lacking) quality of the consent.

At this point a few objections come to mind. First, it may be objected that if a token of consent does not change our duties in the way we would normally expect, then that consent *is* defective; that token of consent is not capable of doing the thing consent is meant to do, so it is lacking in some way. To be charitable to the 'defective consent' view, we should consider the possibility that 'defective' could be used by them just to mean 'not *fully* valid' or 'not affecting others' directed duties in the normal way'. One need not necessarily claim that the 'defect' is somehow internal to the consent or the consent-giver. But in this case the view that consent is defective would apply also to parental consents that fail promote a child's best interests. Here, we have a difference of terminology, not of substance. However, speaking of 'defectiveness' and 'ineffectiveness' is clearer in establishing what goes wrong with consent, in my view.

Second, suppose you disagree with the analysis above that children's consent is not moot. It might be argued that children's consent under the concurrent consents doctrine might be invalid in another way, and therefore unable to change our duties. We might think that children's consent against this background is moot, and that moot consent fails the validity condition that requires that the consent-giver possesses sufficient information about the thing to which she is proposing to consent. David Archard suggests that this means that the consent-giver knows 'everything that would make a real difference to whether or not she consented'.[76] Tom Dougherty expresses the idea in terms of deal-breakers. A deal-breaker is any feature, *F*, of some act, φ, that makes a 'decisive difference' to the consent-giver's decision to consent to φ.[77] As Woodard notes, '[w]e can test for a "decisive difference" counterfactually: if the agent had known about *F*, she would not have agreed to φ'.[78] Others have pointed out in criticism of Dougherty's view, that his idea of

[74] Tom Dougherty, 'Affirmative Consent and Due Diligence'.

[75] For some (other) views on special duties see e.g. Mianna Lotz, 'The Real Value of Child–Parent Vulnerability'. *Ethics and Social Welfare*, 13 (2019), 244–60 and Colin Macleod, 'Paradoxes of Children's Vulnerability', *Ethics and Social Welfare*, 13 (2019), 261–71.

[76] David Archard, *Sexual Consent* (Boulder, CO, Westview Press, 1998), p. 46.

[77] Tom Dougherty, 'Sex, Lies, and Consent', *Ethics*, 123 (2013), 717–44 at 731. The formulation used here is Woodard's.

[78] Woodard, 'Mistreated Consent', See also Emily C. R. Tilton and Jonathan Ichikawa, 'Not What I Agreed To: Content and Consent', *Ethics*, 132 (2021), 127–54. A virtue of this kind of view is that the counterfactual test for deal-breakers is similar to and seems to map onto the legal test for causation in cases concerned with assessing whether someone's failure to provide sufficient information about risks attaching to an intervention undermines consent, e.g. in negligence.

deal-breakers might be hard to generalise such that we get agreement regarding what kinds of facts constitute them. But this is not a problem here, for, as Woodard notes, there is plausibly agreement among most agents that one's consent being moot *would* be a deal-breaker.[79] Plausibly, this would be the case for children, too. We might think, then, that if a child knows that her consent will be moot, this would deter her from consenting, and the consent she gives without this knowledge would be invalid.

But (perhaps unlike other deal-breakers) it is not obvious in the medical treatment context that knowing that one's consent to φ is moot would deter one from consenting to φ.[80] As Woodard notes, 'some agents *do* prefer to consent in [moot consent] cases', for example, to exercise normative control in respect of whether they are wronged by φ (though the claim is not that they *should* do so).[81] We might think that there is something problematic about such consent, but it does not obviously fail the validity condition that requires the consent-giver to be sufficiently informed.[82] Many (or most) cases involving medical interventions will be uncomplicated, the child will consent to the intervention, and her consent will be acted upon. The fact that there is a background condition by which another party's consent can override or supplant the child's consent does not seem to entail that her consent in these uncomplicated cases should be taken as invalid, even if her consent is in some sense moot.

Third, it might be objected that if we accept the duties-based explanation, it justifies too much; it might justify too many instances of not acting on valid consent, beyond cases involving children. In response, it might be said that there are ways to distinguish duties to children from duties to adults. We have more stringent duties to act positively in respect of the former on most views, which can help us resist spillover from children's consent to other consents. We might also justify differential treatment on other grounds, for example that children and adults fare well in different ways, and that autonomy is more important to adult well-being. Moreover, we might think that it is not so bad if the duties-based view applies to some situations involving adults too. One way of taking seriously the idea that children's consent is not special because standard consent's ability to change the directed duties of others is limited too ('constrained consent') might be to accept that concern for others' welfare has a role to play in determining when it is permissible to act on someone else's consent more generally. It seems somewhat plausible that even if A is fully autonomous and consents to [harmful act by B] φ, A's consent does not completely extinguish B's duty not to harm A by φ-ing her. And it is more plausible

[79] Tilton and Ichikawa note that it is implausible that idiosyncratic and uncommunicated deal-breakers undermine the validity of consent: Tilton and Ichikawa, 'Not What I Agreed To', 134.

[80] Woodard, 'Mistreated Consent'.

[81] Woodard, 'Mistreated Consent'. In some cases our pre-emptively consenting to things that will happen to us anyway seems problematic, but this may not always be the case.

[82] There might be other things wrong with moot consent in concurrent consents cases, e.g. insufficient options.

to locate the justification for such limits in our duties than in (deficiencies in) the consent given.[83] It seems to provide a better explanation for when it is wrong to act on someone's consent, which might also be generalisable to, for example, cases in which consent is given in circumstances of exploitation, but where the consent given may nevertheless not be invalid. It is also in line with other recent literature in paying more attention to the role of the consent-receiver.[84] It seems plausible that whether someone consents does not (always) provide a full answer to the question of whether we are doing the right thing when we act on someone's consent, even in terms of *interpersonal morality*.[85]

Fourth, it might be objected that this kind of view might make it less certain when we, as consent-receivers, can permissibly act on someone's consent. I am happy to bite this bullet. We should, as consent-receivers, worry more about when we can permissibly act on someone's consent. This does not mean that we should be more inclined to override someone's consent; just that we should think more carefully about when to act on it.[86]

These objections—and the third and fourth objections in particular—leave some unanswered questions, but they also show how thinking about how children's consent functions can illuminate how consent functions, and what we value in consent, *in general*, beyond children. Regardless of whether we accept the explanation that focuses on the way in which concern for children's well-being structures our duties to children, we should accept that it is more plausible to locate differences between the normative power that children's and adult consent has to affect our duties and reasons for action rather than in deficiencies in the consent-giver.

[83] It might also seem more plausible to locate the source of limitations in the effectiveness of A's consent to φ in B's duties to A than in A's duties to herself, or the idea that, due to the nature of φ, A is not capable of giving valid consent to it, but this is not something I can pursue here.

[84] See e.g. Renzo, 'Defective Normative Powers'; Tilton and Ichikawa, 'Not What I Agreed To'; Woodard, 'Mistreated Consent', etc.

[85] Note that this is not just the claim that someone's consent does not provide all things considered justification. The claim is that someone's consent does not always provide full justification in respect of my action vis-à-vis them as the person against whom I act. I may not wrong them by non-consensually interfering with them, but there may nevertheless be something morally wrong with what I do to them as fellow agents such that it is not permissible for me to act on their consent.

[86] This translates to sexual consent, and consent more generally. Some people may object that the *Me Too* movement has 'gone too far', and resulted in a position where, for example, men are in a constant state of worry regarding whether it's appropriate to hug women or what they can permissibly say to them. It seems doubtful that the *Me Too* movement has had any such effects. But if it were to have had such effects, that would be good. It is right that it is the agent acting towards someone that should be worried and go out of their way to make sure that the person they act towards is really consenting, and whether their consent is really valid (rather than the entire burden falling to women, worrying about whether they come across in such a way that they might be taken to consent).

# Part III

# Children's Responsibility

# 13

# The Prospective Stance: Children and Responsibility

MEGHAN WINSBY

CHILDREN PRESENT A persistent challenge to theories of moral responsibility. Consider the following cases:

> *Shoplifting.* An Ohio woman asked to have the police called when she caught her six-year-old daughter, Shiane, shoplifting. Shiane had stolen a $3.11 package of temporary tattoo stickers and was taken to the station in the back of a police cruiser at the request of her mother.[1]
>
> *Rescue.* Six-year-old Elspeth 'Beanie' Mar of Sacramento, CA, noticed her friend choking on an apple. Beanie got up, walked over, and 'performed the Heimlich manoeuvre on her pal Aniyah Rigmaiden, dislodging the apple and saving her friend's life'.[2] Beanie received a certificate for her heroism, and was praised as a hero within the community and across news outlets and social media.
>
> *Vandalism.* A father finds his six-year-old daughter has damaged his office desk by writing all over it in permanent marker. She has done this either 'thoughtlessly or mischievously'. It is written into this case that we are to assume she '*should* have known better, and *could have done* better'.[3] Let's call her Brydie. According to Tamar Schapiro, Brydie's father would likely 'superficially' respond to her as an equal—by demanding an apology or something similar—but would not feel resentment toward her, only disappointment in her conduct.

[1] 'Mom Calls Cops on Shoplifting Daughter', CBS News, 23 December 2009. https://www.cbsnews.com/news/mom-calls-cops-on-shoplifting-daughter/ (accessed 13 July 2025).

[2] Elspeth 'Beanie' Mar, 6-Year-Old, Saves Friend From Choking', Huffpost, 4 May 2012. https://www.huffpost.com/entry/elspeth-beanie-mar-6-year-old-saves-friend-choking_n_1478650 (accessed 13 July 2025).

[3] T. Schapiro, 'Childhood and Personhood', *Arizona Law Review*, 45 (2003), 575–94 at 578. Emphasis mine.

*Proceedings of the British Academy*, **279**, 253–271, © Authors 2025.

*Shoplifting* and *Rescue* are real-life cases; *Vandalism* is a hypothetical scenario provided by Schapiro.[4] It is not by coincidence that these cases involve six-year-old children. By this age, children are well aware of rules prohibiting certain behaviours. As Michael Tiboris notes, at six years of age children are clearly not infants. However, they are young children and still 'uncontroversially fall short of *full* moral responsibility'.[5] Except perhaps for the case of Beanie, the above scenarios will be familiar to most parents and caregivers. They are examples of the typical ways we involve children in moral practices like blaming and praising.

According to much of the philosophical literature on moral responsibility, the children in *Shoplifting*, *Vandalism*, and *Rescue* are not fully morally blameworthy or praiseworthy. They are excused or exempted from full moral responsibility on the grounds that they are not the kinds of creatures who are the appropriate targets of full moral blame. This status is explained and/or justified on various grounds. The question of whether young children act knowingly and freely in morally significant ways and whether they are able to understand and respond to moral demands figure heavily into these justifications. Another important consideration is whether young children are able to act from a morally objectionable—or laudable—*quality of will*. On one prominent normative conception of childhood, children are viewed as defective adults. It is only when these defects are remedied that children emerge as participants in the moral community, as agents to be included among those who are the apt targets of full-blown praise and blame.[6] On the empirical side, most views understand children as advancing through a series of developmental stages characterised by the presence or lack of various (adult) capacities and/or abilities. Young children are often—among other things—inexperienced and practically incompetent, unreflective, unresponsive to moral reasons, etc. *Very* young children are Frankfurtian wantons, ruled by instinct and subject to their bare first-order desires.[7]

The capacities that would warrant treating children as morally responsible vary according to which normative account of responsibility one takes on, and range from self-perception and reflection to forming stable commitments to goals and principles—the ability to speak from one's own 'deliberative perspective'.[8] A stance of paternalism towards children permits adults to treat them as though

[4] Schapiro, 'Childhood and Personhood', 577.

[5] M. Tiboris, 'Blaming the Kids: Children's Agency and Diminished Responsibility', *Journal of Applied Philosophy*, 31 (2014), 77–90 at 89 (Note 3). Emphasis mine.

[6] Broadly, the 'Aristotelian conception' of childhood, which views childhood as a series of stages characterised by developing capacities of various kinds. For a recent and thorough discussion of the traditional (Aristotelian)/deficiency views, as well as more recent views which propose that children have unique capacities/access to sources of value, see A. Gheaus, 'Childhood: Value and Duties', *Philosophy Compass*, 16 (2021), 1–11.

[7] Schapiro, 'Childhood and Personhood', 589.

[8] For something like the first view, see J. M. Fischer and M. Ravizza, *Responsibility and Control: A Theory of Moral Responsibility* (Cambridge, Cambridge University Press, 1998). For the second view, see Schapiro, 'Childhood and Personhood', 589.

their lives are, in Schapiro's words, 'not quite [their] own to lead, and … [their] choices are not quite [their] own to make'.[9] This is the idea found in Schapiro's own account of what it means to be a child, where childhood is a 'temporary deviation from the norm of adulthood',[10] and the 'predicament' of the child is one in which they may not be included in relationships characterised by a fundamental interpersonal respect owing to their primary deficit: an inability to self-govern—the lack of a *will*. Children will not be agents until they 'pull themselves together'; that is, until they possess the capacity to take responsibility for their actions and their beliefs.[11]

The claim by Schapiro and others that children are to be disciplined, rather than resented or blamed, and managed, rather than held responsible, echoes P. F. Strawson's view that we by and large adopt an *objective* stance toward them. Young children ought to be *exempted*—and thereby excluded—from participation in the kinds of practices that hold people accountable for their actions.[12] So, while the scenarios depicted in *Shoplifting*, *Vandalism*, and *Rescue* present adults—parents, in particular—with opportunities to discipline and train children, children are not to be considered the appropriate targets of 'reactive attitudes' like gratitude or resentment on this received picture. An attitude of *disappointment* and not *resentment* is appropriate toward Brydie in *Vandalism*—and toward young children in general.[13] This is consistent with regarding them as beings to be 'managed or handled or cured or trained',[14] rather than as moral agents, and the sense of being wronged by them is diminished or absent altogether.[15]

[9] T. Schapiro, 'What Is a Child?', *Ethics*, 109 (1999), 715–38 at 715.

[10] Schapiro, 'What Is a Child?', 735.

[11] Schapiro, 'What Is a Child?', 728.

[12] It is worth bringing up David Shoemaker's recent work in quality of will responsibility in connection with the idea that responsibility involves holding someone 'accountable'. In *Responsibility from the Margins*, Shoemaker identifies three different interpretations of 'will' in the quality of will literature and explains our ambivalence in certain 'marginal' cases of responsibility as stemming from mistaking these individual interpretations to be exclusive of each other. The three interpretations are quality of *character* (David Hume, Jeanette Kennett), quality of *judgement* (T. M. Scanlon), and quality of *regard* (P. F. Strawson, G. Watson). On each theory, one either meets the quality of will requirement or one does not. The 'marginal' cases for which Shoemaker aims to account are psychopaths (Strawson's moral idiots), high-functioning autistics, and those suffering from mild-to-moderate Alzheimer's dementia. The three distinct types of 'will' targeted by our responsibility responses generate three distinct types of responsibility: attributability (targeting character), answerability (targeting judgment), and accountability (targeting regard). Though I focus on regard (accountability responsibility) in my discussion here, any of the types of will Shoemaker describes may be targeted from the prospective stance. See D. Shoemaker, *Responsibility from the Margins* (Oxford, Oxford University Press, 2015).

[13] 'Disappointment', in this sense, is the displeasure or anger which responds to unmet expectations. Resentment joins disappointment with the sense that one has been *wronged*.

[14] P. F. Strawson, 'Freedom and Resentment', in G. Watson (ed.), *Free Will* (New York, Oxford University Press, 1962/2003), pp. 72–93 at 79.

[15] It should be noted that in cases of praise without responsibility, we seem to have a more limited vocabulary (and are perhaps completely missing a term for the distinct sense in which we are pleased when benefited analogous to 'disappointment' when we are harmed or let down). Thank you to Isra Black for this point, and to Viktor Ivankovic for the suggestion that something like 'acknowledgement', if not 'approval', might fit here.

The Strawsonian idea is that moral responsibility consists in the deployment of these reactive emotions and our willingness and/or unwillingness to target each other with them. It has largely been taken for granted that young children are inappropriate targets of such participant reactive attitudes, excusing them from participation in responsibility practices. What has been missing from discussions on the grounds of children's partial excusal and/or exemption from responsibility has been a nuanced look at how we in fact *do* include them in our responsibility practices. By 'responsibility practices', I mean these frequently discussed practices of blaming and praising/punishing and rewarding, as in the cases outlined above. However, I also have in mind more robust practices relying on our readiness to hold and express reactive attitudes: practices like promising and trusting.[16]

In the remainder of this chapter, I will lay out and discuss some received views of the *grounds* on which children are typically excused and/or exempted from responsibility practices.[17] Next, I revisit the three cases—*Shoplifting*, *Rescue*, and *Vandalism*—detailed above, and challenge whether the received accounts capture adequately our everyday moral practices with children. I then take up and defend Tiboris' 'normative competence' view of the grounds of moral responsibility, presenting his view as a more realistic alternative when we consider developing moral agents. In the subsequent sections, I switch from discussion of the grounds on which to excuse, exempt, or include children in our moral practices to the perceptual/attitudinal stance we take toward them, having established (broadly) the kind of moral beings they are. Upon finding the Strawsonian participant and objective stances unsatisfying in this regard, I will propose what I call the *prospective* stance. Rather than involving detachment from interpersonal participation and/or 'refuge from the strains of involvement' characteristic of the so-called objective stance toward others, the prospective stance involves a distinctive practice of proleptic involvement with, and patterns of engaged attention toward, children's burgeoning moral agency. In these ways this stance is distinct from the full participant and objective stances—or 'attitudes'—first articulated by Strawson. The prospective stance amounts to a recognition of children *as children*, insofar as they are somewhere along a continuum toward being the appropriate targets of full-blown reactive attitudes. Proleptic engagement with developing moral agents (punishing and rewarding, demanding apologies, etc.) may *always* be the appropriate mode of treatment, but whether this engagement aligns with the prospective stance will depend on the extent to which we are acknowledging the individual developing moral agents as such.

[16] For example, Bennett Helm explores the idea that trust is itself a 'forward-looking' reactive attitude in 'Trust as a Reactive Attitude', in D. Shoemaker (ed.), *Oxford Studies in Agency and Responsibility*, Volume 2 (Oxford, Oxford University Press, 2014), pp. 187–215. Elsewhere, I argue that promising—insofar as it implicates/exploits trust and opens one up to betrayal (a reactive attitude)—is a responsibility practice in this broader sense, and one that also includes young children.

[17] Making use of Tiboris' recent (very succinct) formulations of these views in, 'Blaming the Kids'.

## Children as moral agents: received views

A link between maturity and personal moral responsibility has traditionally been taken for granted. Immaturity, or the simple plea that one is 'only a child',[18] has served as an excusing or exempting condition on responsibility, albeit not without some acknowledgement of its difficulties. In response, Stephen J. Morse, Schapiro, and more recently Tiboris have pointed out that biological age itself is not what matters when it comes to moral responsibility. Instead, what truly matter on this traditional view are the deficiencies in capacity or ability considered necessary for moral responsibility, and it is these deficiencies for which age is very often treated as a proxy. The received explanations for the leniency we show children as compared with adults, then, tend to focus on children's relative shortcomings.[19] Children—and especially young children—are presumed to be non-rational and impulsive, inexperienced, and unresponsive to moral reasons. Moreover, they lack the ability to regulate themselves emotionally. However, these deficiencies do not uniformly index to biological age, as we see variation in capacity and ability between children at any given increment.

Tiboris helpfully divides these received justifications for excusing, exempting, and/or reducing children's personal moral responsibility into two (related) views: the *moral communication* view—roughly associated with Strawsonian-inspired accounts of responsibility—and the *self-constitution* view, an explicitly Kantian conception of childhood articulated in depth by Schapiro and taken up by others concerned with the moral status of children. Tiboris states the moral communication view as follows:

> *The moral communication view*. Children are not morally communicative agents of the kind that can participate in our practice of holding one another responsible, and therefore they cannot be appropriate targets for responsibility.[20]

To clarify the sense of 'morally communicative', it is helpful to consider Gary Watson's notion of a *basic demand*.[21] This is the demand for 'reasonable regard … addressed to a moral agent … capable of *understanding* the demand',[22] and is most often involved in the deployment of the negative reactive attitudes, which makes these attitudes 'not (as fully) appropriately directed to those who do not fully grasp the terms of the demand'.[23] That is, on Watson's account, young children are exempted from full-fledged blame and associated responsibility practices owing to

[18] Strawson, 'Freedom and Resentment', 78.

[19] We show a child leniency in addition to other ways we may be 'treating someone like a child'.

[20] Tiboris, 'Blaming the Kids', 79.

[21] G. Watson, 'Responsibility and the Limits of Evil: Variations on a Strawsonian Theme', in F. Schoeman (ed.), *Responsibility, Character and the Emotions: New Essays in Moral Psychology* (Cambridge, Cambridge University Press, 1987), pp. 256–86 at 264–5.

[22] Watson, 'Responsibility and the Limits of Evil', 264. Emphasis mine.

[23] Watson, 'Responsibility and the Limits of Evil', 264.

their undeveloped moral understanding—an understanding of the proposition(s) contained in second-personal claims and demands. So, the basic demand is a standing, moral demand for reasonable regard, and the apt addressee of this demand understands the terms of that demand. Agents' abilities to 'fully grasp the terms' of the basic demand will provide the basis on which we sort those toward whom the general participant stance is globally appropriate from those toward whom temporary excuses and outright exemptions apply. On this picture, then, participants in moral practice are the appropriate targets of an expectation of good will or regard—a basic demand—that when violated becomes negatively 'reflected in our ordinary reactive attitudes'.[24]

On this view, it is *unfair* to make and enforce demands on those who cannot grasp the nature of those demands. Additionally, fairness aside, it is futile to attempt to press such a moral demand on them.[25] The reactive attitudes communicate disapproval, and disapproval arises when one perceives that the demand for good will has not been met. In the case of children, who lack full moral understanding, the full message contained in resentment, blaming anger, and expressions of these simply cannot be received.[26]

A second kind of argument for reduced moral responsibility in children—the self-constitution view—is expressed as follows:

> *The self-constitution view*. Children's agency is not sufficiently well-established—they lack the kind of autonomy-generating rational agency to which we can plausibly attribute responsibility.[27]

Here, the justification both for an objectivity of attitude toward child transgression and for limiting children's freedom to choose for themselves—treating a child 'like a child'—comes down to children's inability to commit to and act on the basis of stable values they adopt for themselves. Without this ability, children lack the stable self-concept required for rational agency and moral responsibility. Simply put, children lack wills of their own and so the question of whether they can demonstrate an objectionable (or admirable!) quality of will has to have a negative answer. As noted earlier, this view of the normative distinction between child and adult has been labelled the 'predicament' view.[28] This is so owing to the child's (alleged) lack of 'authority over her deliberative perspective',[29] and her resulting state of subjugation to the will(s) of adults.

On Schapiro's influential articulation of this view, children are *obligated* to 'grow up'—to exit the state of childhood and enter into and become proper citizens

[24] Strawson, 'Freedom and Resentment', 78.

[25] This is not to say, or course, that *punishing* children is futile.

[26] Watson notes here that the notion of moral understanding on the part of children raises a host of issues.

[27] Tiboris, 'Blaming the Kids', 81.

[28] For a recent defence of this view, see S. Hannan, 'Why Childhood Is Bad for Children', *Journal of Applied Philosophy*, 35 (2018), 11–28.

[29] Tiboris, 'Blaming the Kids', 82.

of the moral community. For Schapiro, this is analogous to the Kantian obligation to exit the state of nature to form and/or enter into civil society. Adult relationships with children, then, mainly focus on management, and the predicament in which children find themselves is one that obligates adults—and parents in particular—to a set of child-directed duties aimed at expediting their transition fully into the moral community. In the practice of managing children, we do not 'take child action seriously'.[30] Instead we hold them less, if at all, responsible for their actions—so that where an adult may be *resented* or blamed for her behaviour, a child is to be *disciplined.* Following Strawson, Schapiro observes that 'the knowledge that an agent is a child rather than an adult often prompts [one] to modify [one's] "reactive attitudes" toward her … at least insofar as [one decides] to treat her as a child'.[31]

Both the moral communication and self-constitution views entail that it is unfair and/or inappropriate to blame young children for wrongdoing, though neither view explicitly or in any great detail addresses whether it is appropriate to praise them for their good or exceptional deeds. This is likely just an extension of the relative lack of philosophical attention on praise in its connection with moral responsibility, though it may also reflect some deeper asymmetries between praise and blame themselves.[32] In any case, the idea that praising and blaming young children is a form of management and pedagogy from a dispassionate 'objective' stance seems not to fit our practices, as I will discuss below.

## Blaming and praising children

Before turning to a third view of child responsibility—Tiboris' own *normative competence* view—it may be helpful to review *Shoplifting*, *Rescue*, and *Vandalism.* These are cases in which our ordinary moral reactive attitudes may be tested in the case of children, as each case of child action elicits at least some mixed feelings about the degree to which one ought to respond to the child as an equal and hold her responsible. It is unclear which, if any, moral reactive attitudes are appropriate. To be sure, intuitions differ in these and other cases involving children and their transgressions or achievements. However, taken together, these cases draw out some ambivalence when it comes to holding children responsible in the sense of directing moral praise and blame toward them. The point of these cases is really to illustrate the fact that it is common to take up a participant (as in Beanie) or participant-like attitude toward the children in them, and that the fittingness or appropriateness of gratitude or resentment depends on the specific child with whom one is involved.

[30] Schapiro, 'What Is a Child?', 717.

[31] Schapiro, 'What Is a Child?', 717.

[32] This is not to say that the disproportionate attention to blame and moral responsibility or the asymmetry between praise and blame has gone unacknowledged or unaddressed.

In *Shoplifting*, it seems appropriate for Shiane's mother, Diane, to take Shiane's theft as an opportunity to include her in responsibility practices. Shiane is at least *treated* as if she were a full participant in the moral community, complete with a rather grown-up punishment for her crime. However, to what extent do Shiane's mother, the shopkeeper, and the officers involved in her 'arrest' *feel resentment* toward her? Though Diane is no doubt angry, the degree to which this anger is blaming—or resentful—anger will likely depend on how she views Shiane. If, as in *Vandalism*, Diane believes (correctly) that Shiane *should have known better* and *could have done better*, it seems wrong to say further that Shiane is not responsible, and unworthy of blaming anger. However, it may be worth exploring whether there is a distinct kind of let-down that falls short of full-blown resentment, but which exceeds mere disappointment in cases where the child is *not* viewed as someone who could and should have done better than she did. This attitude may be described as a second-personal disappointment that responds to the quality of Shiane's will, at least to some extent, but is also attentive to her stage of development toward full moral participant. When it comes to Diane's treatment of Shiane, some may find calling the police an overreaction. To this, Diane says, 'I don't think I went too far'. She believes a 'light spanking' would not have sent a strong enough message, and that Shiane is very unlikely to repeat the offence 'because of all that [Diane] did'. It is worth emphasising that Diane believes herself to have been sending a message, and that she believes that message to have been received. At any rate, the stance Diane takes toward Shiane can hardly be described as objective.

In *Rescue*, it seems appropriate to praise Beanie for her life-saving actions whole-heartedly. Further, it seems inappropriate to ask to what extent all those involved in this incident feel gratitude toward her. In this case—even though Beanie is a six-year-old like Shiane and Brydie—it seems the *full* participant attitudes of gratitude and appreciation are apt. While there is certainly an instrumental reason to lavish praise on young children—by praising them heartily, children are more likely to act similarly in the future—this reason is present when we praise or blame *anybody*. Again, although reflection may yield differing intuitions, I think it plausible that the reactive feelings of gratitude or appreciation toward Beanie are not grounded merely in instrumentalist considerations, any more than they would be for a full-blown adult. Arguably, some feature of Beanie's quality of will—her altruism and *goodwill*—garners praise in addition to her know-how and quick thinking in the situation. Beanie is not excused or exempted from full-throated praise on the basis that she is 'only a child', though, given her age and level of experience, she is certainly correctly perceived to be one.

In *Vandalism*, Brydie is perceived by her father as someone who 'should have known' not to scribble all over the desk, and who 'could have' refrained from doing so. Schapiro claims Brydie's father would not feel resentment toward her; rather he would merely feel disappointed. I do not think this is obvious. While Schapiro's intuition that he would experience something less than full-blown resentment may be right, I think some measure of reactive (blaming) anger would not be inappropriate. If he believes truly that she acted thoughtlessly or mischievously—and that she was capable of more—this assessment of the quality of her will would make her the apt target of at least some degree of blaming anger. He certainly engages her in a practice of holding responsible (demanding an apology) that is consistent with the participant stance. Whatever else, his feeling less-than-participant resentment while at the same time treating her as an equal (albeit 'superficially') and demanding an apology involves, I think, viewing her as a creature both potentially and increasingly capable of participating in moral life: as a site of possibility and development.[33] This way of viewing her—this stance toward a child with burgeoning agency—fits well with the third account of child responsibility outlined below.

## The normative competence view

The ambivalence one may feel when considering *Shoplifting*, *Rescue*, and *Vandalism* is consistent with Tiboris' account of children's responsibility, which grounds the extent to which one is the appropriate target of reactive attitudes in normative competence. In the case of children, perceived immaturity has been the intuitive ground on which a plea of 's/he is only a child' has been exempting or excusing. Exactly which features of immaturity justify this exclusion from full moral blame is the task set for those trying to develop a theory of responsibility that adequately accounts for children's reduced participation in our responsibility practices. On the moral communication view, this feature is moral understanding and on the self-constitution view, this feature is the possession of an independent will: a stable will from which to exercise authority over one's own choices must be present.

Tiboris draws from developmental psychological research to challenge the empirical assumptions about young children on which the moral communication and self-constitution views rely. What we know from this research undermines the idea that children—even very young ones—lack the basic capacity to understand and apply moral reactive attitudes and emotions. For example, 'socioemotional competence'—the ability to recognise that others' emotional responses are rule-governed and impose rules on our own responses—develops during early childhood (ages 2.5–6).[34] This finding challenges the assumption in the moral communication view that children lack the ability to comprehend the moral demands made on us by the reactive attitudes. Further, longitudinal studies showing that children maintain a more or less 'stable' set of personality traits linked to self-conception from age 3–15 also undermine to a large extent the idea that children lack the stability

[33] C. Agule, 'Blaming Kids', Presentation at the *Annual Meeting of the Canadian Philosophical Association*, 2 June 2019, Vancouver, BC, Canada.

[34] M. Cole, S. R. Cole, and C. Lightfoot, *The Development of Children*, 5th edn (New York, Worth Publishers, 2005), p. 283, as cited in Tiboris, 'Blaming the Kids', 80.

of self-concept necessary to issue action from a robust 'deliberative perspective'.[35] The upshot is that the normative adult/child distinction is developmental and progressive, along with the capacity for moral agency. The normative competence view is comfortable with the conclusion that received views have been trying to avoid:

> children, even very young ones, have access to moral agency and can be genuinely morally responsible for their actions. There is likely no difference between adults and children with respect to the moral agency necessary for responsibility. Plausible features of moral agency are present far before what we intuitively consider normative adulthood.[36]

A view of young children that takes their moral agency—and responsibility—to be present from a very young age does not entail that we treat them equally in all ways and in all cases. We still ought to consider young children, presumptively at least, as partially excused from full-blown moral responsibility. The basis for this is formulated as follows:

> *The normative competence view.* Children's responsibility is diminished because (and to the degree that) they are less competent at using features of their moral agency to meet social demands.

This view holds that the ability to recognise and respond to normative information provides the (relatively low) threshold for moral agency. While children—even young ones—meet this threshold, they more than likely have reduced normative *competence*. If we think of moral competence as a skillset, this skillset takes time and opportunity to hone. Children have diminished moral competence in relation to adults largely due to inexperience. Though there will be some variation from child to child, it is safe to assume that a six-year-old is relatively inexperienced.

This third way of grounding our tendency to excuse children from moral responsibility goes some way toward vindicating our reactions of blaming anger toward six-year-olds—or even younger children—and also our eagerness to engage children in responsibility practices. For one thing, according to Tiboris, locating the grounds for partial excuse from moral responsibility in normative competence implies that there is 'nothing deeply problematic about saying that very young people can be fully morally responsible in some contexts'.[37] Whether they are depends on the extent to which they have developed their *skills*—their normative competence—which allows them to navigate complex social demands. This, of course, comes only with experience and practice and will vary from child to child, and from circumstance to circumstance. In the case of *Shoplifting* and, I think, for similar reasons *Vandalism*, Shiane and Brydie are morally responsible and likely worthy of participant moral blame on the normative competence view.[38] At this age,

[35] Tiboris, 'Blaming the Kids', 82.
[36] Tiboris, 'Blaming the Kids', 85.
[37] Tiboris, 'Blaming the Kids', 88.
[38] In fact, Tiboris is explicit that a six-year-old who has shoplifted is more than likely fully responsible and 'a potential target for real blame' ('Blaming the Kids', 86).

Shiane and Brydie are aware of the norms that govern their respective behaviours and have, in Tiboris' words, 'organising principles of action that issue from [their sense] of what [they value]'.[39] Diane's confidence that the message contained in her punishment will have its intended effect indicates that she is confident that Shiane is aware that she has done wrong. Similarly (and Schapiro makes this explicit), Brydie's father judges her to be capable of better behaviour than that which she demonstrates: she should have known better.

The normative competence view of childhood is in line with taking up a much more engaged overall stance toward children: a stance that contrasts with the cool disengagement implied by the suspension of participant reactive attitudes like resentment and gratitude. The stance that is unique to children is one marked by distinctive, forward-looking patterns of attention which aim to engage them appropriately in the practices of praise and blame. As Craig Agule argues, the patterns of attention we owe children ought to dispose us to 'notice opportunities for future projects, developing capacities, encouraging development, and developing individuality'.[40] Child action—at least insofar as it evinces these various developments—ought to be taken seriously and at the very least, on this view, children receive the recognition respect of being regarded *as they are* rather than merely in light of what they lack—again, considered here as sites of possibility and development.

If this is right, the normative competence view makes sense of the ambivalence we feel toward child responsibility in particular cases. Further, it invites a third kind of perceptual/reactive stance from which to regard children. Where responsibility is primarily concerned with the exchange of reactive attitudes (Strawson), this view of children challenges the standard assumptions made about the kinds of agents who can participate in these exchanges. When we perceive a child, we perceive a being requiring an environment rich with opportunities to practise exercising their moral agency. This (normative) perceptual stance differs from both the full participant and objective stances, as Strawson and others have articulated them. Taking the objective stance toward children—even young ones—out of hand is inappropriate given the kinds of creatures they are. The full participant stance, too, does not recognise the developing nature of children's moral agency. This failure of recognition from either stance is a failure of respect for children as they are.

## The participant and objective stances

In Strawson's own words, the 'responsibility responses' are 'essentially reactions to the quality of others' *wills* toward us, as manifested in their behaviour: to their good or ill will or indifference or lack of concern'.[41] One is morally responsible,

[39] Tiboris, 'Blaming the Kids', 86.

[40] Agule, 'Blaming Kids'.

[41] Strawson, 'Freedom and Resentment', 83. Emphasis mine.

on Strawson's view, just in case one is the apt target of these *participant* reactive attitudes (barring any excusing, exempting, or justifying conditions—or 'pleas'). When one withholds or suspends these reactive attitudes toward another or others, one adopts the so-called objective stance. A *sustained* objective stance is appropriate toward others one regards as having absent or diminished agency. Strawson includes young children on the list of those toward whom sustaining the objective stance is appropriate, exempting them from responsibility and viewing them as 'excluded from ordinary adult human relationships'.[42] He does not universally exempt children from responsibility practices without noting the difficulty in doing so, and it is fair to add, further, that though he does not always state it explicitly, he means *young* children.

As I understand it here, the participant stance describes the general background attitude we hold toward those with whom we typically interact. At least this is the sense according to Strawson; the kinds of attitudes and relationships he has in mind are those which are 'ordinary'. So, on his account, in the *ordinary* case, we would naturally and justifiably feel resentment toward someone who intentionally causes direct harm to us or someone else, breaks a specific promise, or violates basic trust or some other norm. We may seek to *express* blame in various ways—from minor scolding to state-sanctioned punishment. Whether or not we do seek to express this resentment, we nonetheless perceive the target to be fitting for this reactive emotion, and a fitting recipient of blaming modes of treatment. Likewise, if someone were to benefit us, we would naturally feel gratitude and may seek to express this to her. Taking the participant stance thus adds an interpersonal dimension to our perception of some benefits or injuries. For Strawson, this is all holding each other responsible requires. Whether the expectation and exchange of moral reactive attitudes (holding responsible) is in fact *all there is* to moral responsibility is a question that has received a good deal of discussion, but also one I need not pursue here. In any case, the idea that adopting a stance of objectivity toward agents involves withholding participant reactive attitudes has become widely accepted since Strawson's articulation of these ideas.

It is important to note that Strawson claims it would be 'practically inconceivable' to give up the participant stance in favour of the objective one *altogether*,[43] and some later responsibility theorists further hold that letting go of participant reactive attitudes—if this were even possible—would result in a kind of tragedy.[44] Giving up our practices of targeting each other with reactive attitudes like resentment and gratitude is not merely a question of changing our habits but rather one of profoundly altering the quality of our interpersonal relationships. It seems

[42] Strawson, 'Freedom and Resentment', 81.

[43] Strawson, 'Freedom and Resentment', 81.

[44] A notable exponent of this view is Susan Wolf. See S. Wolf, 'The Importance of Free Will', *Mind*, 90 (1981), 151–6.

natural to view our experiences and expressions of praise, blame, resentment, anger, esteem, and so on as ineliminable from the relationships that matter most to us. Relationships like friendship and romantic love rely heavily on appraisals of character and esteem, and it is hard to imagine what these relationships would look like without these appraisals.

Though this background worry about a global objectivity of attitude persists, it is equally important to acknowledge an objection to this worry. Overemphasising the importance of participant reactive attitudes may blind us to a more serene way of engaging with each other. Tamler Sommers urges that there is a lot of hyperbole surrounding the idea of a global objectivity of attitude, and that a world without blaming anger or exalted praise would still have room for genuine appreciation, warm feelings, and love. In fact, the world would be a more humane one, in which we are quicker to forgive and slower to punish harshly. We might add to this that, if we were to adopt the objective stance toward everyone, all the time, we would also be less likely to hold on to painful regrets and grudges. Sommers believes that Strawson, Susan Wolf, and others have failed to make their case for a 'bleak', 'cold' or 'isolated' interpersonal existence lived from the objective stance and contends that '[t]he conclusion is simply assumed, and then underscored with gloomy metaphors'.[45] There is certainly some weight to the argument that our raw reactive emotions, unmitigated by reflection and judicious expression, can steer us awry.

However, it does seem plausible that abandoning the attitudes central to relationships of romantic love, friendship, and mutual respect would, at the very least, greatly *alter* a source of value and meaning in our lives. Even if we weaken Strawson's charge of practical inconceivability to one of mere psychological difficulty and accept, with Sommers, that there may be *some* benefit, there is still reason to think a universal objectivity of attitude would be undesirable, all things considered. When we take up the objective stance toward another, we refuse to acknowledge the power of the other's will. That power, as Michelle Mason argues, is the power to govern oneself in light of social demands and expectations. Further, 'in taking up the objective stance, one usurps a meaning-giving, authorial power for which the competent correctly demand recognition and whose exercise they have reason to value'.[46]

But what about the non-competent: psychotics, moral idiots, and children? If recognition—the acknowledgement of the quality of one's will—is of such great value in the 'ordinary' case as to serve as an ineliminable part of our interpersonal relationships, putting a stop to any thoroughgoing consequentialist grounding of our responsibility practices, then we want to make sure we are getting it right for everyone—including these 'borderline' cases.

[45] See T. Sommers, 'The Objective Attitude', *Philosophical Quarterly*, 57 (2007), 321–41 at 332.

[46] M. Mason, 'Reactivity and Refuge', in D. Shoemaker (ed.), *Oxford Studies in Agency and Responsibility*, Volume 2 (Oxford, Oxford University Press, 2014), pp. 143–62, at 161.

## The global objective stance

Those toward whom we take a sustained objective stance are *exempted* from participant reactive attitudes. Gary Watson gives a succinct general characterisation of the kinds of pleas we take to be exempting as follows: 'they present the other either as acting uncharacteristically due to extraordinary circumstances, or as psychologically abnormal or morally undeveloped in such a way as to be incapacitated in some or all respects for "ordinary adult interpersonal relationships"'.[47]

In this category, Strawson includes those who are psychotic, hypnotised, under tremendous strain, 'moral idiots', and children.[48] For Strawson, these agents are to be controlled, managed, or trained—and not to be blamed or esteemed. These are agents for whom the more global withdrawal of participant reactive attitudes is appropriate, and toward whom the objective stance is to be sustained.

With the inclusion of the problematic case of children alongside cases where we may think adopting the objective stance intuitively apt, Strawson acknowledges certain limitations of his view as he presents it. He acknowledges the seemingly dichotomous nature of his account and that at the very least the outline of his view does not capture all the nuances of our responsibility practices. He points out that his view admits of anomalous cases, which he situates on the 'borderline', so that in particular, when dealing with young children, we engage in some 'compromise' between the objective and participant stances. The compromise employs both participant and objective stances, so that:

> parents and others concerned with the care and upbringing of young children cannot have to their charges either kind of attitude in a pure or unqualified form. They are dealing with creatures who are potentially and increasingly capable both of holding, and being objects of, the full range of human and moral attitudes, but are not yet truly capable of either. The treatment of such creatures must therefore represent a kind of compromise, constantly shifting in one direction, between objectivity of attitude and developed human attitudes.[49]

The contrast between the participant and objective stances is stark, with an 'attitude (or range of attitudes) of involvement or participation in a human relationship', on one hand, and a stance from which we view another as an object of social policy—a subject of treatment— 'to be managed or handled or cured or trained; perhaps simply to be avoided',[50] on the other hand. The idea that maintaining the detached, objective stance precludes involvement in ordinary human relationships is an isolating one, and it is this depersonalising of our human relationships that

[47] Watson, 'Responsibility and the Limits of Evil', 260 (here quoting Strawson's phrase: 'ordinary adult interpersonal relationships').

[48] 'Moral idiots' refers to individuals with what we would now consider some form of antisocial personality disorder.

[49] Strawson, 'Freedom and Resentment', 88.

[50] Strawson, 'Freedom and Resentment', 79.

is meant to count against accepting a strictly consequentialist justification for our responsibility practices. There are many morally important relationships in which we stand—and practices in which we engage—with other people, which are shaped and coloured by a whole range of these attitudes and their expressions. It is in these engagements with each other that Strawson wishes to emphasise 'how much we actually mind, how much it matters to us, whether the actions of other people—and particularly of some other people—reflect attitudes towards us of goodwill, affection, or esteem on the one hand or contempt, indifference, or malevolence on the other'.[51] It is plausible to think, in light of our everyday interactions with children, that a stance of objectivity would deprive both adults and children of a meaning-giving relationship characterised by the expectation and exchange of distinctive reactive attitudes: attitudes constituting a perspective on children as beings whose opportunities for moral growth and development rely on our (adults') attending carefully to the ways in which they have developed and must continue to develop as prospective members of the moral community.

## A prospective stance

It will be helpful at this point to look to Strawson's comments about children and how they fit into his overall picture. As mentioned above, Strawson takes children to be creatures who are both full of potential and are increasingly capable of holding and being the targets of the reactive attitudes. This is consistent with any of the normative views of child responsibility outlined above. However, he says, children are not yet *truly* capable of either. He focuses on our *treatment* of children but states that it must involve a *compromise* between the objective stance and the participant stance with respect to the reactive attitudes. He adds to this that '[t]he punishment of a child is both like and unlike the punishment of an adult', in that adults take up *rehearsals* with children, and these rehearsals modulate 'towards true performances'. So, in punishing children, we are treating them *as if* they are participants, but we need not target them with the 'adult' reactive attitudes. At least, not always. While 'constantly shifting', as Strawson calls it, between objective and participant stances may be one sort of compromise, I think conceiving of the stance we take toward children this way is unsatisfactory for at least the following reasons.

For one thing, the compromise he describes seems a somewhat cursory answer to a broader difficulty with the dichotomous participant and objective stances. Strawson does anticipate this problem—stressing that his presentation stands only as a rough 'schema'—which glides over 'a great intricacy of phenomena'. However, it may be pressed that it is precisely in these, again to use his words, 'ever interesting varieties of case', that much of our moral experience in fact occurs. The specific problem he is confronting is that children seem to fit comfortably into neither the

[51] Strawson, 'Freedom and Resentment', 76.

class of creatures toward whom we adopt his objective stance (globally), nor the class toward whom we adopt the participant stance.[52] If the challenge is to defend this all-or-nothing view from the charge that these two stances are not exhaustive, the idea that we constantly shift from on the one hand withholding reactive attitudes to the other (directing them fully) toward children glosses over the problem.

Relatedly, the idea that the stance we take toward children—even young ones—represents a departure from what is considered 'ordinary' in our moral lives does not do justice to the substantial role children play in our everyday moral experience, regardless of whether we are ourselves parents. *Shoplifting*, *Rescue*, and *Vandalism* illustrate the need to develop a more nuanced account of the stance we take toward children—with respect to the reactive attitudes we often hold toward them as well as the ways we express these attitudes in practice. Though Beanie's rescue of her friend may not be an example of an everyday case in which a child may deserve praise, we can think of many commonplace examples of six-year-old children helping or soothing others, giving compliments or unbidden gifts, etc. The praise or gratitude prompted by these actions seems apt, and not merely strategically deployed to encourage future good deeds. Considering this, I will attempt to elaborate Strawson's 'compromise'; although, on my view, this is a kind of *third way*.

The prospective stance I am proposing is a non-participant, non-objective stance from which I think we quite naturally, as well as justifiably, regard developing moral agents. These are agents who have something like what Robert Noggle terms 'prospective membership in the moral community' and/or those who are still developing specific moral competencies. In other words, this is the stance we take toward children, wherever we perceive them.[53] As from the objective stance, we are prepared to withhold or diffuse our participant reactive attitudes; however, unlike from the objective stance, we are prepared to engage the child in responsibility practices, paying close attention to her developing moral competencies for opportunities to shift into participant-regarding attitudes. This requires taking up a much more engaged overall stance toward children, rather than an objectivity of attitude. This forward-looking stance recognises children as developing moral participants—with developing qualities of will—rather than as either fixed co-participants in our responsibility practices or as exempt from them. Children need to be regarded as 'sites of possibility and development', and any reactive attitudes or modes of treatment directed toward them must be consistent with viewing them this way. The prospective stance therefore motivates us to deploy proleptic attitudes, which require forward-looking, engaged patterns of attention.

Consider again *Shoplifting*, *Rescue*, and *Vandalism*. In *Shoplifting*, either Shiane understands the moral 'message' encoded into her punishment (her 'arrest')

[52] Children at least, but perhaps some adults and non-human animals are ill accommodated by this dichotomous picture.

[53] Here, I want to leave room for further discussion about what it is to perceive a child.

or she does not. If she does, then she is morally responsible and the apt target of blame (as a reactive attitude) as well as fit to receive her punishment on the moral communication view. Alternatively, she (qua young child) does not understand the moral message (i.e. that the basic demand for good will must not be violated) and blaming her—holding her morally responsible—is unfair. On the self-constitution view, Shiane does not possess adequate authority over her choices—her will is not free owing to her lack of stable commitments—and so she ought not be treated as an equal. On both the moral communication and self-constitution views, Diane's treatment of Shiane could be interpreted as a means (merely) to train and manage Shiane's future behaviour. However, this does not seem to comport with the assumptions we make about our children when we send them these kinds of messages. When asked about whether she felt she overreacted, Diane responded that the message needed to be sent the way that it was. Diane's response strongly suggests that she views Shiane as progressively morally competent, and that she chose the punishment she did in order to seize an opportunity to include Shiane in an 'ordinary adult human relationship'. Treating Shiane *as if* she were a full moral participant contains a message that is a reinforcement of what she *already knows:* i.e. that her theft of the stickers violates the rules governing a specific domain of social life. Diane is neither viewing Shiane as a full participant, nor adopting an attitude of objectivity toward her. Rather, she is viewing her as a site of possibility and development and is attending to the opportunity for moral development presented by Shiane's transgression—adopting a prospective stance.

In the case of *Rescue*, Beanie has undoubtedly performed an exceptional act of first aid know-how. Additionally, her recognition of her friend's need (before any teacher(s) or adults in the room) is admirable. As to whether the moral communication or the self-constitution views adequately account for the fact that Beanie seems the appropriate target of whole-hearted praise, I think it is difficult to say given that they lack an explicit treatment of praise. If proponents of either view were to take the stance that we praise Beanie merely (or even mostly) in order to train her—and not at least in part out of a genuine regard for her good will—I think this would be disingenuous. There are further things we might say pertaining to the praise of children, however. Leaving aside broader asymmetries between praise and blame, there is one asymmetry that seems distinctive of the set of reactive attitudes we withhold or deploy in our dealings with children. Where children and adults are differentially blamed for similar wrongdoings, it is also often the case that children and adults are differentially praised for similar good deeds—though in the other direction: children are praised more generously for similar good deeds than their adult counterparts. One obvious explanation, as discussed, is that targeting children with excessive praise encourages future similar behaviours and acts as a moral pedagogical tool. But we often wholeheartedly experience pride and gratitude toward young children for their altruistic and/or meritorious behaviours, even where these children fail to qualify as responsible or even agential on the received views. A disposition to over-praise and/or to feel excessive pride in young children warrants further investigation, I think, in connection with the moral reactive attitudes, and the special relationship(s) between adults and children—parents and their children especially.

To return to *Vandalism*, I think the case as described makes it clear that Brydie's father is not taking the objective stance toward her. Though Schapiro contends that he does not feel blaming anger toward her, I think that the presence or absence of this reactive emotion will depend on the child. However, if, as is stipulated in the case, Brydie's father believes Brydie should know better and could do better than scribbling on his desk, I think it is unlikely that he would respond with *mere* disappointment. I think some measure of resentment directed toward young children who (knowingly) act mischievously or maliciously is realistic, and in many cases justified. Again, this will vary from child to child according to her demonstrated competence with normative skills. Further, Brydie's father—treating her *as if* she were a co-participant in this responsibility practice—demands an apology for her action. Rather than a slap on the wrist, time-out or the deprivation of a toy or other cherished item, Brydie's father engages her in the moral practice of *taking* responsibility. Though there may be some question as to whether full-throated blame is apt, it is unlikely that he adopts a dispassionate regard for her intentions believing that she lacks a will of her own. Additionally, Brydie's father must view her as responsive to moral communication in making this demand of her. Doing so, I believe, involves taking the prospective stance toward her and her receptivity to moral overtures.

Treating children *merely* proleptically, absent a fitting reactive attitude that responds to their burgeoning moral regard (or character, or judgement), fails to show them the respect they are owed as participants in responsibility practices. It fails to acknowledge a key feature of what it is to be a child, morally speaking—to be a locus of possibility and development. I am not alone in my view that respecting children requires paying closer attention to the kinds of moral beings that they are. Paul Bou-Habib and Serena Olsaretti, for example, argue that limits to treating children paternalistically, or 'acting for the sake of one's children', ought to be grounded in their autonomy *as children*.[54] This view distinguishes itself from others in that children are taken to possess a capacity for autonomy, *to various and increasing degrees*, and that effective childrearing can override children's preferences while still respecting this autonomy. Likewise, including children in responsibility practices proleptically shows recognition respect when one is disposed to hold some measure of reactive resentment (blame, or even betrayal) or gratitude (praise, or even admiration), according to the child's normative competence.

[54] Paul Bou-Habib and Serena Olsaretti, 'Autonomy and Children's Well-Being', in Alexander Bagattini and Colin MacLeod (eds), *The Nature of Children's Well-Being* (New York, Springer, 2015), pp. 15–33.

## Conclusion

In this chapter, I have begun to redescribe the stance we take with respect to children to better account for the varied and nuanced ways we engage with them in moral responsibility practices. As a starting point, our readiness to engage children as participants in these practices—in the present case, to praise or to blame them—is an underdiscussed departure from the notion that morally responsible or non-responsible agents are viewed appropriately from the participant and objective stances, respectively. It suggests a third stance from which we are not necessarily prepared to target children with the full range of reactive attitudes but *are* prepared to engage with them in moral rehearsals nonetheless. Further, in some cases, we may be prepared to and justified in holding fully fledged participant reactive attitudes toward young children, and we are disposed to do so on a case-by-case basis. This third, prospective, stance prepares us to engage with some children as full participants in some contexts. Whether we do so depends on how far along in the development of their normative competence we view them to be. This represents at least a partial rehabilitation of child responsibility, though the attitudes we do experience and express are often hindered by a certain degree of ambivalence. This is consistent with Strawson's view that, when it comes to young children, it is 'essentially a borderline, penumbral area that we move in',[55] yet it is inconsistent with an all-or-nothing, in-or-out background stance toward children *as such*.

When we recognise our role with respect to children and adopt the prospective stance, we acknowledge in them their developing moral agency and engage proactively with them so as to offer moral opportunity, as in the case of soliciting promises, and/or proleptically *as though* they were already full participants.[56] We ought to take child action seriously, especially where it demonstrates the development of normative competency and/or offers us the opportunity to facilitate this development. Ultimately, the stance we take toward children is far from objective, and it is marked instead by a rich and unique kind of engagement.

[55] Strawson, 'Freedom and Resentment', 88.

[56] There is more to be acknowledged in Schapiro's view here; in particular, Schapiro's discussion of the *paternalistic* stance is relevant to this idea that adults have a role-based obligation to facilitate the moral development of children.

14

# Consent and Responsibility: How (Not) to Justify Diverging Thresholds for Minors

MAXIMILIAN KIENER*

On Friday 12 February 1993 in Liverpool, UK, Robert Thompson and Jon Venables murdered the two-year-old James Bulger. At the time of their appalling crime, Thompson and Venables were only ten years old, an age at which they would have been unlikely to be able to rebut the presumption of decision-making incapacity and thus give legally valid consent to their own healthcare.[1] Yet, the authorities considered them criminally responsible and made them the youngest convicted murderers in 20th-century Britain.[2]

Although this is an extreme case, it illustrates a more general fact: the age at which children become criminally responsible is often considerably lower than the age at which they become able to give legally valid consent. Nona Noroozi, Ilina Singh, and Minal Fazel found that in 80 per cent of countries with clearly defined ages for consent and responsibility, the age of criminal responsibility was about two to eight years lower than the age of consent to healthcare.[3]

* I gratefully acknowledge the support of the European Research Council, under the European Union's Horizon 2020 research and innovation programme (Project ID: 789270) and the support of the Leverhulme Trust through an Early Career Fellowship (ECF-2021-176). I am also very grateful for the exceptionally helpful comments on earlier drafts from Holger Baumann, Joseph Bowen, Matthias Braun, Alena Buyx, Thomas Douglas, Lisa Forsberg, Gabriel de Marco, Stuart McLennan, Lukas Meier, Peter Schaber, Daniel Tigard, Meghan Winsby, and other members of the audiences at the TU Munich, the University of Oxford, and the University of Salzburg, as well as especially to the editors of this book, Isra Black, Lisa Forsberg, and Anthony Skelton, and an anonymous reviewer.

[1] *Gillick v West Norfolk and Wisbech AHA* [1986] AC 112.

[2] *Wikipedia*, 'Murder of James Bulger'. https://en.wikipedia.org/wiki/Murder_of_James_Bulger (accessed 13 July 2025).

[3] Mona Noroozi, Ilina Singh, and Mina Fazel, 'Evaluation of the Minimum Age for Consent to Mental Health Treatment with the Minimum Age of Criminal Responsibility in Children and Adolescents: A Global Comparison', *Evidence-Based Mental Health*, 21 (2018). https://doi.org/10.1136/ebmental-2018-300032.

In this chapter, I want to determine whether these diverging age thresholds can be justified. But instead of focusing on the law, namely on *legally* valid consent and *criminal* responsibility, I will pursue a moral inquiry, analysing the conditions of *morally* valid consent and the conditions of *moral* responsibility. Thus, I ask whether the differences between legally valid consent and criminal responsibility can be traced back to the same differences between morally valid consent and moral responsibility. By morally valid consent, I mean the exercise of the normative power that generates for another person the (*pro tanto*) moral permission to do what they would otherwise not be permitted to do;[4] and by moral responsibility, I mean the moral accountability that renders one a fitting target of praise or blame.[5]

I will proceed as follows. First, I outline the views of H. L. A. Hart and Heidi Hurd to support a strong connection between the conditions of consent and responsibility, both in the legal and moral domain. More specifically, I will claim that both consent and responsibility require competence, information, and voluntariness. Second, I will analyse each of these conditions in detail and claim that, despite considerable overlap, there are also crucial differences in how they apply to morally valid consent and moral responsibility respectively. To account for these differences, I will suggest a novel view that features the norms of interpersonal relationships, which I will take to be the norms that specify what we owe to each other as consenting parties and as members of a moral or legal community. I will argue that such an approach not only deepens our understanding of morally valid consent and moral responsibility, but also provides a fresh perspective on the diverging ages for legal consent and criminal responsibility. Thus, I propose to use a general inquiry into the relation between consent and responsibility to understand the particular situation of children and adolescents better. On this basis, I will conclude that great differences between the ages of legal consent and criminal responsibility, as is the case in the UK, lack moral support.

Before I proceed, it is worth clarifying my methodological approach. My key examples in the second section deliberately concentrate on paradigmatic consent cases with adults rather than children. Doing so helps me articulate a broader argument about the relationship between consent and responsibility, one that is not restricted to the domain of minors. Yet, at the same time, it sets a robust framework from which the implications for children, particularly regarding diverging age thresholds for consent and responsibility, can be more effectively drawn and understood. Thus, my envisaged progression from a general (adult-centric) focus in the second section to a more specific (children-centric) focus in the fourth section aims to clarify the complex dynamics of consent and responsibility, reinforcing the overall argument with a comprehensive perspective across different debates in normative ethics and legal theory.

[4] Tom Dougherty, 'Yes Means Yes: Consent as Communication', *Philosophy & Public Affairs*, 43 (2015), 224–53 at 232; V. Tadros, *Wrongs and Crimes* (Oxford, Oxford University Press, 2016), p. 201; Peter Schaber, 'Consent and Wronging a Person', in Peter Schaber and Andreas Müller (eds), *The Routledge Handbook of the Ethics of Consent* (London, Routledge, 2018), pp. 55–64 at 56.

[5] David Shoemaker, *Responsibility from the Margins* (Oxford, Oxford University Press, 2015).

## Hart and Hurd on responsibility and consent

H. L. A. Hart claims that there is an 'analogy between conditions that are treated by criminal law as *excusing* conditions and certain similar conditions that are treated in another branch of the law as *invalidating* certain civil transactions such as wills, gifts, contracts, and marriages'.[6] He further elaborates:

> a will, a gift, a marriage, and (subject to many complect conceptions) a contract may be invalid if the party concerned was insane, mistaken about the legal character of the transaction or some 'essential' term of it, or if he was subject to duress, coercion, or undue influence of other persons. These are the obvious analogues of mistake, accident, coercion, duress, insanity which are admitted by criminal law as excusing conditions.[7]

Hart makes an astute observation: what invalidates civil transactions, including consent, and what excuses criminal wrongdoing seem to be the same factors: insanity, certain mistakes (or ignorance), and coercion (alongside other forms of pressure). What is more, this is not a coincidence: the analogy exists, Hart argues, because both the law on civil transactions and the law on criminal wrongdoing purport to respect individuals as 'choosing being(s)',[8] namely, they purport to make the legal consequences of an individual's action depend on whether that individual had a fair opportunity to act or not act as they did. Hart also goes on to explain the advantages of such an approach, namely, that individuals have the power to determine, by their own choice, what will happen to them and thereby predict their futures. However, Hart also stresses that such 'a *choosing* system'[9] is, more fundamentally, a matter of respecting individuals and protecting them against the claims of society.

However, Hart states only an 'analogy' between excusing and invalidating conditions, not an 'identity'. In other words, insanity, ignorance, and pressure may invalidate as well as excuse, but they may apply differently to consent and responsibility. This is because, as Hart explains, what invalidates consent is 'qualified or limited by other principles'[10] than those that excuse wrongdoing. For instance, some pressure or mistake may invalidate consent, yet not excuse wrongdoing, or vice versa.

Unfortunately, Hart remains vague about these qualifying principles. Regarding responsibility, he says only: 'the law, like every other human institution, has to compromise with other values besides whatever values are incorporated in the recognition of some conditions as excusing'[11] and mentions considerations 'concerning the limits of human *capacity* to control behaviour. (…) [and] difficulty of

[6] H. L. A. Hart, *Punishment and Responsibility*, 2nd edn (Oxford, Oxford University Press, 2008), p. 29, original emphasis.

[7] Hart, *Punishment and Responsibility*, p. 34.

[8] Hart, *Punishment and Responsibility*, p. 49.

[9] Hart, *Punishment and Responsibility*, p. 44, original emphasis.

[10] Hart, *Punishment and Responsibility*, p. 34.

[11] Hart, *Punishment and Responsibility*, pp. 33–4.

*proof*.[12] Regarding consent, Hart primarily emphasises the importance of taking into account the perspective of the other party in a consent transaction: 'Those who enter in good faith into bilateral transactions of the kind mentioned with persons who appear normal (i.e. not subject to any of the relevant invalidating conditions) must be protected, as must third parties who may have purchased interests originating from a transaction that on the face of it seemed normal.'[13] Thus, further inquiry into the conditions of consent and responsibility is needed.

Heidi Hurd pursues such an inquiry, finding much common ground with Hart, even though she never refers to him explicitly.[14] Like Hart, Hurd defends a connection between excusing and invalidating conditions. Like Hart, she argues that what excuses and invalidates is insanity, mistakes, and pressure.[15] And, like Hart, Hurd thinks that the convergence of excusing and invalidating conditions is not a coincidence. Although Hurd does not use Hart's term of 'choosing beings', Hurd stresses that both excusing and invalidating conditions purport to protect an individual's choice: both sets of conditions should indicate whether a person's '*choice* [was rendered] insufficiently autonomous to be praiseworthy or blameworthy (…) [or] render[ed] (…) insufficiently autonomous to have moral force',[16] i.e. the moral force of valid consent.

However, *unlike* Hart, Hurd adopts a *moral* and not just a legal perspective. She claims a connection between the conditions of *morally* valid consent and the conditions of *moral* responsibility (in the accountability sense).[17] By contrast, Hart focused on '*legal* responsibility'[18] and *legal* transactions only, explicitly rejecting any extrapolation of his view to the moral domain. But Hurd seems to be correct here. *Morally* valid consent and *moral* responsibility, as defined earlier, are also undermined by incompetence, ignorance, and pressure.

Finally, unlike Hart, Hurd not only presents an 'analogy' between the conditions of consent and responsibility but boldly asserts 'identity': 'the conditions under which prima facie consent is defeated *are identical to* the conditions under which defendants are properly excused from moral blame, and, to the extent that the law mirrors morality, from legal liability'.[19]

Hence, for Hurd, the conditions that invalidate consent and those that excuse wrongdoing are the *same*, and not just *analogous*.[20] Therefore, Hart's 'qualifying

[12] Hart, *Punishment and Responsibility*, pp. 32–3.

[13] Hart, *Punishment and Responsibility*, pp. 34–5.

[14] Heidi M. Hurd, 'The Moral Magic of Consent', *Legal Theory* 2 (1996), 121–46.

[15] Hurd, 'The Moral Magic of Consent', 140.

[16] Hurd, 'The Moral Magic of Consent', 140.

[17] Hurd, 'The Moral Magic of Consent', 140.

[18] Hart, *Punishment and Responsibility*, p. 53.

[19] Hurd, 'The Moral Magic of Consent', 122, emphasis added.

[20] See Mandava and Millum who adopted this view too, although without referring to Hurd. 'When is a threat controlling, such that it would invalidate consent? We suggest that it reaches this point when we would no longer consider the threatened person morally responsible for her actions [in the sense of deserving praise or blame]': Amulya Mandava and Joseph Millum, 'Manipulation in the Enrollment of Research Participants', *Hastings Center Report*, 43 (2013), 42.

principles' do not play a role in Hurd's view as they would only detract from the identity of excusing and invalidating conditions that Hurd is keen to emphasise.

Thus, both Hart and Hurd emphasise a close connection between the conditions of consent and responsibility: Hart proposes a (legal) 'analogy', whereas Hurd states (moral and legal) 'identity'. Both Hart and Hurd present a clear challenge to the different ages for criminal responsibility and legal consent: if there really is such a close connection between consent and responsibility, as Hart and Hurd maintain, how could one justify setting the ages for consent and responsibility so differently? To answer this question, and further test Hart's and Hurd's positions from the moral perspective of this chapter, I will now look more closely at each of the conditions of morally valid consent and moral responsibility. Henceforth, I will label these conditions Competence (as precluded by insanity), Information (as precluded by mistakes or ignorance), and Voluntariness (as precluded by pressure).

## Analysing the three conditions of consent and responsibility

### Competence

To give morally valid consent, and to be morally responsible, a person must be competent, by which I mean that they must possess the mental capacities for comprehending their specific situation and engaging in adequate reasoning about it. Being insane, for instance, precludes one's competence.

However, competence is *issue-specific*, which means that the required capacity depends on the issue under consideration: a person may have the capacity to give valid consent to a minor medical procedure, yet lack the capacity required to consent to major surgery.[21] In *A NHS Foundation Trust v Ms X*, for instance, a woman was found competent to make a decision about her alcohol consumption, yet not competent to make a decision about how her anorexia nervosa ought to be treated.[22] Similarly, in the context of responsibility, a kleptomaniac may lack the competence to be held morally responsible for theft (given their medical condition) but still possess the capacity to be held responsible for, say, rape.[23]

Looking at children confirms these points. The doctrine of *Gillick* competence states that children and adolescents can provide legally valid consent only when their maturity and capacity match the complexity of the medical decision under

[21] Tom L. Beauchamp and James F. Childress, *Principles of Biomedical Ethics*, 7th edn (New York, Oxford University Press, 2013), p. 115; Alan Wertheimer, *Consent to Sexual Relations* (Cambridge, Cambridge University Press, 2003), p. 217; Allen E. Buchanan and Dan W. Brock, *Deciding for Others: The Ethics of Surrogate Decision Making* (Cambridge, Cambridge University Press, 1989), pp. 299–334 at 18.

[22] *A NHS Foundation Trust v Ms X* [2014] EWCOP 35..

[23] W. Sinnott-Armstrong and K. Levy, 'Insanity Defenses', in J. Deigh and D. Dolinko (eds), *The Oxford Handbook of Philosophy of Criminal Law* (Oxford, Oxford University Press, 2011), pp. 299–334 at 308.

consideration,[24] and the same is true for morally valid consent. Thus, an adolescent may possess the maturity needed to decide with respect to a low-stakes, routine medical procedure but not the maturity required to make a decision about treatment options when their life is at stake. Similarly, children's maturity also needs to match the kind of wrongdoing they are accused of, or otherwise they could not be morally responsible for it.[25]

Hence, so far, the aspect of issue-specificity applies equally to consent and responsibility. But there are also principled differences between consent and responsibility with regards to competence. The first difference is that competence to consent primarily requires *prudential* capacity, i.e. the capacity to understand *one's own* situation, values, and interests, whereas competence to be responsible also requires *moral* capacity, i.e. the capacity to understand the situations of *others* and their moral significance. By way of illustration, Tom Beauchamp and James Childress explain that a person's competence for medical consent requires 'the capacity to understand the material information, to make a judgment about this information in light of their values, to intend a certain outcome, and to communicate freely their wishes to caregivers or investigators'.[26] In contrast, competence for responsibility, as David Shoemaker explains, requires 'the capacity to understand, apply, and/or respond to *moral* reasons'.[27] For this reason, someone may be competent to consent, yet not competent to be responsible, as the following case shows:

> *Psychopath*. James, a psychopath, is unable to appreciate or be motivated by moral reasons. Yet, James fully understands his own situation and prudential interests. One day, James consents to getting a tattoo on his forehead despite having promised his partner Janet not to do so. After getting the tattoo, James shows up at an important work meeting of Janet's and embarrasses her.

James' consent to the tattoo is valid. Yet, given the impairment of his moral capacity, he may not properly be held responsible for breaking the promise to Janet and embarrassing her.

A second key difference concerns *tracing*, which applies to responsibility but not to consent. In the context of responsibility, tracing means that a person can be responsible for committing a wrong, even if she did not satisfy the conditions of responsibility *at the time* of committing that wrong, *as long as* she satisfied these

[24] Jonathan Herring, *Medical Law and Ethics*, 8th edn (Oxford, Oxford University Press, 2020), pp. 189–91.

[25] T. M. Scanlon, *Moral Dimensions: Permissibility, Meaning, Blame* (Cambridge, MA, Belknap Press of Harvard University Press, 2008), p. 156.

[26] Beauchamp and Childress, *Principles of Biomedical Ethics*, p. 116. Concerning sexual consent, see Wertheimer, *Consent to Sexual Relations*, p. 215 ff.

[27] David Shoemaker, 'Moral Address, Moral Responsibility, and the Boundaries of the Moral Community', *Ethics*, 118 (2007), 71, emphasis added; cf. Jonathan Herring, 'The Age of Criminal Responsibility and the Age of Consent: Should They Be Any Different', *Northern Ireland Legal Quarterly*, 67 (2016), 343–56; Wertheimer, *Consent to Sexual Relations*, p. 222. However, there are also cases where consenting requires regard for others, rather than oneself, e.g. when parents consent to medical treatment for their child. But even here, the regard for the child is still primarily *prudential* in the sense of being concerned with what is in the child's best interests. Thanks to Thomas Douglas for this pointing this out to me.

conditions at an earlier point in time and, at that point, culpably caused her failure to satisfy them later on. In other words, one can be responsible for a wrong which one committed while lacking competence if one's lack of competence can be *traced back*, and was caused by, some suitably culpable behaviour in the past. The paradigmatic example is drunk driving, where a person may not be competent *while* driving drunk, but *was* competent before intoxicating herself and, by doing so, risked harming others.[28]

In the context of consent, however, tracing does not apply. Even if someone culpably caused her failure to satisfy the conditions of consent, consent may still be invalid. Consider the following case, which brings out the contrast between consent and responsibility in this regard:

> *Drunk Sex.* Jane drinks a lot at a conference and meets Bill at a bar. Bill clearly sees that Jane is heavily intoxicated. Yet, Bill still obtains Jane's consent to sex and acts on it.

Jane lacks the capacity to consent due to her inability to make a reasoned decision about whether to have sex with Bill. For this reason, Jane's consent is insufficiently autonomous, invalid, and does not create the permission Bill would need to have permissible sex with her. If Bill *did* go ahead and sleep with Jane, he would violate Jane's rights and exploit her. The fact that Jane voluntarily intoxicated herself is not significant in this regard.

Yet, Jane may still be responsible for having sex with Bill. For instance, Jane's spouse, Walter, may blame Jane for becoming drunk and cheating on him, especially if Jane has had a history of similar events in the past. But Walter can blame Jane only if she herself drank too much and thereby risked losing control and having sex with another man. By contrast, if Bill spiked Jane's non-alcoholic drink so that she would lose competence, Walter could no longer justifiably blame Jane. Thus, even if the object of consent and responsibility is the same, i.e. sex with Bill, there can be situations in which consent may be invalid without the person being excused.

I suggest that this contrast between consent and responsibility is best explained in terms of tracing. However, even those scholars who deny that responsibility has a tracing condition can recognise an important contrast between consent and responsibility here. These scholars, including Manuel Vargas[29] and Matt King,[30] would still argue that there is an important difference between the situation in which Jane gets drunk by her own decision (and then drives or has sex with Bill) and the situation

[28] John Martin Fischer and Mark Ravizza, *Responsibility and Control: A Theory of Moral Responsibility* (Cambridge, Cambridge University Press, 1998), pp. 49–51; John Martin Fischer and Neal A. Tognazzini, 'The Truth About Tracing', *Noûs*, 43 (2009), 531–56.

[29] Manuel Vargas, 'The Trouble with Tracing,' *Midwest Studies In Philosophy*, 29 (2005), 269–91.

[30] Matt King, 'Traction without Tracing: A (Partial) Solution for Control-Based Accounts of Moral Responsibility', *European Journal of Philosophy*, 22 (2014), 463–82.

in which someone else spikes Jane's drink. Only in the former situation would they consider Jane responsible and their explanation for Jane's responsibility would refer to aspects such as negligence or recklessness, instead of tracing.[31] However, whatever the relevant considerations regarding Jane's responsibility are, they could not equally explain the validity of Jane's consent. For the validity of Jane's consent to having sex with Bill, it is irrelevant whether Jane became drunk by her own decision or whether someone else spiked her drink. Jane will be incapable of giving valid consent regardless of how she became intoxicated. Thus, for those readers who are sceptical about tracing, I leave open that there are other ways of explaining the contrast between responsibility and consent that is at play here. But for the remainder of this chapter, I will rely on the widely accepted notion of tracing.

Hence, I conclude: the conditions of competence for consent and responsibility significantly overlap: both require the ability to grasp key information and reason accordingly. Yet, they also diverge: the capacity for consent is primarily prudential, whereas that for responsibility is primarily moral, and tracing (or some alternative) applies to responsibility but not to consent.

## Information

Second, to give morally valid consent, and to be morally responsible, a person must also be aware of what it is that he is actually doing, namely, that he is, in fact, *consenting to X* or, for instance, that his conduct is *harmful to others.* Certain types of ignorance preclude both valid consent and moral responsibility. With consent, this is often developed into an explicit requirement for information, especially in the medical context about *informed* consent,[32] whereas in the context of responsibility it is often called the *epistemic condition* of responsibility.[33]

Yet, there are also key differences. First, for consent but not responsibility, the relevant information can depend on an individual's own values. For instance, for a professional pianist, the risk that a medical procedure causes slight harm to a finger is highly significant and therefore requires disclosure. Ignorance of it can preclude valid consent.[34] Relatedly, in the context of sexual consent, Tom Dougherty argues that withholding information that would be a 'deal-breaker' for this person will invalidate her consent, so that, again, the relevant information can depend on that individual's own values and preferences.[35] By contrast, an individual's own values are normally irrelevant to determining whether ignorance excuses wrongdoing. The

[31] King, 'Traction without Tracing'.

[32] Beauchamp and Childress, *Principles of Biomedical Ethics*, pp. 125–37.

[33] Philip Robichaud and Jan Willem Wieland, *Responsibility: the Epistemic Condition*, 1st edn (Oxford, Oxford University Press, 2017).

[34] Maximilian Kiener, 'Artificial Intelligence in Medicine and the Disclosure of Risks', *AI & Society*, 36 (2021), 705–7.

[35] Tom Dougherty, 'Sex, Lies, and Consent', *Ethics*, 123 (2013), 717–44.

relevant ignorance is of the facts concerning the harmfulness of one's actions and perhaps also, as a minority of scholars have added, whether one was aware of the existence of certain norms.[36] However, a person's own values and preferences are not significant.[37]

A second key difference concerns tracing, which again applies to responsibility but not to consent. Ignorance excuses only when it is not itself culpable, i.e. when it is not the individual's fault that they are relevantly ignorant. Yet, the same is not normally true for consent. If a person culpably fails to read important information about deciding whether to undergo certain medical procedures, such ignorance can still invalidate consent even if it does not excuse. Consider the following case:

> *Clinical Trial.* Jim participates in a clinical trial that carries the risk of contracting a sexually transmissible disease. Therefore, participants are given information about this risk and are asked to abstain from unprotected sexual intercourse during the duration of the trial. The investigator of the trial hands over an information sheet to Jim, who promises to read it. When Jim and the investigator meet again, Jim has forgotten to read it. Although the investigator notices Jim's ignorance, she does not care and proceeds to obtain Jim's consent. Later, Jim contracts the disease and infects his partner.

Jim's ignorance of the risk of contracting the disease may not excuse him for infecting his partner. He had all the relevant information and negligently failed to read it. Jim's partner can hold him accountable. Yet, Jim's ignorance may still invalidate the consent, at least if the investigator was under a duty to ensure that Jim understood all relevant information. Thus, ignorance can invalidate consent, even if it does not excuse, and this is because tracing normally applies to responsibility but not to consent.

Finally, the requirement of information for consent and responsibility reacts differently when the stakes increase.[38] When stakes increase in decisions of consent, people need *more* information to give valid consent. In medical contexts in particular, undergoing especially intrusive medical procedures requires significant disclosure of information, most notably about the key risks, benefits, and relevant alternatives, whereas the protocol for minor medical procedures, e.g. a blood draw, may not even mention informed consent at all. In the context of responsibility, however, things are different. When the stakes increase, such that one's action could be especially risky or harmful, people are, if anything, under more demanding

[36] cf. F. Rudy-Hiller, 'The Epistemic Condition for Moral Responsibility', in Edward N. Zalta and Uri Nodelman (eds), *Stanford Encyclopedia of Philosophy* (Palo Alto, Metaphysics Research Lab, Stanford University, 2022).

[37] Herring, 'The Age of Criminal Responsibility and the Age of Consent', 349.

[38] There is a debate about whether the same is true for competence, namely, whether increasing stakes also increases the required level of competence, at least in the context of consent. For instance, Beauchamp and Childress deny that stakes are significant in this way (Beauchamp and Childress, *Principles of Biomedical Ethics*, p. 120), whereas Buchanan and Brock argued that they are (Buchanan and Brock, *Deciding for Others*, p. 55). Since this has remained a very controversial area and is not key to my argument in this chapter, I will not discuss it here.

obligations to inform themselves and *fewer* mistakes would actually excuse them. This is because, in high-stakes situations of responsibility, ignorance may more easily reflect insufficient regard for others than it would in low-stakes situations.

Thus, regarding the requirement of information, there is not only overlap between consent and responsibility, in the sense that both require people to be aware of certain key aspects, there are also three key differences concerning the significance of an individual's values, tracing, and the impact of increasing stakes.

### Voluntariness

Finally, morally valid consent and moral responsibility require voluntariness, which means the absence of certain types of pressure, such as coercion or manipulation. Regarding consent, Joseph Millum claims that 'valid consent requires that the person who has the authority to make a decision make that decision herself'.[39] However, when someone is subject to illegitimate controlling influences, e.g. coercion or severe manipulation, she is 'not making the decision (…) herself'[40] and, therefore, her consent is invalid.[41] Regarding responsibility, Hart explains that people acting under coercion lack a fair opportunity to comply with relevant norms and therefore do not deserve blame and punishment,[42] e.g. someone who commits perjury because someone threatened them that they would otherwise be 'cut up'.[43]

However, there are also key differences between consent and responsibility. First, tracing applies to responsibility again, but not to consent. Coercion excuses only if one did not culpably put oneself in a situation where one would be (foreseeably) subject to it. If one joins a criminal gang and is subsequently coerced into committing wrongs, one cannot (at least not normally) rely on such coercion to excuse one's wrongdoing. By contrast, the same is not true for consent. Entering a relationship with an abusive boyfriend does not preserve the validity of one's coerced consent to sex, even when such coercion was foreseeable.

The second difference concerns the effect of increasing stakes. Suppose that I am threatened to be beaten unless I trample my neighbour's flowers. Such a threat might excuse (or even justify) my trampling the flowers. But if the same threat aims to make me kill my neighbour, and I subsequently do kill my neighbour, then the threat may no longer excuse my action, let alone justify it. In such a case, I would

[39] Joseph Millum, 'Consent Under Pressure: The Puzzle of Third Party Coercion', *Ethical Theory and Moral Practice*, 17 (2014), 118.

[40] Millum, 'Consent Under Pressure', 118.

[41] To be clear, although the consenter, literally speaking, still has a choice, the coercion is such that it deprives the consenter of a *meaningful* choice. For further elaboration on literal and meaningful choice, see also John Hyman, *Action, Knowledge, and Will* (Oxford, Oxford University Press, 2015), ch. 4.

[42] Hart, *Punishment and Responsibility*.

[43] *Hudson and Taylor* [1971] 2 QB 202. See also J. Dressler, 'Duress', in J. Deigh and D. Dolinko (eds), *The Oxford Handbook of Philosophy of Criminal Law* (New York, Oxford University Press, 2011), pp. 269–98.

be morally expected to show greater fortitude. Hence, in the context of responsibility, increasing stakes require greater fortitude, and fewer instances of pressure will excuse wrongdoing.

The reverse is true for consent: when stakes increase, some pressure may invalidate consent, even if the same token of pressure would not invalidate consent in a situation with lower stakes. By way of illustration, suppose a patient must decide whether to undergo major surgery or accept the risk of serious exacerbation of his disease. In this context, the physician is under an increased obligation to assist, or at least not sabotage, the patient's decision-making. If the physician *does* sabotage the patient's decision-making, e.g. by body-shaming him in order to obtain consent to the surgery, the physician seriously wrongs the patient. More precisely, the wrong caused by such body-shaming is also more serious in a high-stakes situation than it would have been in a low-stakes situation, e.g. when the physician uses this tactic to make the patient consent to a new diet. This is because, in a high-stakes situation, manipulative conduct displays even greater disrespect for the patient's autonomy and well-being. However, when exerting pressure becomes more seriously wrong, it is also more likely that such pressure invalidates consent, since the illegitimacy of the exerted pressure has a bearing on the validity of consent.[44]

Hurd objects to such reasoning and claims the opposite: 'the greater the interest we have at stake, the greater should be the coercion required to tempt our compromise of it'.[45] In her view, when people are 'willing to sacrifice an important interest to avoid a fairly trivial threat', they are 'pathetic' and make 'bad choices'. Yet, they '[do not] manifest a lack of autonomy' that would invalidate their consent.[46] In addition, Hurd says, judging the consent of these people to be invalid in response to low pressure can be 'condescending (…) [and] paternalistic'.[47] It can be condescending because this would portray a person's autonomy as more fragile than it actually is, and it can be paternalistic because it risks taking away from people the power to give valid consent when it is most important to them. Here, Hurd suggests that the higher the stakes are for a person, the more resilient she will be.

To be clear: I agree with Hurd that trivial threats should not invalidate consent, and there has to be some threshold below which pressure does not affect the validity of consent.[48] Otherwise, the conditions of consent may indeed be condescending

[44] Millum, 'Consent Under Pressure'; Alan Wertheimer, 'Voluntary Consent: Why a Value-Neutral Concept Won't Work', *Journal of Medicine and Philosophy*, 37 (2012), 226–54; Maximilian Kiener, 'Consent and Living Organ Donation', *Journal of Medical Ethics*, 47 (2021), 1–4; Maximilian Kiener, 'When Do Nudges Undermine Voluntary Consent?', *Philosophical Studies*, 178 (2021), 4201–26; Tom Dougherty, 'Why Does Duress Undermine Consent?', *Nous* (2019), 317–33. Also, note that the previous three paragraphs contained verbatim phrases from my book *Voluntary Consent: Theory and Practice* (London, Routledge, 2023), ch. 5.

[45] Hurd, 'The Moral Magic of Consent', 143.

[46] Hurd, 'The Moral Magic of Consent', 143.

[47] Hurd, 'The Moral Magic of Consent', 145.

[48] For discussion of this view, see Dougherty, 'Sexual Misconduct on a Scale: Gravity, Coercion, and Consent,' *Ethics*, 131 (2021), 319–44.

and paternalistic. However, I disagree with Hurd that higher stakes should require more serious pressure because people do not normally become more resilient when the stakes increase, and they are certainly not pathetic when they give in to less serious pressure. For instance, when the stakes for patients increase, they are often already in pain or fear and therefore not likely to be more resilient to pressure than someone who has to decide over minor procedures, e.g. whether to have a wisdom tooth pulled out. A similar situation arises for children and adolescents. When stakes increase, they might be intimidated and more deferential to adults rather than more resilient. Children are, to use Keating's words, particularly 'liable to be vulnerable and impressionable'[49] in these contexts. Thus, Hurd's claim about increased resilience is, as a matter of empirical fact, doubtful. Furthermore, her claim that people who give in to less serious threats tend to be 'pathetic' is not convincing either: a patient who succumbs to body-shaming or a child who becomes exceptionally deferential in a high-stakes situation may show weakness but not pathetic character. For this reason, we should reject Hurd's view and side with my suggestion that increasing stakes can lower the requirements for pressure to invalidate consent.

Finally, regarding the requirement of voluntariness, there are some additional anomalies that require an explanation. In cases of third-party coercion, i.e. those where A consents to B performing a certain act only because the third-party C coerced A into consenting, A's consent can still be valid, depending on the role of the consent-receiver.[50] Consider the following case (inspired by Millum[51]):

> *Tattoo.* Coercer threatens to injure Victim severely if Victim does not consent to receiving a tattoo from Recipient. Recipient cannot help Victim escape this situation in any way other than executing the tattoo. Victim therefore consents to Recipient going ahead.

Since Recipient can assist Victim solely by providing the tattoo, and given Victim's request on these grounds, Recipient can permissibly administer the tattoo. More precisely, Recipient can do so without *wronging* Victim, that is, without infringing upon Victim's rights. However, a widely shared principle in the ethics of consent, which we may term the *Permissibility Principle*, stipulates that the permissibility of certain actions (e.g. administering a tattoo), specifically in the sense that there is no wronging, requires valid consent. Therefore, this scenario illustrates that we cannot presuppose that coercion invariably invalidates consent, regardless of the source. Instead, this case prompts a closer examination of the relation between consent and coercion.

[49] Heather Keating, 'The Responsibility of Children in the Criminal Law', *Child & Family Law Quarterly*, 19 (2007), 186.

[50] Mollie Gerver, 'Consent and Third-Party Coercion,' *Ethics*, 131 (2021), 246–69; Dougherty, 'Why Does Duress Undermine Consent?'.

[51] Millum, 'Consent Under Pressure'.

As I argue elsewhere,[52] coercion invalidates consent only if consent was 'obtained by' coercion but not if consent was 'merely motivated by' coercion. Consent is 'obtained by' coercion when the consent-receiver (1) exerts or collaborates in exerting the coercion, (2) exploits the coercion, or (3) facilitates the success of the coercion in some other significant, morally culpable sense (e.g. by omitting to provide help when doing so is possible and feasible). In *Tattoo*, Recipient did none of this. On the other hand, consent is 'merely motivated by' coercion' if a person's reason for consenting is to prevent a threat from being carried out but the threat came from a third party and the consent-receiver neither contributed to it nor wronged the victim in any of the three ways outlined above. And this was the case in *Tattoo.*

Thus, if this is correct, then coercion does not always invalidate consent. Whether it does depends on the role of the person receiving consent. But things are different when we look at responsibility. If, in the case *Tattoo*, Victim previously promised to their spouse never to get a tattoo, Victim could still be excused on the grounds that there was severe coercion. Thus, cases like *Tattoo* show that even if coercion does not invalidate consent it may still provide an excuse.

Further divergence between consent and responsibility is illustrated in the following case:

> *Scam.* Bill and Cameron share a bank account, with each of them having the authority to permit certain transactions unilaterally. One day, Bill gets a phone call and a bluffing threat makes him transfer money to another bank account. Due to the threat, Bill's consent is not valid. Yet, Cameron may still blame Bill for falling for the scam. Cameron may justifiably hold Bill to a standard that requires that Bill not give in to such manipulation. Such a bluffing threat had already been made a couple of times to Bill, and Cameron had warned Bill about it previously, but Bill panicked and did not think about it.

Here, the object of consent and responsibility is the same: transferring money. And I take it that the threat invalidates Bill's consent, while, at least in some such circumstances, it may not excuse Bill's conduct. Consent is invalid because Bill is severely wronged in how his consent is obtained. However, Bill may not be excused, at least not vis-à-vis Cameron, if the situation is such that Bill ought to have known better and withstood the threat. Bill's excuse will, to some extent, depend on the norms that govern his relation to Cameron and, potentially, also on further details of the case. But I suggest that there is a plausible reading of the case in which Bill would not be excused for this action.

To conclude the discussion of voluntariness: consent and responsibility do indeed share voluntariness as a key condition. But there are also key differences concerning tracing, the effects of increasing stakes, and further anomalies peculiar to consent and responsibility, as illustrated by *Tattoo* and *Scam.*

[52] Maximilian Kiener, 'Consenting under Third-Party Coercion', *Journal of Moral Philosophy*, 19 (2021), 361–89.

## A novel relationship-based view

So, let us take stock. Morally valid consent and moral responsibility share the conditions of competence, information, and voluntariness. Moreover, these conditions make similar demands for consent and responsibility: people need to possess the capacity to grasp material information and reason accordingly, they need to be aware of what they are doing to various degrees, and they need to be free from illegitimate pressure, such as coercion. Thus, from this perspective, Hart and Hurd are right to point out a strong parallel between consent and responsibility, not only from a legal (Hart) but also from a moral (Hurd) perspective.

Yet, my analysis has also highlighted key differences between consent and responsibility. Some of them are easy to explain. For instance, recall that competence is always issue-specific. Thus, if the 'issue' of responsibility is wrongdoing and the 'issue' of consent is the pursuit of one's interests, it is easy to see that the capacity for responsibility is primarily *moral* whereas that for consent is primarily *prudential*. Moreover, for the same reason, the information relevant to consent can depend on a person's *own* values, whereas the information relevant to responsibility does not.

However, other differences cannot be explained so easily, most notably why tracing only applies to responsibility but not to consent, why increasing stakes affect consent and responsibility differently, and what lies behind the anomalies in my examples *Tattoo* and *Scam*. In what follows, I will present a unified explanation of these differences and thereby elaborate on Hart's idea that there is indeed a close 'analogy' between the conditions of consent and responsibility, albeit not 'identity' in Hurd's sense.

### Tracing

Responsibility has a tracing condition because, as members of a moral community, we can expect each other not to create circumstances that make it more likely that we wrong and harm others. Therefore, people have to bear the risk of blame and punishment when they intoxicate themselves, culpably fail to inform themselves, or put themselves in a position where others will foreseeably coerce them into wrongdoing. In so acting, a person shows insufficient regard for, or commitment to, the interests of others and thereby rules out an excuse for their behaviour.

By contrast, the same reasoning does not apply to consent. Even if a person intoxicates herself (*Drunk Sex*), culpably fails to acquire relevant information (*Clinical Trial*), or puts herself in a position where others will coerce her (the example of the abusive boyfriend), another person may not normally obtain valid consent from this person on the grounds that the consenter herself brought about her situation. This is because, in the role of a consent-receiver, people are obliged, at a minimum, not to take advantage of the consent-giver's weakness. I take this to be a norm fundamental to the consenter (consent-giver)–consentee (consent-receiver) relationship. Although the norms of this relationship may vary across contexts, e.g. the medical and sexual contexts, they will always shape what people owe each other, and thereby also affect the conditions of valid consent.[53]

Thus, to understand the differences between consent and responsibility with regards to tracing, we need to attend closely to the relevant relationships: when thinking about responsibility, the relationship between members of a moral or legal community is central, while thinking about consent requires that we focus on the relationship between consenter and consentee.

## Increasing stakes

This line of reasoning can also help to explain the differences concerning the effect of increasing stakes. When stakes increase in the context of responsibility, members of a moral community can demand from each other not to fail to abide by the moral norms too easily, so that the values of the moral or legal community will be sufficiently protected. George Fletcher and Antony Duff highlight this aspect clearly in the legal context. When Fletcher discusses duress, he claims that the relevant question is 'what we can fairly expect of each other in a civilized society',[54] where the term 'civilised society' purports to highlight the norms of this specific legal community; and when Duff discusses duress, he claims that the relevant question is what 'kind and degree of courage we can properly demand of citizens'[55] when crucial values and interests are at stake, thereby also stressing the community of citizens as the decisive factor in determining whether an excuse is available. My own view expands on these thoughts. Whereas Fletcher and Duff argue that *legal* responsibility is shaped by the norms of the *legal* community, and I argue that *moral* responsibility is shaped by the norms of the *moral* community.

A similar rationale explains why increased stakes affect consent differently, namely, why they may make requirements more demanding so that even *lower* pressure could invalidate consent. Consider the medical context again: for reasons previously outlined, when a patient has to make a very important decision, the physician's obligation not to sabotage the decision-making becomes more stringent. This obligation is a central norm in the patient–physician relationship and is especially important in the context of obtaining consent. So, the ultimate explanation of why the consent requirements change in the way they do when stakes increase has, once again, to do with the norms of the relationship between the consenter (patient) and consentee (physician). If the physician violates these norms and thereby induces the patient to consent, she disqualifies herself as someone receiving the patient's permission to proceed, and therefore cannot obtain valid consent.

[53] Kiener, 'When Do Nudges Undermine Voluntary Consent?'.

[54] George P. Fletcher, *Basic Concepts of Criminal Law* (New York, Oxford University Press, 1998), p. 83.

[55] Antony Duff, 'Rule-Violations and Wrongdoings', in S. Shute and A. Simester (eds), *Criminal Law Theory: Doctrines of the General Part* (Oxford, Oxford University Press, 2002), pp. 47–74 at 64.

Thus, the explanation of the different effects of increasing stakes for consent and responsibility is ultimately the same as the explanation of why tracing normally only applies to responsibility but not to consent. In both cases, the norms of the relevant relationship shape the conditions of consent and responsibility.[56]

### Further anomalies

Finally, the cases concerning third-party coercion also show that the validity of consent can crucially depend on the norms of the consenter–consentee relationship. Consent is valid in cases of third-party coercion if and only if the consentee complies with what he owes to the consenter in this interaction. Thus, it is not a coincidence that, for consent, it is the person exerting coercion who plays a fundamental role. The same is not true for responsibility, where different relational norms play a role. For this reason, the consent given to *Recipient* in *Tattoo* could be valid, yet consenting to the tattoo may be something that the person is excused for vis-à-vis other members of the moral community or, per my example, vis-à-vis a particular person who received the consentee's promise not to get tattooed.

Finally, these aspects concerning relationships also explain the intuitively plausible verdict in *Scam*: consent is invalid since the process by which it was obtained violates norms which the consentee must abide by. Yet, even if this is correct, the person giving invalid consent may still be responsible to others for succumbing to certain influences, as the norms which govern the relationship to those others may justifiably hold the consenter to a higher standard. Thus, explaining the divergence of the conditions of consent and responsibility in these cases again requires that we take into account the specific norms of the relationship.

### Relevant relationships

In conclusion, I therefore suggest that we can explain the differences between consent and responsibility by analysing the norms of the relevant relationship, namely, that of either the consenter–consentee relationship or of the moral/legal community. The key idea here is that understanding the conditions of consent and responsibility requires not just an *intra*-personal perspective, i.e. looking at a person in isolation, but also an *inter*-personal perspective, i.e. looking at a person *in relation to others*.

The consenting person relates to others as a *source* of demands and the *content* of such demands includes that others respect the consenter's vulnerability and not take advantage of her, even when she, for instance, culpably intoxicates herself. By contrast, the (allegedly) responsible person relates to others as an *addressee* of demands and the *content* of such demands includes that *she* show sufficient

[56] The previous three paragraphs contained verbatim phrases from my book Kiener, *Voluntary Consent*, ch. 5.

resilience, fortitude, and diligence in complying with the norms of the moral/legal community.

These demands are interpersonal, or second-personal, in the sense that they concern what people may demand *from each other*. They constitute the moral backbone of relationships: the consenter–consentee relationship is shaped by the moral fact that the consenter is a source of demands for consideration and against exploitation, whereas the relationship between responsible agents is shaped by the moral fact that everyone is an addressee of demands for fortitude and resilience.

Once we allow the norms of these relationships to have a bearing on the conditions of consent and responsibility, we can neatly explain the relevant differences. In *Drunk Sex*, Jane culpably intoxicated herself. Yet, her consent is still invalid because obtaining such consent would disregard Jane as a source of the demand against exploiting her situation. In cases of drunk driving, however, the culpably intoxicated drivers are still responsible because they remain addressees of the demand for diligence in complying with important moral or legal norms. Thus, when we determine *how* the conditions of competence, information, and voluntariness apply to consent and responsibility, respectively, we need to adopt an interpretation of these conditions that conforms with the norms of the respective relationship, i.e. the consenter–consentee relationship or of the moral/legal community.

Finally, note that this proposal not only explains why the validity conditions for consent differ from the excusing conditions for moral wrongdoing. It can also make sense of the substantial overlap since, on this view, both sets of conditions ultimately depend on how the person under consideration relates to others. Thus, understanding the conditions of consent and responsibility requires an inter-personal approach, sensitive to the norms that govern the moral relations between people, either as consenting parties who can create permissions or as responsible agents who can be liable to blame.

## Re-evaluating the age differences for responsibility and consent

Let me now use my results to return to the differences in age for criminal responsibility and legally valid consent. My proposed view suggests a two-pronged approach, according to which we can evaluate the difference in ages on psychological (or descriptive) grounds and on normative grounds.

### Psychological grounds

The psychological grounds follow on from my discussion of competence. I argued that competence for consent and responsibility is issue-specific. Thus, if the object of consent, that is, what a person consents to, and the object of responsibility, that is, the wrong a person is responsible for, differ in relevant respects, then the required psychological capacity for consent and responsibility will differ too. Thus, age differences for consent and responsibility could be justified if, as a matter of fact, the competence needed for moral responsibility is lower than the competence needed for consent.

However, there is considerable controversy here. Lyons argues that the capacity needed for consent and responsibility is essentially the same: there 'seems little difference in the capacities required to be prospectively responsible for choices or actions that pertain to either criminal acts or one's personal healthcare decisions'.[57] Barry Lyons mentions the fictitious case of the 15-year-old Mary who can be convicted of murder but cannot refuse her own life-saving treatment. Lyons claims that, in both cases, Mary needs to understand the concepts of death and fatal action, and it is therefore inconsistent to hold Mary responsible for murder but then deny her ability to validly refuse treatment for herself.

By contrast, Jill Craigie and Alicia Coram suggest that the capacity for responsibility may be more demanding than the capacity for consent: 'from the perspective of ascribing culpability, the competent agent has capacities *over and above* those that are currently considered relevant in the context of the right to make one's own treatment decisions',[58] and Craigie makes explicit that this speaks in favour of 'adopting a more demanding standard for criminal responsibility [than for valid consent]'.[59] Keating builds on this point and states that the moral capacity needed for responsibility, especially the capacity to understand right and wrong, is demanding. It is not just a 'matter of rote learning—it is wrong to steal, it is wrong to fight [but rather a matter of more fundamentally] *understanding* the difference between right and wrong',[60] where right and wrong are genuine moral categories and do not just mean 'naughty', 'disapproved of by others', or 'likely to attract censure'.

Finally, Jonathan Herring holds the opposite view and suggests that the capacity needed for criminal responsibility is lower than the capacity needed for valid consent. He says: 'It may well be that children, through the education system, will develop more quickly an awareness of the rules of society [as required for criminal responsibility], than the kind of self-knowledge needed to adopt their own values [as required for valid consent].'[61]

This dispute will depend on empirical facts to a considerable extent, namely when exactly children develop the respective capacity for consent and for responsibility, and I cannot therefore settle this dispute here. Yet, I can draw a more general conclusion from my previous results: the diversity of different objects of consent and

[57] Barry Lyons, 'Dying to Be Responsible: Adolescence, Autonomy and Responsibility,' *Legal Studies*, 30 (2010), 257–78 at 275.

[58] J. Craigie and A. Coram, 'Irrationality, Mental Capacities, and Neuroscience', in N. A. Vincent (ed.), *Neuroscience and Legal Responsibility* (Oxford University Press, 2013), pp. 89–105 at 100, emphasis added.

[59] J. Craigie, 'Against a Singular Understanding of Legal Capacity: Criminal Responsibility and the Convention on the Rights of Persons with Disabilities', *International Journal of Law and Psychiatry*, 40 (2015), 6–14 at 12.

[60] Keating, 'The Responsibility of Children in the Criminal Law', 193, original emphasis.

[61] Herring, 'The Age of Criminal Responsibility and the Age of Consent', 350.

responsibility makes it unlikely that, from a moral (as opposed to a legal) point of view, the age of responsibility should *always* be lower or higher or the same than the age of consent. It is precisely the relativity to the issue under consideration that requires a more fine-grained analysis. It could be that a child may be competent to decide over simple medical procedures, yet not be competent to be responsible for a more complex form of wrongdoing, or that the child lacks competence for a complicated medical procedure but has competence for simple and salient types of wrongdoing. Thus, even if the law has reasons to set a *general* age for consent and responsibility, my moral analysis of competence does not support this either way. In fact, the point about issue-specificity suggests that an approach like that of *Gillick* competence would be appropriate to account for diverse situations and levels of maturity, not only in relation to consent but also in relation to responsibility. Therefore, from the perspective of my analysis, the view that the age threshold for responsibility should generally be lower than that of consent cannot find support.

## Normative grounds

However, in addition to psychological grounds, my view also allows for normative considerations to play a role in determining the conditions for consent and responsibility. This is because my discussion of tracing, increasing stakes, and further anomalies (as illustrated by *Tattoo* and *Scam*) showed that relationship norms can shape the conditions of consent and responsibility too, beyond mere psychological considerations about capacity. Accordingly, we could ask if the values and normative considerations that underpin the conditions of responsibility and consent justify the diverging ages.

To test this route, let us ask what the normative considerations behind a lower age of responsibility would be and whether these are consistent with, or are even supported by, the considerations that my analysis has highlighted.

Craigie explained that the reasons behind a lower age of criminal responsibility could be twofold, namely, about 'being "tough on crime" (…) [and] being committed to substantive views on the value of life and health'.[62] Being tough on crime means sending a clear signal to children and adolescents that their wrongs will be prosecuted and punished, assuming that such a signal will deter and reduce crimes. Yet, this assumption presupposes that children possess sufficient competence to understand the signal. Therefore, this approach cannot justify a lower age of responsibility independent of a psychological assessment of children's competence. If children at 10 years old cannot sufficiently understand relevant moral and legal norms, there is simply no point in sending them 'a clear signal'. To corroborate this suggestion, consider the 10-year-old Thompson, one of the children who killed James Bulger, who is reported to have asked the police whether they took his victim James to the

[62] Craigie, 'Against a Singular Understanding of Legal Capacity', 12.

hospital 'to get him alive again'.[63] Such a child is very unlikely to have understood the fatal nature of his acts, let alone their moral repugnance. Thus, being tough on children like him is very unlikely to deter children of similar competence.

At this point, however, one may concede that punishing Thompson may not deter children *like him*, who also lack sufficient maturity, but one may still insist that it could deter other, more mature adolescents, thereby making clear to them that they will also be held responsible for their crimes, and this message could have an overall deterrent effect. I leave open whether this is, empirically speaking, correct because my objection to this view goes deeper. If the punishment of Thompson becomes a means to deter others from crime, Thompson would be instrumentalised in the sense that the authorities would not address him on an interpersonal basis, i.e. as a member of the moral community capable of guiding his actions with appropriate reasons and of responding to the authorities' charges adequately. Nor would they put Thompson's interest and well-being at the centre of their deliberation. Rather, they would use him as a carrier of a message to others. But if my previous analysis is correct, most notably that the conditions of moral responsibility, including appropriately holding someone morally responsible, is crucially shaped by the norms governing the relationships between people as moral agents, then this instrumentalisation of Thompson lacks moral justification and speaks against holding him responsible.

Furthermore, T. M. Scanlon may have an even stronger objection to punishing children like Thompson. He might say that, even if Thompson *were* competent, punishing him like an adult is unjustified because it neglects the special relationship that society has with children. He says:

> Even when children understand full well why they should not do something, they may not be blamed for doing it in the same way that an adult would be. I believe that the explanation lies in the ways in which our normal relationship with a child (our own child or even someone else's) differs from our relationship with normal adults. Our relationship with children is an unequal one because of the child's relative lack of development, including moral development. It is a tutelary relationship: we are to understand that children are 'just learning' and to help them grow. Our relationships with children thus lack certain elements of our relationships with normal adults.[64]

Hence, the 'tough on crime' approach illegitimately instrumentalises children (my argument), and potentially also fails to acknowledge their special position within that community (Scanlon's argument). Therefore, 'being tough on crime' does not provide a justification for having a very low age of responsibility in comparison to the age of consent.

But what about the value of life? If we want to save lives, it seems that we should be strict when it comes to the commission of wrongdoing, such as physical violence, i.e. we should hold people with a low level of competence responsible, but not when it comes to consenting to medical treatment or withholding consent

[63] *Wikipedia*, 'Murder of James Bulger'.

[64] Scanlon, *Moral Dimensions: Permissibility, Meaning, Blame*, p. 156; see also Meghan Winsby, 'The Prospective Stance: Children and Responsibility', in this volume, pp. 253–71.

in a serious medical context as too low a competence level could lead to self-harm or death. Thus, a low responsibility level and a high consent level may best protect people's health and lives.

But again, it is doubtful whether holding those with low levels of competence responsible for their actions really saves lives and protects others. It is still an open question as to whether low responsibility levels prevent wrongdoing. Moreover, it could be detrimental to those incompetent perpetrators whose experience in penal rather than educational facilities could make their lives considerably worse, could increase recidivism, and could harm them in significant, even life-threatening, ways. On the other side, it is equally doubtful whether high levels of competence for consent best protect the consenter, or whether they deprive at least a significant number of individuals of very valuable opportunities to exercise their autonomy. Thus, it seems that, here too, we would need a more flexible, *Gillick*-style approach to do justice to the individual under consideration. But most importantly, these different standards for consent and responsibility would neither respond to an individual's traits nor to his or her normative relationship with others, but rather just impose on individuals a certain conception of what is deemed valuable or desirable by the society. As a result, the conditions of consent and responsibility would fail to address individuals interpersonally, i.e. as reasoning members within a certain community, and thereby threatens to instrumentalise juvenile offenders just as the goal of 'being tough on crime' did.

Thus, I conclude that, from the perspective of my moral analysis, the strict rule that the age of responsibility is lower than the age of consent cannot be justified. We need a more fine-grained approach and should be particularly critical of wide age gaps, like those in the UK, where the age of criminal responsibility is 10 years, the age at which a minor is found *Gillick* competence will often be higher, and the age of consent to sex is 16 years.

## Conclusion

This chapter compared the conditions of morally valid consent with the conditions of moral responsibility (as accountability). After analysing Hart's *analogy* account and Hurd's *identity* account, I focused on the three shared conditions of consent and responsibility in detail: competence, information, and voluntariness. On the basis of significant differences between consent and responsibility, I rejected Hurd's identity view but developed a novel *analogy* account, which was based on, but also went beyond, Hart's claims. I argued that relationship norms allow us to explain the differences between the conditions of consent and responsibility without relinquishing the view that there is a close connection between consent and responsibility. I finally used this view to propose a two-pronged approach in the evaluation of different ages for criminal responsibility and legally valid consent. I argued that different ages are morally justifiable in principle, yet a great divergence between them, such as that which exists in the UK, is unlikely to be justified.

# 15

# What's Special About Juvenile Justice?

DAVID O. BRINK*

THE WAR ON crime in the United States that began in the 1980s and 1990s included demands to get tough on juvenile crime. A significant part of the war on juvenile crime was the trend to transfer juvenile offenders to adult criminal court, where the length and nature of sanctions are much more punitive than in juvenile court. Though enthusiasm for the war on crime has abated somewhat recently, many of those laws—including the transfer trend—are still on the books in many jurisdictions and a feature of juvenile justice in the United States.

The trend to transfer juvenile offenders to adult criminal court treats juvenile offenders as on a par morally and legally with their adult counterparts. Many commentators find the transfer trend deeply problematic and claim that we ought to recognise a moral *asymmetry* in our treatment of juvenile and adult crime such that all else being equal juvenile crime deserves less punishment than adult crime. The transfer trend is problematic because it denies this asymmetry. This chapter explores different rationales for this asymmetry and its significance.

A *political rationale* claims that the disenfranchisement of juveniles compromises *the state's authority* to punish juveniles in the way it may punish adults. The political rationale employs a conception of *democratic* legitimacy and appeals to the categorical difference in the voting rights of juveniles and adults. By contrast, a *developmental rationale* claims that juveniles *deserve* to be punished less than adults because their immaturity makes them less responsible and, hence, less culpable for their wrongdoing. The developmental rationale appeals to retributive

* This chapter develops ideas in my earlier work on juvenile justice—David O. Brink, 'Immaturity, Normative Competence, and Juvenile Transfer', *Texas Law Review*, 82 (2004), 1555–85; David O. Brink, 'The Moral Asymmetry Between Juvenile and Adult Offenders', *Criminal Law and Philosophy*, 14 (2020), 223–39; and David O. Brink, *Fair Opportunity and Responsibility* (Oxford, Clarendon Press, 2021), ch. 12. I would like to thank Craig Agule, Amy Berg, Isra Black, Lisa Forsberg, Erin Kelly, Robert Leventer, Stephen Morse, Anthony Skelton, and Gideon Yaffe for helpful feedback on earlier versions of this material.

*Proceedings of the British Academy*, **279**, 293–315, © Authors 2025.

ideas about punishment and plausible claims about the way in which immaturity affects responsibility and culpability. This chapter explores limitations in the political rationale and defends a qualified version of the developmental rationale for the moral asymmetry between juvenile and adult offenders.

This qualified developmental rationale underlies recent Supreme Court cases recognising upper limits on the severity of juvenile punishments in which the Court has defended limitations on the application of the death penalty and life imprisonment without the possibility of parole (LWOP) to juvenile offenders. However, the developmental rationale for the moral asymmetry of juvenile and adult offenders has more radical implications for both juvenile and adult sentencing. The need for such sentence limitations for juveniles only arises because of the transfer of juveniles to adult criminal court, which is itself in tension with recognising the moral asymmetry of juvenile and adult offenders. Moreover, the Court's broadly retributive recognition of the need to condition juvenile sentencing on a determination of the offender's degree of maturity and culpability is equally applicable to adult sentencing. Like juveniles, adults are owed sentences that reflect their degree of culpability, which argues against mandatory minimum sentences altogether. If the argument of this chapter is correct, there is something special about juvenile justice that explains a moral asymmetry between juvenile and adult offenders. That rationale not only condemns the transfer trend but also has important implications for sentencing within adult criminal court.

## The traditional juvenile court

Prior to the adoption of a separate juvenile court, adolescents or teenage minors were treated by the law as adults. But in the 20th century new ideas about child development, education, and socialisation led to a rethinking of appropriate institutional responses to juvenile misconduct. A developmental perspective led many legal analysts to treat juvenile offenders as immature in ways that made them less accountable and culpable for their wrongdoing than their adult counterparts and to see them as more corrigible than adult offenders. These changes led to the adoption of a separate juvenile court.[1]

The traditional juvenile court is different from adult criminal court in significant ways. Whereas defendants in adult criminal court can elect to have jury trials, the trials in juvenile court are bench trials, conducted by judges with experience in juvenile justice. Defendants in juvenile court experience different sentencing

[1] See e.g. John Whitehead and Steven Lab, *Juvenile Justice*, 9th edn (Boston, MA, Routledge, 2018) and Howard Snyder and Melissa Sickmund, *Juvenile Offenders and Victims: 2006 National Report* (Washington, DC, Department of Justice, Office of Juvenile Justice and Delinquency Programs, 2006), ch. 4.

and incarceration outcomes. Unless extended through the use of blended sentencing, sentences in juvenile court expire at the age of majority, and so are much shorter than sentences for comparable offences in adult court. Juvenile criminal records are sealed, whereas there is public access to the criminal records of adult offenders. Juveniles do not suffer post-incarceration penalties that are imposed on adult felons, such as disenfranchisement, loss of public assistance, and the duty to report conviction to potential employers. Finally, juvenile offenders are sentenced to juvenile correctional facilities, which are less dangerous than adult correctional facilities and which are supposed to address the developmental, nutritional, physical, educational, and vocational needs of juvenile offenders.

## The transfer trend

In response to perceived increases in violent youth crime in the United States, especially associated with drug trafficking, the 1980s and 1990s witnessed a national trend toward getting tough on youth crime and holding juvenile offenders more accountable. A central element in this national trend is the transfer of juveniles to adult criminal court, where the consequences of conviction are in various ways much more severe than they are in juvenile court.

The most traditional mechanism for trying juveniles as adults is the *judicial waiver* or transfer of the juvenile to adult criminal court. The judicial waiver occurs in a juvenile court hearing, decided on a case-by-case basis. The Model Penal Code §4.10 contemplates that the waiver will occur only in cases in which the juvenile is at least 16 years old. It does not specify the conditions in which such a waiver is appropriate. Traditionally, juvenile court judges have taken into consideration the age and maturity of the accused, the prior record of the accused (e.g. whether he is a repeat offender), and the severity or seriousness of the offence. Several states have passed legislation that affects the judicial waiver, effectively expanding its scope. For instance, several states have lowered the age at which the judicial waiver can be issued either as a general matter or for certain categories of offence. In effect, the judicial waiver, as traditionally conceived, creates a presumption in favour of trying the accused juvenile as a juvenile, a presumption which could only be rebutted on a case-by-case basis when it was shown that the juvenile was sufficiently mature and had already shown signs of sufficient incorrigibility as to justify treating him as an adult. Recently, several states have also expanded the scope of the judicial waiver by shifting the presumption from juvenile jurisdiction to adult jurisdiction for certain ages and categories of offence. Partly as the result of such statutory changes the scope of the judicial waiver has expanded considerably.

Another mechanism of transfer to adult court involves *prosecutorial discretion.* Legislation in several states gives prosecutors the authority, either as a general rule or in special circumstances relating to the age of the accused and the category of offence, to determine whether to bring the case in adult court. This mechanism allows the prosecutor to bypass the need for a judicial hearing and waiver. Recent legislation has simultaneously expanded prosecutorial discretion—expanding the pool of cases in which prosecutors can exercise their discretion to try juveniles as adults—and restricted it—by creating presumptions for transfer for certain ages and categories of offence. Both kinds of change in prosecutorial discretion have had the effect of increasing the number of transfers.

Judicial waiver and prosecutorial discretion do not amount to mandated transfer. Even when there is a presumption in favour of transfer, it can be rebutted in individual cases. Perhaps the most significant and disturbing aspect of the transfer trend is the legislative adoption in many states of *mandatory transfer* statutes that exclude certain cases from juvenile court and require such cases to be processed in adult criminal court, bypassing both judicial and prosecutorial scrutiny over the appropriate forum for the accused. Typically, mandatory transfers lower the age at which juvenile cases go to adult court either as a general rule or for special categories of violent offence, such as murder, rape, and aggravated assault. Many states have now adopted some kind of mandatory transfer regime.

The situation in California, where juvenile transfer has been and is evolving, is instructive. Adoption of Proposition 21 in 2000 added a mandatory transfer to the California Welfare and Institutions Code §707(b) requiring that juveniles 14 years of age or older be tried as adults in cases where they are accused of murder or various sexual offences, including rape, forcible sodomy, and lewd and lascivious acts with a child under the age of 14. Subsequently, the provisions of Proposition 21 and §707(b) were amended by the adoption of Proposition 57 in 2016, permitting the transfer of juveniles as young as 14 accused of §707(b) offences to adult criminal court but making the transfer conditional on prosecutorial petition and judicial approval. Proposition 57 shows that enthusiasm for mandatory transfer has abated. But it still permits transfer, subject to prosecutorial and judicial discretion, of juveniles as young as 14. In 2018, Senate Bill 1391 went further than Proposition 57, eliminating authority to transfer juveniles who are 14 or 15. In 2019, the California Courts of Appeal upheld the constitutionality of SB 1391.[2] As California illustrates, attitudes toward the transfer trend are changing.[3] But California is more progressive than many jurisdictions; in many jurisdictions the transfer trend is still strong, and even in California discretionary forms of juvenile transfer for 16 and 17-year-olds remain in effect.

The net result of such departures from the Model Penal Code provisions for juvenile transfer is that more juveniles are being transferred to adult court at younger ages for a broader variety of crimes.[4] Though enthusiasm for the transfer

[2] *People v Superior Court* (S.L.), Court of Appeal of California, Sixth Appellate District (2019).

[3] Many thanks to Commissioner Robert Leventer for explaining developments in juvenile transfer in California since the adoption of Proposition 21 in 2000.

[4] The trend is well documented in P. Griffin, P. Torbert, and L. Szymanski, *Trying Juveniles as Adults in Criminal Court: An Analysis of State Transfer Provisions* (Washington, DC, Office of Juvenile Justice and Delinquency Prevention, 1998); Snyder and Sickmund, *Juvenile Offenders and Victims*, ch. 4; and Whitehead and Lab, *Juvenile Justice*, ch. 8.

trend may have lessened somewhat in the last decade, the legacy of the transfer trend is still with us, especially in jurisdictions with mandatory transfer of young adolescents still on the books.

It is this broad trend to try juveniles as adults and, in particular, the trend to try ever-younger juveniles as adults on account of the seriousness of their offences that ought to raise serious jurisprudential concerns. The transfer trend denies that there is anything special about juvenile justice. The extreme expression of this trend would be the *abolition* of the juvenile court altogether, treating juvenile offenders exactly the same as their adult counterparts. Those of us who think that the abolition of the juvenile court and the transfer trend are unjust need to explain what is special about juvenile justice. We need to explain the moral asymmetry between juvenile and adult offenders.

## A democratic rationale for asymmetry

If the moral asymmetry between juvenile and adult offenders is a categorical one with clear and sharp boundaries, we might consider a political rationale for the asymmetry, specifically, one that appeals to democratic constraints on political legitimacy. Unlike adults, juveniles cannot vote. There is a worry about the political legitimacy of the abolition of the juvenile court and the transfer trend given the fact that juveniles do not have the vote. Just as American revolutionaries appealed to democratic legitimacy in complaining about taxation without representation, so, too, juveniles might object to the transfer trend by complaining about incarceration without representation.[5]

Democratic principles give citizens a voice in determining institutions and policies that affect them, and we might say that institutions and decision-making mechanisms are democratic insofar as they reflect the will of the governed. For this reason, democratic principles favour extending the franchise and making it universal, or nearly so. Democratic principles are compelling, and can be defended from a wide variety of normative perspectives—on *procedural grounds* as part of a fair procedure, on *substantive grounds* as leading to substantively more just or optimal outcomes, or by a *mixture* of procedural and substantive perspectives.[6] If we accept

[5] Disenfranchised felons might also complain about incarceration without representation. However, in their case, disenfranchisement, whether right or wrong, is the consequence of conviction and incarceration. By contrast, juvenile offenders are incarcerated without ever having had the franchise.

[6] For a sample of justifications of democracy, see Charles Beitz, *Political Equality: An Essay in Democratic Theory* (Princeton, NJ, Princeton University Press, 1989); Thomas Christiano, *The Rule of the Many* (Boulder, CO, Westview Press, 1996); Philip Pettit, *Republicanism: A Theory of Freedom and Government* (Oxford, Clarendon Press, 1997); Richard Arneson, 'Democracy Is Not Intrinsically Just', in K. Dowding, R. Goodin, and C. Pateman (eds), *Justice and Democracy* (Cambridge, Cambridge University Press, 2004), pp. 40–58; and David Estlund, *Democratic Authority* (Princeton, NJ, Princeton University Press, 2007).

democratic principles for any of these reasons, we might doubt the political legitimacy of the transfer trend.

1 The state can legitimately enforce laws only against citizens who have had a say in enacting those laws in the sense that they have had an opportunity to influence the adoption of those laws.
2 Juveniles lack the right to vote and so lack the opportunity to influence the adoption of laws that affect them.
3 Hence, the state is not justified in enforcing laws against juveniles as it is in enforcing laws against adults.

Do our democratic commitments compromise the political legitimacy of the state punishing juveniles as it does adults?[7] Despite the initial appeal of this argument from democratic legitimacy to explain what is special about juvenile justice, it faces several problems.

One worry about the democratic objection to the transfer trend is that it proves too much. If laws can be legitimately enforced only against those who have had a say in enacting them, then the disenfranchisement of juveniles might seem to imply that the state has *no authority* to enforce *any* laws against juveniles. But the claim that democratic states lack legal authority altogether over disenfranchised juveniles is a very radical claim, much more radical than the claim that juveniles deserve to be punished less than their adult counterparts. We should be able to resist the transfer trend without completely relinquishing authority over disenfranchised youth.

Another worry that the democratic rationale proves too much is that it would seem to apply equally well to other non-voting groups that nonetheless seem to be subject to the law, such as resident aliens, foreign nationals, and other visitors. The proponent of the democratic rationale for what is special about juvenile justice might claim that foreign visitors effectively agree to be subject to the host country's laws when they voluntarily enter that country, thus waiving any complaint of democratic legitimacy that they might otherwise make later in response to prosecution for non-compliance with the laws of the host country. According to this suggestion, host countries retain democratic authority over foreign visitors by virtue of their tacit consent to be subject to the laws of the host country.

However, it's not clear that this solves the problem with the democratic rationale. Why assume that the decision of foreign visitors to visit constitutes consent to

[7] Gideon Yaffe, *The Age of Culpability* (Oxford, Clarendon Press, 2018) develops a complex version of the democratic rationale for moral asymmetry and criticises the developmental rationale for failing to provide a rationale for a categorical moral symmetry. In this chapter, I express reservations about the democratic rationale and defend a non-categorical version of the developmental rationale. I cannot discuss the details of Yaffe's arguments here. For fuller discussion of his views, see Brink, 'The Moral Asymmetry of Juvenile and Adult Offenders' and *Fair Opportunity and Responsibility*, ch. 12.

be governed by all the laws of the host country? We can't answer that this is the condition that the host country places on visitation. If that is an adequate answer here, then the proponent of the transfer trend has an answer to the appeal to democratic legitimacy. For the state can equally say that full criminal penalties are a condition that it places on non-compliance with the criminal law. Then, when a juvenile commits a crime, the state can say that the juvenile's non-compliance constitutes consent to be subject to the same penalties for non-compliance that adults are subject to. The stipulation about implied consent seems no more plausible in the case of foreign visitors than it is in the case of juveniles. If so, this seems to be an unresolved problem in the democratic rationale for why juvenile justice is special and what is wrong with the transfer trend.

Finally, there is a worry about whether democratic legitimacy could constitute a free-standing rationale for the special treatment of juvenile justice that does not presuppose the plausibility of the developmental rationale. If the only thing wrong with the transfer trend is that disenfranchised juveniles are treated the same as enfranchised adults, there's an obvious solution. Give juveniles the vote. There are two problems with this. First, anyone attracted to the developmental rationale will think that even if juveniles had the vote, there would still be reason to view many of them as deserving less punitive treatment on account of their immaturity. Second, even if we could be persuaded that it was legitimate to treat some 17-year-olds or perhaps even 16-year-olds as adults, provided they had the right to vote, most of us would be reluctant to think that it would be permissible to treat much younger juveniles as adults if only they had the right to vote. Surely, it would be objectionable to treat eight-year-olds as adults if only we gave them the vote. The importance of the developmental rationale explains both objections. We would think that there was something problematic about treating many juveniles as adults, even if they had the vote, because we believe that their immaturity explains their reduced responsibility and desert. Moreover, the same immaturity that explains why it would be wrong to treat enfranchised juveniles as adults explains why there are lower limits on how early the franchise should be granted. It may well be that 18 years of age is not the only plausible age threshold for the vote, but it seems quite plausible that eight-year-olds are developmentally below the threshold.

## Predominant retributivism and fair opportunity

These doubts about the democratic rationale for the moral asymmetry of juvenile and adult offenders give us reason to explore the developmental rationale. That rationale claims that it is the immaturity of juvenile offenders that makes them less responsible and, hence, less culpable for their wrongdoing than their adult counterparts. Because the developmental rationale appeals to the reduced culpability and desert of juvenile offenders, it appeals to broadly retributive assumptions about punishment, which themselves depend on assumptions about the nature of responsibility. These are complex issues. But one way to fund the developmental rationale is by appeal to *predominant retributivism* and the *fair opportunity* conception of responsibility.[8]

A broadly retributive conception of blame and punishment claims that blame and punishment should be proportional to *desert*, where desert is understood to be the product of two independent variables—wrongdoing and responsibility or culpability.

$$P \alpha D (= W x R)$$

Some version of retributivism provides a natural fit with our understanding of exculpatory affirmative defences. The two main exculpatory defences in the criminal law are *justifications* and *excuses*; they each deny one of the two independent variables in the retributivist desert basis for blame and punishment. Justifications deny wrongdoing, claiming that although the agent's conduct satisfies the conditions of a criminal offence, nonetheless in the circumstances in question the conduct is not inconsistent with the law's larger aims and purposes and, hence, is all-things-considered permissible. Excuses concede wrongdoing but deny that the agent is blameworthy for her misconduct by denying the agent's responsibility or culpability for the wrongdoing.

*Predominant retributivism* provides one way of articulating retributivist essentials. It makes the following three claims.

1 Desert in the form of culpable wrongdoing is a necessary condition of punishment.
2 Proportionate justice sets an upper limit on permissible punishment.
3 Punishment is a fitting response to culpable wrongdoing in the sense that there is a strong *pro tanto* case for punishment that is proportionate to desert. However, there may be good forward-looking reasons for punishing less than the offender deserves.

The first two claims are *negative* retributive theses. (1) insists that desert in the form of culpable wrongdoing is a necessary condition on justified punishment, which implies that punishment is impermissible in the absence of culpable wrongdoing. (2) treats proportionate justice as setting an upper limit on permissible punishment. (3) is the *positive* retributive thesis that desert provides a reason to hold culpable wrongdoers accountable by punishing them.

Predominant retributivism makes these negative and positive retributive claims but leaves the form of punishment open, provided it does not exceed proportionate justice, and insists that desert-based reasons for punishment must sometimes compete with non-desert reasons to punish less than desert. In this way, predominant retributivism is a *mixed* theory of punishment, combining forward-looking consequentialist considerations about punishment—involving deterrence, rehabilitation,

[8] For fuller discussion, see Brink, *Fair Opportunity and Responsibility*.

moral education and norm enforcement, and restorative justice—and backward-looking retributive considerations about desert. But predominant retributivism treats these consequentialist considerations as non-desert factors that are constrained by desert.

Claims about culpability are funded by a conception of responsibility. A plausible working hypothesis is that responsibility and excuse are inversely related. An agent is responsible for conduct for which she has no excuse, and she is excused for conduct for which she is not responsible. If so, excuse is a window onto responsibility and vice versa.[9] The criminal law recognises two main kinds of excuse—*incompetence* excuses, such as insanity, and *duress* excuses. Incompetence involves impairment of an agent's internal capacities. By contrast, duress involves a situation in which wrongful interference by another with the agent's options deprives her of the fair opportunity to act on her own deliberations about how to behave. In this way, standard excuses reflect impairment of the agent's *capacities* or *opportunities*.

If we treat excuse as a window onto responsibility, we should factor responsibility into capacities and opportunities. Specifically, we might conceive of responsibility in terms of *normative competence* and *situational control*. Normative competence involves a kind of reasons-responsiveness that factors into *cognitive competence*—the ability to recognise moral and criminal norms—and *volitional competence*—the ability to conform one's conduct to this normative knowledge. Normative competence and situational control are individually necessary and jointly sufficient for responsibility, because significant impairment of either condition results in an excuse. These forms of impairment are excusing, because punishment despite these forms of impairment would violate the norm that punishment is appropriate only when the agent had the *fair opportunity to avoid wrongdoing* (see Figure 15.1).

This fair opportunity conception of responsibility and excuse is attractive for several reasons. It provides a plausible principled reconstruction of our reactive attitudes of praise and blame, and it fits our considered judgments about when agents are responsible and when they should be excused. Moreover, it draws on and synthesises the best elements in two traditions. Within philosophy, the fair opportunity conception draws on the reasons-responsive wing of the compatibilist tradition about free will and responsibility, which reconciles responsibility and determinism by grounding responsibility in the capacities of agents to respond to normative requirements that bear on their conduct.[10] Within the criminal law, the

[9] Michael Moore, *Placing Blame* (Oxford, Clarendon Press, 1997), p. 548, describes excuse as 'the royal road' to responsibility. It's important to recognise that it is a two-way street.

[10] See Susan Wolf, *Freedom within Reason* (New York, Oxford University Press, 1990); R. Jay Wallace, *Responsibility and the Moral Sentiments* (Cambridge, MA, Harvard University Press, 1994); John Fischer and Mark Ravizza, *Responsibility and Control* (New York, Cambridge University Press, 1998); Dana Nelkin, *Making Sense of Freedom and Responsibility* (Oxford, Clarendon Press, 2011); David O. Brink and Dana K. Nelkin, 'Fairness and the Architecture of Responsibility', *Oxford Studies in Agency and Responsibility*, 1 (2013), 284–313; Manuel Vargas, *Building Better Beings* (Oxford, Clarendon Press, 2013); and Brink, *Fair Opportunity and Responsibility*.

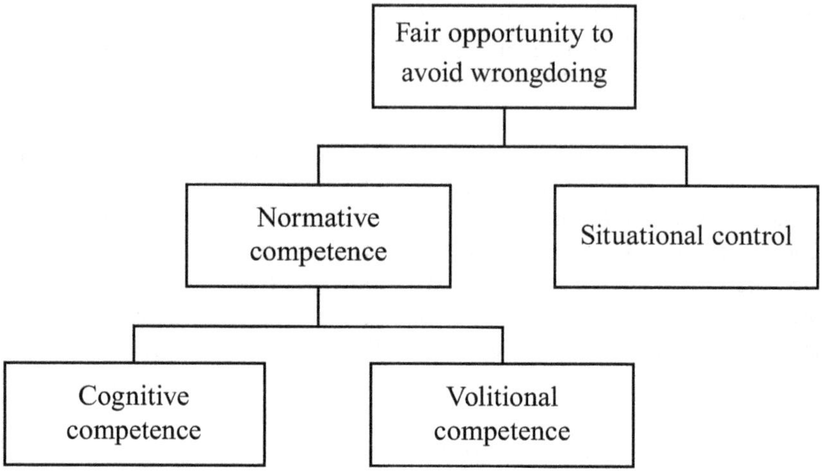


**Figure 15.1** Responsibility as fair opportunity

fair opportunity conception draws on the fair choice tradition in criminal jurisprudence, which understands responsibility in terms of the choices of agents with rational capacities and the fair opportunity for them to exercise those capacities.[11]

## A developmental rationale for asymmetry

Predominant retributivism and the fair opportunity conception of responsibility provide the philosophical and jurisprudential infrastructure for the developmental rationale for the moral asymmetry between juvenile and adult offenders. Proponents of transferring juveniles to adult criminal court appear to be moved by the magnitude of wrongdoing in juvenile crime normally associated with adult crime. The motto seems to be that adult crime calls for adult penalties. But insofar as we are retributivists about whom to punish and how much to punish, we should see a problem with the trend to try juveniles as adults on account of the seriousness of their crimes. It is true that the retributive formula implies that all else being equal—in particular, holding responsibility and culpability constant—the worse the wrong the greater should be the punishment. But all else is not equal when we are comparing juvenile and adult crime. Wrongdoing and responsibility are *independent* factors in the retributivist desert basis for punishment. Juveniles can

[11] See H. L. A Hart, *Punishment and Responsibility* (Oxford, Clarendon Press, 1968); Moore, *Placing Blame*; and Stephen Morse, 'Culpability and Control', *University of Pennsylvania Law Review*, 142 (1994), 1587–660 and 'Uncontrollable Urges and Irrational People', *Virginia Law Review*, 88 (2002), 1025–78.

engage in the same crimes as adults, committing the same wrongs, but typically they bear less responsibility for the harm they cause. This is because for developmental reasons they typically possess reduced normative competence in relation to their adult counterparts. Insofar as they possess reduced normative competence, juveniles will be less responsible and, hence, less culpable than adults. Insofar as they are less culpable for their wrongs, they deserve less blame and punishment. This is the retributive element in the developmental rationale for what is special about juvenile justice.[12]

The fair opportunity conception of responsibility recognises that normative competence has both cognitive and volitional dimensions. Responsible agents must be able to recognise reasons bearing on their conduct and make suitable normative discriminations, and they must be able to conform their conduct to this normative knowledge. If so, normative competence involves a variety of psychological capacities. It involves cognitive capacities to recognise the relevant norms and to grade their comparative urgency, so as to navigate potential moral conflicts. It also involves volitional capacities, including capacities for impulse control necessary to implement one's judgments about what is best despite temptation and distraction and independence from peer pressure for conformity. These capacities are *scalar* insofar as they can be possessed to different degrees. Of course, adults can vary in the degree to which they possess these capacities. But we believe that most normal adults have these capacities to a sufficient degree to make them responsible for their actions. By contrast, the gradual development of normative competence is what marks normal normative progress through childhood and adolescence to maturity. Though not all individuals mature at the same rate, and some individuals never mature, this sort of normative maturation is strongly correlated with age.

There is widespread agreement among developmental psychologists that the period between 12 and 18 years of age is a time of very significant physical, cognitive, and emotional development.[13] Older adolescents may have many of the cognitive abilities that adults have, but they lack the wealth of experience and factual information that adults typically possess. Even when older adolescents share cognitive abilities with adults, they typically lack familiar forms of emotional and social maturity and control. They are less able to represent the future adequately, with the

[12] Our focus here is on how immaturity affects normative competence, responsibility, and desert. A different concern is how immaturity affects the competence of juveniles to stand trial—to understand the charges, to assist counsel in preparing a defence, and to make plea decisions. See e.g. Richard Bonnie and Thomas Grisso, 'Adjudicative Competence and Youthful Offenders', in T. Grisso and R. Schwartz (eds), *Youth on Trial: A Developmental Perspective on Juvenile Justice* (Chicago, IL, University of Chicago Press, 2000), pp. 73–103.

[13] See, generally, Laurence Steinberg, *Adolescence*, 11 edn (New York, McGraw-Hill, 2017); E. Scott, N. Reppucci, and J. Woolard, 'Evaluating Adolescent Decision Making in Legal Contexts', *Law and Human Behavior*, 19 (1995), 221–44, and in Grisso and Schwartz (eds), *Youth on Trial: A Developmental Perspective on Juvenile Justice*.

result that they are more impulsive and less risk-averse.[14] They also tend to be more susceptible to the influence of peers, with the result that they lack a key ingredient in normative competence.[15] Finally, there is emerging evidence that the neurological correlates of these cognitive, emotional, and social capacities are undergoing crucial development throughout adolescence and well into late adolescence and young adulthood.[16] If normative competence is a condition of responsibility, then the reduced or diminished normative competence of juveniles calls into question many of the punitive reforms to juvenile justice embodied in the transfer trend.

## Immaturity and forward-looking rationales for punishment

In this way, immaturity is directly relevant to the retributivist's backward-looking rationale for punishment. Immaturity involves reduced normative competence and, hence, reduced culpability and desert. All else being equal, juveniles tend to be less responsible than their adult counterparts. But immaturity is also relevant to the forward-looking rationales for punishment, especially those involving rehabilitation and deterrence.

Rehabilitative goals have a legitimate role in adult criminal justice, in which offenders are fully responsible for their crimes. They have an even more important role in juvenile justice, in which the immaturity of offenders renders them simultaneously less responsible but more corrigible. Adolescence is a pivotal period both because it is a time of enormous cognitive and emotional growth and maturation and because it is a time when enduring intellectual, emotional, and social skills and habits are being established. This means that adoption of the rehabilitative stance toward juvenile offenders is not only especially appropriate but also especially consequential. This makes it imperative that juvenile offenders be sentenced to special juvenile facilities that avoid the brutality of adult prisons, that provide significant educational, vocational, and avocational training, and that make provisions for the

[14] See e.g. P. Finn and B. Bragg, 'Perception of the Risk of an Accident by Young and Older Drivers', *Accident Analysis and Prevention*, 18 (1986), 289–98; M. Tester, W. Gardiner, and E. Wilfong, 'Experimental Studies of the Development of Decision-making Competence', in *Children, Risks, and Decisions: Psychological and Legal Implications* (New York, American Psychological Association, 1987); and Scott *et al.*, 'Evaluating Adolescent Decision Making in Legal Contexts'.

[15] See e.g. T. Berndt, 'Developmental Changes in Conformity to Peers and Parents', *Developmental Psychology*, 15 (1979), 608–16; S. Steinberg and S. Silverberg, 'The Vicissitudes of Autonomy in Early Adolescence', *Child Development*, 57 (1986), 841–51; Scott *et al.*, 'Evaluating Adolescent Decision Making in Legal Contexts'.

[16] See e.g. S. Anderson, A. Bechara, H. Damasio, D. Tranel, and A. Damasio, 'Impairment of Social and Moral Behavior Related to Damage in Human Prefontal Cortex', *Nature Neuroscience*, 2 (1999), 1032–7; F. Benes, 'The Development of Prefontal Cortex: The Maturation of Neurotransmitter Systems and their Interactions', in C. Nelson and M. Luciana (eds), *Handbook of Developmental Cognitive Neuroscience* (Cambridge, MIT Press, 2001), pp. 79–92; and William Hirstein, Katrina Sifferd, and Tyler Fagan, *Responsible Brains: Neuroscience, Law, and Human Culpability* (Cambridge, MA, MIT Press, 2018), ch. 8.

special nutritional and developmental needs of adolescents. Adult correctional facilities rarely address rehabilitative goals with adult offenders. They are even more poorly suited to address the special rehabilitative needs and opportunities posed by juvenile offenders. But then the trend to try juveniles as adults and incarcerate them in adult correctional facilities runs afoul of rehabilitative ideals of punishment.

We can also see how immaturity changes the operation of deterrent values within juvenile criminal justice. Deterrence is usually understood in terms of sanctions that create incentives to comply with the law, thus deterring crime. By attaching sanctions to criminal activity, we make it less attractive; the greater the sanctions, the more unattractive we make such activity. In the case of *specific* deterrence, applying sanctions to the wrongdoer is supposed to deter *him* from further criminal conduct. In the case of *general* deterrence, applying sanctions to the wrongdoer is supposed to deter *others* from criminal conduct.

Immaturity seems likely to affect the deterrent value, both general and specific, of sanctions for juveniles. The deterrent effect of sanctions crucially depends on potential criminals being rational calculators of expected utility. No doubt, this is an idealising assumption even for adults. But it is an especially unrealistic assumption for juveniles. Younger adolescents not only lack the cognitive capacities of adults, but also, and more importantly, they lack the ability to vividly represent the future and are prone to discount the significance of future benefits and harms out of proportion to their actual magnitude and, as a result, to engage in irrational risk-taking. But this means that sanctions that might, in principle, work for adults won't have the same deterrent value for juveniles. In fact, there is evidence from Florida and other states that use of harsher, adult criminal sanctions for minors actually increases recidivism rates.[17] If so, considerations of specific deterrence actually speak against the transfer trend. In the juvenile context, deterrence is more likely to be served by establishing better schools for the social sentiments both inside and outside of correctional facilities than by ratcheting up the severity of the sanctions for violating the law.

## Two tracks in juvenile justice

There is evidence that adolescence involves a period of increased risk-taking and antisocial impulses that are normally outgrown. The historically robust fact that juvenile crime constitutes a disproportionate amount of all crime committed means that most deviance is limited to adolescence.[18] Most deviant adolescents do not become deviant adults. Whereas most teenage offenders do not become career

[17] See Donna Bishop, Charles Frazier, Lonn Lanza-Kaduce, and Lawrence Winner, 'The Transfer of Juveniles to Criminal Court: Does It Make a Difference?', *Crime and Delinquency*, 42 (1996), 171–91.
[18] See e.g. Barry Feld, *Bad Kids: Race and the Transformation of the Juvenile Court* (New York, Oxford, 1999), pp. 221–2.

criminals, younger preteen arrest is the best predictor of career criminality. This suggests that the class of juvenile offenders divides roughly into two subclasses—a small number of juveniles whose antisocial tendencies begin before puberty who are strongly disposed to become career offenders and a much larger number of juveniles whose deviance is confined to adolescence and who, under normal circumstances, would outgrow these deviant tendencies.[19] Whereas specifically adolescent deviance is more common and represents a temporary phase, significant preteen deviance is strongly correlated with cognitive and emotional disabilities and the presence of domestic dysfunction and other environmental stress for which it is difficult to correct. Indeed, significant preteen violence is predictive of antisocial personality disorder and psychopathy. This two-track model of juvenile deviance has implications for what is distinctive about juvenile justice.

On the one hand, few people think that normal preteens—those who suffer from no special cognitive, affective, or conative deficits—are fully responsible, and the trend to try juveniles as adults typically does not extend to preteens.[20] If preteen crime is mostly committed by children who suffer from severe psychological deficits, then there is even less reason to treat them as normatively competent and even less reason to treat them as responsible for the offences they commit. The absence of responsibility for their offences means that they do not meet the retributive condition for punishment. But preteen criminality, especially violent criminal conduct, demands intervention in the form of counselling, monitoring, and detention if the child poses a significant danger to himself or others.

By contrast, adolescence-specific deviance is potentially culpable, but at least with younger adolescents, we have reason to think that their normative competence is significantly diminished. When we note that such deviant behaviour is normally outgrown, this might incline us to view it as part of the process of normative maturation, experimentation, and education. This isn't to normalise juvenile criminal conduct, especially violent misconduct, but it suggests that criminal conduct

[19] See e.g. Terrie Moffitt, 'Adolescence-Limited and Life-Course-Persistent Antisocial Behavior: A Developmental Taxonomy', *Psychological Review*, 100 (1993), 674–701 and Thomas Grisso, 'Society's Retributive Response to Juvenile Violence: A Developmental Perspective', *Law and Human Behavior*, 20 (1996), 229–47.

[20] The earliest transfer, with which I am familiar, is the famous case involving Lionel Tate, who as a 12-year-old killed a 6-year-old family friend in daycare, imitating what he had seen in professional wrestling on television. Tate was tried as an adult and convicted of first-degree murder, which in Florida carries a mandatory sentence of life in prison without the possibility of parole. Tate was offered a chance to plead to second-degree murder and a reduced sentence, but his mother insisted that he refuse the plea bargain on the ground that Lionel did not intend to kill his friend. In response to public outcry over Tate's sentence, he was granted a retrial and accepted substantially the same plea deal that he had earlier refused. See *Tate v Florida* 864 So 2d 44, 46–7 (Fla Dist Ct App 2003). Another case involving 12-year-olds occurred in Wisconsin, when 12-year-olds Morgan Geyser and Anissa Weier tried to kill their friend Payton Leutner, stabbing her 19 times, in an attempt to appease the (fictional) Slender Man. Geyser and Weier were tried as adults but acquitted by reason of insanity and committed to psychiatric care for a minimum of 40 years (Geyser) and 25 years (Weier). See e.g. 'Teenager in "Slender Man" Stabbing Gets 40 Years in Mental Hospital', *New York Times*, 1 February 2018.

might be the manifestation of developmentally normal psychological mechanisms involving risk-taking and experimentation. Moreover, this isn't a reason not to hold juveniles accountable and punish their misconduct. Indeed, appropriate reactive attitudes, intervention, and punishment may be essential if juveniles are to learn important moral lessons and outgrow their deviance. But recognition that most juvenile crime is adolescence-specific gives us reason to respond to age-specific juvenile misconduct in ways that encourage moral learning and don't foreclose the possibility of a normal adult life.

## Qualifying the developmental asymmetry

So far, I have defended a developmental rationale for the moral asymmetry thesis that, all else being equal, juveniles should be treated differently and punished less harshly than their adult counterparts. This rationale for what is special about juvenile justice has fairly revisionary legal and policy implications, especially in undermining the legitimacy of many aspects of the transfer trend. Despite its reformist implications, the developmental rationale draws on familiar and plausible assumptions about punishment, responsibility, and adolescent development—indeed, some of the very reasons for establishing a separate juvenile court in the first place.

However, we need to be cautious about how exactly to frame the conclusion of the developmental rationale and what it implies about the ways in which juvenile justice is special. The idea that there is a moral asymmetry between juvenile and adult offenders is a useful generalisation or slogan, but it requires various qualifications.

First, we should not expect the developmental rationale to provide a purely principled justification of a categorical asymmetry between juveniles and adults, without resort to pragmatic considerations. For instance, we are unlikely to be able to justify treating everyone over 18 in adult criminal court and everyone under 18 in juvenile court without appeal to such considerations. This is because when the underlying normatively relevant factors are scalar, thresholds and bright lines will be somewhat arbitrary, because they attach enormous significance to small differences straddling the threshold and ignore large differences above and below the threshold. There will typically be little difference in normative competence between a young 18-year-old and an older 17-year-old, though a categorical asymmetry would treat them very differently. Moreover, there will be individual variation, with some juveniles being more normatively mature for their age than other juveniles the same age and perhaps than other young adults. In order to maintain a categorical asymmetry between juveniles and adults, we would need to resort to pragmatic considerations. For instance, the case for a categorical asymmetry is stronger if the following claims are plausible.

1 Age is a generally reliable proxy for normative maturity.
2 Most 18-year-olds are sufficiently mature to be held responsible.

3 Normatively precocious juveniles are rare.
4 It is difficult to identify normatively precocious juveniles reliably.
5 Blackstone's asymmetry: mistakes of over-punishment are worse than mistakes of under-punishment.[21]

Together, these claims make the best case for embracing a categorical asymmetry between juveniles and adults in which we treat all juveniles differently than adults. Because it relies on empirical claims, especially about our epistemic limitations, it is a partly pragmatic rationale for a simple categorical asymmetry between juveniles and adults.

Second, even if this is a reasonable pragmatic solution to handling individual variation, it does nothing to address reliable differences between older and younger juveniles and similarities between older juveniles and younger adults. If we assume that most 18-year-olds have reached a threshold of sufficient normative competence to be tried in adult court, we may wonder whether a categorical asymmetry between 18-year-olds and 17-year-olds makes sense, given their similarities. It's not clear if their modest differences in normative competence and Blackstone's asymmetry justify categorically different treatment. In this connection, it is noteworthy that the Model Penal Code does not embrace a categorical asymmetry between juveniles and adults. As we have seen, the Model Penal Code presumes that all juveniles should be tried in juvenile court but allows that presumption to be rebutted in a case-by-case manner for juveniles between 16 and 18 years of age based on a judicial determination that the juvenile in question demonstrates culpability comparable to an adult (§4.10). Because the judge has limited discretion and must rebut a presumption in favour of 16–17-year-olds being tried in juvenile court, this limited use of judicial waiver is a modest departure from categorical asymmetry, one that aims to better track developmental facts about competence and culpability.

Third, another well-motivated departure from a categorical asymmetry between juvenile and adult crime concerns the selective use of *blended sentencing* that combines a juvenile sentence until the age of majority and an adult sentence subsequent to the juvenile one. Older mature adolescents will often be significantly, if not fully, normatively competent. This will be true of many 17-year-olds. So they can be largely, if not fully, responsible for committing crimes, both serious and less serious. Under the traditional juvenile sentencing rules that require juvenile sentences to expire by the age of majority, such offenders are unlikely to receive sentences commensurate with their desert, at least in the case of serious offences. Indeed, there is a puzzle for the traditional juvenile sentencing system that the older and more responsible the offender—the closer to being 18 years old—the less time he can serve for

[21] The English jurist William Blackstone famously claimed that it is worse to punish the innocent than to let the guilty go free. See William Blackstone, *Commentaries on the Laws of England* (London, Strahan & Woodfall, 1791) Book IV, Chapter 27, p. 358. A corollary of Blackstone's asymmetry is that all else being equal it is worse to over-punish than to under-punish.

his crimes. Blended sentencing provides a solution to this puzzle insofar as it allows mature adolescents who are substantially culpable for serious crimes to serve limited adult sentences in addition to their comparatively short juvenile sentences. The actual use of blended sentencing in jurisdictions that employ it may not always have conformed to the retributive formula of proportionality. But the retributive conception of proportionality endorses the selective use of blended sentencing.

We could try to defend a simple categorical asymmetry between juvenile and adult crime by appeal to both the developmental rationale and pragmatic considerations. However, we should recognise that the developmental rationale does not support a simple categorical asymmetry. Seventeen-year-olds will often be as competent as young adults, especially for egregious crimes involving what we might call manifest illegality. Moreover, a retributive understanding of the developmental rationale requires the selective use of blended sentencing for serious crimes committed by older adolescents. These are well-motivated departures from a simple categorical asymmetry between juvenile and adult crime and are fully consistent with the Model Penal Code position that treats the asymmetry as a presumption that can be rebutted on a case-by-case basis for older adolescents and especially serious crimes. The developmental rationale should embrace these deviations from a strict asymmetry.

However, the transfer trend far outstrips these modest departures from strict asymmetry, transferring young adolescents to adult court for a wide variety of offences. That trend pushes the age at which normative competence might be established much further back, to ages where it strains credulity to think that the case for normative immaturity could be successfully rebutted. This is bad enough, but an important strand in the transfer trend actually inverts the presumption so that many juveniles accused of certain crimes now bear the presumption of showing that they should be tried in juvenile court. Worse still are the mandatory transfer laws that automatically transfer comparatively young juveniles accused of certain crimes to adult court. It is hard to see how such transfer policies could be defended by appeal to the scalar nature of normative competence and individual variability in normative maturation. An irrebuttable 18-year-old cut-off, which few endorse, would be problematic in some of its applications, but at least it would generally, if imperfectly, track the facts about normative competence that matter. To replace an irrebuttable 18-year-old threshold in favour, for example, of an irrebuttable 14-year-old threshold is ridiculous. It, too, fails to achieve individualised justice, but it also greatly multiplies the number of individual injustices. For while an 18-year-old threshold for adulthood will be both under-inclusive and over-inclusive at the margins, a 14-year-old test will be massively over-inclusive. This is bad enough. If we assume, as Blackstone does, that it is better to weight the criminal justice system so that errors of over-punishment are seen as worse than errors of under-punishment, then the transfer trend must seem especially unjust. This means that the appeal to accountability that is often made to support the trend to try juveniles as adults, so far from supporting that trend, actually undermines it.

## Constitutional limits on juvenile sentencing

In the context of the developmental rationale for the moral asymmetry of juvenile and adult offenders and doubts about the transfer trend, it is worth discussing issues raised in comparatively recent Supreme Court decisions that uphold sentence limitations on juvenile crime in capital and other cases involving serious crimes. Three cases are of special interest. First, *Roper v Simmons* (2005) interprets the Eighth Amendment's prohibition on cruel and unusual punishments to impose a categorical prohibition on capital punishment for juveniles convicted of homicide.[22] Second, *Graham v Florida* (2010) interprets the Eighth Amendment to impose a categorical prohibition on LWOP for juveniles convicted of non-homicide offences.[23] Third, *Miller v Alabama* (2012) interprets the Eighth Amendment to prohibit mandatory LWOP sentences for juveniles convicted of homicides.[24]

These sentence limitation cases bear an interesting relation to the transfer trend. On the one hand, because they recognise a developmental rationale for differential sentencing for juveniles and adults, these cases resist at least the most extreme implications of the transfer trend. On the other hand, the issues addressed in these cases would not even arise without the transfer trend because they all involve appropriate sentences for juveniles who have been tried in adult criminal court. When juveniles are tried in adult court, they become subject to sentencing possibilities—including mandatory sentencing—that run afoul of the reduced culpability of juvenile offenders recognised in these cases.

In *Roper*, 17-year-old Christopher Simmons and a friend kidnapped a woman from her home and threw her off a bridge, where she drowned. Simmons was tried as an adult, and under Missouri law was sentenced to death. Justice Kennedy's majority opinion interprets the Eighth Amendment to impose a categorical prohibition on capital punishment for juveniles convicted of homicides. He appeals to societal consensus against the use of the death penalty for juveniles, as reflected in legislative changes in state criminal codes that have in many cases eliminated the possibility of the death penalty for juveniles and changes in penal practice of sentencing juveniles to the death penalty even in jurisdictions where that is permissible. But Kennedy also relies on the Court's own reading of the evidence about juvenile culpability to argue that the Eighth Amendment's demand for proportionate punishment precludes the execution of offenders who were juveniles at the time of their crimes. Kennedy embraces a version of the developmental rationale for treating juveniles differently than adults, citing reduced impulse control, reduced independence of judgment (reduced ability to resist peer pressure), and underdeveloped character as factors reducing juvenile culpability and undermining deterrence

[22] *Roper v Simmons* 543 US 551 (2005).
[23] *Graham v Florida* 130 S Ct 2011 (2010).
[24] *Miller v Alabama* 132 S Ct 2455 (2012).

rationales for capital punishment. On this basis, he defends a categorical ban on capital punishment for juveniles convicted of homicide, while conceding that some juveniles may be as mature as normal adults, appealing to our inability to identify these exceptional cases reliably.

In dissent, Justice O'Connor questions the appropriateness of adopting categorical bans on capital punishment for juveniles when it is conceded that some older juveniles are sufficiently culpable to justify capital punishment. She claims that categorical sentencing limitations are in tension with the commitment to individualised justice in sentencing.

Terrance Graham was 16 when he attempted armed robbery in Florida. Graham was tried as an adult, but he expressed remorse and a resolve to do better and was sentenced to probation. However, while on probation, he committed additional crimes in which his companions used firearms. His probation was revoked, the trial court judge claimed he was incorrigible, and he was sentenced on the earlier charges to LWOP. Kennedy's majority opinion mostly follows the script of *Roper*. He appeals to both societal consensus, as reflected in legislative changes and penal practice, and to the Court's own reading of the evidence about juvenile culpability to argue that the Eighth Amendment's demand for proportionate punishment precludes LWOP for juvenile offenders in non-homicide cases. Kennedy says the same developmental factors that reduced juvenile culpability in *Roper*—reduced impulse control, lack of independence of judgment, and underdeveloped character—also reduce culpability for non-homicide offences. Perhaps more clearly here, Kennedy defends a categorical ban, while conceding that some older juveniles may be sufficiently mature to be tried as adults, by appeal to our inability to reliably identify these exceptional cases.

Chief Justice Roberts concurs in the conclusion that Graham's sentence was constitutionally disproportionate while rejecting the majority's categorical ban. Roberts points out that Graham's sentence of LWOP for attempted robbery is far more severe than sentences for comparable crimes by adults. Moreover, he agrees with the developmental claim that immaturity does in general diminish culpability and so should be relevant to proportional sentencing. But Roberts claims that there are some cases—involving especially heinous offences and older juvenile offenders who are sufficiently mature and competent—in which LWOP is as fitting for juveniles as for adults. He focuses on cases in which the crimes are serious and involve manifest immorality, the juvenile is 17, and there is no reason to believe that there is significant lack of culpability. In such cases, he thinks, LWOP can be proportionate for juveniles.[25] Roberts assumes that we will know the exceptional cases in which defendants are mature enough to be treated the same as adults when we see them.

25 Roberts discusses three such cases, involving Milagro Cunningham, Nathan Walker, and Jakaris Taylor. See *Graham*, at 2041–2.

*Miller* involved two Alabama cases in which 14-year-olds were tried and convicted as adults for homicide. Under mandatory sentencing laws in Alabama, they were sentenced to LWOP. In one case, the youth (Jackson) was convicted of homicide under the felony-murder rule—when Jackson and friends went to rob a video store, he stayed outside, and his friend shot the store clerk. Justice Kagan writes for the majority, interpreting the Eighth Amendment to prohibit mandatory LWOP sentences for juveniles convicted of capital crimes. She says that the result here is the product of two distinct lines of cases—the categorical sentence limitations in *Roper* and *Graham* and other cases that call for individualised sentencing. Kagan says that the categorical ban in *Graham*, though it applied there only to non-homicides, applies here to homicides, citing factors of diminished culpability that have wider application, including to homicides. In principle, that might support a categorical ban on LWOP sentences for any juvenile offender for any type of crime, including homicide. But she does not draw that stronger conclusion. Instead, she notes that proportionate sentencing must consider the potentially reduced culpability of juvenile offenders. So whereas *Graham* adopted a categorical ban on LWOP in non-homicide cases, *Miller* requires that such sentences cannot be categorically required in homicide cases. The result in *Miller* does not prevent sentencing some juvenile killers to LWOP, but it does say that this cannot be mandatory and can happen only after explicit consideration of the maturity of the juvenile defendant and in light of the way in which immaturity can diminish responsibility.

*Roper* and *Graham* both involve categorical limits on juvenile sentencing, whereas *Miller* rejects a categorical limit in favour of individualised sentencing. But the three cases are united by a concern about the danger of over-punishing juvenile offenders, in relation to adult offenders, on account of their reduced normative competence. Whereas the first two cases find that reduced juvenile competence is sufficient to justify categorical bans on the most severe punishments, the third case appeals to the same facts to justify consideration of reduced normative competence among juveniles as part of the sentencing process for homicides by juveniles.

## Categorical limits and individual desert

Our discussion of juvenile justice has endorsed the developmental rationale for thinking that other things being equal punishment of juvenile crime should be less severe than for comparable adult crime. Though forward-looking considerations about rehabilitation, deterrence, and the adolescence-specific character of crime support this asymmetry between juvenile and adult crime, the primary factor in the developmental rationale is retributive. It is because adolescents are cognitively and volitionally immature that they deserve to be punished less for their crimes than their adult counterparts. The traditional juvenile court is one way to recognise this asymmetry and guard against the blind spot the general public seems to have for the independence of wrongdoing and culpability.[26] These same developmental considerations underlie Supreme Court cases recognising sentence limitations that apply to juveniles that do not apply to adults.

However, the factors that underlie the developmental rationale are all scalar and allow for variation among juvenile cohorts (17, 16, and 15-year-olds) and among individuals within a given cohort. This fact raises questions about whether the categorical rule for assignment to juvenile or adult court and the categorical rules imposing sentence limitations for juveniles are consistent with individual just deserts. We may be confident that normal 14-year-olds are developmentally immature in relation to normal 19-year-olds in ways that are normatively significant and justify differential treatment, but the differences between 17-year-olds and 18-year-olds are less sharp, especially since only a single day might separate members of these two cohorts. Moreover, given individual variation, some 17-year-olds will be at least as normatively competent as some 18-year-olds. How then can their categorically different treatment be squared with the criminal law's interest in individual desert? Won't this result in some older adolescents being under-punished and some young adults being over-punished? To some extent, these concerns about individual desert animate the concerns of O'Connor and Roberts about categorical limits on juvenile sentencing.

Let's focus for a moment on the worry about under-punishing adolescents. As we have seen, one could try to defend categorical differences between juveniles and adults in their application to all juveniles on partly pragmatic grounds. One might insist we need bright lines here, even if the underlying factors are scalar. To maintain a categorical asymmetry between juveniles and adults, we could argue that (1) age is a generally reliable proxy for normative maturity; (2) most 18-year-olds are sufficiently mature to be held responsible; (3) normatively precocious juveniles are rare; (4) it is difficult to identify normatively precocious juveniles reliably; and (5) mistakes of over-punishment are worse than mistakes of under-punishment. If these conditions are met, there is a reasonably strong pragmatic rationale for a simple categorical asymmetry between juveniles and adults. Indeed, we might claim that by following this categorical rule about assignment to juvenile or adult court, we are likely to maximise just deserts overall, even if it means that in some cases we would under-punish. This is the sort of argument that Kennedy advances against O'Connor and Roberts.[27]

[26] Jury studies suggest that assessments of the severity of punishment appropriate for crimes are surprisingly insensitive to information about the age and maturity of the wrongdoer. See e.g. C. Crosby, P. Britner, K. Jodl, and S. Portwood, 'The Juvenile Death Penalty and the Eighth Amendment: An Empirical Investigation of Societal Consensus and Proportionality', *Law and Human Behavior*, 19 (1995), 245–61 and S. Ghetti and A. Redlich, 'Reactions to Youth Crime: Perceptions of Accountability and Competency', *Behavioral Sciences and the Law*, 19 (2001), 33–52.

[27] For further discussion, see Amy Berg, 'Bright Lines in Juvenile Justice', *Journal of Political Philosophy*, 29 (2021), 330–52.

However, even if this pragmatic rationale explains why we should be firm about not treating younger adolescents as adults, it does not explain why we should treat older adolescents, for instance 17-year-olds, so differently from young adults. This is where we invoked departures from the categorical asymmetry between juveniles and adults involved in the use of blended sentencing for older adolescents and the Model Penal Code provision for judicial waiver for older adolescents. Especially if the presumption is in favour of trying older adolescents as juveniles, the selective use of blended sentencing or the judicial waiver must rebut that presumption on a case-by-case basis and for cause. Why not similarly treat the constitutional limits on juvenile sentencing as rebuttable presumptions, rather than categorical limits? In effect, *Miller* does treat the prohibition on LWOP sentences for all crimes, even homicide, as a rebuttable presumption, insofar as it claims that LWOP cannot be mandatory, even for homicide, and in the case of homicide must be conditioned on an assessment of the juvenile's maturity and normative competence. So the question is whether the rules laid down in *Roper* and *Graham* would be better construed as rebuttable presumptions, rather than categorical rules.

I suspect that sympathy with the categorical versions of these sentence limitations is fuelled by doubts about whether capital punishment is ever, or at least usually, a justified response to homicide and whether LWOP is ever, or at least usually, a justified response to crimes that are not homicides. Of course, this would raise questions about the permissibility of these punishments for adults, too. If we *stipulate* that capital punishment is sometimes justified for homicides such as murder and that LWOP is sometimes justified for crimes other than homicides for adults, then I think we have reason to recognise the possibility that such punishment might be deserved for some older adolescents, and we should treat the rules forbidding such punishments as rebuttable presumptions.

However, this analysis of constitutional limitations on juvenile sentencing has implications for permissible sentencing of young adults and the use of significant mandatory minima for adults. If we are going to allow departure from rules about the differential treatment of juveniles when we are dealing with older juveniles and allow that the presumption against treating them as adults can be rebutted if they can be shown to be normatively competent, shouldn't we allow adults, especially young adults, the opportunity to show that they should not be subject to full adult punishments if their normative competence is diminished in some way? Perhaps the presumption should be that all adults should be subject to punishment specified for crimes that are not fully justified or excused, but this should be a rebuttable presumption. If *Miller* is right that sentencing older juveniles to LWOP for murder can only take place after individual culpability assessments in light of the mitigating character of immaturity, then we might think that maximal sentences for adults, especially young adults, should likewise be conditional on individual culpability assessments about the offender's normative competence and situational control. But this is a problem for all mandatory sentencing schemes for adults, such as mandatory minima and three-strikes laws, because they prevent the consideration of individual culpability.[28] If so, the reform of juvenile justice suggests broader reforms for criminal law.

## Conclusion

If we want to justify the moral asymmetry of juvenile and adult offenders, we cannot rely exclusively or even primarily on the democratic rationale that appeals to the disenfranchisement of juveniles. Instead, we need to rely on a version of the developmental rationale that stresses how immaturity tends to reduce the desert of juvenile offenders and tends to provide more opportunities for the rehabilitation and moral education of juvenile offenders. These developmental facts explain what is wrong with the trend to transfer juveniles to adult court because it fails to recognise that young adolescents are substantially less responsible and, hence, less culpable for their misconduct than their adult counterparts. However, the developmental rationale is unlikely to support a categorical form of asymmetry in which all juveniles are less culpable than all young adults and in which all juveniles have the same degree of culpability as each other. Though younger adolescents will be less culpable for their misconduct than older adolescents, there may be little or no difference in culpability between some older adolescents and some younger adults. We could perhaps defend categorical sentence limitations for juveniles of the sort recognised in *Roper* and *Graham* on largely pragmatic grounds. But *Miller* suggests that at least some sentencing rules are best thought of as presumptions that can be rebutted based on individualised culpability assessments. Once we appreciate the way in which long sentences for juveniles are either categorically impermissible or justifiable only on the basis of individual desert assessments, we can see that the same sentencing protocols should apply to adults, or at least young adults. This excludes various kinds of adult sentencing provisions that impose significant mandatory minima and ignore variations in individual desert.

What is special about juvenile justice is that all else being equal the immaturity of juveniles renders them less culpable for their misconduct than their adult counterparts, and this difference makes them less deserving of the same sentences appropriate for their adult counterparts. But the same retributive rationale for making the punishment of juveniles proportionate to their degree of responsibility and culpability explains why we should also find the criminal law's use of categorical sentencing rules for adults in the form of steep mandatory minima problematic. The same retributive principles that rationalise criminal justice reforms for juveniles rationalise criminal justice reforms for adults.

[28] This concern about mandatory minima is connected with the need to take partial responsibility and excuse seriously. For discussion, see Brink, *Fair Opportunity and Responsibility*, ch. 15.

# Index

www.ingramcontent.com/pod-product-compliance
Lightning Source LLC
Chambersburg PA
CBHW072002241025
34505CB00003B/297
* 9 7 8 1 8 3 6 2 4 5 6 7 4 *